T0318250

Adam Smith

Adam Smith (1723–1790) is widely regarded as one of the great thinkers of the Enlightenment period. Best-known for his founding work of economics, *The Wealth of Nations*, Smith engaged equally with the nature of morality in his *Theory of Moral Sentiments*. He also gave lectures on literature and jurisprudence, and wrote papers on art and science.

In this outstanding philosophical introduction Samuel Fleischacker argues that Smith is a superb example of the broadly curious thinkers who flourished in the Enlightenment—for whom morality, politics, law, and economics were just a few of the many fascinating subjects that could be illuminated by naturalistic modes of investigation.

After a helpful overview of his life and work, Fleischacker examines the full range of Smith's thought, on such subjects as:

- epistemology, philosophy of science, and aesthetics
- the nature of sympathy
- moral approval and moral judgement
- virtue
- religion
- justice and jurisprudence
- governmental policy
- economic principles
- liberalism.

Including chapter summaries, suggestions for further reading, and a glossary, *Adam Smith* is essential reading for those studying ethics, political philosophy, the history of philosophy, and the Enlightenment, as well as those reading Smith in related disciplines such as economics, law, and religion.

Samuel Fleischacker is LAS Distinguished Professor of Philosophy at the University of Illinois at Chicago, USA. His books include *The Ethics of Culture* (1994), *On Adam Smith's Wealth of Nations: A Philosophical Companion* (2003), *A Short History of Distributive Justice* (2004), *The Good and the Good Book* (2015), *What Is Enlightenment?* (Routledge, 2012), and *Being Me Being You: Adam Smith and Empathy* (2019).

Routledge Philosophers

Edited by Brian Leiter

University of Chicago, USA

Routledge Philosophers is a major series of introductions to the great Western philosophers. Each book places a major philosopher or thinker in historical context, explains and assesses their key arguments, and considers their legacy. Additional features include a chronology of major dates and events, chapter summaries, annotated suggestions for further reading and a glossary of technical terms.

An ideal starting point for those new to philosophy, they are also essential reading for those interested in the subject at any level.

Also available:

Darwin
Tim Lewens

Rawls
Samuel Freeman

Spinoza
Michael Della Rocca

Russell
Gregory Landini

Wittgenstein
William Child

Heidegger
John Richardson

Adorno
Brian O'Connor

Husserl, second edition
David Woodruff Smith

Aristotle, second edition
Christopher Shields

Kant, second edition
Paul Guyer

Hume
Don Garrett

Dewey
Steven Fesmire

Freud, second edition
Jonathan Lear

Habermas
Kenneth Baynes

Peirce
Albert Atkin

Plato
Constance Meinwald

Plotinus
Eyjólfur Emilsson

Einstein
Thomas Ryckman

Merleau-Ponty, second edition
Taylor Carman

Leibniz, second edition
Nicholas Jolley

Bergson
Mark Sinclair

Arendt
Dana Villa

Cassirer
Samantha Matherne

Adam Smith
Samuel Fleischacker

For more information about this series, please visit: https://www.routledge.com/The-Routledge-Philosophers/book-series/ROUTPHIL

Samuel Fleischacker

Adam Smith

LONDON AND NEW YORK

First published 2021
by Routledge
2 Park Square, Milton Park, Abingdon, Oxon OX14 4RN

and by Routledge
52 Vanderbilt Avenue, New York, NY 10017

Routledge is an imprint of the Taylor & Francis Group, an informa business

British Library Cataloguing-in-Publication Data
A catalogue record for this book is available from the British Library

Library of Congress Cataloging-in-Publication Data
Names: Fleischacker, Samuel, author.
Title: Adam Smith / Samuel Fleischacker.
Description: Abingdon, Oxon; New York, NY: Routledge, 2021. |
Includes bibliographical references and index.
Identifiers: LCCN 2020057104 (print) | LCCN 2020057105 (ebook) |
ISBN 9780415787567 (hardback) | ISBN 9780415787550 (paperback) |
ISBN 9781315225876 (ebook)
Subjects: LCSH: Smith, Adam, 1723–1790.
Classification: LCC B1545.Z7 F539 2021 (print) | LCC B1545.Z7 (ebook) |
DDC 192—dc23
LC record available at https://lccn.loc.gov/2020057104
LC ebook record available at https://lccn.loc.gov/2020057105

ISBN: 978-0-415-78756-7 (hbk)
ISBN: 978-0-415-78755-0 (pbk)
ISBN: 978-1-315-22587-6 (ebk)

Typeset in Joanna
by codeMantra

Contents

Abbreviations

When citing Smith, I will use page numbers, rather than the sub-divisions provided in the standard Glasgow edition. I will also refer to all the works listed below by abbreviation and page number. If I cite a text several times in a row, I will use its abbreviation the first time but give just a page number after subsequent references.

Works by Adam Smith

CAS   *Correspondence of Adam Smith,* ed. EC Mossner, Ian Simpson Ross, (New York: Oxford University Press, second edition, 1987)

EPS   *Essays on Philosophical Subjects,* ed. WPD Wightman, JC Bryce, (Oxford: Oxford University Press, 1980); first published in 1795

LJ   *Lectures on Jurisprudence,* ed. RL Meek, DD Raphael, PG Stein, (Oxford: Oxford University Press, 1978). Unpublished in the author's lifetime.

LRBL   *Lectures on Rhetoric and Belles-Lettres,* ed. JC Bryce, (Oxford: Oxford University Press, 1983). Unpublished in the author's lifetime.

TMS   *Theory of Moral Sentiments,* ed. DD Raphael, AL Macfie, (Oxford: Oxford University Press, 1976); first published in 1759

WN   *An Inquiry into the Nature and Causes of the Wealth of Nations,* ed. RH Campbell, AS Skinner, WB Todd, (Oxford: Oxford University Press, 1976); first published in 1776

Other Works

AVE   Charles Griswold, *Adam Smith and the Virtues of Enlightenment*, (Cambridge: Cambridge University Press, 1999)

EHU   David Hume, *Enquiry Concerning Human Understanding*, in Hume, Enquiries, eds. LA Selby-Bigge and PH Nidditch, third edition, (Oxford: Clarendon, 1975)

EMP   David Hume, *Enquiry Concerning the Principles of Morals*, in Hume, *Enquiries*.

ES   Emma Rothschild, *Economic Sentiments*, (Cambridge: Harvard University Press, 2001)

ET   Anthony Waterman, "Economics as Theology: Adam Smith's *Wealth of Nations*," Southern Economic Journal 2002, 68 (4).

IP   Dennis Rasmussen, *The Infidel and the Professor: David Hume, Adam Smith, and the Friendship that Shaped Modern Thought*, (Princeton: Princeton University Press, 2017)

LAS   Ian Ross, *The Life of Adam Smith*, (Oxford: Clarendon Press, 1995)

SL   Knud Haakonssen, *The Science of the Legislator*, (Cambridge: Cambridge University Press, 1981)

T   David Hume, *Treatise of Human Nature*, eds. LA Selby-Bigge and PH Nidditch, second edition, (Oxford: Clarendon Press, 1978)

Chronology

Preface

This is a book on Adam Smith as a philosopher. That's quite different from a book on Smith as an economist, which is the respect in which most people today know him. Smith is widely regarded as a founder of the discipline of economics, and excerpts (short excerpts, generally) from his *Inquiry into the Nature and Causes of the Wealth of Nations* figure in many introductory textbooks to the discipline. But Smith also wrote an important book in moral philosophy—*The Theory of Moral Sentiments*—as well as papers in aesthetics and the philosophy of science. Moreover, he began working on the *Wealth of Nations* in his capacity as a professor of moral philosophy. To be sure, the phrase "moral philosophy" was more capacious in his day than it is in ours, including much that today we might regard as social science. Still, questions about the aims of human life, the nature of the self, conscience, virtue, and the relationship of morality to religion and politics, were central to it, as they are to moral philosophy today. And those questions will be central to our exploration of Smith's work.

We will also explore Smith's work in a philosophical *way*. Here the relevant contrast is with the approach of an intellectual historian. Historians try to figure out what an author intended to say, and how what he said arises from his social context and influenced later social contexts. Philosophers tend to abstract from the social context of an author, to a considerable extent, and are interested in how one might criticize and defend an author's positions as well as what those positions were. Our exploration, accordingly, will attend relatively little to Smith's historical context—although that will come in at various points—while spending more time than a historian would on laying out potential arguments for and against Smith's views.

Time was when Smith was well known for his moral philosophy. In his own day, it had a wide readership in France, Germany, and the American colonies. The Wealth of Nations was indeed originally greeted with excitement in large part because it came from the pen of the author of The Theory of Moral Sentiments. As we'll see, placing the Wealth of Nations in the context of Smith's moral philosophy also sheds a transformative light on it: Smith's policy proposals, especially, make best sense in that light. Over time, however, Smith's achievement in economics seems to have eclipsed his own work in philosophy. One of my main aims is to help correct that imbalance.

I anticipate that readers of this book will primarily be either philosophers and students of philosophy who are unfamiliar with Smith, or economists, political scientists, and intellectual historians who have read a lot of Smith but never really engaged with him as a philosopher. In writing the book, accordingly, I have tried to assume little either about what Smith said or about how philosophy works. The result may at times appear a bit too basic to one or the other set of readers, but I hope that few readers will feel lost. Smith says at one point that he takes "the utmost pains that [he] can to be perspicuous" in his writing (WN 46). I have tried to do the same in writing about Smith.

I have worked on Smith for many years and consequently owe thanks to more people than I can remember. As regards this book in particular, however, I owe a special debt of gratitude to two groups of people. Michael Guidot, Cody Hatfield-Myers, Taylor Kloha, Hannah Martens, and Alex Sarappo gave me terrific feedback as students in the graduate seminar on Smith that I gave at UIC in 2019, as did Stephen Engelmann, Tony Hernandez, and Tyler Sproule who sat in on that seminar. Then, in the summer of 2020, Alex and Tony joined Olivia Bailey, Remy Debes, Nir Ben Moshe, Fonna Forman, Ryan Hanley, Zac Harmon, Dennis Rasmussen, and Geoffrey Sayre-McCord in giving over hours of their time to a series of Zoom discussions of the manuscript; Nir in addition gave me detailed written comments on practically every chapter. Further input came from the participants in a session on part of this manuscript at the Liberty Fund in 2019, as well as the participants in a 2019 Liberty Fund seminar on Smith, and the audience for my lecture on "Smith and Religion" at the 2020 conference on "Religion and Enlightenment in Eighteenth Century Scotland" sponsored by the Eighteenth Century Scottish Studies Society and the Institute for the Study of Scottish Philosophy; my thanks to Doug den Uyl, Amy Willis, James Foster, and Rick Sher for setting up these events. Smith is right to stress the importance of friendship to happiness. What he doesn't stress is the importance of friendship to scholarship. I feel very lucky to be able to count so many incisive and lively Smith scholars among my friends: my book has certainly gained from their input.

It goes without saying that none of these people is responsible for the remaining errors or confusions to be found in this book. They are my own special contribution. I just hope that what I say about Smith is true enough—and interesting enough—to inspire readers to turn away from my book on him and engage with his writings on their own.

One
The sage of Glasgow

1.1 Smith in his time and ours

Few figures in the history of Western thought have been simultaneously as well known and as poorly understood as Adam Smith. Smith is generally thought of only as a founder of economics. In fact he was first and foremost a moral philosopher, and his great book on economics arose out of courses he taught on moral and political philosophy. He is also generally thought of as a champion of selfishness—a forerunner of Ayn Rand. In fact, his moral philosophy is devoted to *countering* the view of human nature as selfish put about by his predecessors Thomas Hobbes and Bernard Mandeville.[1] And some scholars have characterized him as holding traditional Christian beliefs, appealing among other things to "Providence" to guarantee that the invisible hand of the market will distribute goods amply and fairly. In fact, he contributed to the Enlightenment's critique of Christianity, and his religious beliefs seem to have been limited to a modest theism.

Smith looms so large in public discourse about capitalism (a word he never used) that one may also get the impression that he played a significant role in shaping the economic policies of his day. This impression is not wholly false—he knew many of Britain's leading politicians, was consulted by some of them on tax policy and free trade with Ireland, and may have written a position paper for the Attorney General on how the rebellion in America ought to be handled— but his political influence was mostly indirect. He neither entered politics nor wrote pamphlets on behalf of any cause, leading instead a quiet life as a professor, a tutor to a young nobleman, an independent scholar, and, in his final 12 years, a Commissioner of Customs.

Smith lived during the height of the Scottish Enlightenment, a period running roughly from 1725 to 1800 in which perhaps the most important Anglophone work in philosophy, history, economics, and political science was done in Edinburgh and Glasgow, rather than London or Oxford. Until fairly recently, the fact that Scotland was such a distinctive and important centre of the Enlightenment was overlooked by most people. But over the past generation or two, that oversight has been corrected. One relatively early contributor, in philosophy, to the revival of interest in this period was Alasdair MacIntyre, who writes in *After Virtue*:

> [W]e too often understand [the Enlightenment] as primarily an episode in French cultural history. In fact France is from the standpoint of that culture itself the most backward of the enlightened nations. The French themselves often avowedly looked to English models, but England in turn was overshadowed by the achievements of the Scottish Enlightenment. The greatest figures of all were certainly German: Kant and Mozart. But for intellectual variety as well as intellectual range not even the Germans can outmatch David Hume, Adam Smith, Adam Ferguson, John Millar, Lord Kames and Lord Monboddo.[2]

To this list, one might add the philosophers Frances Hutcheson and Thomas Reid, the biographer John Boswell, the inventor James Watt, the physicist Joseph Black, and the chemist James Hutton. Hutcheson was moreover Smith's teacher, Boswell his student, Reid his successor, and he was a good friend and colleague of Watt, Black, and Hutton. Hume was his closest friend. Smith was therefore situated squarely at the heart of the Scottish Enlightenment, observing if trying to stay out of its controversies, and engaged in active dialogue with practically all its other major figures.

1.2 Early life; professorship at Glasgow; The Theory of Moral Sentiments

Smith was born on or shortly before June 1723—the exact date is unknown but he was baptized on June 5th—in the small Scottish town of Kirkcaldy. His father, also named Adam Smith, and also, for some time, a customs official, had died six months earlier. Smith was his mother's only child, and he was extremely close to her, living with her in Kirkcaldy for extended periods as an adult, and describing her, upon her death, as the person "who certainly loved me more than any other person ever did or ever will love me; and whom I certainly loved and respected more than I ever shall either love or respect any other person" (CAS 275). As these lines imply, Smith never married, nor is he known to have had so much as a single love affair.

When he was 14, Smith entered Glasgow University, where he particularly enjoyed mathematics and physics but also studied moral and political philosophy with the "never to be forgotten" Francis Hutcheson (Smith's description), whose chair he would later occupy. At Glasgow, he was awarded a Snell Exhibition: a fellowship to Balliol College, Oxford designed for Scottish students who planned to enter the Anglican clergy. Smith didn't like Oxford much. In his first surviving letter, he remarks to his guardian that "it will be his own fault if anyone should endanger his health at Oxford by excessive study," and he abandoned any interest he might once have had, if he ever did have any, in entering the clergy (LAS 59). In the words of his first biographer, Dugald Stewart, he found "the ecclesiastical profession [un]suitable to his taste."[3] Instead of attending to theology, he spent his time at Oxford drafting a series of essays on the history and philosophy of science.

He also spent a good deal of his time reading David Hume's *Treatise of Human Nature* (IP 39–40). Hume eventually came to be widely regarded as the greatest philosopher who ever wrote in English, but in his own day he was looked on largely with suspicion—as a sceptic of religion at best and very possibly an atheist. A well-known story has it that Smith was found with the *Treatise* by some of his professors at Balliol, who seized it and "severely reprimanded" him for reading it (IP 39). Some say that this incident, as well as the ideas he found in Hume, helped lead him away from the clergy. In any case, Smith was an early reader of Hume and came to be deeply influenced by him. Nicholas Phillipson says that Smith became "the perfect Humean" at Oxford, and remained that for the rest of his life.[4] This is a mistake if it is meant to suggest that most or all of Smith's major doctrines are borrowed from Hume. Smith criticizes

Hume vigorously in many respects, and almost never fully agrees with him. But it is true that Smith works within Hume's naturalistic framework in practically everything he writes, eschewing appeals to God's purposes and trying to account for all human practices in terms of our emotions, material and psychological needs, and history. Smith's distinctive views of sympathy, moral judgment, religion, and politics can moreover be properly appreciated only if they are compared and contrasted with Hume's.

Smith returned to Scotland in 1746, living with his mother for a couple of years and giving a series of lectures in Edinburgh on rhetoric and belles-lettres, and on law and jurisprudence. Then, in 1751, the Chair of Logic came open at Glasgow University, and Smith was appointed to fill it. Almost immediately, the successor to Francis Hutcheson, Thomas Craigie, stepped down from the Chair of Moral Philosophy, however, and Smith moved to that Chair. He taught moral philosophy at Glasgow for the next 12 years, where his students included John Millar, later to be an important political philosopher in his own right, and James Boswell, the biographer of Samuel Johnson. Smith's colleagues at Glasgow included the chemist Joseph Black, the physician William Cullen, and James Watt, famous for developing the steam engine. All three were friends of Smith; he also became good friends with Hume, although the two lived in different cities. Through Glasgow's Political Economy Club, he came in addition to know some of Scotland's leading merchants. Besides the Political Economy Club, Smith participated, along with Hume, Adam Ferguson, Hugh Blair, and William Robertson, in Edinburgh's Philosophical Society, Select Society, and Poker Club: the most prominent gathering places for Scotland's literati.

Smith's lectures at Glasgow followed the same general plan as those of his teacher and predecessor Hutcheson, beginning with the foundations and nature of morality,[5] moving from there, via the moral principles that underlie law, to a variety of legal topics, and concluding with "police." By the latter term, Smith meant public policy, which he described as concerned with "cleanliness, security, and cheapness or plenty" (LJ 486). Practically all his attention, in this regard, was devoted to "cheapness or plenty." It is easy to see how the first section of Smith's lecture course informed his first book, *The Theory of Moral Sentiments* (TMS) and the last was a source for his second book, *An Inquiry into the Nature and Causes of the Wealth of Nations* (WN). Indeed, a good deal of the content of both books comes out of his Glasgow lectures. The intervening material, on jurisprudence, was also supposed to become a book—"a sort of theory and history of law and government" (CAS 287)—but Smith never completed that manuscript, and asked that it be burned upon his death. Had he completed the trilogy, it might have been more obvious that his moral and economic systems were meant to fit together: that he conceived them as two parts of an overarching account of the workings of morality and society.

The Theory of Moral Sentiments appeared in 1759, after Smith had been teaching for eight years. It comprised an account of sympathy, moral judgment, justice, the self, and the nature of social ties. In many respects, these accounts differ from those of Hutcheson and Hume, but the overall contours of the book fit well within their moral sentimentalist school of thought. Like Hume and Hutcheson, and as against rationalists like Ralph Cudworth or Samuel Clarke, Smith saw morality as rooted in our sentiments rather than our reason, although he made some room for reason too to shape our moral judgments. Like Hume and Hutcheson, and as against Thomas Hobbes and Bernard Mandeville, Smith also stressed our innate sociability—our natural inclination, independent of self-interest, to benevolence—although he saw the ideal of virtue as lying in a balance between self-interest and altruism, rather than in altruism alone, as Hutcheson had insisted. (In this Smith shows the influence of Lord Shaftesbury and Bishop Butler as well as Hume.) He agreed with Hutcheson, however, that selfishness is the greatest threat to morality: "[T]o feel much for others and little for ourselves,... to restrain our selfish, and to indulge our benevolent affections, constitutes the perfection of human nature" (TMS 25).

TMS was a great success, quickly making Smith's name in Britain, becoming part of the college curriculum in the American colonies, and getting translated into both French and German.[6] Largely on the strength of TMS, Smith became acquainted with powerful figures in British politics, and well-known writers and thinkers in France; when WN came out in 1776, it carried an advertisement for a new edition of TMS right after its title page (LAS 270). Smith himself is also said to have regarded TMS as a better book than WN (LAS 177).

It's worth bearing all this in mind when reading WN, since it makes clear that Smith must have expected the initial readers of his treatise on economics to approach it, as he did himself, well aware that the pursuit of our self-interest needs to be put within a moral framework—that we must take care to "restrain our selfish, and... indulge our benevolent affections." The popular idea today that the author of WN was a rational egoist, uninterested in or sceptical of human tendencies toward altruism, has been made possible by a fading of TMS from the public eye, something that was unimaginable to Smith's readers in his own day.

1.3 The making of the *Wealth of Nations*

In 1764, one admirer of TMS, Charles Townshend, offered Smith a new position: travelling companion and tutor to the young Duke of Buccleuch, over a period of some years in France. Townshend was the Duke's stepfather and guardian; he was also a Member of Parliament, former Lord of the Admiralty, and, later, Chancellor of the Exchequer. Smith left Glasgow to take up this position, partly because he wanted to see more of the world. He also gained from it a solid income for the rest of his life, since Townshend continued to pay him even after he ceased to tutor the Duke. At first he found it difficult to meet people in France, however, and was bored. "I have begun to write a book to pass away the time," he said—probably WN.[7] But after a while, Smith's social connections improved. He got to know the leading French *économistes*, including Jacques Necker, Anne Robert Jacques Turgot, and François Quesnay, and became "a habitué of the leading salons" in Paris, where he encountered such figures as Denis Diderot, Jean-Baptiste le Rond d'Alembert, and the Baron d'Holbach. He also met Voltaire on a visit to Geneva.[8]

Still, by the end of 1766, Smith was homesick. "I long passionately to rejoin my old friends," he told his publisher, and advised Hume, who was toying with the possibility of retiring to France, to make his home in London or Edinburgh instead (CAS 121). Shortly thereafter, Smith was given reason of another, tragic sort, to end his stay in France. The Duke's younger brother Hew Campbell Scott, who had come for a visit, caught a fever and died. Smith was at Campbell Scott's bedside throughout his illness, sending detailed letters about his condition daily to his mother and stepfather, and he and the Duke returned to Scotland immediately after his death, bearing his body with them.

The next ten years Smith spent either with his mother in Kirkcaldy, or in London, working on WN. Writing was a long, difficult process for Smith. "I am a slow a very slow workman," he said, "who do and undo everything I write at least half a dozen of times before I can be tolerably pleased with it" (CAS 311).[9] He also felt he needed to consult a wide variety of arcane sources—church and monastery account books, for instance, going back to the thirteenth century (see CAS 145–50)—before he had the evidence he needed for the broad historical claims he wanted to make about Europe's political economy. In early 1776, Hume worried that Smith was in addition too caught up in the crisis in the American colonies to finish his book. "If you wait till the Fate of America be decided," Hume wrote to Smith, "you will wait long" (CAS 185).

But in March 1776, Smith's *Inquiry Concerning the Nature and Causes of the Wealth of Nations* finally appeared. Smith's friends, eagerly awaiting it for years, wrote to tell him that it exceeded their expectations. "One writer after another [on political economy] did nothing but puzzle me," wrote Hugh Blair, while "You have given me full and Complete Satisfaction" (CAS 188). And the clarity and comprehensiveness of the book is very much what other readers have valued in it, from Smith's day to our own. Beginning with a thorough-going analysis of the foundations of economics—the division of labour, the workings of markets, the components of price, the nature of stock (capital), and of banking—it went on to give a history of European political economy from the fall of the Roman Empire onwards, detailing the obstacles put in the way of economic growth by feudalism. Analysis and history then came together to underwrite an attack on the prevailing theories of what governments should do to promote wealth: whether that be propping up manufacturing, as the mercantilists maintained, or propping up agriculture, as the Physiocrats urged. Smith argued that governments should abstain from promoting any particular industry or economic sector: "the obvious and simple system of natural liberty," leaving economic choices as much as possible up to economic agents themselves, was by far the best way to promote wealth. The book concluded with a series of policy recommendations. These included a proposal for widespread public education as well as discussions of the need for standing armies, the low quality of government-supported universities (Smith repeated here the complaints he had made years before about Oxford), and reasons why governments should not establish churches.

WN has been called "the most influential of all Enlightenment contributions to human science."[10] One of Smith's initial readers compared him to Newton, seeing WN as providing a *Principia* of the laws of wealth.[11] Some say that it contains few if any radically new economic ideas,[12] but the quality and scope of its analytic framework nevertheless made it the founding document of the discipline we now know as economics. And while it achieved extraordinary fame only after Smith's death, it was well received immediately. Warm letters poured in to congratulate Smith within a month of its publication from Hume, Blair, Joseph Black, and Adam Ferguson; a recent governor of Massachusetts, Thomas Pownall, wrote an extended response to it within six months. The first edition also sold out within six months, and Smith made revisions for a second edition in 1777.[13] WN was translated into German in the same year that it first came out, and into French and Danish within the next four years (LAS 362, 365; CAS 250). Lord North, the British Prime Minister, acknowledged its influence on him in his budget speech of 1777 (CAS 378n), and many leading figures in the new United States read it avidly. James Madison put it on a list of core books for a proposed congressional library in 1783.[14]

It is interesting to note which features of WN's argument drew negative attention from Smith's contemporaries. Hume thought Smith wrongly made rent an independent component of price. Pownall defended some protectionist measures, arguing that Smith had not taken seriously enough the value of nurturing infant industries until they could succeed on their own (CAS 358–9). Blair (himself an Anglican minister) thought Smith was wrong to argue for a complete separation of church and state. Adam Ferguson (also a minister, but one who did not object to Smith's account of the church) said that Smith was likely to have the universities, the churches, and the merchants all against him, but that he, Ferguson, would defend him against all these critics. The one group he felt Smith had wrongly offended was the advocates of militias. Ferguson and Smith were both members of the Poker Club, which had been formed to promote the importance of a militia in Scotland, and Ferguson thought Smith should not have claimed that standing armies were superior to militias (CAS 193–4). None of these critics—and no-one else at the time, as far as I am aware—accused the author of WN of having presented a system based on self-interest, or of being unconcerned about the poor. And the idea that Smith's "system of natural liberty" could be contrasted with an alternative system designed to eliminate class hierarchies was not on the table at all.

1.4 Hume's death and Smith's encomium to him

In 1776, the same year that WN appeared, David Hume's health began to decline sharply. He told Smith in February that he had lost 70 pounds, and by April, many of Smith's friends began to write him anxious letters about Hume's health. It is not clear exactly what his final illness was, but nothing seemed to improve the condition for long, and Hume became convinced that he was dying. He remained quite cheerful, however, joking with Smith that he had been unable to come up with good excuses to give to Charon, the mythical ferryman to the underworld, for why his death should be postponed. Finally, he came up with one possibility:

> I thought I might say, Good Charon, I have been endeavouring to open the eyes of people; have a little patience only till I have the pleasure of seeing the Churches shut up, and the Clergy sent about their business.

But, Hume said, he knew exactly what Charon's response would be: "O you loitering rogue: that wont happen these two hundred years; do you fancy I will give you a lease for so long a time? Get into the boat this instant." Smith detailed this conversation in a letter to another friend, remarking that "Poor David Hume is dying... with great chearfulness and good humor, and more real resignation to the necessary course of things, than any Whining Christian ever dyed with pretended resignation to the will of God" (CAS 203–4). Hume told Smith that he had written a short autobiography that he would like to have published after his death; Smith proposed to add some details about Hume's death to that work, including the conversations about Charon. Hume agreed to this, and shortly after he died, Smith's publisher William Strahan put out a little pamphlet with both the autobiography and a letter from Smith describing Hume's death (but with the phrase "seeing the downfal of some of the prevailing systems of superstition" in place of Hume's "seeing the Churches shut up, and the Clergy sent about their business").[15] The pamphlet closed with a moving encomium from Smith to his friend: "Upon the whole, I have always considered him, both in his lifetime and since his death, as approaching as nearly to the idea of a perfectly wise and virtuous man, as perhaps the nature of human frailty will permit" (CAS 221).

The reaction to this little pamphlet was uproar. Pious people could not believe that a mocking infidel like Hume could die peacefully, and certainly refused to accept the idea that anyone could be "wise and virtuous"—let alone a model of wisdom and virtue—who was at best sceptical about the existence of God. Smith said that the "single, and as I thought very harmless Sheet of paper" that he had written to Strahan brought on him "ten times more abuse" than he had received for his entire attack on Britain's commercial system.[16]

If Smith really thought his encomium to Hume was "harmless," that would explain what is otherwise a highly unusual moment in his public relationship to faithful Christians. Exactly what his own religious beliefs amounted to is hard to say, but he was certainly very cautious, normally, about the public expression of heresy. (He was cautious about public controversy generally, advising Hume not to engage publicly with Jean-Jacques Rousseau when that paranoiac repaid the kindnesses Hume had done him by supposing that Hume was the mastermind of a grand conspiracy against him.[17]) Smith was a professor at Glasgow in 1751, when Hume applied for a position there, and although he said that he would "prefer David Hume to any man for a colleague," he worried about what the public would think if Hume were appointed (CAS 5–6). Later, when Hume asked Smith, in his last few months, to shepherd his *Dialogues Concerning Natural Religion* into print, Smith firmly refused—indicating to others, moreover, that he did not think it should be published at all (CAS 211). In the end, Hume's nephew took care of the publication, and Smith tried to turn down the money Hume had left him in his will, taking it to be compensation for the task he had refused to carry out. Hume's brother John did not think the bequest should be seen that way, however, and pressed Smith to accept it (CAS 214–5).

1.5 Final years

Upon becoming a Commissioner of Customs in 1777, Smith asked the Duke of Buccleuch to stop sending him an annuity. But the Duke, who had been instrumental in getting Smith the position at Customs, argued that "he never would want it to be suspected that he had procured an office for his friend, in order to relieve himself from the burden of… an annuity" (CAS 252–3). As a result, Smith had an excellent income from 1777 onwards. He was, in his own words, "fully as affluent as I could wish… to be," and he used this money in part to acquire a substantial townhouse in Edinburgh, where he lived with his mother and his cousin Janet until their deaths in the 1780s.

It was a bit odd for such a promoter of free trade to serve in a customs office. Edward Gibbon, who had become a friend, wrote Smith a teasing letter upon hearing of the appointment. "Among the strange reports, which are every day circulated in [London], I heard one to-day so very extraordinary, that I know not how to give credit to it," he began:

> I was informed that a place of Commissioner of the Customs in Scotland had been given to a Philosopher who for his own glory and for the benefit of mankind had enlightened the world by the most profound and systematic treatise on… trade and revenue which had ever been published.
>
> (CAS 228)

Gibbon presumably found the appointment a bit of a come-down in the world, but he was also surely amused that the "profound" treatise written by the new Customs Commissioner did not have much use for the sorts of work that customs offices carry out. Nevertheless, Smith seems to have enjoyed the work, and to have used the opportunity to learn more about how the commercial system he had criticized actually worked. He gained expertise on smuggling, for one thing, which he had maintained was encouraged by high tariffs.[18]

At this time, Smith also took up botany—"in which however I made no great progress"—and "some other sciences to which I had never given much attention before" (CAS 252). He continued to participate in Scotland's club life and became known for hosting large Sunday night dinners for his friends. Meanwhile, he wrote some papers on the imitative arts and worked on two large projects that he never finished. "I have two... great works upon the anvil," he told the Duc de la Rochefoucauld in 1785 (CAS 286–7), "a sort of philosophical history of all the different branches of literature, of philosophy, poetry and eloquence" (perhaps a descendant of the lectures on rhetoric and belles-lettres he had given early in his career) and "a sort of theory and history of law and government" (almost certainly a descendant of the lectures he had given on jurisprudence). He also carried out substantial revisions of both WN and TMS, for new editions of these works. The final edition of TMS, in particular, put out in 1790 just before Smith died, contains an entire new section on virtue as well as large additions to earlier chapters.

Occasionally, during these years, Smith was consulted by the British government on political or economic issues (the American crisis, a proposal by the Irish for a free trading arrangement), and in 1787, he was elected Rector of Glasgow University. His life in the 1780s seems to have been comfortable and busy, but he lamented the steady loss of his friends and relatives. "My friends grow very thin in the world," he wrote to Strahan in 1784 (CAS 275), "and I do not find that my new ones are likely to supply their place." As his cousin Janet, who was also his housekeeper, was dying in 1788, he said that her loss "will leave me one of the most destitute and helpless men in Scotland" (CAS 432). Two years later, he came down with a stomach complaint from which he could not recover, and he died on July 17, 1790.

1.6 Posthumous publications

Smith is of course best known for the two great books he published in his lifetime, but he did allow his literary executors, Joseph Black and James Hutton, to publish versions of a few of the pieces he had originally written as a young man, when he had planned to put together a "philosophical history" of science and the arts. This volume, which Black and Hutton entitled *Essays on Philosophical Subjects* (EPS), includes at least one piece, the "History of Astronomy," that not only contributes interestingly to the philosophy of science, but also sheds light on Smith's own social-scientific methodology. We shall consider it, and other elements of EPS, in Chapter 2.

Black and Hutton did faithfully carry out Smith's request that the manuscripts he had drafted for the two grand projects he had had "upon the anvil" be burned upon his death. A set of student notes on Smith's lectures on jurisprudence came to light about a century after Smith's death, however, and another set of such notes,[19] as well as student notes on his lectures on rhetoric and belles-lettres, were discovered in the twentieth century. These have all now been published, in the standard edition of Smith's works. They give us some sense of what Smith might have included in his two projects "upon the anvil," but how far they represent Smith's settled views on jurisprudence and literature is an open question. The different sets of notes on the jurisprudence lectures cohere with one another, and with sections of WN, very well, and can therefore I think be used as good evidence for how Smith was thinking about jurisprudence in the 1760s. But there is a gap between that and the views he might have held had he revised the lectures to a point he regarded as fit for publication in the 1780s. The lecture notes on rhetoric and belles-lettres are even harder to assess, given that we have just one set of them and very little in his published record with which to compare them.[20] I shall make only limited use of these sources.

1.7 Smith's personality

What sort of a person was Adam Smith? It's not altogether easy to answer that. On the one hand, he had a number of warm friendships, especially with Hume, participated actively in the rich social life of Scotland's literati, and seems always to have enjoyed a convivial dinner. "[A] fine time it was," wrote Alexander Carlyle, "when we could collect David Hume, Adam Smith, Adam Ferguson, Lord Elibank, and Drs. Blair and Jardine [in a tavern for dinner], on an hour's warning."[21] Smith's correspondence also displays an urbanity, tact, and concern for others that bespeaks a person well-attuned to the niceties of social interaction.[22] In addition, when writing to his close friends, Smith sometimes displays a dry wit. He praises a young man to one of his friends by saying that all his qualities should help him make progress in the world except his modesty and sincerity: "and these, it is to be hoped, experience and a better sense of things may, in part, cure him of" (CAS 7). When asking Strahan to go through the first edition of The Theory of Moral Sentiments and point out errors, he says

> I shall at the same time preserve the pretious [sic] right of private judgment for the sake of which our forefathers kicked out the Pope and the Pretender. I believe you to be much more infallible than the Pope, but as I am a Protestant my conscience makes me scruple to submit to any unscriptural authority.
>
> (CAS 67–8)

Then, upon going through the manuscript for errors himself, he tells Strahan that he is sending him a list of "the manifold sins and iniquities you have been guilty of in printing my book," calling the worst of them "sins against the holy Ghost" (CAS 73). Some years later, writing to Hume from France, he tells him that the Duke of Buccleuch

> has read almost all your works several times over, and was it not for the more wholesome Doctrine which I take care to instill into him, I am afraid he might be in danger of adopting some of your wicked Principles.
>
> (CAS 105)

On the other hand, the reports we have of how Smith behaved in the presence of people suggest that he could be startlingly unsociable. Carlyle, even while recollecting what a "fine time it was" when he could dine with Smith, Hume, Blair, et al, characterizes Smith as a poor conversationalist—lecturing at people, albeit quite well, rather than engaging with them—and as "the most absent man in company I ever saw, moving his lips and talking to himself, and smiling, in the midst of large companies."[23] A newspaper account, upon Smith's death, said that "his appearance was ungracious, and his address awkward," and that "his frequent absences of mind gave him an air of vacancy, and even of stupidity."[24] The word "absent" appears particularly often in descriptions of Smith,[25] and tales of his absent-mindedness abound. Sir Walter Scott, who spent time in Smith's household as a teenager, recounted an incident in which Smith

> put an elderly maiden lady, who presided at the tea-table, to sore confusion, by neglecting utterly her invitation to be seated, and walked round and round the circle, stopping ever anon to steal a lump from the sugar basin, which the venerable spinster was at length constrained to place on her own knee, as the only method of securing it from his… depredation.[26]

Another woman who hosted Smith recounted in her diary that one morning Smith, concentrating on something he was saying rather than his breakfast,

> took a piece of bread & butter, which, after he had rolled round & round, he put into the teapot & poured water upon it; some time after he poured it into a cup, & when he had tasted it he said it was the worst tea he had ever met with.[27]

These descriptions suggest that Smith may have been somewhere on the autism spectrum. In any case, he seems to have lived to an extraordinary degree within his own head. Dugald Stewart, whose memoir of Smith is the main source for later biographers, describes him as "habitually inattentive to familiar objects, and to common occurrences," but says that his peculiarities—combined with "the artless simplicity of his heart" and "the warm interest he felt to the last, in every thing connected with the welfare of his friends"—endeared him to those who knew him.[28] Stewart adds, unsurprisingly, that Smith was "not fitted for the general commerce of the world, or for the business of active life,"[29] but it may yet be true, as Smith's first full biographer, John Rae, claimed, that "few men were ever by nature more entirely formed for friendship than Smith."[30] Smith had, in any case, many of the social virtues that he analyzed and praised in TMS. He was scrupulously honest, refusing payment wherever he thought it was not his due,[31] and a concerned and devoted tutor, son, and friend. But for someone who wrote so much and so incisively about society, he seems to have been a surprisingly solitary person, comfortable only in small groups of intimate friends, and content to spend most of his time reading or writing, when not engaged with professional duties.

1.8 Enlightenment humanist

Setting Smith's personality aside, now, what sort of thinker was he? Was he first and foremost a moral philosopher, who happened to turn to economics for part of his career? Or was he first and foremost the pioneering founder of economics, who happened to have a background in moral philosophy? I think he is best seen as neither of these things, exactly, but rather a superb example of the sort of broadly curious thinker who flourished in the Enlightenment, interested in everything from rhetoric to botany, for whom morality and politics and economics were just a few of the many fascinating subjects that could be illuminated by naturalistic modes of investigation. Smith himself characterizes philosophers as people who take a general interest in things rather than focusing on any specific thing. They are "generall observers," he says, "whose trade it is, not to do any thing, but to observe every thing; and who, upon that account, are often capable of combining together the most distant and dissimilar objects."[32] Smith also thinks that this wide-angle view on things enables philosophers to come up with inventions. The example he gives is "the fire engine," by which he probably meant the steam engine invented by his friend James Watt. But he may also have been thinking of his own policy proposals, on everything from public education to taxation to the American crisis, which similarly arose from the broad overview he developed of politics and political economy.[33] In any case, it seems clear that the simple willingness to "observe every thing" and to compare "the most distant and dissimilar objects"—to *notice* things that other people take for granted, and put them in the context of other features of human life—is for him the prime mark of philosophical work. And that gift for observation, rather than the derivation of foundational principles, is the main achievement of both TMS and WN. Nicholas Phillipson rightly calls WN "the greatest and most enduring monument to the intellectual culture of the Scottish Enlightenment,"[34] and it is the *breadth* of that culture, and the pride it took in observing things impartially—independently of political or religious prejudice—that Smith represents especially well. The Swiss naturalist Charles Bonnet once called Smith "the sage of Glasgow" (CAS 180). Bonnet was himself an excellent example of a well-rounded Enlightenment thinker—trained in law, he was best known for contributions he made to psychology and biology (including botany, as it happens)—and this compliment, from one *lumiére* to another, nicely captures Smith's place in the world of letters.

If that is right, however, it will be a mistake to assimilate Smith's philosophy to the systematic work of Descartes or Locke or Hume. It will also be a mistake to assimilate his political economy to the more systematic work of his successor Ricardo. If we are looking for rigorous system-building, or the foundationalist arguments that make such systems possible, we are likely to be disappointed in Smith. If we see him as the broadly curious Enlightenment humanist that he took himself to be, and appreciate the many fine observations he makes and insightful connections he draws, we will get a much better sense of his achievements.[35]

There are two other advantages of regarding Smith as a broad Enlightenment intellectual rather than (simply) a philosopher or political economist. One is that we can then better grasp the importance, to his work, of debunking popular prejudices. His political economy, in particular, is striking for the degree to which it is directed against prejudice: against corn dealers,[36] against the poor,[37] and in favour of mercantilist projects like the East India Company, especially. But a prejudice—a "pre-judgment," literally—is a belief based on such poor grounds that exposing it to the light, laying out clearly the subject matter that it misconstrues, should lead it to evaporate. Precisely this is what Smith seems to think will happen to, for instance, the prejudice against corn dealers once their role in the larger economy is properly appreciated. Observing a wide variety of things, and bringing them together, thus serves the paradigmatic Enlightenment goal of combatting prejudice.

The second advantage of placing Smith in his Enlightenment context is that we can more clearly appreciate the importance of history to his work. Naturalistic, critical history—an attempt to narrate the past from which the present has arisen in a clear-eyed way, free from religious or political bias—was central to the "light" that Enlightenment figures hoped to shed on their social world and Smith was good friends with a number of these historians: above all, William Robertson, Edward Gibbon, and David Hume (whose *History of England* is what really brought him fame in his own time).[38] Moreover, everything Smith himself either wrote or planned to write was in significant part historical. He began his career by writing histories of astronomy, physics, and metaphysics. TMS contains, in its Part VII, perhaps the first extended history of moral philosophy in a volume on that subject. A history of corn prices from the sixteenth to the eighteenth centuries, and a history of European economies from the Roman Empire onwards, play central roles in the argumentation of WN. And Smith described his two projects in his later years as "a sort of theory and history of law and government" and "a sort of philosophical history" of belles-lettres. The idea that the history of a practice or institution will shed important light on its social function, and its success or failure in fulfilling that function, is a central commitment of the Enlightenment, and one of which Smith is an outstanding representative.

1.9   Ideological agendas?

What light does Smith's life shed on his moral and political philosophy? This is another question that it is hard to answer. Were Smith, say, a merchant or a director of the East India Company, like his predecessor Thomas Mun, we might expect his economic theories to reflect the biases typically developed in that role. Were he a politician or political activist, like Edmund Burke and Thomas Paine, we might expect his political views to reflect the parties or causes he represented. Were he a minister, or someone known, like his friend Hume, for public polemics against church doctrine, we might expect his views of religion to reflect these roles. Smith was, however, none of these things—we do not even know what political party he supported, although he is usually taken to be some sort of

Whig—and was in fact reluctant to speak up publicly on any major controversy of his day, or even to express such views, in any detail at least, in his private interactions and correspondence.

There are two significant exceptions to this rule. One is Smith's open commitment to the American side in the war between Britain and its colonies. Dennis Rasmussen writes that most Scottish intellectuals firmly supported the British government's attempt to hold on to the colonies, calling Smith and Hume "almost the lone dissenters on this score" (IP 178). Smith's dissent came in the form of recommending, in WN, that the colonists be given representation in the British parliament (even suggesting that the capital of Britain might eventually move to the other side of the Atlantic: WN 625–6), although privately he seems to have urged more modest concessions to the rebels.[39] He closed WN by urging Britain to reconcile itself to what in fact was about to happen: the loss of the colonies to independence.

Smith's avowal of these views does little to change how we would otherwise read him, however. Everything he wrote about politics and economics comports with an opposition to colonialist projects, which he explicitly criticizes in a long chapter of WN. So there is nothing surprising about the fact that he favoured the Americans in their struggle with their homeland, nor any reason to think that he tailored his theories to meet a prior political commitment.

The same does not go for the other respect in which Smith's private views may interact with his published work. It is said by many scholars that Smith was an agnostic or atheist, and by others that he was a traditional Christian.[40] If he was the first, then his tributes to Providence and remarks on the value of believing in God in TMS are in bad faith; if he was the second, then these passages can be seen as meant to bring in their train a richer religious commitment than he explicitly avows. What Smith believed, privately, about religion can therefore play a significant role in how we interpret his work.

I stand between the extremes on this matter. As we have seen, Smith made some fun of traditional Protestant as well as Catholic beliefs in his private correspondence, and scoffed at "whining Christians" and their "pretended resignation" to God; as we have also seen, however, he was careful to tone down Hume's aspersions on churches in the tribute to Hume that he prepared for the public.

He also omitted an approving passage on Christ's atonement for our sins from the final edition of TMS, and there are passages in both TMS and WN criticizing the moral qualities of Christian clerics almost as harshly as Hume was wont to do (see, for instance, TMS 133–4; WN 771, 802–3). Indeed, if we set aside the passage on atonement that Smith removed from TMS, and a passing compliment in WN to the clergy of Presbyterian churches, I can think of no favourable comments on specifically Christian doctrines or institutions anywhere in Smith's oeuvre.[41] In WN, Smith expresses a hope that one day "that pure and rational religion, free from every mixture of absurdity, imposture, or fanaticism, [that] wise men in all ages of the world wished to see established" would reign everywhere (WN 793). But the only "pure and rational religion" that wise people "in all ages of the world" could possibly be said to have praised is some broadly Stoic theism, not Christianity.

So it seems clear that Smith was no traditional Christian—no Christian of any sort, perhaps, by the end of his life. But it doesn't follow from this that Smith rejected the idea of a God or an afterlife. Both of those ideas were part of "rational" or "natural" religion, as that was understood in Smith's day, and Smith explicitly affirms those ideas in TMS. I shall argue in Chapter 8 that Smith is best read as a believer in some sort of rational or natural religion. But neither his writings nor his biography makes his religious beliefs particularly clear.

I do not think that Smith deliberately hid what he believed. Some scholars dismiss every hint of religious belief in Smith as an insincere sop to the populace. They offer no evidence for this claim, however, and no evidence for it can be found in Smith's writings, whether private or public; nowhere is there a sceptical critique of arguments for God along the lines of say, chapter XI in Hume's first Enquiry. To assume that Smith must nevertheless have been an atheist or agnostic is I think simply to read into him the commitments of modern-day, secular academics. I am in any case averse to "hidden doctrine" readings of a text unless there is evidence, in the style or content of that text or in the author's private writings, that it should not be taken at face value.[42] Otherwise, such readings are conducive to a free-wheeling imputation to the author of whatever a reader wants to see in the text, indeed to a collapse of the distinction between author and reader—a collapse that I regard as the abandonment of the project of interpretation.

What we can safely say is that Smith avoided open religious controversy. That may reflect a reserved character, but it also fits well with his generally modest conception of what philosophers can accomplish—with his interest, not in sparking theoretical or practical revolutions, but in providing a comprehensive, impartial view of our moral and social world, from which small corrections to prevailing beliefs can be made. Smith was an Enlightenment intellectual who hoped that a fuller understanding of things would lead to gradual, slow change in the beliefs of ordinary people. In his thought as in his life, he demonstrated an unusual humility, and we appreciate him best if we start by recognizing that humility.

1.10 A moderate radical

Jonathan Israel has drawn a distinction between a "radical" Enlightenment, laying the groundwork for the revolutions against monarchy, aristocracy, religious oppression, and slavery that were to begin in 1789, and a "moderate" Enlightenment that was far more conservative, urging reform rather than revolution, and trying to preserve at least the basic structure of the institutions that the radicals sought to overturn.[43] And Smith, for him, belongs firmly with the moderates rather than the radicals. But while it is true, as we've just seen, that Smith was a "moderate" in many ways, Israel's reading of the Enlightenment in terms of this distinction is highly misleading, and makes a particularly bad mess of Smith. Israel sees metaphysical materialism, moral rationalism, atheism, republicanism, opposition to slavery, and support for revolution as belonging together in one neat package, and characterizes all his "radicals" as endorsing the package while all his "moderates" oppose it. There are many reasons for rejecting this schema. Contrary to Israel's claims, for instance, Benjamin Rush, John Millar, and Thomas Jefferson, three of his radical heroes, were all moral sentimentalists, not rationalists (all three were indeed highly influenced by Smith).[44] Israel also insists that radicals had to reject traditional religion. He writes, for instance, that radicalism "had to be anchored in forms of philosophy built on blanket denial of a prior transcendental order."[45] Rush was quite religious, however—Israel says that he "proposed stripping away practically all traditional theology" from Christianity, but that is not true[46]—and the minister Richard Price, one of Israel's main heroes, can certainly not be described as denying "a prior transcendental order to the world."[47] At the same time, Israel struggles mightily to attribute to Hume—one of his "moderates"—much greater respect for religion than he actually had.[48] A classificatory system that counts Rush and Price as radical challengers to traditional Christianity, but Hume as one of its defenders, has gone seriously wrong somewhere.

When it comes to Smith, Israel seems simply not to have read either Smith's own writings, or the secondary literature on those writings, with any care. He claims that "emancipating enslaved blacks is simply not an issue that figures at all substantially in [Smith's] perspective,"[49] blithely ignoring the texts in which Smith decries slavery, especially of black people in the Americas (TMS 206–7; LJ 181–5). He presents Smith as a friend of aristocracy, but in fact Smith regularly characterizes aristocrats as vain fools, who have "usurped ... unjust advantage[s] over ... their fellow-citizens."[50] He presents Smith as a friend of empire, but a vehement critique of empire runs through WN—which ends with a recommendation that Britain give up its fantasies of world dominion.[51] And he dismisses Smith's strong concern for the well-being of the poor by way of jaw-dropping misreadings of what Smith says on this subject.[52]

A better sense of where Smith belongs in the struggle for more egalitarian societies that got underway in the Enlightenment—and for more naturalistic ones, less bound by traditional religions—can be gained from the fact that he was admired by such egalitarian figures as Millar, Rush, Tom Paine, Jeremy Bentham, the Marquis of Condorcet, Mary Wollstonecraft, and William Godwin. He was also, however, admired by more conservative figures, like Edmund Burke and William Pitt: probably in large part for his moderation, his preference for gradual reform over revolution. But a preference for a moderate rather than a revolutionary pace of change could go along quite well with a set of radically egalitarian political ideals, in the Enlightenment, and one's stance on traditional Christianity could come apart from one views on either the proper pace or the proper direction of political change. The intellectuals of the Enlightenment were far more complex than Israel's portrayal of them suggests, and many were radicals on political but not religious questions, or vice versa, or were radical in some political and religious respects but not in others. Smith is one of the most complex, and most independent-minded, of these intellectuals and we appreciate him best if we separate him from any religious or political party and try instead to let his writings speak for themselves. That will be our project in the ensuing chapters.

1.11 Summary[53]

Smith was a central figure of the Scottish Enlightenment, educated in its ethos and close friends with many of its leading figures, especially David Hume. This context helps us see why it is a mistake to see him as either just a philosopher or just an economist. He was, rather, a broadly curious Enlightenment humanist with interests in a wide array of subjects. It's also a mistake to identify him with any strong religious or political agenda. In both his writings and his conversation, he stayed instead away from controversy for the most part, and he cannot easily be characterized as either a religious sceptic or a religious believer, either a challenger to the political and social order of this day or a defender of it.

Notes

1 He is also said to have been, personally, extremely generous. See LAS 407.

2 Alasdair MacIntyre, *After Virtue*, 2nd ed. (Notre Dame: University of Notre Dame Press, 1984), 37. MacIntyre provides a nice account of the social context out of which the Scottish Enlightenment arose in his *Whose Justice? Which Rationality?* (Notre Dame: University of Notre Dame Press, 1988), chapters 12 and 13. See also A. Broadie and C. Smith (eds.), *The Cambridge Companion to the Scottish Enlightenment*, 2nd ed. (Cambridge: Cambridge University Press, 2019) and John Robertson, *The Case for Enlightenment: Scotland and Naples 1680–1760* (Cambridge: Cambridge University Press, 2005). Robertson notes that

> Before 1960 [the Scottish Enlightenment] was scarcely recognized at all. Few remembered even that David Hume and Adam Smith were Scottish; that their contemporaries included Francis Hutcheson, Adam Ferguson, William Robertson, Thomas Reid, Lord Kames, and John Millar was long forgotten by all except a handful of specialists.
>
> (24–5)

3 Stewart, "Account of the Life and Writings of Adam Smith," EPS 272.

4 Nicholas Phillipson, *Adam Smith: An Enlightened Life* (New Haven: Yale University Press, 2010), 71.

5 Actually this was preceded by some discussion of "natural theology," but we have no idea of what Smith said under this heading. No notes have survived of it, and no part of it found expression in his writings. See Stewart, "Account," 274 for a description of Smith's course.

6 See the editors' introduction to TMS 29–33, and my "Philosophy and Moral Practice: Kant and Adam Smith," *Kant-Studien* 82/3 (1991) and "Adam Smith's Reception among the American Founders, 1776–1790," *William and Mary Quarterly* 59/4 (2002).

7 CAS 102, and editor's note thereto. But see also LAS 202–3.

8 Phillipson, *Adam Smith*, 192.

9 See also CAS 140, where he compares his work with "the web of penelope."

10 Robert Wokler, quoted in IP 160.

11 Thomas Pownall, "A Letter from Governor Pownall to Adam Smith," in CAS 337, 354.

12 Joseph Schumpeter, *History of Economic Analysis*, ed. E.B. Schumpeter (New York: Oxford University Press, 1954), 184–5.

13 It was to go through four further editions in Smith's lifetime, and he revised it for a sixth edition just before he died.

14 Fleischacker, "Adam Smith's Reception among the American Founders," 901.

15 The published "Letter to Strahan" also omits the very warm salutation on Hume's last letter to Smith: "Adieu My dearest friend."

16 The best account I know of the controversy sparked by the "Letter to Strahan" is IP, Chapter 12. For a collection of documents relevant to the controversy, see also Dennis Rasmussen (ed.), *Adam Smith and the Death of David Hume* (Lanham: Lexington Books, 2018).

17 On this affair, see IP, chapter 7.

18 See CAS 246, 272–3, 410–1; WN 882, 884, 898, 903.

19 A third, rather short set of notes—known as the "Anderson Notes"—has also come to light. It is not included in LJ, but can be found in Ronald Meek, "New Light on Adam Smith's Glasgow Lectures on Jurisprudence," *History of Political Economy* 8/4 (1976).

20 Lecture 3 of LRBL was worked up into Smith's "Considerations Concerning the Formation of Languages."

21 Alexander Carlyle, *Autobiography of the Rev. Dr. Alexander Carlyle, Minister of Inveresk*, 2nd ed. (Edinburgh: William Blackwood, 1860), 275.

22 Much of it is devoted to introducing his students or the children of his friends to potential mentors; one long exchange consists of an attempt to help his friend Adam Ferguson receive an annuity that was due him (CAS 416–23).

23 Carlyle, *Autobiography*, 227.

24 Phillipson, *Adam Smith*, 56. See also Ross, quoting Horace Walpole on hearing that Charles Townshend had selected Smith as a traveling companion for his stepson:

> I am afraid … Townshend will make a very indifferent *compagnon de voyage* out of a very able professor of ethics. Mr. Smith has extensive knowledge … but he is awkward and has so bad an ear that he will never learn to express himself intelligibly in French.
>
> (*LAS* 196)

25 Boswell called him an "accurate, absent man"; Dugald Stewart said that he was "habitually inattentive to familiar objects, and to common occurrences; and he frequently exhibited instances of absence"; Lady Mary Coke, recounting the tea episode below in her diary, called Smith "the most Absent Man that ever was" (IP 48, 147; Stewart, "Account," 329).

26 Quoted in LAS 310.

27 Quoted in IP 147.

28 Stewart, "Account," 329.

29 Stewart, "Account," 329.

30 Quoted in IP 49.

31 Recall his attempt to refuse the money that Hume left him, given that he had refused to publish Hume's *Dialogues*, and his attempt to persuade the Duke of Buccleuch to stop his annuity: §§ 3 and 4, above.

32 LJ 347; WN 21; Compare LJ 492, 570 (from the "Early Draft" of WN), and EPS 45: "Philosophy is the science of the connecting principles of nature."

33 See WN 21n22 and my *On Adam Smith's Wealth of Nations* (Princeton: Princeton University Press, 2004), 244–5.

34 Phillipson, *Adam Smith*, 237.

35 Hume and Rousseau were of course broad Enlightenment humanists as well—the one writing histories and political essays, the other operas and novels, in addition to philosophy. Both also wrote philosophy in highly inventive and fluid literary styles, something that Smith did not do.

36 Smith explicitly compares the prejudice against corn dealers to medieval prejudices against witches: WN 534.

37 See for instance WN 143–4, on the intellectual skills of the "common ploughman."

38 One might also include Adam Ferguson and John Millar. Both carried out their work primarily by way of history.

39 The "Thoughts on America" (included in CAS as Appendix B) suggest going back to the pre-Townshend status quo, and then gradually letting the colonies go.

40 See Chapter 8, below.

41 There is a nod to the idea that we are made in God's image and a couple of nods to the Golden Rule in TMS (25, 165–6, 171) but these are ideas that advocates of natural religion in the eighteenth century (as well as Jews and Muslims) would

have shared. On TMS 301 Smith describes a variety of Christian "divines" as being "of the most eminent piety and learning and of the most amiable manners": but it is notable that he has picked these figures out, not as Christians, but as believers in a Platonist conception of God as a perfectly benevolent being.

42 Smith himself shared this aversion, by the way, indignantly rejecting the idea that Plato should be read as holding a "double doctrine"—an esoteric teaching that contradicted his exoteric meaning—in a long footnote to the "History of Ancient Logics and Metaphysics" (EPS 121–3n). (I am indebted to Dennis Rasmussen for pointing out that this footnote can support my anti-esoteric reading of Smith himself.)

I don't mean to deny that *some* writers have an esoteric doctrine. There are authors whose style and content give us reason to look for hidden meanings behind their texts. Maimonides explicitly tells his reader that he will be hiding some of his teachings, in the introduction to his *Guide for the Perplexed*, and Lord Shaftesbury, Hume, and Gotthold Lessing, to take but three eighteenth-century examples, not infrequently use irony, literary framing devices, and, sometimes, obvious contradictions, as hints to the reader against taking what they say at face value. The same is rarely if ever true of Smith. He is a very straightforward writer, committed above all to being "perspicuous" (his term: WN 46), and not at all given to the jokes and literary games in which his friend Hume, among others, delighted.

43 Jonathan Israel, *Radical Enlightenment* (Oxford: Oxford University Press, 2001), *Enlightenment Contested* (Oxford: Oxford University Press, 2006), *Democratic Enlightenment* (Oxford: Oxford University Press, 2011) and *A Revolution of the Mind* (Princeton: Princeton University Press, 2010).

44 For Israel's use of moral rationalism as a criterion of radicalism, see RM 19–20. For his inclusion of Rush, Millar, and Jefferson among the radicals, see *Democratic Enlightenment*, 229 (here he also draws an exaggerated distinction between Smith and Millar), 475–6 and *Revolution of the Mind*, 15, 41–9. For Millar's sentimentalism, see John Craig's "Life of John Millar, Esq" in Millar, *The Origin of the Distinction of Ranks*, ed. A. Garrett (Indianapolis: Liberty Fund, 2006), 20–4; for Jefferson's, see his letter to Peter Carr, on August 10, 1787, in Thomas Jefferson, *The Life and Selected Writings of Thomas Jefferson*, eds. A. Koch and W. Peden (New York: Random House, 1993). Most of what Rush says about our moral faculties evokes Hutcheson and Hume (and at one point draws explicitly on Kames) rather than their rationalist opponents. See Benjamin Rush, *Lectures on the Mind* (Philadelphia: American Philosophical Society, 1981), 460–76, esp. 472:

> the moral faculties distinguish and separate in an instant the objects of moral feeling, from those of intellectual perception; hence we find their first decision, like that of an external sense, is always just, whereas the first decisions of the intellectual faculties are frequently erroneous.

45 Israel, *Enlightenment Contested*, 591.

46 Israel, *Revolution of the Mind*, 43. A glance at Rush's "Defence of the Bible as a School Book" (in his *Essays, Literary, Moral and Philosophical* [Philadelphia: Thos. and William Bradford, 1806]) will show that Israel has Rush badly wrong. Rush insists there on the importance of the "doctrines" of the Gospels, not just their moral teachings (the moral teachings, he says, rest on the doctrines)—in particular the doctrine of "the vicarious life and death of the Son of God" (105).

47 He was also not a metaphysical monist, insisting instead that we have an immaterial free will.

48 He says, for instance, that Hume thought it indispensable to morality to believe that the world has "an intelligent Creator and supervisor" who promises us "reward and punishment in the hereafter" (*Democratic Enlightenment*, 211; *Enlightenment Contested*, 690). Israel pulls this extraordinary claim out of an ambiguous passage in Hume's *Natural History of Religion* that most commentators (including ones in Israel's own footnotes) take to be disingenuous, and that in any case says nothing about either morality or reward and punishment. In fact Hume argues throughout his writings that secular motivation is perfectly adequate for keeping people virtuous, and religious commitments are largely harmful to that motivation. Consider, for instance, his attack on "monkish virtues" in the second *Enquiry*, or Philo's response to Cleanthes' suggestion that religion (because of its promise of reward and punishment in an afterlife) is necessary as "a security to morals":

> How happens it then … that all history abounds so much with accounts of its pernicious consequences on public affairs? Factions, civil wars, persecutions, subversions of government, oppression, slavery: these are the dismal consequences which always attend its prevalence over the minds of men. If the religious spirit be ever mentioned in any historical narration, we are sure to meet afterwards with a detail of the miseries which attend it. And no period of time can be happier or more prosperous than those in which it is never regarded or heard of.
>
> (*Dialogues Concerning Natural Religion*, ed. R. Popkin, 2 ed.
> [Indianapolis: Hackett, 1998], 82)

49 Israel, *Democratic Enlightenment*, 240.

50 WN 385. See also TMS 53–4, 62–4, 149–50, 181–5; WN 265, 385–6, 418–9. Smith does think that an aristocracy of wealth and fortune helps maintain civil order (see especially WN 710–4), but this seems more a descriptive claim than a normative one. Given his moral disapproval of aristocrats, and of the effect of aristocracy on the moral sentiments of all of us, it is hard to imagine that he would fail to embrace a more democratic way of maintaining order, if he could be shown one that was effective.

51 WN 947. See also 448, 561–2, 582–90, 613–8, 626, 634–41, 752–4 and Sankar Muthu, "Adam Smith's Critique of International Trading Companies," *Political Theory*, 36 (April 2008).

52 Unwilling to accept the general view among scholars that Smith was a "friend
    of the poor," Israel insists that Smith's "occasional remarks expressing indig-
    nation at how law and institutions are manipulated by the rich at the expense
    of the poor mostly occur in unpublished papers and remained marginal to
    his thought" (Democratic Enlightenment, 238). It's hard to know where to start, in
    pointing out the errors and distortions in this claim. First, Israel backs it up
    by citing Emma Rothschild's Economic Sentiments (ES), but in the pages he cites
    Rothschild largely discusses WN, not "unpublished papers." (He cites ES 61–2,
    which has seven references to WN.) Second, Smith does not just make "occa-
    sional remarks" about the well-being of the poor. A polemic on their behalf
    runs through WN, and shows up in much of TMS as well. (See my On Adam
    Smith's _Wealth of Nations_, section 51). Nor is this a personal commitment inde-
    pendent of Smith's main lines of thought. TMS contains a careful analysis of just
    why our moral sentiments tend, balefully but inevitably, to overlook the poor
    (TMS I.iii), and one of WN's central themes is that economies should serve the
    bulk of the population—overwhelmingly poor, in Smith's time—rather than
    national glory, or the interests of merchants or aristocrats. Ignoring all of these
    elements of Smith's thought, Israel claims instead that for Smith "success in
    business, like aristocratic birth, should be regarded as a sign of divine favour"
    (Democratic Enlightenment, 238–9). It's hard for a scholar of Smith to imagine how
    one could possibly read him this way. Israel manages it by misreading a passage
    from TMS (166–7) that actually argues just that the rewards proper to skill in
    business are different from those proper to moral virtue (a passage which he
    indeed mis-cites, attributing the phrases he quotes to two other sections of TMS
    (239n24)—which, ironically, make precisely the opposite point from the one he
    tries to put in Smith's mouth! Indeed, they include Smith's famous claim that
    the admiration of riches is "the great and most universal cause of the corruption
    of our moral sentiments.")

53 The format of these Routledge books on great philosophers includes a summary
    of each chapter at its end. In some cases, I found that I could integrate that fairly
    smoothly into the chapter's conclusion; in other cases, the summary has been
    added to a chapter whose content was already complete. I have signalled this by
    entitling the final section "Conclusion and summary" in the first sort of case,
    and simply "Summary" in the second.

Further reading

Nicholas Phillipson, Adam Smith: An Enlightened Life
John Rae, Life of Adam Smith
Dennis Rasmussen, The Infidel and the Professor
Ian Ross, The Life of Adam Smith
Dugald Stewart, "Account of the Life and Writings of Adam Smith"

Two

Epistemology; philosophy of science; aesthetics

It no doubt looks odd to group epistemology, philosophy of science, and aesthetics together. The combination is less surprising, however, when we consider that Smith's writings about scientific and philosophical theories mostly concern the sentiments that lead us to accept such theories: sentiments, after all, are crucial to our admiration of art. In any case, the small volume published after Smith's death under the title *Essays on Philosophical Subjects* (EPS) is a collection of pieces on astronomy, physics, metaphysics, and the arts. The editors of that volume, Smith's old friends Joseph Black and James Hutton, say in their preface to it that the essays "appear[...] to be parts of a plan [Smith] had once formed, for giving a connected history of the liberal sciences and elegant arts" (EPS 32). So Smith himself seems to have thought that science and art belong together.

Now the pieces in EPS do not fit well under the headings of what we call either epistemology or aesthetics today. But in Smith's day, philosophy and science were not sharply distinguished, and much that went under the heading of "philosophy" overlapped with what we would call "social science": psychology, sociology, economics, anthropology, or political science. This is true not only of Smith's writings, but of Hutcheson's, Hume's, Rousseau's, and even Kant's.

One concern we have today about running philosophy and social science together is that that may blur the distinction between the descriptive and the normative. And the relationship between these two ways of approaching a subject is a vexed one for many eighteenth-century thinkers. The problem of how to distinguish philosophy from social science arises in a particularly acute way for

Smith's pieces in EPS, moreover. There may be a mix of descriptive and normative points, and a tendency to blur the lines between these things, even in Hume's and Kant's writings on knowledge and beauty, but they clearly do address normative questions—questions about what sorts of claims *rightly* count as claims to knowledge or claims of taste—as well as descriptive ones. Smith explicitly tells us at the opening of the "History of Astronomy" that he is not going to do that in this piece. "Let us examine… all the different systems of nature, which, in these western parts of the world… have successively been adopted by the learned and ingenious," he says, "… without regarding their absurdity or probability, their agreement or inconsistency with truth and reality" (EPS 46). He proposes instead to consider these systems entirely as regards their capacity to "sooth the imagination": to satisfy the *psychological* impulses that lead us to construct or accept scientific explanations. This programme characterizes the other essays in EPS as well. They abstract from the normative questions that have traditionally been the focus of philosophy, and consider claims about what is real or beautiful largely from the perspective of the tendencies in the human mind that lead us to make such claims. So Smith seems to be doing something much closer to psychology than to philosophy in EPS.

Nevertheless, there are philosophical insights of considerable interest scattered throughout EPS, and these insights shed light on Smith's methodology in TMS and WN. For that reason—as well as the fact that some of these pieces seem to have been among Smith's first writings—we will begin with these essays. I'll offer a quick overview of their contents, then draw out a series of philosophical themes running through them. I'll also say a little about Smith's essay on language, which is not included in most editions of EPS, and his lectures on rhetoric and belles-lettres: materials that are similarly helpful for understanding Smith's methodology.

2.1 The contents of EPS and the "considerations on language"

The most famous essay in EPS is known as "The History of Astronomy," although it is really the first of three essays on "The Principles Which Lead and Direct Philosophical Enquiries."[1] The history of astronomy is simply supposed to *illustrate* the principles that guide philosophical enquiries,[2] just as the second essay in the collection illustrates those principles by way of the history of ancient physics, and the third uses ancient logic and metaphysics (mostly the latter) to illustrate them. Once again, it is worth bearing in mind that by "philosophical," Smith means in part what we would today call "scientific," and that he uses "principle" to refer primarily to psychological tendencies—sentiments, for the most part—not rules of reason. So "the principles which lead and direct philosophical enquiries" means, in modern terms, "the psychological tendencies which lead and direct scientific and philosophical inquiries."

We should also bear in mind that Smith tells us that he will set aside the plausibility, even the truth, of the theories he takes up and consider simply the sentiments that lead people to accept them. Smith says that "philosophy… may be regarded as one of those arts which address themselves to the imagination," and he is looking for the principles—psychological tendencies, again — that make theories appealing to our imaginations (EPS 46). Smith's over-arching hypothesis is that astronomical, physical, and metaphysical theories are sparked by our sentiment of "wonder"—a disturbing, if sometimes also exhilarating, response to anomalies—and are regarded as successful if they allay that wonder: if they enable our imagination to place the events that disturbed it into regular patterns. Once the theory succeeds in this, however, new anomalies that it cannot account for are likely to arise, our imaginations will again be disturbed by them, and a new theory will be needed to allay this new discomfort.[3] The astronomy essay, much longer and more detailed than the others, lays out various ancient, medieval and early modern "systems" for explaining the heavens, showing how each solved problems that its predecessors could not solve. It ends with a superb account of the Newtonian system, and how it provided a far simpler, and therefore more satisfying, explanation of motion in general—both on earth and in the heavens—than had Galileo, Descartes, or any other previous theorist. Then, in its final lines, the essay reminds us that even Newton's system is but an "invention… of the imagination," not "the real chains Nature uses" to connect its constituent parts, so it may one day be superseded by another such invention.

The remaining two essays in the "philosophical principles" series deal with ancient physics and metaphysics. The first of these turns from the heavens to the earth, and traces doctrines about basic substances—from the reduction of everything to earth, water, air, and fire to the Stoic idea that a world-mind gives reality to everything—while the second mostly recounts debates over universals and essences from Plato through Malebranche. Both essays are quite short, do not go into the modern period as much as the astronomy essay does, and make little use of the appeal to how systems "sooth the imagination" that runs through the astronomy essay. The essays do however show that Smith had a rich knowledge of the history of philosophy, and was interested in some of its most arcane debates.

Aside from the series on philosophical principles, the epistemological content of EPS consists of an essay on the external senses.[4] This is the piece that comes closest to a strictly philosophical essay in our modern sense, focused as it is on the question of what kinds of sensation lead us to posit an object as independent of our minds. Unsurprisingly, touch turns out to be the primary basis for making such judgments: "As we feel [a thing] as... altogether external to us," says Smith, "so we necessarily conceive it as... altogether independent of us" (EPS 136). "Solid" and "substantial" are indeed synonyms in "common language," he points out, and this linguistic fact reflects the criterial role that touch plays in establishing external reality. (This appeal to common language runs through Smith's work.) The question of whether something we see or hear or smell or taste is real therefore comes down to a question about how closely we can tie our experience of it to our ability to touch it.

The remaining extended piece in EPS concerns what Smith calls "the imitative arts."[5] Smith opens this essay by noting that a mere copy of a carpet would not be considered beautiful by virtue of being a copy. Indeed, that would take away from any merit it has. Yet we consider a painting beautiful even when its subject is humdrum or ugly, as long as it imitates that subject with great skill. What accounts for this difference? What makes imitation, in the latter case but not the former, something that leads us to call a thing beautiful? Smith's answer is that it is precisely the difficulty we encounter in imitating a three-dimensional world using a two-dimensional canvas that makes for the beauty in painting. We take pleasure in *imitation that overcomes disparity*, and more pleasure in that imitation the greater the disparity it overcomes. Smith then uses this idea as a clue for explaining the beauty in a wide variety of arts: music, dancing, poetry, even topiary. Disparities here play roughly the role that anomalies play in the "History of Astronomy": overcoming them soothes our imagination and thereby gives us pleasure. Smith acknowledges that this is not the only thing that the arts do, and when he comes to music, he says that instrumental music isn't properly imitative at all; we take a more direct pleasure just in the way it arranges sound. (He says this, however, only after proposing a fascinating, extremely perceptive account of how music may be said to imitate the rhythms of our mental life, coming back again and again to certain themes just as certain ideas re-appear again and again in our reflections, and developing joyous or sad motifs in an arc that parallels the way we experience these emotions (EPS 191–2, 196–8).) But the guiding idea of the essay is that the joy we take in art is fundamentally a cognitive one—that art appeals to the same mental faculties that we use to construct scientific theories. In this, Smith anticipates the contribution to aesthetics that was soon to be made by Kant. And the theory he advances, emphasizing the formal features of painting and sculpture and music, can make sense of a great variety of artistic styles, including modern ones.

Black and Hutton added a short essay that Smith had begun on "the affinity between certain English and Italian verses" to their initial edition of EPS. Subsequent versions of the book sometimes also included Smith's "Considerations Concerning the Formation of Languages" (EPS 29); the current edition does not include that but adds Smith's "Letter to the *Edinburgh Review*" (his first publication, in 1755–6), his "Review of Johnson's Dictionary," and his preface and dedication to a collection of William Hamilton's poems. The "Letter to the *Edinburgh Review*," which urges that journal to extend its purview beyond Scotland and pay attention, in particular, to French thought, is interesting for its extensive engagement with Rousseau's *Second Discourse*, then little known in Britain. Here, as elsewhere, Smith seems to find the Genevan thinker simultaneously fascinating and irritating.[6] The essays on English and Italian verses, the review of Johnson's dictionary, and the preface to Hamilton, are brief and minor pieces. It is indeed surprising that Black and Hutton, well aware of Smith's aversion to having his unpolished work put before the public, included the essay on verses, which is in very rough draft. Nevertheless, even these pieces are interesting for the evidence they give of Smith's abiding, strong interest in the workings of language. The review of Johnson's dictionary, which complains that Johnson did not do a careful enough analysis of the differences among the meanings of a word, also suggests that Smith thought that philosophical attention could fruitfully be given to language.

That point comes out clearly in Smith's "Considerations" on the formation of languages. The focus of this essay is essentially Smith's version of the theory of general ideas proposed by Berkeley and Hume[7]—their answer to the question, difficult for all empiricists, of how, if all mental contents come originally from the perception of particular objects, we are ever able to formulate general or abstract ideas. But while Berkeley and Hume proposed their solution to that problem as a matter of how our *minds* work (essentially, that our habits of association enable a particular idea to evoke, in our memory, many similar objects), Smith proposes his solution as a matter of how *language* works: he investigates, not general *ideas* but general *terms*. The central point of the "Considerations" is that words for particular things must have preceded words for abstractions from those things. People must first have used "cave" or "tree" as names for a particular cave or tree, says Smith, and only later generalized the word to cover similar objects (LRBL 203). Adjectives, which express qualities, and prepositions, which express relations, must have developed yet later, and indeed have been modifications of nouns before they were hived off into words of their own (Smith notes that many qualities and relations are built into noun forms in Latin, while separate words are used for them in Italian). Verbs may have begun as names for complete events—Smith has his reader imagine that "venit," in Latin, first meant "the lion comes" and was only later used for anything that approaches (216)—and the agents of those events may have been separated from what they did later on. Many of these developments came about, Smith speculates, once peoples and their languages began to intermingle and the difficulties they found in communicating with one another were minimized by having separate terms replace the complex inflections that had hitherto signified quality, relation, and agency. He supports these speculations with differences between Latin and Italian, Latin and

French, and French and English: languages formed, in the first two cases, by the mingling of Latin with the languages of the Lombards and Franks, and in the last case by the mingling of French with the language of the Anglo-Saxons (220–3).

This is an interesting contribution to the eighteenth-century's speculations on the origins of language, but it is unclear how much it helps to resolve the problems that the empiricists had in accounting for comparison and abstraction. Smith seems simply to posit *that* at some point we become capable of such activities, rather than showing *how* they are possible (LRBL 205–7, 209–11). The very fact that he shifts the terrain on which these problems should be addressed from an investigation of the mind to an investigation of language is however something of an advance on Berkeley and Hume. David Pears says that "it would be a fair verdict" on Hume's theory of general ideas "that it tacitly relies on unexamined features of language. [Hume] follows his chosen psychological path under the guidance of language, but never stops to examine the features of the guide."[8] Smith does stop to examine features of language as a guide to how we think, even if his consideration of these features, from the perspective of our contemporary philosophical world—which has focused intensely on language for over a century—is not terribly sophisticated.[9]

2.2 EPS and Smith's methods (I): cross-cultural comparisons

Several themes run through the essays in EPS that recur in Smith's other writings. First, Smith takes a considerable interest in cross-cultural comparisons. The little essay on Italian and English verses is of course devoted to such a comparison, and the "Considerations" moves among English, Greek, Latin, and Italian, and even makes reference to Armenian, Hebrew, and Gothic (LRBL 211, 214, 216). In his review of Dr. Johnson's dictionary, Smith implicitly criticizes the venerable English writer for not proceeding in a similarly comparative way. Smith gives two examples of what he thinks Johnson should have done. As regards the first, the simple conjunction "but," Johnson had given its Saxon derivation followed by a variety of definitions illustrated exclusively by examples from English literature. Smith begins his own treatment of the word with a general comparison between it and terms that function similarly in Latin and French, then compares each of its particular English uses with Latin and French forms. Similarly, Smith discusses Dutch painting, Italian instrumental music, and French opera in "Imitative Arts," making reference as well to non-European music and dance on several occasions (187, 209, 213); he even claims to "have seen a Negro dance to his own song" at one point (209; cf. WN 776).[10]

This interest in other cultures and societies, including non-European cultures and societies, will continue in TMS and WN. TMS contains copious allusions to French literature, as well as a famous passage on the virtues of African and Native American societies (205–7). WN includes extensive discussions of the economies of China and India, some treatment of the social organization of Tartars, Arabs, and Native Americans, and comparisons throughout among the economies of Britain, France, Spain, and Holland.

The reason for this interest is clear. In practically everything he writes, Smith tries to find general human patterns of sentiment, and general human modes of organizing society, and to do that he draws on the historical and anthropological materials at his disposal as fully as possible. He may sometimes present an inadequate or distorted picture of societies beyond his ken. But he is at least vividly aware that he can make claims about general tendencies in human nature, on his own empiricist terms, only if he makes every effort to look beyond his own time and place. He rarely if ever employs *a priori* argumentation in defence of his claims, and he never simply projects Scottish habits or characteristics onto everybody else in the world. The nineteenth-century writer Walter Bagehot's caricature of Smith as trying to show how, "from being a savage, [man] rose to be a Scotchman"[11] is amusing, but entirely unfair. Indeed, Smith was far less Eurocentric than most of his contemporaries. Throughout his work, he shows a broad respect for cultures other than his own, including African and Native American cultures.

2.3 EPS and Smith's methods (II): language

A second theme of EPS is that Smith regards the development of language as a clue to the development of thought. This idea will re-appear throughout his work. In the "History of Astronomy," he takes the coining of "general name[s]" to be a prime example of how our imagination tries to find broad rubrics of classification and explanation that reduce anomalies (EPS 38). In "External Senses," as we have noted, he adduces the synonymity of "solid" and "substantial" "in common language" (EPS 136) as evidence for his hypothesis that the sense of touch is our main criterion for establishing independent objecthood. And in TMS, he takes the fact that the notion of a moral sense has not "got a name in any language" (TMS 326) to indicate the artificiality of that notion—to suggest that it is an invention of philosophers, rather than something rooted in human nature.

On the other hand, Smith often takes ordinary language to be ambiguous or confused. The first sentence of the "History of Astronomy" tells us that "Wonder, Surprise and Admiration are words which [are]… often confounded in our language" (EPS 33). In his review of Johnson's dictionary, Smith says that "there is no standard of correct language in conversation" and recommends frequent use of the dictionary "to all those who are desirous to improve and correct their language" (241). In TMS, he says that "language wants names" to mark all the fine distinctions in kinds of friendship (TMS 328–9). And in WN, he remarks that the confused tendency to equate wealth with money is enshrined in everyday language: "wealth and money… are, in common language, considered as in every respect synonymous" (WN 429).

Moreover, Smith takes confusions of this sort to lead to serious social problems. The popular equation of wealth and money is worrying to Smith because mercantilists exploit it to make their case for the false notion that national policy should be geared towards amassing gold and silver: "In consequence of these popular notions, all the different nations of Europe have studied, though to little purpose, every possible means of accumulating gold and silver in their respective countries" (WN 431). Elsewhere, Smith suggests that philosophers have exploited linguistic confusions to advocate bad moral systems. Mandeville, he says, erased the distinction between necessity and luxury by way of "ingenious sophistry… covered by the ambiguity of language" (TMS 312). Smith also thinks that features of language lead philosophers to fool themselves. Plato's doctrine that essences or "universal natures are more real than particular things," he says, "seems to have arisen, more from the nature of language, than from the nature of things" (EPS 125).

So Smith has an ambivalent relationship to common language. But whether he relies on it or he criticizes it, he takes language throughout his writings to be of central importance to human life. In WN he suggests that our tendency to "truck, barter, and exchange" with one another—the tendency that makes possible all our economic activity—arises from our capacity for speech, and he develops this point at length in LJ. Only language, he argues there, enables us to realize that we can pursue our self-interest by working together with other human beings: other animals work together in hunting down prey, but then kill each other over the spoils (LJ 352). Smith also implies strongly, in WN, that language is what enables us to treat one another with respect, and ourselves with self-respect: to "address" one another in terms of the other's needs, rather than trying to gain their help with "servile and fawning attention[s]" (WN 26).[12] The centrality of speech to our lives, and the idea that it is "the characteristical faculty of human nature," is indeed the subject of one of Smith's last additions to TMS (TMS 335–7).[13] Even if he does not offer any striking new analysis of language in EPS and the "Considerations" then, his attention to it shows that the Aristotelian conception of humanity as a linguistic animal was an early and consistent theme of his philosophical writings. Which does not preclude, as we have noted, a belief that one job of the philosopher is to correct how we commonly use language.

2.4 EPS and Smith's methods (III): common life

Closely connected to Smith's tendency to find philosophical ideas in everyday language is his tendency to root his theories in our common-life judgments. This theme too shows up prominently in EPS. A guiding idea of the "History of Astronomy" and its sequels is that scientists—natural philosophers—are driven to try to make sense of unfamiliar phenomena in terms of objects and processes "with which the mind [is] extremely familiar" (EPS 107; see also 42, 44, 46–7). In "External Senses," Smith is at pains to show that the distinction that philosophers like Locke and Berkeley had brought out between what belongs purely to our sensations and what belongs to the objects that those sensations represent is already built into "the opinions of the vulgar" (141–4). What we think in common life seems to be a good starting point for what we *should* think, for Smith in EPS. Philosophy need not, and perhaps cannot, have a deeper foundation than that.

This idea guides the way Smith does philosophy in TMS. Early on in the book Smith tells us that "philosophers, of late years" have thought about our moral sentiments chiefly in terms of the consequences to which they give rise, scanting the question of whether they are appropriate to the circumstances that cause them. But "in common life," when we make moral judgments, we "consider [sentiments] under both these aspects" (TMS 18). This becomes Smith's reason for developing a moral theory that can evaluate the "propriety" of our feelings—their fittedness to the circumstances that arouse them—as well as their consequences. What we actually think in common life is once again a touchstone for what we *should* think.

Now when Smith invokes "common life" moral judgments at the beginning of TMS, he is fairly clearly targeting Hume. It was Hume who, he thinks, had been concerned too much with the effects that our sentiments tend to produce,[14] to the exclusion of their propriety. At the same time, Hume had himself suggested that morality is and should be rooted in the judgments we make in common life. Having come to extremely sceptical conclusions about the nature of substance, reason, and personal identity, in Book I of his *Treatise*, Hume closed that Book by saying that he was going to turn away from metaphysics to "the sphere of common life": to "the principles of moral good and evil, the nature and foundation of government" and other subjects that come up in the course of "daily conversation and action" (T 270–1). We may read Smith as accepting this move but then turning it against Hume himself. If "the principles of moral good and evil" are to be found in "the sphere of common life," then surely we should attend to the fact that in common life we judge of feelings in accordance with their propriety and not just their effects. This is a nice rebuke of Hume in Hume's own terms—something that Smith is fond of doing.

But we may be able to take a broader lesson away from this contretemps with Hume: that Smith accepts Hume's general critique of metaphysics, could see no way around it at least, and does not believe that philosophers can provide *a priori* foundations for the way we ordinarily reason, either in science or in morality. That would explain why Smith never takes up metaphysical questions himself, except to describe what ancient philosophers thought about them, and why he devotes himself in his "philosophical principles" series to considering the way in which scientific theories satisfy or fail to satisfy our imaginations rather than what makes them true. I think Smith believes that some scientific theories, Newton's especially, *are* true—truer than their predecessors, at any rate. I don't think he is an anti-realist, denying that our theories reflect a reality outside of them (more on that below). But he prefers giving us what we might call a phenomenology of the acceptance of scientific theories—and, in "External Senses," a phenomenology of how we judge of external reality—to engaging with foundational disputes over realism. Which is to say that he works out from common-life assumptions, from the presuppositions of "daily conversation," rather than trying to question, or defend, such beliefs against the background of a deeper epistemic foundation. He may not have called himself a "common sense" philosopher, as his successor Thomas Reid did, and he did not explicitly lay out a view of philosophy as rooted in common sense. But he seems clearly to view it that way, and in effect operates like a common-sense philosopher. Indeed, one might argue that this label fits him more fully than it does Reid. A true common-sense philosopher should not *argue* for the foundational importance of common sense, after all. Arguments of that sort are themselves an engagement with foundational disputes of the sort that the common-sense philosopher is supposed to avoid. And they are certainly not something we engage in as *part* of common sense.

This point, if correct, sheds an interesting light on Smith's method in both TMS and WN. In TMS, Smith says that systems of moral philosophy must cohere with what we pre-theoretically believe about morals. Scientific systems can gain adherents even if they defy much of what we ordinarily think, he says, since they concern matters very distant from our ordinary lives. Such systems are like reports by a traveller of a distant country that we have never visited ourselves. But any system that "proposes to explain... our sentiments of approbation and disapprobation" concerns "affairs of the very parish we live in," and thus cannot convince us unless it fits, to some large degree, with what we already believe about such affairs (TMS 313–4). The implication is that moral theories should simply clarify, organize, and explain our common-sense moral ideas—exactly as Smith himself does in TMS. To expect a *new* system of morality, upending many of the moral ideas we already have, is then to misunderstand what moral philosophers can accomplish.

As for WN, central to the free trade position at its core is the idea that "every individual... can, in his local situation, judge much better than any statesman or lawgiver can do for him" (WN 456). More generally, WN argues throughout for the soundness of the judgment of everyday people, in most circumstances, as against that of the legislators who seek to control their choices (see, for instance WN 138, 346). When Smith comes to the duties of a political sovereign, moreover, he describes them as "plain and intelligible to common understandings" (687). A polemic in favour of an economic and political realm that respects our common-sensical judgments thus runs through WN.

At the same time, Smith makes efforts at a number of points to correct our common-sense judgments. The "popular notion" that wealth is money, as noted earlier, is a particular target of his. He describes this notion as a "prejudice" (WN 471), a term he often uses for the ideas he is trying to combat. A statute that restricts the corn (flour) trade, he says, "authorizes two very absurd popular prejudices": prejudices that he indeed compares to "popular terrors and suspicions of witchcraft" (533, 534). He also uses "prejudice" to describe the popular disdain for actors and opera-singers and the contempt that "some political writers" heap on shopkeepers and tradesmen (361). But a "prejudice" is not merely an incorrect belief. It is a "pre-judgment," a belief we hold without properly judging at all: something we cling to without adequately thinking about it. Smith says explicitly, about the prejudice that equates wealth with money, that "[i]t would be too ridiculous to go about seriously to prove, that wealth does not consist in money... but in what money purchases" (438). He says similarly, about mercantilist arguments that make it look as if international trade is a zero-sum game, that the contrary idea—that "the great body of the people" in every nation can only gain by commerce with other nations—"is so very manifest, that it seems ridiculous to take any pains to prove it": "Nor could it ever have been called in question, had not the interested sophistry of merchants and manufacturers confounded the common sense of mankind" (493–4). This gives us an important clue to how Smith regards prejudices: they are blockages to common sense, sometimes fostered by disingenuous thought leaders, which common sense itself can dissolve. The job of the philosopher is then to *alert* common sense to the fact that it is blocked in a certain way, to point out the prejudice and highlight its absurdity,[15] and thereby to enable us, using our common sense, to overcome it. Sometimes, Smith mocks mercantilist prejudices, noting for instance that the argument that gold and silver are important because they are durable could just as well justify accumulating pots and pans (WN 439–40). Often, he tries to make "perspicuous" (46) the basic principles of economic activity, such that what is wrong with various prejudices will become obvious. Both of these techniques involve deploying common sense against its own blockages: not exactly *arguing* against prejudices—that would be fruitless since prejudices are held prior to and independently of argument—so much as *exposing* them, bringing them into a clear light, in which they should disappear.

If this is right, then Smith deploys common sense even where he recognizes how common sense can go wrong. We should see him as offering an immanent critique of common sense, drawing on the fact that common sense contains means of correction within itself. I submit that this is his method throughout his work. In the "History of Astronomy," he says that "philosophy is the science of the connecting principles of nature"—that it makes sense of the irregular, the unfamiliar in terms of the regular and the familiar (EPS 45–7). In WN, he tells us that he is willing to take "the utmost pains... to be sure that I am perspicuous" (WN 46). Clarifying the unfamiliar in familiar terms, putting things together so that we have a "perspicuous" view of a range of phenomena: this, rather than making new discoveries or finding a principle to ground our familiar beliefs and experience, is the task of philosophy for Smith. He works out from our common-life beliefs, whether about the cognitive import of sensation ("External Senses"), the nature of morality (TMS), or the workings of political economy (WN), towards a more coherent, and clearer, system of these beliefs.

2.5 EPS and Smith's methods (IV): particularism

Smith's commitment to common sense is bound up in good part with a fourth theme in his work, evident already in the "Considerations" and the lectures on rhetoric and belles-lettres, which we may describe as his particularism. As we have seen, the "Considerations" suggests that our ways of expressing general qualities and relations began originally as names for particular objects and events. The lectures stress that attending to particulars is crucial to the effectiveness of oratory, painting, and the description of emotions and characters. In literary descriptions especially, says Smith, "we ought to choose out some minute circumstances" that illustrate the emotion or character trait we are trying to capture.[16] These points anticipate his claim in TMS that we can sympathize with the suffering of others only if we "adopt the whole case of [our] companion with all its minutest incidents" (TMS 21).

Empiricism is a mode of epistemology that always emphasizes the particular (that's what we experience, after all) and Smith's version of it is more explicitly particularist than most. For Smith, we have a firm grasp only of particular cases, and generalizations are more or less unfirm to the degree to which they abstract from the detail of these cases.[17] In TMS, Smith tells us that general moral rules are "founded upon experience of what, in particular instances, our moral faculties ... approve, or disapprove of" (TMS 159), and that "it is in particular instances only" that the propriety or impropriety of actions is clear (188). In WN, he tells us that economic agents succeed only when they pay "exact attention to small savings and gains" (385), when they lavish care on "particular portions" of stock (928), when, like the corn merchant, their interest "makes [them] study" to carry out a particular task "as exactly as [they] can" (534). Interest and exact attention are linked in this last passage in the way that perception and the sentiments moving one to act are linked in Aristotle's theory of animal motion: I perceive details *insofar as* I am worried about achieving a certain end to which they are relevant.[18] And, in general, judgment— Smith's term for the kind of knowledge we need most in our ordinary lives[19]—requires "exact" and "vigilant" attention (385, 530, 755).

It follows that we ought to be suspicious of the very general claims about human nature characteristic of the systems built by philosophers and social scientists, and of policies based on such systems. As regards philosophy and social science, we may say, with Knud Haakonssen, that Smith gives priority to "contextual knowledge" over "system knowledge." Contextual knowledge is "the kind of concrete knowledge which arises from specific situations and which gives rise to common-sense ideas of behaviour wherever people live together" (SL 79). "System knowledge"—scientific knowledge—of human societies must for Smith always begin from, and account for, the contextual knowledge "people have of themselves and others" (SL 81; cf. WN 768–9). As regards policy, Smith's particularism underwrites his suspicion of what governments can effectively do. The claim that "every individual can, in his local situation, judge much better than any statesman or lawgiver can do for him" (WN 456) is the basis for his broadly hands-off approach to economic policy: his preference for "the system of natural liberty" over systems that try to micro-manage the economy.

This contextual, particularist view of knowledge helps explain Smith's fondness for common sense. In his lectures on rhetoric and belles lettres, Smith proclaims that common law is more equitable than law based on statutes because "what is founded on practice and experience must be better adapted to particular cases than that which is derived from theory only" (LRBL 175). Exactly this can also be said about common sense, which is after all also a mode of thought "founded on practice and experience." Common sense is fluidly self-corrective, about practical matters, because it responds quickly and precisely to empirical particulars. Ordinary people, even if they lack formal education, constantly adjust their beliefs to accord with what they see and hear. And this is sufficient, Smith believes, for them to work out most of what they need to know about their fellow human beings, especially those they observe often. For that reason, "every individual can, in his local situation, judge much better than any statesman or lawgiver can do for him" (WN 456).

2.6 EPS and Smith's methods (V): imagination

A fifth theme: the importance of imagination. Smith tells us in the "History of Astronomy" that "[p]hilosophy... may be regarded as one of those arts that address themselves to the imagination" (EPS 46).

Given his love of literature and music, it seems safe to suppose that he took pleasure in this fact, that he liked regarding himself as similar to the writers and musicians he admired. At any rate, the role he attributes to the imagination, as regards appreciating the arts, is very similar to the role he gives it as regards accepting scientific theories. A work of imitative art is beautiful to the extent that it overcomes the obstacles to our recognition of similarity that our imagination puts up, and a scientific theory is worthy of acceptance to the extent that it overcomes the obstacles to a smooth flow of associations that our imagination puts up. In both cases, the imagination is soothed in the face of difficulty. Our imagination is gratified by a work of imitative art that overcomes a great "disparity" between the medium of the imitation and the object being imitated, just as it is by a scientific theory that fits together initially jarring events or objects into a familiar pattern. So the pleasure we take in beauty is a cognitive pleasure, for Smith, something that gratifies the same faculties that we use in science. At the same time, we accept scientific theories in part because of their aesthetic qualities: their simplicity and beauty.[20]

To a considerable degree, Smith is following in Hume's footsteps. Hume famously understood causality as a customary connection among objects forged in our imagination (e.g. T 102–5, 108, 172), belief as a bestowal of "vivacity" by the imagination on hitherto faint ideas (T 94–123; see especially 117, 122–3), and personal identity as a "fiction" constructed by the imagination (254, 259). We should bear in mind that imagination, in seventeenth- and eighteenth-century philosophy, is not something that simply invents things. It is rather the faculty of "images," as the name implies. The imagination takes in and arranges everything we sense, thus providing us both with sensory information and with fictions crafted out of sensory information. All our mental pictures, visual and aural—whether of a horse or a unicorn, of a car horn or the song of the Sirens—come from the imagination. That said, Hume's predecessors had often contrasted the imagination unfavourably with reason, intellect, or understanding. Unlike reason, the imagination was seen as unreliable and prone to confuse reality with fantasy. For Hume to insist that our basic ideas of reality, as regards both external objects and ourselves, come from the imagination was thus a mark of his scepticism, his willingness radically to unsettle the line between fiction and reality. It is hard to imagine any reader in Hume's time not being shocked by his claim that "'Tis not solely in poetry and music, we must follow our taste and sentiment, but likewise in philosophy" (T 103).

I don't think that Smith's emphasis on the role of the imagination in science and philosophy is meant to bear this sceptical freight. Smith certainly alludes to Hume in his series on philosophical principles, talking at one point of "the association of ideas" and of a "customary connection" between purported causes and effects (EPS 41), and characterizing the connection we attribute to causal relationships as one to which we are "accustomed" (44, 79, 91, 96, 104, 107, 128). But he never defends Hume's doubts about causality, external reality, reason, or personal identity. At the same time, he never attempts to refute those doubts. I'll argue in a moment that Smith was a realist about the external world and he seems clearly to take for granted a robust conception of personal identity throughout TMS. But by and large he simply finesses the metaphysical issues about reality and selfhood that Hume had raised. Remember, he is believed to have read Hume's *Treatise*, with avid attention, as a student at Balliol. Perhaps he was so impressed by Hume's brilliance, as regards epistemology and metaphysics, that he did not dare try to refute him. Or perhaps he decided that Hume had gone as far as anyone could go in trying to provide an empirical grounding for notions like substance, causality, or personal identity, and that if Hume did not succeed, he himself was unlikely to do better. In any case, he never addressed these matters. Instead, he marked out for himself the task of examining the workings of the imagination that is so important to Hume *from within* those workings—doing a phenomenology of them, as we might say today.

And that is a task well-suited to his skill set. Smith is a remarkably astute psychological observer who produced a rich picture of what goes on in our imaginations. He also proposed a more substantial role for the imagination in sympathy and morality than Hume himself had acknowledged, and probably saw his "system" of political economy in WN as overcoming anomalies in the way we imagine wealth, trade, money, and the like. Throughout his work, Smith sees the imagination as central to the way we think and conduct ourselves, both in everyday life and in the loftiest of theoretical projects. The fact that the imagination is so much a part of common life also links this theme with the endorsement of everyday language and common sense that we considered above. Smith's point in construing the imagination as central to theory is to stress that theory is less distant from common sense than his predecessors had supposed.

2.7 Realism

I have said several times now that Smith remained far more of a realist about scientific theories than Hume. What evidence is there for this claim? When we look at the end of the "History of Astronomy," we may doubt that Smith is a realist at all. Having laid out Newton's astrophysics in detail, Smith describes it as having "a degree of firmness and solidity" that no other system has achieved. He adds that the "most sceptical cannot avoid feeling" this firmness and solidity. But just because we "feel" this firmness and solidity does not mean it is really there. Smith goes on to question his own favourable judgment of the Newtonian system, suggesting that

> even we, while we have been endeavouring to represent all philosophical systems as mere inventions of the imagination..., have insensibly been drawn in, to make use of language expressing the connecting principles of this one, as if they were the real chains which Nature makes use of to bind together her several operations.
>
> (EPS 105)

Is this not a declaration that all philosophical systems, including Newton's are fictional? Is Smith not leaving us with an ironic, teasing suggestion that even theories that feel perfectly "firm" and "solid" are mere products of the imagination? Charles Griswold uses this passage to argue that Smith is "a nondogmatic skeptic" rather than a realist, a philosopher uncommitted to determining "how things 'really are'" (AVE 169). Is Griswold not clearly right?

I don't think so. We need in the first place to read this concluding passage of the "History of Astronomy" together with what precedes it. For instance, when laying out the difficulty that our imaginations experience in dealing with events that follow one another "in an uncommon order," Smith asks us to conceive what would happen if "a person of the soundest judgment… whose imagination had acquired those habits, and that mold, which the constitution of things in this world necessarily impress upon it" were transported to a planet "where nature was governed by laws quite different from those which take place here" (EPS 43, my emphasis). In this passage we are told that the imagination is shaped by external things "impressing" themselves upon it, and that there are laws of nature governing our world, which our habits of mind reflect. Later in the essay, Smith explicitly invokes a correspondence account of truth. His readers need to await the return of Halley's comet in 1758, he says, in order to determine whether Newton's theory "corresponds as happily to this part of the [solar] system" as it does to all its other parts (103). Similarly, in the "Ancient Physics" essay, Smith talks about our ideas of the universe as "being confirmed by… observations" or "[by] facts and experiments" (109), and in "External Senses," Smith says we conceive solid bodies as "independent of us" and has no hesitation about endorsing that conception (136, see also 140–1). All of these passages use realist language to describe our beliefs and sensations. They pre-suppose that there is something to go wrong about, when we represent or make claims about the world beyond us, and that we aim, in representation and theorizing, to get that world right, not merely to satisfy the internal drives of our imaginations.

Elsewhere, Smith is yet more explicitly a realist. In a passage of TMS that alludes to the histories recounted in the "Astronomy" essay, Smith tells us that systems of natural philosophy "may appear very plausible, and be for a long time very generally received in the world, and yet have no foundation in nature, nor any sort of resemblance to the truth." He gives Descartes's system of vortices as an example. This theory was regarded for a long time as "a most satisfactory account" of astronomical phenomena, he says, but it has now "been demonstrated, to the conviction of all mankind, that these pretended causes of those wonderful effects do not actually exist."[21] And he goes on to say that in moral philosophy a system cannot "depart so far from all resemblance to the truth" and yet convince any large number of people (TMS 313). The language of truth and falsehood, of reality and appearance, is at the forefront of this passage.

The same is true of many passages in WN. Smith tells us for instance that "In some parts of Lancashire it is pretended... that bread of oatmeal is a heartier food for labouring people than wheaten bread," but adds, "I am, however, somewhat doubtful of the truth of [this doctrine]" (WN 177). He accuses mercantilist writers of passing off an "absurdity" as "a certain and undeniable truth" (449–50), and says that the system of the Physiocrats, "with all its imperfections, is, perhaps, the nearest to the truth that has yet been published upon the subject of political economy" (678). In the last two cases, it is essential to Smith's critique of other political economists to contrast what is true with what is merely held to be true. Elsewhere in WN, he is concerned just about the truth of various factual claims—but that too, of course, is essential to the case he is making for his own economic theory.[22] His case is, in short, a thoroughly realist one: never does he defend his views by appealing to their beauty or simplicity, or how they "sooth the imagination."

But when we bring these stretches of Smith's writing, as well as the realist notes in the "Astronomy" itself, together with the ironic passage at the end of the "Astronomy," we are called upon to find a realist reading of that passage as well. This is not hard to do. When examined closely, it is clear that in the ironic passage Smith is admonishing us—and himself—not to get carried away into thinking that Newton's system is the culmination of all science, that it will never be superseded, as its predecessors have been. Like all other "philosophical systems," Newton's system provides a series of "connecting principles" that attempt to *represent* "the real chains with which Nature... bind[s] together" events—which is to say that those principles are not *identical with* the real chains they represent. So a new system, representing the real chains of nature more adequately, is likely to come along some day, superseding Newton even as he has superseded his predecessors. But that is not to deny that the earlier systems improved on one another—as Smith in fact portrays them as doing: each system takes account of anomalies that the previous ones had failed to account for—nor that the new system, when it arrives, will improve on Newtonianism. Smith's point throughout the essay is that we *accept* systems on the basis of how they sooth our imaginations, but nothing about that point is meant to deny their truthfulness. Nor is that his point at the end of the essay. He just wants to stress that the work of soothing the imagination is never done and we should anticipate that even Newtonianism will some day give way to a new system. Smith is a thorough-going fallibilist about scientific theory, who does not believe that science will ever come to a full explanation of nature. But he is not a sceptic, much less an anti-realist. For Smith, nature "impresses" itself upon us, and we accordingly develop theories that reflect it—with increasing, if never complete, accuracy. We respond to reality in our theorizing. We are not confined within our own thoughts and imaginings.

This realist, if robustly fallibilist, conception of theorizing continues into TMS and WN. When Smith talks favourably of moral philosophers who recognize "a real and essential distinction between vice and virtue" (TMS 306), and unfavourably of the "licentious" philosophers who dismiss or blur that distinction, he indicates that there is truth and falsehood in moral as well as scientific thought. And he presents what he takes to be a true account of how political economy works, while fending off a variety of fictions about it, in WN. That project is fully compatible with a recognition that in political economy, as in physics, the imagination comes up with "connecting principles" to bring together otherwise puzzling phenomena. That is just how truth is found, for Smith, in all sciences. Or at least that is how truth is *approximated*, how we get *closer* to truth in our theories, without ever arriving at full truth. There is every reason to think that Smith was just as thorough a fallibilist about the connecting principles he proposes in WN as he was about Newton's physics, fully prepared for the eventuality that his own "connecting principles" will be superseded one day by other economic explanations, prompted by anomalies for which his theories cannot account. But there is no reason to think that he took himself to be describing phenomena that are real only from a human perspective, let alone the perspective of a particular society or period in time, much less that he dismissed the importance of judgments of truth and falsehood.

2.8 A moral sceptic?

The main point of Griswold's portrayal of Smith as a non-dogmatic sceptic is that Smith, according to Griswold, rejects any realist grounding for morality, not for science. Griswold also sees Smith as concerned to bury his scepticism out of the sight of ordinary readers because he recognized that widespread scepticism about morality could undermine everyday moral practice (AVE 156–78, 369). In being aware of such a problem, Griswold suggests, Smith rightly saw the dangers of Enlightenment teachings, but did not adequately respond to them. Griswold proposes that we can best overcome some of the problems in Smith's legacy by developing a version of moral realism that does not appeal to Platonic Forms (372–6). He cites work by David Wiggins and John McDowell as offering the kind of philosophical justification for morality that might be both plausible in modern terms and successful in overcoming Smithean scepticism.

Even though I consider it a mistake to call Smith a sceptic about morality, I agree with Griswold to a considerable extent on these issues. I certainly agree that Smith was concerned to root moral theory in pre-philosophical moral thought, and that, especially if one conceives of moral theory in these terms, Wiggins and McDowell provide the most promising sort of justification for morality to be found nowadays. But I think Smith is already much closer to their views than Griswold allows.

To begin with, the evidence that Smith is a moral sceptic is extremely thin, as Griswold himself admits. Griswold acknowledges that Smith nowhere calls himself a sceptic, and rests the plausibility of his reconstruction of Smith's philosophical commitments "primarily on its fit with [Smith's] work" (AVE 170). But a non-, even an anti-sceptical understanding of Smith's fundamental commitments fits the work much better. Smith never betrays sceptical worries. He was a close friend of Hume, and his moral philosophy is deeply indebted to Hume's. But he rarely so much as alludes to Hume's epistemic scepticism, and never mentions Hume's doubts about the self or the existence of God. Nor does he ever express any worry to the effect that the spread of philosophy among ordinary people might lead them to become sceptical of morality. On the contrary, he recommends that philosophy be widely spread, as a corrective to the "poison of [religious] enthusiasm and superstition" (WN 794). Griswold maintains that Smith is a sceptic in his metaethics, because he sees morality "as arising 'from us,' not as established by nature or the divine" (AVE 161). But in fact Smith repeatedly suggests that moral sentimentalism is compatible with a belief in divinely established moral distinctions: that the moral emotions can properly be regarded as "vicegerents" of God, divinely set up within us (TMS 130, 165–6). In addition, even if we set aside these suggestions, why should a view of morality as arising from us count as a *sceptical* view? The thought is presumably that ordinary moral judgments and emotions pre-suppose some more robust, more "mind-independent" notion of moral reality, but Smith gives us no reason to hold such a picture of ordinary moral thinking (pace AVE 166–8, 173). Rather, like Hutcheson, he seems to think that ordinary moral thought is *itself* sentimentalist at its core. Here, as throughout his writings, Smith attributes considerable philosophical sophistication to ordinary thought, and criticizes philosophers for losing touch with the facts of ordinary experience rather than criticizing ordinary people for making philosophical errors.

Indeed, it seems to me most plausible to understand Smith as rejecting the antirealism about morality associated with Hume, even as providing an implicit answer to it. Consider the opening of TMS. Smith declares that sympathy, which Hume had understood to be a sort of contagion by which your feelings transfer over to me, actually consists in my imaginatively projecting my feelings into your situation: how would I feel if I were in your shoes? He goes on from here to say that the distinction between the sympathetic feelings I imaginatively acquire on your behalf and the feelings I perceive you to have yourself allows for the possibility that I might judge your feelings to be the *wrong* ones—to be, for instance, too weak or too strong for your situation. To this he adds that you and I seek a mutual harmony of feelings, so if I am right that your feelings are unsuited to your circumstances, you will be inclined to correct them so that they come into accord with my judgment, and in the long run to have just the feelings, in such circumstances, that an impartial but sympathetic spectator would have.

These claims constitute a sophisticated revision of Hume. Hume had maintained that a "passion is an original existence," without "reference to any other object." Since reason can only evaluate relationships among ideas, or between an idea, something that makes "reference" to another object (that is representational), and the object to which it refers, the passions are therefore independent of reason (T 415, 463–7). But if morality is ultimately founded, as Hume insists, in a set of passions, our basic moral judgments must be independent of reason: must be neither correct nor incorrect. Smith responds to this by showing how passions can in fact be representational: they represent appropriate or inappropriate responses to a situation. So each passion *does* make "reference to another object," for Smith: the object constituted by the feelings of a sympathetic impartial spectator. Accordingly, there is room for talk of correct and incorrect passions. One notable feature of TMS is how much it restores to moral sentimentalism the language of the moral realists whom Hume and Hutcheson opposed—of Ralph Cudworth and Samuel Clarke and William Wollaston. Smith describes passions as "suitable or unsuitable," "proportionate or disproportionate," "fitted or not fitted" to their objects (TMS 16, 18–19, 31, 67, 75, 88, 113–4), compares moral approval with cognitive agreement (TMS 17, 20), and invokes a correspondence relationship between passions much like that standardly held to obtain, for true statements, between thought and object (TMS 18, 48). If, as McDowell suggests in an important paper, reality can be attributed to any property that is independent of the subjective state in which we experience it at a given moment,[23] then Smith's account of sympathy and the passions allows us to see the moral import of a feeling as real: to assess the feelings we have in reaction to our situations, and the feelings by which we approve or disapprove of other people's feelings, as correctly or incorrectly fitted to those situations. Far from being a sceptic, Smith may thus have anticipated the most sophisticated modern responses to scepticism. He seems himself to have felt that by restoring a full-bodied notion of corrigibility to sentimentalist ethics, he had saved it from the incompatibility with common life with which it was threatened by Hume.

At times, Griswold seems to recognize this, acknowledging that Smith saw Hume's philosophy as being too distant from the perspective of common life (AVE 54), that Smith understands our emotions as "in some way cognitive," that his moral emotivism has more room for objectivity than other versions of that view (87, 115, 129–30), and that he may have regarded the search for a fuller metaphysical grounding for ethics as philosophically misguided (173, 364). But Griswold never pulls these insights together into a case for regarding

Smith as the very opposite of a moral sceptic. I think Smith at least glimpsed the possibility that scepticism in the end undermines itself—that it is no more justifiable than, and indeed implicitly rests on, the foundationalist views it challenges.[24] One can come through scepticism to the other side, as it were, asking, as followers of Wittgenstein often do, "from what position can the sceptical challenge itself be launched?" Is the sceptic not herself holding out an untenable, metaphysically grounded view of what truth ought to be, by which she judges all actual modes of attributing truth to be inadequate? We should probably hesitate to put quite such questions in Smith's own mouth, but he certainly devoted much of his work, both in moral philosophy and in political economy, to displaying the rationality of common life, to mapping common life from within and correcting it, where necessary, with its own tools, rather than trying either to justify or to criticize it from an external standpoint. He accepts the standpoint of common life without Hume's air of resignation, without treating it as a collection of useful fictions and constructs that we accept only when philosophy fails to provide us with something better. It is true of Hume, but not of Smith, that the endorsement of common life comes with a bit of a wink and a nod, and with a scepticism in reserve that pops up periodically to remind us of the hollowness of our common beliefs. Griswold's admonition that such a philosophy is ultimately incompatible with ordinary life can thus be properly directed at Hume. But Smith has already grasped both the problem and its solution, I think, which explains how he can recommend that philosophy be given a larger, not a smaller, role in ordinary people's lives. Philosophy, for Smith, can get beyond scepticism, can issue in a full-throated endorsement of the general standpoint, if not all the specific beliefs, with which we already live.

2.9 A religious sceptic?

Is Smith a sceptic, at least, about the existence of God? Griswold characterizes the sceptical view he attributes to Smith as above all "an intellectual stance toward certain kinds of metaphysical arguments, in particular, those about 'reality' and 'substances' such as 'Forms' and God" (AVE 169). In a similar vein, Dennis Rasmussen points to the harshly dismissive language Smith uses about the origins of polytheism in the "History of Astronomy"—Smith describes the belief of ancient peoples that intelligent beings cause phenomena like thunderstorms as arising from "cowardice and pusillanimity" and as "the lowest and most pusillanimous superstition" (EPS 48, 50)—and notes that Smith recalls this passage just before beginning to talk, in the "History of Ancient Physics" about the "idea of an universal mind, of a God of all, who originally formed the whole, and who governs the whole by general laws" (EPS 113). Says Rasmussen:

> Although he does not stress the point, it appears that Smith considers this belief… to be just as much of an invention of the imagination, driven by human desires, as earlier polytheistic superstitions and later scientific theories were. Once again, the order is not so much observed in the world as imposed on it, by us and for the sake of our own mental comfort.
>
> (IP 43)

Rasmussen goes on to say that Smith "soft-pedaled" this assimilation of monotheism to polytheism because of the uproar that a critique of the notion of an intelligent designer would have aroused among his readers.

But to run together Smith's treatment of polytheism and monotheism in this way is to miss what Smith is up to in the passage that Rasmussen discusses. For when Smith comes to the development of a notion of "an universal mind, a God of all" in the "Ancient Physics," his point is precisely to contrast this idea with the "pusillanimous superstition" of the polytheism that had preceded it. The idea of "a God of all" went with an idea of nature as fundamentally unified, he says, and as capable of being rationally explained (EPS 113). Indeed, it is the unity and rationality of nature that led people to a belief in God. So just "as ignorance begot superstition, science gave birth to the first theism that arose among those nations, who were not enlightened by divine Revelation" (114). And Smith goes on to expound Platonic and Stoic conceptions of God as a unifying, rational, and good principle of the universe: very much the conception of God that he would himself advance for the rest of his life.[25]

There is therefore, at the very least, a great difference in tone between the way Smith describes polytheism and the way he describes (mono-)theism. Moreover, it is a mistake to lump polytheistic superstitions, theism, and scientific theories together as equally "invention[s] of the imagination," for Smith. For on Smith's view of science, the "connecting principles" to which our imaginations give rise *respond to the way that nature impresses itself upon us* and therefore approximate, even if they never fully grasp, the "real chains" that bind the events in nature itself. To say that "science gave birth to... theism" is therefore to associate theism with the imaginative activities by which we most sensitively and effectively respond to a reality beyond ourselves (and with the courage it takes to face truth, not the "cowardice and pusillanimity" that leads us to hide from truth), rather than turning theism into an "invention" of the same kind as a belief in Jupiter or "in demons, witches, genii [and] fairies" (EPS 49). Unlike Rasmussen, then, I read Smith in the "Ancient Physics" as endorsing the belief in an intelligent designer common in his day rather than criticizing or mocking it.

This point also makes for a response to Griswold. It is not quite clear to me what Griswold means by saying that Smith takes up a sceptical stance towards arguments for God. If he means just that Smith does not himself give any such arguments, I agree, and agree also that that may be a respect in which he was influenced by Hume. But if it means that Smith does not *believe* in God, and is sceptical of all tendencies that lead people towards a belief in God, it seems to me that the passage from "Ancient Physics" points in the other direction. It suggests both that the sort of belief in God held by Plato and the ancient Stoics was reasonable and that the fact that the scientific views they developed led them in that direction was a good thing. This is not enough to show definitively that Smith himself was a theist, and we will see in Chapter 8 that Smith's views on God's existence are difficult to pin down precisely. But the essays in EPS, to the extent that they touch on this subject, give us some reason to think that his answer to the question, "does God exist?" was "yes" rather than "no."

2.10 Conclusion and summary

Adam Smith would surely not still be read today if his writings had consisted solely of the pieces in EPS and the "Considerations." They are not substantial enough to constitute a major contribution to aesthetics, epistemology, or the philosophy of science.[26] If they are meant to show a close connection between aesthetics and epistemology, they do not make that point clearly or plausibly enough for it to have had an impact on subsequent philosophers. If they are meant to represent either the "nondogmatic skepticism" that Charles Griswold attributes to Smith or the Wittgensteinian post-scepticism that I see in him, they come nowhere near clarifying or defending those positions. Nevertheless, they are useful in that they bring up themes that will reverberate throughout Smith's later writings, and that provide an intriguing framework in which to interpret those writings. They also bring out Smith's astonishing erudition, his deep knowledge of the history both of philosophy and of physics, and his love of the arts, especially literature and music. The latter point, especially, is worth bearing in mind when considering his reflections on wealth in TMS and WN. This is not a man who would lump pushpin and poetry together, as Jeremy Bentham did, or who was interested largely in material goods or power. He was instead very much a broad Enlightenment intellectual, putting great store on the cultivation of the mind by way of philosophy, history, science, and the arts. A rich life, for him, was one filled with these things, and a wealthy nation was one that had plenty of resources for people to pursue them.

Notes

1 Rasmussen draws attention to this feature of the essay: IP 40.
2 Black and Hutton note, at the end of the astronomy essay, that

> it must be viewed, not as a History or Account of Sir Isaac Newton's Astronomy, but chiefly as an additional illustration of those Principles in the Human Mind which Mr. Smith has pointed out to be the universal motives of Philosophical Researches.
>
> (EPS 105)

3 Many commentators have suggested that the idea that new theories are sparked by gaps or anomalies in previous theories foreshadows the work of Thomas Kuhn.
4 Placed immediately after the series on philosophical principles in modern editions, but placed at the end of the book in its first edition (see https://archive.org/details/essaysonphiloso00stewgoog/page/n13).
5 See James Chandler, "Adam Smith as Critic," in C. Berry, M. Paganelli and C. Smith (eds.), *The Oxford Handbook of Adam Smith* (Oxford: Oxford University Press, 2013), for a penetrating and illuminating investigation of this piece.

6 Smith's relationship to Rousseau has now become the subject of a substantial scholarly literature. See especially Michael Ignatieff, *The Needs of Strangers* (New York: Viking, 1984), chapter 4, Ryan Hanley, "Commerce and Corruption: Rousseau's Diagnosis and Adam Smith's Cure," *European Journal of Political Theory* 7 (2008), Dennis Rasmussen, *The Problems and Promise of Commercial Society: Adam Smith's Response to Rousseau* (University Park: The Pennsylvania State University Press, 2008) and Charles Griswold, *Jean-Jacques Rousseau and Adam Smith: A Philosophical Encounter* (London: Routledge, 2018).

7 T I.i.vii, following George Berkeley, *Principles of Human Knowledge*, in *The Empiricists* (New York: Anchor Books, 1974), Introduction §§ 6–20. The immediate source for Smith's thinking in the essay seems however to have been not Hume or Berkeley, but Rousseau, whose *Second Discourse* he cites repeatedly (LRBL 205, 213n) and follows in his account of the development of adjectives and verbs.

8 David Pears, *Hume's System* (Oxford: Oxford University Press, 1990), 29.

9 Nir Ben Moshe has pointed out to me that Locke's account of abstraction makes explicit reference to language:

> The use of words ... being to stand as outward marks of our internal ideas, and those ideas being taken from particular things, if every particular idea that we take in should have a distinct sense, names must be endless. To prevent this, the mind makes the particular ideas received from particular objects to become general; which is done by considering them ... separate from all other existences , and the circumstances of real existence .... This is called ABSTRACTION; whereby ideas taken from particular beings become general representatives of all of the same kind; *and their names general names*, applicable to whatever exists conformable to such abstract ideas. ... Thus the same colour being observed to-day in chalk or snow, which the mind yesterday received from milk, it considers that appearance alone, makes it a representative of all of that kind; *and having given it the name <u>whiteness</u>*, it by that sound signifies the same quality wheresoever to be imagined or met with.
>
> (John Locke, *An Essay Concerning Human Understanding*, ed. *A.C. Fraser*
> (New York: Dover, 1959), II.xi.9; 206–7, my emphasis)

But note that Locke moves here *from* a mental process *to* language, while Smith—anticipating modern philosophers—moves from language to the mind.

10 I can't imagine where Smith did see any such thing, I must say, and have found no discussion of the remark in biographies of Smith.

11 Walter Bagehot, *Collected Works*, ed. N. St. John-Stevas (Cambridge: Harvard University Press, 1968), vol. 3, 91.

12 See the discussion of this passage in Sections 10.4 and 12.1, below.

13 Nicholas Phillipson discusses this passage, and the importance of conversation to Smith's moral theory in general, in "Adam Smith as Civic Moralist," in I. Hont and M. Ignatieff (eds.), *Wealth and Virtue* (Cambridge: Cambridge University Press, 1983), 188–9.

14 See for instance T 589–90:

> [Our moral] sentiments may arise either from the mere species or appearance of characters and passions or from reflexions on their tendency to the happiness of mankind, and of particular persons. My opinion is that both these causes are intermix'd in our judgments of morals ... Tho' I am also of opinion, that reflexions on the tendencies of actions have by far the greatest influence, and determine all the great lines of our duty.

15 Smith often uses "absurd" or "absurdity" for views that he opposes: see, e.g., WN 101, 124, 151, 174, 267, 377, 384, 396, 458, 467, 488.

16 "The orator insists on every particular, exposes it in every point of view" (LRBL 35);

> We should not only make our circumstances all of a piece, but it is often proper to choose out some nice and curious ones. A painter in drawing a fruit makes the figure very striking if he not only gives it the form and colour but also represents the fine down with which it is covered. ... In the same manner in description we ought to choose out some minute circumstances which concur in the general emotion we would excite and at the same time but little attended to. Such circumstances are always attended with a very considerable effect.
>
> (LRBL 72; *see also* 79–80, 83)

17 Smith's account of language is permeated by this assumption: see especially LRBL 204–5, 214, 215–6, 218, 224.

18 "For [Aristotle] the mark of practical thinking is that it is concerned with particulars, and that some of the premises in practical reasoning are premises about particulars. ... It is as animals endowed with needs, desires, and the power of voluntary locomotion that we are alive to particular facts through sense perception. By nature animals perceive or otherwise apprehend pretty much what they need to in order to act so as to live and propagate. Thus, to be one who takes in the particulars of one's circumstances is already to be an agent or an incipient agent."—Sarah Broadie, "The Problem of Practical Intellect in Aristotle's Ethics," in *Proceedings of the Boston Area Colloquium in Classical Philosophy*, vol. 3 (1987). See also Terence Irwin, *Aristotle's First Principles* (Oxford: Clarendon Press, 1988), 118–20, 261–3. For further examples of the linkage between interest and attention to detail in Smith, see WN 833, 836, 838–9, 844, 885.

19 See Chapter 6 of my *Third Concept of Liberty* (Princeton: Princeton University Press, 1999).

20 A view with considerable currency in modern-day philosophy of science. See for instance Peter Kivy, 'Science and Aesthetic Appreciation," *Midwest Studies in Philosophy* 16/1 (1991), James McAllister, *Beauty and Revolution in Science* (Ithaca: Cornell University Press, 1999) or the essays in *Thinking about Science, Reflecting on Art: Bringing Aesthetics and Philosophy of Science Together*, eds. O. Bueno, G, Darby, S. French, and D. Rickles (London: Routledge, 2017).

21 Compare also LRBL 146: "[T]he Cartesian Philosophy ... tho it does not perhaps contain a word of truth ... nevertheless [was] ... universally received by
   all the Learned in Europe at that time."
22 For further realist language in WN, see, e.g., WN 108, 430, 517, 524, 739,
   771, 823.
   An intriguing additional text relevant to Smith's realism is LRBL 91:

> A well contrived Story may be as interesting and entertaining as any
> real one ... but still as the facts are not such as have realy existed, the
> end proposed by history will not be answered. The facts must be real,
> otherwise they will not assist us in our future conduct, by pointing out
> the means to avoid or produce any event. Feigned Events and the causes
> contrived for them, as they did not exist, can not inform us of what
> happend in former times, nor of consequence assist us in a plan of future
> conduct.

   Of course a modern anti-realist may treat "really existing" as a form of rhetoric
   that some society or group within a society uses to highlight what it would like
   people to believe. But Smith himself shows no inclination to do that. On the
   contrary, both here, and in the passages from TMS and WN quoted above, his
   aim seems to be precisely to *emphasize* the difference between what some social
   group considers to be real—"constructs" as truth—and what, independent of
   their beliefs and constructions, *is* real or true.
23 John McDowell, "Values and Secondary Qualities," in *Mind, Value, and Reality*
   (Cambridge: Harvard University Press, 1998), 134, 136. McDowell speaks of
   the "veridicality" of value properties—their suitedness to judgments of truth
   and falsehood—rather than their "reality."
24 See Ludwig Wittgenstein, *On Certainty*, trans. G.E.M. Anscombe and D. Paul, eds.
   G.E.M. Anscombe and G.H. von Wright (New York: Harper & Row, 1969), for a
   version of this view.
25 See Chapter 8 below.
26 But see Chandler, "Adam Smith as Critic," and Peter Jones, "The Aesthetics
   of Adam Smith," in H. Mizuta and C. Sugiyama (eds.), *Adam Smith: International
   Perspectives* (New York: St. Martin's Press, 1993) for interesting engagements with
   Smith's essays on aesthetics.

Further reading

James Chandler, "Adam Smith as Critic"
Charles Griswold, *Adam Smith and the Virtues of Enlightenment*, chapters 1 and 4
Dennis Rasmussen, *The Infidel and the Professor*, chapter 2
Eric Schliesser, *Adam Smith: Systematic Philosopher and Public Thinker*, chapters 3 and 11

Three
Moral sentimentalism

3.1 Moral philosophy in Smith's time

Let's begin our consideration of Smith's moral philosophy where Smith himself began his lectures on morality[1]: with a look at the history of moral philosophy. That will help us both identify what was most distinctive in its time about TMS, Smith's book on moral philosophy, and explain why Smith proceeds as he does in developing the argument of that book: why, in particular, he draws his account of morality out of an account of sympathy.

Those of us who teach university courses called "Introduction to Moral Philosophy" nowadays are generally anxious, early on, to explain the distinction between consequence-based and intention-based ways of evaluating actions, and especially between utilitarianism and deontology, the two main examples of these moral systems. Utilitarian systems, we tell our students, judge that action best that makes for the greatest happiness for the greatest number of people. Deontologists, by contrast, judge actions according to the intentions that go into them, assessing those intentions in accordance with a formal principle of duty. We usually give Immanuel Kant as the main example of a deontologist, and Jeremy Bentham and John Stuart Mill as paradigmatic advocates of utilitarianism.[2] We tell students that the debate between these two approaches to ethics continues vigorously today, and that they are by far the most prominent philosophical ways of handling ethical questions.

What matters about this debate for the purposes of a book on Smith is that it is quite new. It is, in particular, not how questions about morality were framed in Smith's day. Francis Hutcheson and David Hume may be seen as proto-utilitarians, helping to shape the arguments and vocabulary that Bentham later took up,[3] and Smith in some ways looks forward to Kant.[4] But both Hume and Smith are closer to the ancient philosophers who developed what today gets called "virtue ethics"—stressing how we live on the whole over our individual actions and resisting the idea that determinate rules can tell us, in most cases, how to act—than to the rule-governed systems that Bentham and Kant developed. That alone should signal that the categories we now use to define moral philosophy do not fit the mid-eighteenth century well. Their questions were not ours.

What were their questions? Two, above all: first, whether human beings are irremediably selfish or have in addition some capacity for altruism, and second, whether morality is properly grounded on reason or on sentiment. Thomas Hobbes proposed a thoroughly egoistic groundwork for morality in the mid-seventeenth century—moral norms (not sharply distinct, for Hobbes, from political norms) represent the ground rules that egoistic but rational creatures agree to so that they will not destroy one another. Bernard de Mandeville suggested in the early eighteenth century that moral norms are the invention of political leaders, and that we adhere to them unthinkingly or hypocritically, really wanting to pursue our own interests alone. Both moral rationalists like Ralph Cudworth, Samuel Clarke, and William Wollaston and moral sentimentalists like Lord Shaftesbury, Francis Hutcheson, and David Hume responded to these views by rejecting the egoistic portrayal of human nature on which they depend, arguing that we have some tendencies to care for others for their own sake, and that morality is and must be built in large part on these tendencies. Some of these people—Shaftesbury and Hume, for instance—considered it a part of virtue to take care of oneself; Hutcheson insisted that only benevolence could count as virtue, although he allowed that taking care of oneself was in many cases morally innocent, and might even be indirectly required by virtue (I can't care for others adequately, after all, if I am sick or starving). But all the philosophers I've just mentioned argued against the egoistic picture of human nature promoted by Hobbes and Mandeville, on both descriptive and normative grounds.

The rationalists and the sentimentalists disagreed, however, about the source of our commitment to moral principles. For Cudworth and Clarke, moral principles were like mathematical truths: they exist eternally, and can be discerned *a priori* by reason. Our inferiority to God immediately entails a duty of obedience to Him, Clarke thought, and our equality with one another immediately entails duties of respect for one another. These propositions seemed to him just as self-evident as the fact that 3 is less than 5 and equal to 2 + 1.[5] Wollaston instead compared moral principles to empirical facts. If I steal your horse, he thought, that is as if I am saying that your horse is mine. Immorality, for Wollaston, is always a form of falsehood.[6]

To all this, Hutcheson and Hume responded (a) that moral principles are not analogous to either mathematical or empirical facts (Hume's famous "no ought from is" principle appears in this context) and (b) that the rationalists have no plausible story to tell about what motivates us to be moral. Clarke seemed to think that "the very same" reason that "forces" us to affirm the equality of two lines also makes us feel obliged to do to others as we would have done to ourselves.[7] Hutcheson and Hume denied that reason has this motivating impact on us.[8] Morality is centrally a guide to action, they stressed; nothing can count as a moral principle if it cannot move us to action.[9] So if our sentiments are the source of our actions, moral principles must affect our sentiments. How can they do that unless they themselves express a sentiment or set of sentiments? Inspired by a hint in Shaftesbury that we have a "moral sense"[10]—Shaftesbury himself is an odd figure, combining elements of rationalism and sentimentalism[11]—Hutcheson proclaimed that we approve and disapprove of others' actions by way of a sensory organ analogous to our organs for sight, hearing, and touch. And what that organ approves of is the quantity of benevolence in each action; correlatively, it disapproves of malevolence, and indifference to others' well-being.[12] Hume rejected the idea that we have anything akin to a literal sense for morality (T 473),[13] and maintained that we approve and disapprove morally of certain kinds of concern for oneself as well as benevolence. But he agreed that approval and disapproval are emotional conditions and that their proper objects are likewise states of feeling. A similar position was held by Smith and Lord Kames, who together with Hutcheson and Hume comprise the core of the Scottish moral sentiment school of philosophy.

3.2 Attractions of sentimentalism

One feature of moral sentimentalism that made it appealing to moral philosophers in the Scottish Enlightenment is that it comports well with empirical, broadly naturalistic approaches to the world. If we begin our account of morality from the empirical facts about moral practice, it seems very much to be a sentimentalist enterprise: we feel attached to certain norms and are horrified by their violation. We do not normally experience ourselves, when trying to make a moral decision, as engaged in some kind of calculative process, or a process of scientific discovery; we try instead to determine what *feels* right. To say that we are or should instead be seeking out eternal moral truths that resemble eternal mathematical truths sounds odd.

The moral rationalism of the early eighteenth century was in addition hard to square with the largely *secular* naturalism that came to mark the Enlightenment. The rationalists' contention that there are moral entities out there to be discerned by reason makes far better sense if there is a God to establish or ground eternal truths than if the world is simply a collection of arbitrary empirical facts. At the end of the eighteenth century, Kant was to develop a rationalist theory in which moral principles express *how* we reason about action, rather than being objects for reason to discern. This sort of moral rationalism does not require belief in a God (even if Kant thought that morality can lead us to believe in God). But that is not true for the rationalism of a Cudworth or a Clarke, and it is unsurprising that a religious sceptic like Hume was drawn to a view that does without objects that lie beyond experience. That is not to say that all moral sentimentalists were sceptics about God. Hutcheson was a Protestant minister, albeit a heterodox one (he believed too much in innate human goodness for his fellow believers' taste), and he retained a place for religious faith in his moral system. But sentimentalism was a position more in tune than rationalism with an approach to the world that tried to make do just with natural, rather than super-natural, entities.

The naturalistic cast of moral sentimentalism has indeed given it an enduring appeal to modern philosophers. In various ways and to varying degrees, such figures as Alfred Ayer, John Mackie, Simon Blackburn, and Bernard Williams have all adopted a sentimentalist approach to morality—some of them explicitly proclaiming themselves successors to Hume in the bargain. All of these figures are

committed to a naturalistic approach to philosophy, and are sceptical, at best, about the existence of God.

To be sure, the attraction of the sentimentalist approach goes
beyond its naturalism. By taking certain feelings of approval, on the
part of a spectator, to be criterial of moral goodness or rightness, and
the object of those feelings to be paradigmatically a feeling on the
part of an agent, we can finesse nicely the question of what the *purpose* of morality might be. Sentimentalism thus improves on its main
naturalistic rival, utilitarianism. The idea that morally good actions
must aim to maximize happiness is by no means obvious, and in fact
does not fit the phenomenology of much moral judgment very well.
Moral systems evolve in societies to meet a wide variety of human
needs and interests, and there is no good reason to suppose that all
these needs and interests are directed to a single, universally desired
state called "happiness." In allowing for the view that what makes
an action good is simply the feelings motivating it, independent of its
consequences, moral sentimentalism makes for a better fit with the
way most of us, in most societies, actually judge actions. And Smith's
version of sentimentalism, as we will see, is particularly well suited
to exploit this phenomenological point.

3.2 Smith's contribution to the debates of his time

We are now in position to appreciate how Smith inserts himself
into the history of moral philosophy. Smith sees the debate between
rationalists and sentimentalists as overblown: both sentiment and
reason have a role to play in moral approval, he says, although "the
first perceptions of right and wrong" must come from "immediate sense and feeling" (TMS 319–20). Accordingly, he devotes
little space in TMS to the criticisms of Clarke and Wollaston that
had exercised Hutcheson and Hume, more or less taking over the
meta-ethical views of his teacher and his friend, although he gives
reason a somewhat larger place in moral thought than they did. On
the normative question of whether virtue is a product of self-love
or not, Smith more emphatically sides with Hutcheson and Hume,
rejecting Mandeville, in particular, as having offered a "licentious
system" rather than a proper theory of morality. He does not consider benevolence to be *criterial* of morality, however, as Hutcheson
does. For him, as for Hume, proper self-love is also a part of virtue.

But Smith takes his own major contribution to come in the definition of what "proper" means in that last sentence. Here a detour via Hume is helpful. As we have noted, Hume moved away from Hutcheson's bare posit of a moral sense towards an explanation of how morality might arise from features of our sentiments that are not in themselves laden with normative features. An aspect of Hume's *Treatise of Human Nature* of which he was particularly proud was his account of sympathy—the process by which we come to share the feelings of other people. But if we tend to share the feelings of other people, we will tend among other things to feel pain when they feel pain and pleasure when they feel pleasure. This leads us to approve of those personality traits in a person that lead her to bring happiness to herself or to other people: traits that are "agreeable" or "useful," in Hume's own terminology, to herself or to others.[14]

Smith agreed with Hume that our sense of moral approval emerges from the workings of our capacity for sympathy, and that that capacity is in the first instance non-moral. But Smith had a different account of sympathy from Hume's, and, consequently, a different moral theory. In particular, Smith thought that when we sympathize with others, we imagine ourselves into their circumstances, rather than simply feeling what they feel. This allows us to regard their feelings as "proper"—appropriate to their circumstances—if we think we would feel as they do in their situation, and improper otherwise. More precisely, we think their feelings are proper if we think an *impartial spectator* would share those feelings, in their circumstances. Neither this idea of propriety, nor the analysis Smith gives to it, appears in Hume. We will see the importance of these points in Chapter 5.

3.3 Purposes of moral philosophy

A word, now, on Smith's purposes in doing moral philosophy. Smith appears to have begun his moral philosophy course by telling his students that there are two main questions to consider, as regards the principles of morals:

> First, wherein does virtue consist? Or what is the tone of temper, and tenour of conduct, which constitutes the excellent

and praise-worthy character …? And secondly, by what power
or faculty in the mind is it, that this character, whatever it be, is
recommended to us?

(TMS 265)

Under the first heading, Smith puts Hutcheson's view that virtue
consists in benevolence, Clarke's view that it consists in acting suit-
ably to the various relationships we stand in, and Hobbes' view
that it consists in following the norms to which a rational egoist,
concerned with his or her long-term self-interest, would agree.
Under the second heading, Smith arrays the positions of rationalists
and sentimentalists, as well as the idea that only self-love can recommend virtue to us.[15] Smith also tells us that the way we resolve
the first question can have considerable impact on what we do. The
answers we give to the second question, by contrast, "though of
the greatest importance in speculation, is of none in practice." That
question is "a mere matter of philosophical curiousity" (315).

This division turns out to be confusing when it comes to
Smith's own work. Given that Smith devotes by far the bulk of TMS
to an account of how and why the verdict of a notional "impartial
spectator" is the proper criterion for moral judgement, we might
think that his book is dedicated to the second of his two questions.
And that is indeed how many scholars have read him. But this
answer, I believe, must be wrong. In the first place, it makes no
sense that Smith would deride the second question as "a mere
matter of philosophical curiousity," yet devote his own book on
moral philosophy entirely to it. That would be especially odd given
that Smith, echoing his teacher Hutcheson's insistence that moral
philosophy should contribute to moral practice, says that "the
great purpose of all systems of morality" is to influence "the character and conduct" of those who adopt these systems (TMS 293).
In the second place, Smith gives the first of his questions three
times as much space as the second, in the history of moral philosophy that he provides in TMS.[16] And in the third place, in the
course of that history, Smith identifies his views more closely with
Plato's and Aristotle's views of what virtue consists in than with
any view on what faculty in the mind leads us to approve of virtue
(270–1, 293, 306).

These points can help clarify what Smith means by his two questions. In telling us that the criterion of virtue is the judgment of a sympathetic impartial spectator, Smith thinks he is *also* telling us what virtues we should have.[17] The fact that a sympathetic impartial spectator will disapprove of our being wholly selfish is enough to show that we should be benevolent, for instance, while the fact that a sympathetic impartial spectator will expect us to take care of ourselves shows that benevolence is not the whole of virtue. Smith thinks that his criterion for virtue shows that virtue itself consists in a balance of self-love and love for others, and in dispositions that make for courage without rashness, self-respect without pride, and magnanimity without arrogance. As he says, this makes his model of a virtuous character very like those of Plato and Aristotle (TMS 270–1), a point that he seems to regard as confirming its correctness.[18] In explaining the means by which we come to approve of virtue, Smith thus takes himself also to be explaining what virtue is. As we learn that we should aim for the approval of an impartial spectator, we also learn how we should earn that approval—what character traits we should cultivate. The core teachings of TMS are thus meant to have a significant impact on moral practice. So they must be meant to respond to the first of Smith's questions rather than the second.

What remains, then, of the second question? Well, Smith appears to understand this question as having mostly to do with the debate between rationalists and sentimentalists, and he is not very interested in that debate. As we have seen, Smith thinks that both sentiment and reason have a role to play in moral approval. "The first perceptions of right and wrong" come from "immediate sense and feeling," but we use reason to draw out from these first perceptions both "general rules of justice" and "more vague and indeterminate ideas" of other virtues, which guide our conduct in many cases (TMS 319–20; compare 326). It is especially characteristic of reason to produce general rules, and the importance of general rules to justice is a point that Smith stresses over and over, throughout TMS as well as his lectures on jurisprudence. He believes that only that generality can defeat our self-deceiving attempts to excuse injustice, display to us our equality with other people, and allow for the fair treatment of everyone in a large society.[19] Reason thus plays an extremely important role in morality for Smith—a role that, especially in the way it displays human equality to us, foreshadows the role it plays in Kant—even if only sentiment can provide us with the initial material on the basis of which we judge right and wrong.

So Smith thinks he offers a fairly easy way of reconciling the views of those who promote reason and those who promote sentiment as the ground of morality. He does that, however, by moving away from what today we call "meta-ethical" questions—whether reason or only sentiment can motivate us, whether sentiment or only reason can have a cognitive function, and whether the objects of moral judgment are rational principles or particulars that must be discerned by sentiment—and trying to substitute, in their place, questions about the roles that sentiment and reason play in moral practice. This move from meta-ethical to ethical questions appears also in his response to the other mental principles he takes up as candidates for the basis of moral approval: self-love, a moral sense, and sympathy. As regards the first, Smith does argue that it is simply not true, as Hobbes had maintained, that our approval of virtue derives entirely from self-love, but he also takes pains to show that wanting someone else's pain to be alleviated out of sympathy cannot be regarded as a selfish concern: thereby fending off the possibility that his own moral views might be assimilated into egoism (TMS 316–7). As against a moral sense, Smith makes some sophisticated meta-ethical points about the phenomenology of moral approval (324–5) as well as about the fact that moral approval can be turned on our faculties of moral approval themselves (323–4, 325).[20] But the upshot of these criticisms is that we should adopt, in place of Hutcheson's benevolence-only view of morality, the complex system of moral judgment that Smith advocates: which has the ethical advantage that it takes account of all the various features that go to make up a balanced character. So it is hard, once again, to separate Smith's meta-ethical from his ethical views. His critiques of both Hobbes and Hutcheson turn at least as much on concerns about moral practice as they do on any theory of moral cognition.

Smith's talk of "the faculty in the mind" that recommends virtue to us is therefore confusing, and only on one construal of that talk are theories about that faculty irrelevant to practice. He would have done well, I think, to have adopted a distinction between meta-ethical and practical theories of our moral faculties, and characterized just the first of these as a matter of mere philosophical curiosity. The term "meta-ethics" did not exist in his day, however, nor were the topics that come under that heading sharply distinguished from first-level ethical questions. Now that we have this term, and the discipline it names, I think we can safely say that the questions Smith regarded as irrelevant to moral practice were meta-ethical ones, and that nothing he says about those questions is meant to dismiss the importance of investigating the nature of the mental faculty by which we decide how to act and cultivate virtues. Explicating the nature of this latter faculty—the sympathetic impartial spectator—constitutes the core of TMS. But in explicating this faculty, Smith takes himself to be simultaneously explaining what constitutes living up to its demands: what constitutes virtue.

3.4 Smith's meta-ethics

All that said, Smith does have some meta-ethical views, and they are of some importance to the content of his moral theory.

In the first place, Smith is a moral particularist, giving our judgment of particular cases ontological and epistemological priority over moral rules.[21] In his history of moral philosophy in TMS he says that "it is altogether absurd and unintelligible to suppose that the first perceptions of right and wrong can be derived from reason" — these perceptions must instead be "the object … of immediate sense and feeling" (TMS 320). In the middle of TMS, when he discusses moral rules, he tells us that we "lay [them] down to ourselves" in response to feelings of great revulsion at certain particular acts, or great admiration for other particular acts (159). They then serve as guides to our conduct, counteracting the self-deceit—the "source of half the disorders of human life" (158)—by which we might otherwise excuse ourselves for actions we would never excuse in others. General rules thus play a crucial role in our practice. But they are grounded in our reaction to particular cases. We would never see what is terrible about the conduct they prohibit, or wonderful about the conduct they mandate, had we not first, by "immediate sense and feeling," responded to particular instances of them.

This particularism meshes nicely with the cognitive particularism I attributed to Smith in Section 2.5, and goes a long way toward underwriting the suspicion of general theories in politics, and of the "man of system" who tries to impose such theories on everyone, for which Smith is famous. But it's worth stressing that Smith does give general rules an important role to play in his moral system. That role is not simply a pragmatic one, moreover. Because they are general— because they apply to each and every human being—they reveal to us human equality: remind us of it anyway. When we are tempted, in self-deceit, to exalt ourselves above others, these rules show us "the real littleness of ourselves," the fact that we are "but one of the multitude, in no respect better than any other in it" (TMS 137, 83).[22] This helps explain another feature of Smith's politics: his emphasis on the importance of general rules to justice, and of justice to the decency and stability of a state.

Smith spends two separate chapters (TMS III.vi and the latter half of VII.iv) on the relationship between his particularism and the role he gives to moral rules. He thinks it is a mistake both to codify rules for virtues like charity, generosity, gratitude, or friendship and to fail to codify rules for justice.[23] He adds that it can be a mistake—made by "the casuists of the middle and later ages of the christian church" (TMS 329–39)—to suppose that even all matters of justice can be pinned down precisely. Whether we are duty-bound to keep promises made to a highwayman is a subject that can make for endless debate among philosophers, for instance, but its proper resolution, like that of many other fine issues about truth-telling, promise-keeping, and respect for property, depends on "feeling and sentiment" rather than "precise rules." (339) Nevertheless, Smith hopes that some general foundations for jurisprudence can be established—some "natural rules of justice independent of all positive institution" (341). He ends TMS with a promise to provide an account of these general principles in a later work (341–2): a promise that he never fully kept, but that provides an important background to his arguments in WN.

3.5 Conclusion and summary

Smith takes his most important contribution to the moral sentimentalism of Hutcheson and Hume to lie in his account of propriety. "Philosophers have, of late years, considered chiefly" the effects of our feelings, Smith says, and attended too little to "the relations which they stand in to the cause which excites them" (TMS 18). He proposes to rectify this balance, showing how our feelings can be and are judged as appropriate or inappropriate to the situations that give rise to them, independently of the results they tend to bring about. And it is on the basis of this propriety or impropriety of a person's feelings that we judge of his or her character—that we come to the sorts of judgments, in favour of well-balanced characters, that Smith says we find in Plato and Aristotle.

But if our main moral concern is the propriety of the motives going into our actions, rather than the effects of those actions, then we will need some way of judging motives without reference to effects. Kant, famously, came up with a rational principle—the categorical imperative—by which to assess those motives. Smith, sticking to the moral sentimental framework in which he had been educated, looks for a mode of judgment that arises from the process by which we share emotions with one another: "sympathy," as he calls it.

Notes

1 Although this became the last part of the book—TMS—that he based on those lectures. See editors' note 1 to TMS 265.

2 Not altogether happily in the case of Mill, I believe: I take him instead to be a moral eclectic (as at one point he described himself) and more a critic than an advocate of the utilitarianism espoused by his father and Jeremy Bentham. But this is a story for another occasion.

3 Hutcheson was indeed the first to enunciate the "greatest happiness" principle: albeit in a context in which it does rather different work than it does for Bentham. See note 12 below.

4 See my "Philosophy in Moral Practice: Kant and Adam Smith," and *A Third Concept of Liberty*.

5 Samuel Clarke, *A Discourse of Natural Religion*, I.3, in D.D. Raphael (ed.), *British Moralists 1650–1800* (Indianapolis: Hackett, 1991), 200–2 (paragraphs 232–3).

6 William Wollaston, *The Religion of Nature Delineated*, I.III–VI, in Raphael, *British Moralists*, 240–50 (paragraphs 275–88). The horse example is on 248–9 (paragraph 287).

7 "[T]he reason which *obliges* every man in *practice*, so to deal always with another, as he would reasonably expect that others should in like circumstances deal with him; is the very same, as that which *forces* him in *speculation* to affirm, that if one

line or number be equal to another, that other is reciprocally equal to it" (Clarke, *Discourse of Natural Religion*, in Raphael, *British Moralists* 207–8 (paragraph 242).

8 Frances Hutcheson, *An Essay on the Nature and Conduct of the Passions with Illustrations on the Moral Sense*, ed. A. Garrett (Indianapolis: Liberty Fund, 2003), Section II, and Hume, T 456–63.

For a challenge to the view that Hume sees reason as inert, see Geoffrey Sayre-McCord, "Hume on Practical Morality and Inert Reason," in R. Shafer-Landau (ed.), *Oxford Studies in Meta-Ethics* (Oxford: Oxford University Press, 2008).

9 It may not in fact do that—we may act immorally—but even to feel guilty about acting immorally, we must be able to see how morality could have moved us.

10 Shaftesbury, *An Inquiry Concerning Virtue or Merit*, Part II, Section 3 and Part III, Sections 1–3, in his *Characteristics of Men, Manners, Opinions, Times*, ed. L. Klein (Cambridge: Cambridge University Press, 1999). See especially pp. 173, 177, 182–3.

11 See Christel Fricke, "Moral Sense Theories and other Sentimentalist Accounts of the Foundations of Morals," in A. Broadie and C. Smith (eds.), *Cambridge Companion to the Scottish Enlightenment*, 2nd ed. (Cambridge: Cambridge University Press, 2019).

12 The language of "quantity" in this sentence is deliberate: it is at this point that Hutcheson introduces his greatest happiness principle, as a way of determining the proper object of our benevolence. Actions are good or bad depending on whether they are willed benevolently, for Hutcheson, not whether they accord with the greatest happiness principle, but the benevolent person will strive to meet the greatest happiness principle, since that captures, mathematically, the maximal object of benevolence.

13 But see Remy Debes, "Hume's Peculiar Sentiment" (unpublished manuscript) for an argument that Hume remains something of a moral sense theorist *malgré lui*.

14 Note the utilitarian strain in Hume's moral thought here, as well as the fact that his moral thought is not limited to that strain: both in that the prime object of moral evaluation is character rather than actions, and in that Hume allows for traits that are merely "agreeable," but not useful, to count as virtues.

15 So Hobbes appears twice in this rubric, once as a normative theorist and once as a meta-ethicist.

16 He spends 48 pages on the first question and 13 pages on the second.

17 In addition to the passages cited in this paragraph, and the whole of Book VI, see TMS 50–66, 78–5, 106–8, 118–22, 132–4, 138–56, 171–8, 189–93 for stretches of TMS in which Smith uses his account of our moral faculties to delineate the virtues that can win the approval of those faculties.

18 He also takes great pains, in the final edition of TMS, to distance his views of virtuous character from those of Stoicism, with which they have nevertheless often been associated. The Stoics, he thinks, over-emphasise the virtue of self-command, making for a character that is unbalanced in point of compassion: see TMS 272–93.

19 See further discussion below, Sections 3.4 and 9.4.
20 Geoffrey Sayre-McCord makes rich use of these passages: see his "Sentiments and Spectators: Adam Smith's Theory of Moral Judgment," in V. Brown and S. Fleischacker (eds.), *The Philosophy of Adam Smith* (Routledge, 2010) and "Hume and Smith on Sympathy, Approbation, and Moral Judgment," in *Social Philosophy and Policy*, 30/1–2 (2014).
21 Ryan Hanley stresses Smith's particularism, linking it persuasively to his admiration for ancient ethical systems: Hanley, *Adam Smith and the Character of Virtue* (Cambridge: Cambridge University Press, 2009), 79–81, 88–9.
22 This is why, I believe, Smith identifies "reason" with "the great judge and arbiter of our conduct," at one famous moment in TMS, and says that it alone can keep us in the paths of justice, preventing us from "prefer[ring] ourselves … shamefully" to others: TMS 137.
23 The first, he suggests, may be compared to literary style and the second to grammar: a good composition will follow the rules of grammar strictly but deploy a much looser and vaguer idea of what counts as good style.

Further reading

Stephen Darwall, *The British Moralists and the Internal 'Ought'*
Christel Fricke, "Moral Sense Theories and Other Sentimentalist Accounts of the Foundations of Morals"
Michael Gill, *The British Moralists on Human Nature and the Birth of Secular Ethics*
Christine Korsgaard, *Sources of Normativity*, chapters 1 and 2

Four
Sympathy

4.1 Differences between Hume and Smith over sympathy

Both Smith and Hume use the word "sympathy" to mean roughly what today we call "empathy."[1] The word "empathy" was not available to them—it was coined only in 1909, by the psychologist Edward Titchener.[2] Had they had that word, they probably would have used it. They speak of sympathy with joy and anger, not just with pain, and are more interested in the sharing of feelings in itself than in any pity that might arise from those shared feelings.[3] But they offer quite different accounts of what it is to share feelings. For Hume, sympathy consists in observing the feelings of another person and coming to have the same feelings oneself, while for Smith, sympathy consists in projecting oneself, in imagination, into the *circumstances* of another person and coming to have the feelings that one thinks one would have there. For Hume, that is, in paradigm cases of sympathy we simply feel whatever the other person seems to feel. If he seems happy, we are happy; if he seems angry, we get angry. Smith's account of sympathy, by contrast, opens up a potential *gap* between what we feel on behalf of another person and what she herself seems to feel. If she seems happy or angry, but I think I would not be happy or angry in her circumstances, my sympathy for her will not consist in having the same feelings that she has. And this gap allows me to evaluate her feelings themselves, rather than just the consequences, for herself or other people, of the actions she might take on the basis of those feelings. Jane is bitterly disappointed that no-one has remembered her birthday, but I, imagining myself into her circumstances, think she is more upset than she should be. Molly, by contrast, is I think less upset than she should be about the humiliations she has experienced at work. Smith's account of sympathy makes sense of these kinds of judgments and thus plays into his moral system. It helps make sense of judgments about the *appropriateness* ("propriety") of feelings to the situations that evoke them, the importance of which he thinks Hume overlooked.

Several other differences between Hume and Smith stem from their different views of sympathy. First, for Smith we more actively employ the imagination to arouse sympathy than we do for Hume: we need deliberately to think our way into other people's circumstances to feel full sympathy for them. This leads Smith to give imaginative literature a greater place in moral development than Hume does. I may, for instance, come by way of a novel or play to sympathize with people in India, or people in great poverty, even though I have never shared their circumstances.

Second, while both think we have greater sympathy with our family and fellow countrymen than with people in general, they explain that greater sympathy differently. For Hume, we feel more similar to people biologically related to us, and people who share our circumstances, than to people in general, and the mechanics of sympathy lead us to share feelings in proportion to the degree of similarity we perceive between ourselves and others. For Smith, we feel more sympathy with people with whom we have already engaged in sympathetic relationships—people whose circumstances we have already imagined ourselves into—and those people will normally be members of our family or communities. So Hume makes better sense than Smith does of how brute biological kinship, and the accident of living together in the same place, can draw us close to other people, while Smith makes better sense than Hume does of how we can feel close to an adoptive family, and why we are likely to feel close with our neighbours only when we make an effort to interact with them sympathetically. As noted above, it is also easier to see on Smith's view how we can extend our sympathies to culturally or socially distant others—imagining ourselves into their circumstances, even if we have not shared them.

Sympathy for Hume thus works in general by way of causes over which we have little control, while for Smith it works by way of processes over which we can have a good deal of control. In a slogan: sympathy is *cast upon* us for Hume, while for Smith it is *cultivated by* us. We *receive* sympathy by way of various causal factors, for Hume; we *achieve* sympathy by way of various imaginative exercises, for Smith. We will explore Smith's account of sympathy via his debate with Hume over it, in this chapter. In the next chapter, we'll turn to the way Smith uses sympathy as a crucial building block for his moral system—a system that is once again in dialogue with Hume's.

4.2 Hume and Smith in the terms of modern theories of sympathy

Most philosophers who write on processes like sympathy today belong to either the "theory theory" or the "simulation theory" camp. Theory theorists say that we learn a folk theory when growing up—a set of folk beliefs, which bears some structural analogies to a scientific theory—about the causes and bodily expressions of various emotions, and then infer that Joey is sad because he's crying (and most people who cry are sad), or sad because he's hurt his finger (and most people who hurt their fingers are sad). Simulation theorists say that we neither need nor in fact employ any such theory to pick up on the feelings of others, that we instead come to know what others are feeling, and/or to share such feelings, by simulating how we would feel in their circumstances. A third, smaller group are called "contagion" theorists. They see the emotions of others, or the expression of those emotions, as simply having an impact upon us by which we feel something similar; no inference or process of simulation is necessary.[4]

Neither Hume nor Smith fits perfectly into any of these categories, if only because they are less interested in how we *know* what others are feeling—the main concern of contemporary philosophers of mind—than in what effects the *fact* that we share other people's feelings has on the rest of our social lives. That said, we can get a good first sense of the differences between Hume and Smith by placing Hume with the "contagion" folks, while aligning Smith with the "simulation" theorists.

Hume is often described as having a contagion account of sympathy, and I will use that label for it, but what he says doesn't entirely fit the label. He certainly does use the *language* of contagion to characterize the sympathetic process. He indeed revels in that language, writing frequently as if we simply catch emotions from one another:

> No quality of human nature is more remarkable ... than that propensity we have to sympathize with others, and to *receive by communication* their inclinations and sentiments, however different from ... our own. ... A chearful countenance *infuses a* sensible complacency and serenity into my mind; as an angry or sorrowful one *throws a sudden damp* upon me.
>
> (T 317, my emphases)

Again: "As in strings equally wound up, the motion of one communicates itself to the rest; so all the affections readily pass from one person to another, and beget correspondent movements in every human creature" (T 576). Other people's emotions "infuse" themselves into my mind; they "communicate" themselves to me; I have their feelings "thrown ... upon me." The language throughout these passages is passive, describing people among whom emotions travel whether they want those emotions or not, in the way diseases pass from one person to another: "contagiously," as Hume says expressly at one point (T 605).[5]

All of this looks much like a modern-day contagion view—feelings simply spread among us, without any intervening cognitive process. But Hume's official account of sympathy looks more like a "theory theory":

> When any affection is infus'd by sympathy, it is at first known only by its effects, and by those external signs in the countenance and conversation, which convey an idea of it. This idea is presently converted into an impression, and acquires such a degree of force and vivacity, as to become the very passion itself ... Tis indeed evident, that when we sympathize with the passion and sentiments of others, these movements appear at first in our mind as mere ideas, and are conceiv'd to belong to another person, as we conceive any other matter of fact. 'Tis also evident, that the ideas of the affections of others are converted into the very impressions they represent.
>
> (T 317, 319)

Here sympathy depends on a causal inference, either from a set of effects—"external signs in the countenance and conversation"—to the passion that likely caused them, or from a set of causes to the passion that will likely arise from them. Elsewhere Hume says this explicitly: "No passion of another discovers itself immediately to the mind. We are only sensible of its causes or effects. From these we infer the passion: And consequently these give rise to our sympathy" (T 576). This looks very like a theory theory. We have a theory about the usual effects and causes of various feelings, and infer that others are experiencing a particular feeling on the basis of that theory.

But if Hume rests sympathy on a causal theory of this sort, a problem arises for him that Smith picks up on. For if, as Hume expressly says in the last passage I have quoted, "no passion of another discovers itself immediately to [our] mind," how does the theory about which feelings, in other people, go with which causes and effects ever get set up? How do I ever come to know which "external signs in your countenance and conversation" signify pleasure or pain or anger in you, if I can never directly witness your pleasure or pain or anger?

This is not merely the methodological problem, of concern to researchers even today, about whether the facial expressions and behaviour of people in other cultures, or with unusual psychological constitutions, signify the same feelings that we would have when manifesting those external behaviours. It is instead a more thorough-going worry that arises for anyone who holds a private access view of the mind. If no-one else can get into my mind, how can I make so much as a good probabilistic guess about what goes on "inside" other people, from any external circumstances whatever? How can I assume any degree of similarity between my internal experiences and theirs? As part of his attack on the private access view of the mind, Ludwig Wittgenstein asks,

> If I say of myself that it is only from my own case that I know what the word 'pain' means—must I not say the same of other people too? And how can I generalize the *one* case so irresponsibly?[6]

But before Wittgenstein, the private access view was widely taken for granted. Certainly, most early modern philosophers seem to hold it—including Hume, as evidenced by his very claim that "no passion of another discovers itself immediately to [our] mind." The prevalence of private access views of the mind may be one reason why the idea of a basic sympathy among human beings, a basic tendency to share one another's feelings, seemed so striking when Hume proposed it. But the prevalence of such views also makes it more than a little odd that Hume assumes that we can make causal inferences about other people's feelings without ever getting to witness, in so much as a single case, both the cause and its effect.

4.3 Smith's critique of Hume in outline

Smith certainly thinks this is odd. "As we have no immediate experience of what other men feel," he says on the opening page of TMS, "we can form no idea of the manner in which they are affected, but by conceiving what we ourselves should feel in the like situation." No causal inference, and no contagion, can tell us how others feel; we must draw on our own resources for that. The paragraph goes on to drive this point home:

> Though our brother is upon the rack, as long as we ourselves are at our ease, our senses will never inform us of what he suffers. They never did, and never can, carry us beyond our own person, and it is by the imagination only that we can form any conception of what are his sensations. Neither can that faculty help us to this any other way, than by representing to us what would be our own, if we were in his case. It is the impressions of our own senses only, not those of his, which our imaginations copy.
>
> (TMS 9)

Two paragraphs into the book, and Smith has already introduced what he regards as his signature contribution to the sentimentalist project on which Hutcheson and Hume were working: a projective account of sympathy, to contrast with Hume's contagious one, from which a different account of moral judgment will flow. Smith insists that mere contagion cannot induce sympathy. In order to sympathize with others, we must actively imagine ourselves in their positions, not passively take in the way they appear to feel. We need to imagine ourselves into the other person's situation, to project ourselves into his or her shoes, in order to experience any sort of sympathy.

But while the fact that Smith disagrees with Hume on sympathy may seem obvious—it did to Smith's initial readers, such as Lord Kames and Dugald Stewart[7]—it is often ignored. Stephen Darwall has contrasted Smith's and Hume's views of sympathy beautifully in a 1998 essay,[8] but others deny that there are any differences between them. In one of the first major modern studies of Smith, Joseph Cropsey presented him as holding exactly the contagion view of sympathy that I have attributed to Hume. He writes, in explication of Smith: "The man who observes the joy of another will himself experience joy, and the spectator of grief or of fear will himself feel … grief or fear."[9] Going in the other direction, Alvin Goldman treats the contagion Hume talks about as if it were just a special case of projecting oneself into the feelings of others.[10] Even such a careful scholar as David Raynor sees the two philosophers as holding much the same view of sympathy.[11] It is therefore worth taking a few moments to lay out in some detail how Smith takes himself to be answering Hume.

4.4 Smith's critique of Hume in detail

Begin with the following lines, in the passage from the beginning of TMS quoted above:

> As we have no immediate experience of what other men feel, we can form no idea of the manner in which they are affected, but by conceiving what we ourselves should feel in the like situation. … It is the impressions of our own senses only, not those of his, which our imaginations copy.

The terms Smith uses here evoke Hume strongly, to anyone who has read the latter's *Treatise* or *Enquiry Concerning Human Understanding*. A contrast between "impressions" and "ideas" is central to Hume's philosophy, and the term "impressions," in particular, is one Hume took pains to note that he was coining.[12] Hume also treats "immediate experience" as a synonym for "impression," and what our imaginations "copy" as a synonym for "ideas." So this paragraph of Smith is suffused with Hume's vocabulary.

Moreover, the point Smith is making, both in this paragraph and throughout the opening chapter of TMS, makes sense only as a critique of Hume. Hume had said that other people's behaviour "convey an idea" to us of what they are feeling (T 317). Smith says that "we can form no idea" of what other people are feeling except "by conceiving what we ourselves should feel in the like situation." Hume says we are overwhelmed with an immediate horror if we witness "the cruel execution of the rack" (T 388); Smith stresses that *even* "when our brother is on the rack," if we ourselves are "at ease" we will never learn of what he suffers through our senses. And the point of these allusions to Hume is one that Smith has excellent reason to suppose that Hume would appreciate. Hume had regularly attacked ideas of importance to other philosophers (causation, substance, the self) by asking, "from what impression does this supposed idea derive?" Smith is asking exactly that of Hume's presumption that we get an idea of other people's feelings from our observation of them. If feelings are essentially private, as he and Hume both believe, how can anything we sense about other people give us an idea of their feelings?[13] The private access view of the mind makes it impossible for us ever to get an impression of their feelings, and without an impression of something, for Hume, we can never get an idea of it. So within the methods prescribed by Humean philosophy, this would seem to be a gotcha moment. Smith is telling Hume that he himself has overlooked the sort of thing that he usually accuses other philosophers of overlooking. We cannot acquire ideas of other people's feelings if we have no impressions of their feelings from which to copy those ideas. Instead, says Smith, the imagination must do *all* the work of sympathy—must provide the original impressions we have of other people's feelings as well as the ideas we form from those impressions.

Smith proceeds, in the rest of TMS's opening chapter, to bolster this gotcha argument for his projection theory with two other attacks on Hume's contagion account. First he offers a response to the most plausible examples Hume gives for the contagion view. Then he musters other cases of sympathy that, he thinks, can be readily be explained by projection but not by contagion.

The first strategy takes up the seven paragraphs that follow the one about our imaginations copying the impressions of our own senses rather than the impressions of the other person. Hume had said that "when the misery of a beggar appears very great, ... we sympathize with him in his affliction, and feel in our heart evident touches of pity and benevolence" (T 387). Smith picks up the same example, but stresses the degree to which we bring ourselves, imaginatively, into the beggar's condition: when the beggar's misery consists in "sores and ulcers," he says, we "are apt to feel an itching or uneasy sensation in the correspondent part of [our] own bodies" (TMS 10, my emphasis). Hume had said that "a chearful countenance infuses a sensible complacency and serenity into my mind; as an angry or sorrowful one throws a sudden damp on me" (T 317). Smith grants that this "may seem" to be true in some cases; grief and joy do "at once affect the spectator with some degree of a like ... emotion."[14] But he goes on to argue, first, that this does not hold, pace Hume, with regard to anger (we are inclined instead to sympathize with the person against whom the anger is directed), and second, that even where it does hold, as with grief and joy, that is "because they suggest to us the general idea of some good or bad fortune that has befallen the person in whom we observe them" (TMS 11). Even as regards grief and joy, then, other people's emotional expressions have an impact on us only because they suggest to us a condition—good or bad fortune—that we can enter imaginatively. Smith adds that we will have but an "extremely imperfect" sympathy with another person's grief or joy before we receive an answer to the question, "What has befallen you?" I need to know what you are experiencing before I can really sympathize with you: "general lamentations, which express nothing but the anguish of the sufferer," do not create "any actual sympathy that is very sensible" (11). So even in Hume's best cases for contagious sympathy, what is really going on is imaginative projection: these are cases in which sympathy "may seem to arise merely from the view of a certain emotion in another person," but that is not what is really going on. Smith summarizes this skirmish with Hume in a crisp statement of the differences between them: "Sympathy ... does not arise so much from the view of the passion, as from that of the situation which excites it" (12).

He then moves to his final point, meant to clinch his victory over Hume: that in some cases we "feel for another ... a passion of which he himself seems to be altogether incapable" (12). Smith gives four examples. The first is when we "blush for the impudence and rudeness of another, though he himself appears to have no sense of the impropriety of his own behavior." Hume had mentioned this sort of thing, in very similar language: "we blush for the conduct of those, who behave themselves foolishly before us, ... tho' they shew no sense of shame nor seem in the least conscious of their folly" (T 371). But for Hume this was a hard case to explain,[15] while for Smith it follows readily from how sympathy works in paradigm cases. We sympathize because we place ourselves in the other's condition and think we would feel shame were we to behave so rudely.

Smith's other three cases do not come from Hume. He mentions (1) a "wretch" who has lost the use of reason, and "laughs and sings" without realizing that a disaster has befallen him; (2) a mother who fears for her sick infant, knowing the real dangers that his illness poses to him and not merely feeling "the uneasiness of the present instant" that the infant is experiencing; and (3) our horror at the fact that the dead can no longer enjoy "the light of the sun" or participate in "life and conversation," even though they themselves are presumably experiencing nothing at all. In none of these cases could the sympathy we feel come, contagiously, from what the other feels, since the other does not feel what we feel for him or her; sympathy must instead arise from a projection into the other's circumstances. And Smith thinks that these cases make clear how sympathy works in general.

I have gone in such detail through the opening chapter of TMS because it is still common for scholars to assimilate Smith to Hume, or to dismiss the anti-Humean argument of the second paragraph of this chapter as an anomaly or exaggeration, and suggest that Smith backs away from it a few paragraphs later, granting that grief and joy do pass contagiously from person to person. In fact, the anti-Humean argument runs through the entire chapter, and even the apparent concession Smith makes about grief and joy turns out not to be a concession two paragraphs later—even grief and joy turn out to work through imaginative projection, for him, not contagion. Moreover, Smith employs his projective account of sympathy throughout TMS, repeatedly equating sympathy with an "imaginary change of situations" (TMS 19, 21, 317), or speaking of "bring[ing] home the case [of others] to ourselves" (e.g., 16, 18, 109, 317), and "enter[ing] into" their conditions.[16] He also uses the fact that it is easier for our imaginations to enter into some kinds of situations than others to explain many facts about sympathy: that we sympathize more with pains of the mind than pains of the body, for instance, or more with joy than with grief (27–31, 43–50). Indeed, Smith's entire moral theory would fall apart were it not for his insistence on the projective quality of sympathy. It is only that quality that allows us to *compare* our sympathetic feelings for others with what they feel on their own behalf, and judge of the "propriety" of those feelings.

4.5 A problem with Smith's account

There may however be a systematic reason why scholars have resisted attributing a purely projective theory of sympathy to Smith. How can we possibly carry out the comparisons I have just referred to, after all, unless we have some access to other people's feelings independent of projection? Moreover, Smith himself seems alive to this point, often talking in a way that suggests we can know what others are feeling by way of a causal inference from their expressions, without projection. We are vexed, he says, if another does not "seem to be entertained" by a book or poem that we like, or if our friends "seem indifferent" about injuries we have suffered. We pick up on the feelings of "a stranger [who] passes us in the street with all the marks of the deepest affliction."[17] Apparently we can, even for Smith, get an idea of what others are feeling from their gestures and behaviour.

How can we square this aspect of Smith with his insistence on a projective account of sympathy? Well, we could just say that Smith is inconsistent, or didn't think out his views fully enough. To some extent, I think this is true of both Hume and Smith on sympathy, even if they have wonderful insights into it. (Nor should they be blamed for this: sympathy is hard to explain, and the private access view from which both start makes it especially hard.) But the fact that Smith needs us to have some non-projective way of grasping other people's feelings in order to make his comparisons work is so glaringly obvious, and Smith seems so fully aware of it, that

I am reluctant to attribute a bald inconsistency to him on this point. Instead, I suggest that Smith believes that only what he might call the "original" of our ideas of other people's passions—the impression that first enables us to grasp what it means for them to feel grief, joy, anger, etc.[18]—must come from imagining ourselves into their situations. Once the idea is in place, we can begin to associate it with external circumstances and infer that a person is angry, happy, sad, etc. from her gestures and behaviour.

Alternatively, we might say that Smith thinks we can know *that* a person is angry, happy, sad, etc. by way of inductive inferences but can know *what it feels like* to be angry, happy, sad, etc. (the "qualia" of these feelings) only by way of projection. Knowing what it feels like to have other people's feelings is in any case what Smith seems to be after in the anti-Humean paragraph at the beginning of TMS: that is what only "our senses," not the senses of the other, can inform us of, what we need the imagination to "form any conception of." Knowing *that* another is undergoing torments of some sort is not something for which we need projection—but it is also not sympathy. Sympathy is "feeling with" another, and Smith insists that that cannot be done by way of causal inference, or of contagion.

So the "theory theory" language that Smith employs in TMS to explain how we know what others are feeling can be squared quite nicely with his insistence on a projective account of sympathy. We need merely to bear in mind that sympathy, for Smith, is not a way of *knowing* something about other people, just of sharing their experiences. And it is the fact that we can and do share other people's experiences that does crucial work in his moral theory.

4.6 Hume or Smith: which account of sympathy is better?

There are reasons to be drawn to the Humean account of sympathy, and reasons to be drawn to the Smithian account. Especially if we stress the contagion language in Hume's account, Hume does a better job than Smith of describing what we might describe as biological sympathy—the kind of automatic sympathy with others in which all human beings engage, along with other animals. Smith does better with what we might call socialized sympathy. Hume doesn't get the phenomenology of our socialized sympathies quite right, doesn't, in particular, recognize how much our judgment of other people's feelings affects our ability to sympathize with them. If I think you are over-indulging in your pain, or are pained about something you shouldn't be pained about (you made an insulting remark, say, and are upset that you were rebuked for it), then I am unlikely to sympathize with you, no matter how sorrowful a countenance you wear. And if I approve of your feelings, I am more likely to enter into them. I may indeed block myself from feeling a sympathy to which I was otherwise inclined if I disapprove of your feelings, and encourage it in myself if I approve. Smith's account gets all these matters exactly right. Smith's account also, because it gets these things right, helps us see how an impulse to moral judgment may be built into the workings of our emotions, rather than having to be generated from an external point-of-view, as it is for Hume.[19]

In addition, there is something very attractive about Smith's idea that imagination produces our sympathies from the ground up, that the deepest source of human bonds is not a mechanism, like the motion passed among "strings equally wound up," but our conscious efforts to see ourselves in each other's shoes. If true, this would give us far more control over how we sympathize, and with whom, than we get on the Humean picture; it would give imaginative literature a central role to play in our ability to expand our sympathies; and it would fit with the fact that much moral insensitivity to other people, both when it comes from greed or selfishness and when it comes from an obstinate pursuit of foolish or bigoted causes, is the result of a lack of imagination. And I think Smith's view is true, up to a point: we do come most deeply to share other people's feelings only after we make the effort to imagine ourselves into their situations, and we expand the range of people with whom we can sympathize only when we picture ourselves in their shoes.

But Smith is right only up to a point. His account begins with what I've called our socialized sympathies; it takes no cognizance of a capacity for sympathy that we may share with other animals. Sympathy does seem to have some roots in our biology,[20] however, independently of what, as socialized adults, we do with our imaginations. The feelings of the people around them affect even babies, and even our pets can be affected by our moods. Yet we don't suppose that babies or dogs can project themselves into our shoes. Hume is right: a "chearful countenance" does almost automatically "infuse" cheer into us, and an "angry or sorrowful" one does "throw a sudden damp" on us, even if we don't want to have these feelings or don't approve of them. I said earlier that we may try to block unwanted or inappropriate sympathies, but even then there must be something to block. Sometimes we share other people's feelings even while wishing we didn't.

The contagious form of sympathy is also our most immediate and intense way of sharing feelings. We feel other people's feelings strongly when we pick them up via contagion, getting very angry when they are very angry, feeling on top of the world when they are joyful, and falling into a funk when they are depressed. Contagious sympathy thus gives us a strong and direct bond with our fellow human beings—we identify with one another, and experience their emotions much as we do our own. And the pervasiveness and intensity of contagious sympathy makes it a powerful tool for explaining social phenomena. Hume was perhaps the first to demonstrate that.

But the advantages of the contagious mode of sympathy come with disadvantages. I can't really help catching other people's emotions, but that is to say that I am passive in the face of contagion. Hume captures this aspect of contagion wonderfully. But if the "chearful countenance" of another "infuses" good feeling into me, if feelings pass from one person to another as movement does among "strings equally wound up," or as diseases do across a densely populated area, then they affect me whether I want them to or not; I will have little or no control over sympathy.[21] So if we seek control over the degree to which we share other people's emotions, we have reason to be wary of contagious sympathy, and hope there is another way of sharing feelings.

Our lack of control over contagion often goes along with an ignorance of the causes of the emotions we are experiencing, moreover, and of whether they are appropriate or inappropriate responses to those causes. When I catch your anger or joy, I needn't know why I am catching it—what has angered or pleased you, or in what light you saw the object of your emotion. Your neighbour said something which you took to be a sneer. But the two of you have a bitter history that can make any remark seem like a sneer. So I might not myself feel anger if I heard the remark. But I didn't. I just see your anger and, liking you, react similarly.

That last qualification, about liking you, brings out a further feature of contagion that can be problematic. We can catch the emotions of any other human being, but we catch those emotions more readily from people we like or feel close to. Hume emphasizes this feature of contagion, using it to explain family relationships, classism, and national characters.[22] And he is right that in these and many other respects, contagious sympathy both draws on and reinforces divisions among human beings, helping us to form or strengthen us/them relationships. Recognizing this helps us account for a variety of social formations. But we may also want to resist or overcome our divisive tendencies, and look for a form of sympathy that does not encourage them.

In all these respects, Smith's projective sympathy improves on contagious sympathy. In order to imagine myself into your situation, I need to do something, not just let your emotions wash over me. Sympathy is not for Smith something that just happens to us; it is something we achieve only when we engage in certain kinds of imaginative activity.[23] And because we are active in arousing it, we can and must *choose* whether, how, and to what degree to do so. I try to imagine, perhaps, how I would feel if I lived in a one-room shack, or if I won the lottery, or if I had to choose between taking care of a medical need and securing a large business deal. I don't necessarily feel what you feel as a result. Perhaps you are inured to the hardships of life in the one-room shack and don't feel its limitations as sharply as I do for you. Perhaps you are overjoyed at winning the lottery, but I see the many factors that will probably lead you to lose your winnings in a few years. Perhaps you are enormously upset about your business deal but it seems to me that I would be, and you should be, grateful at having promptly averted a potential health crisis. But then I wonder whether I have adequately imagined the details of your situation. Maybe your life in the one-room shack is pretty good and it is class or cultural bias that leads me to think otherwise. Maybe you have wise plans for using the lottery money. Maybe your business deal was so important that you are right to be bitterly disappointed at losing it. What exactly I should be projecting myself into is not easy to say, and I may try and then come to think that I have done it badly, and need to try again.

So projective sympathy takes work. We need to set our imaginations in action to engage in it, and may need to extend our imaginations to correct or improve it. Smith says that the sympathetic spectator "must ... endeavour ... to bring home to himself every little circumstance of distress which can possibly occur to the sufferer" (TMS 21). In a lovely recent book called *The Empathy Exams*, Leslie Jamison points out that empathy—by which she means the projective sympathy that Smith describes—calls on us to unearth the full form of the situations in which we are to imagine ourselves: "to bring difficulty into the light." "Empathy isn't just listening," she says, "it's asking the questions whose answers need to be listened to. Empathy requires inquiry as much as imagination."[24] This fits in beautifully with Smith's insistence that sympathy requires me to bring home "every little circumstance of distress which can possibly occur to the sufferer," to "adopt the whole case of [my] companion with all its minutest incidents" (21).

We are thus not passive when engaging in Smithian sympathy. On the contrary, we are intensely active. And we are not, cannot be, unaware of what gave rise to the feelings we have as a result. On the contrary, we have those feelings only *because* we are aware of a set of circumstances that causes or occasions them. What we share with the other is not just a feeling—to the extent that we do share a feeling—but an understanding of the course of experience in which the other had that feeling: of what her life, or a passage in it, is like.

4.7 Smithian sympathy and the self

I want to take note of one more feature of Smithian sympathy before moving on. In Part I of TMS, Smith presents sympathy as something I do by imagining myself, as myself, into your situation. In Part VII of his book, he says something rather different:

> When I condole with you for the loss of your only son, in order to enter into your grief I do not consider what I, a person of such a character and profession, should suffer, if I had a son, and if that son were unfortunately to die: but I consider what I should suffer if I was really you, and I not only change circumstances with you, but I change persons and characters.
>
> (TMS 317)

Here it seems that I imagine myself as you, not as myself, in your situation. It's not clear that Smith himself notices the difference between these two things; he doesn't say anything to flag it. We also cannot surmise that Smith developed his view, between Parts I and VII of TMS. He wrote them both at about the same time (if anything, he drafted Part VII before Part I), and he says nothing after Part I to suggest that further nuances need to be added to the account of sympathy in it.

Some prominent Smith scholars therefore say that Smith had a confused view of sympathy. Charles Griswold, for instance, sees a sharp tension between the sympathy of Part I and the sympathy of Part VII, arguing that there is an internal contradiction in what Smith wants out of sympathy.[25] I submit, to the contrary, that Smith intends these to be flip sides of the same process, or perhaps ends of a spectrum that includes both exercises. After all, it is hard to draw a sharp line between imagining myself as myself into your situation and imagining myself as you into your situation. Suppose I try to feel my way into the shoes of a black person who has been subjected to a racial insult. Can I really enter so much as her situation without thinking about what it is like to be her in that situation? My being subjected to a racial insult is unlikely to have the practical consequences or emotional impact that such a thing would have on a black person. So even to enter the other's situation properly, I must become her to a significant degree—I can't so much as try on her shoes if I remain wholly me in imagination.[26] There is, moreover, no clear limit to how much I must take on board to get her situation right. The effect of a flight delay on an impatient person's life is different from the effect of a delay on a calm person's life;[27] the effect of a setback on the life of a person with a fragile ego is different from the effect of a setback on a person with great self-confidence. What counts as a person's situation cannot be neatly separated from how she feels about those situations, nor can her feelings be separated from her prior history, including her prior psychological history. The situations we are in include our dispositions to react emotionally to various things, and the histories that have bred such dispositions in us. Accordingly, we can't really enter other people's shoes without also imagining ourselves as them, to some degree.

Elsewhere, I have argued that Smith's conception of the self does not allow for a sharp line between these two things. We have no awareness of ourselves—no self-consciousness—until we begin to see ourselves in the "mirror" provided by the people around us, he says, and we acquire that awareness by coming to sympathize with ourselves as if from the perspective of one of those people (TMS 110–1). But on the Cartesian and Lockean views of the self that Smith inherited, my self does not exist if I am not aware of it; a self, on these views, is by *definition* something that reflects upon itself, that is self-aware. So Smith's self cannot so much as exist until it is awakened to such reflection by way of its sympathetic engagement with others. There is then every reason to think that a Smithean self will *consist* in large part of what it sees when it projects itself into the lives of others, and when it imagines itself into its own life from the perspective of others. There will then be no clear distinction between who I am and who you are—hence none between my sympathizing with you as you, and sympathizing with you as me.[28]

Now Smith does not explicitly say that the sympathy of Part I and the sympathy of Part VII are two aspects of the same process, or two ends on a spectrum of sympathetic identification. Given that my reading of him fits in well with both his account of the self and the phenomenology of sympathy, however, we have reason to favour my interpretation over Griswold's. And if we do, we see how thoroughly Smith sees the very nature of our selves as structured by our interaction with others.

4.8 Conclusion and summary

Whatever we say about the relationship between Part I and Part VII of TMS, it should now be clear that Smith's projective account of sympathy offers us a rich alternative to Hume's contagion account, even if Hume captures some facts about how we share feelings better than Smith does. Less clear is what exactly these various views of sympathy have to do with morality. For Smith, the connection between sympathy and morality goes through the pleasure we take in sharing feelings with others: a pleasure that Smith identifies with approval ("approbation") of those feelings. But even that will not quite get us to morality. Not all approval is moral approval; moral approval comes about only when we filter our ways of sharing feelings through the device that Smith calls "the impartial spectator." We take up these topics in the next chapter.

Notes

1 It's worth noting that Smith gives us an account of how we *share* feelings without giving us an account of what our feelings *are*. There is no equivalent in Smith's oeuvre to Hume's *Dissertation on the Passions* (or Book II of Hume's *Treatise*, on which the *Dissertation* is based), or the many other seventeenth and eighteenth century philosophical works devoted to our passions. Instead, Smith tells us in the middle of TMS that we would never attend to our own passions were it not for the judgments on those passions that we receive from those around us. It is in society that a person "first views the propriety and impropriety of his own passions" and it is only from that view that his attention moves from a focus just on the objects of his passions to "the passions themselves, the desires or aversions, the joys or sorrows, which those objects excite[…]" (TMS110). Smith implies here that he thinks a theory of the passions—a grouping of our feelings under categories, and an analysis of how they arise and differ from one another—can take place only within a moral context, that psychology is a science permeated by moral considerations from the get-go. It seems that we must move from moral theory to psychology, for Smith, rather than building up a non-moral psychology first, and then moving on to morality. If this is true, it's a view radically from Hume's and one that leads to a different kind of moral theory. I shall in any case follow Smith's procedure, and consider his view of shared feelings without first laying out a theory of feelings themselves.

  For a different approach, which deliberately inverts Smith's procedure on this score, see Eric Schliesser, *Adam Smith: Systematic Philosopher and Public Thinker* (Oxford: Oxford University Press, 2017), chapter 3.

2 See Rae Greiner, "1909: The Introduction of the Word 'Empathy' into English," and Remy Debes, "From *Einfühlung* to Empathy," in E. Schliesser (ed.), *Sympathy: A History* (Oxford: Oxford University Press, 2015).

3 Smith tells us explicitly, right at the beginning of TMS, that "sympathy" may originally have had the same meaning as pity or compassion, but that he thinks one can now, "without much impropriety," use it "to denote our fellow-feeling with any passion whatever" (TMS 10). See also 43:

> Our sympathy with sorrow, though not more real, has been more taken notice of than our sympathy with joy. The word sympathy, in its most proper and primitive signification, denotes our fellow-feeling with the sufferings, not the enjoyments, of others.

Smith could hardly be clearer about the fact that he is reaching for a word rather different from "sympathy," in its everyday sense.

4 For accounts of contagion, see Elaine Hatfield, "Emotional Contagion and Empathy," in J. Decety and W. Ickes (eds.), *The Social Neuroscience of Empathy* (Cambridge: MIT Press, 2009), and Elaine Hatfield, John Cacioppo, and Richard Rapson, *Emotional Contagion* (Cambridge: Cambridge University Press, 1994).

5 Hume also twice describes other people's emotions as "diffus[ing their] influence over" us (T 386, 592), and in the first of these passages goes on to compare the workings of sympathetic emotions to a system of "pipes" in which no more can flow than what is put in from "the fountain." All through the *Treatise*, Hume's imagery for sympathetic emotions presents us as passive in the face of the sentiments of others, as unable to help but be affected by them, or to consciously shape the direction or strength of that influence. His general, famous summation of this account, when he says that "the minds of men are mirrors to one another" (T 365), is of a piece with this imagery: we stand there, passively reflecting one another's feelings, for Hume, rather than actively putting ourselves into their situations. The contrast with Smith could not be more pronounced.

6 Ludwig Wittgenstein, *Philosophical Investigations*, trans. G.E.M. Anscombe (New York: Macmillan, 1958), § 293.

7 Kames, who knew both men well and had read their work closely, identified the projection view with Smith, in a critique of it that he added to the third edition (1779) of his *Essays*, and defended, against it, a more Humean account of sympathy: Henry Home, Lord Kames, *Essays on the Principles of Morality and Natural Religion*, ed. M. Moran (Indianapolis: Liberty Fund, 2005), I.i.ix, 70–2. Dugald Stewart distinguished between the two in a similar way (and again defended Hume against Smith): see the discussion of Stewart in Ian Duncan's "The Fate of Sympathy: Hume, Smith, Scott, Hogg," delivered at *Re-claiming Adam Smith*, Columbia University, September, 2006.

8 Stephen Darwall, "Empathy, Sympathy, Care," *Philosophical Studies* 89 (1998). See also Darwall, *The Second-Person Standpoint* (Cambridge: Harvard University Press, 2006), 44–6 and footnote 12 to 45.

9 Joseph Cropsey, *Polity and Economy* (South Bend: St Augustine's Press, 2001), 14; see also 17–9.

10 Alvin Goldman, *Simulating Minds* (Oxford: Oxford University Press, 2006), 17. On 299, Goldman also calls Smith a contagion theorist: "Recall Adam Smith's description of a companion's amusement enlivening one's own. This is hedonic contagion." But Smith's point, in the passage Goldman cites (TMS I.i.2.2; 14), is precisely that our companion's amusement enhances our own *if and only if we can imagine the source of the amusement from the companion's point of view*. That, for Smith, is emphatically not contagion.

11 David Raynor, "Adam Smith and the Virtues," *Adam Smith Review* 2 (2006).

12 "Here therefore we may divide all the perceptions of the mind into two classes or species... the less forcible and lively are commonly denominated *Thoughts* or *Ideas*. The other species want a name in our language, and in most others;

I suppose, because it was not requisite for any, but philosophical purposes, to rank them under a general term or appellation. Let us, therefore, use a little freedom, and call them *Impressions*; employing that word in a sense somewhat different from the usual" (EHU 12/18 see also T 1 and 2n).

13 Hume's own answer to this problem seems to be that we are similar enough to one another in general that we can assume that our emotional configurations are also paralleled in other people. "'Tis obvious," he says,

> that nature has preserv'd a great resemblance among all human creatures, and that we never remark any passion or principle in others, of which, in some degree or other, we may not find a parallel in ourselves. The case is the same with the fabric of the mind, as with that of the body.
>
> (T 318)

Someone impressed by the private access problem might insist that this is not in fact obvious, and repeat Wittgenstein's mocking question about inferring from our own case to what goes on in everybody else: "how can I generalize the one case so irresponsibly?" But Hume's comparison between "the fabric of the mind" and the fabric of the body may give us a clue to how he would respond to this complaint: he may consider it a mistake to distinguish sharply between the mind and the body. (Thanks to Louis Loeb for stressing this point to me.) In the "Liberty and Necessity" chapter of his *Enquiry Concerning Human Understanding*, Hume suggests strongly that mind and body are intimately intertwined—pointing out how my mental state can depend on the state of my stomach, for instance (EHU 53/68)—and it is even possible, although he never quite says this, that he shared Spinoza's belief in the identity of the mind and the body. (He is certainly unafraid of materialistic approaches to human beings, as his "On the Immortality of the Soul" makes clear.) But if we don't separate mind from body, there is plenty of evidence for the similarity between our minds and the minds of others: from the evidence for the similarities in our bodies. When we look to the functioning of human bodies, it is obvious that "nature has preserv'd a great resemblance among all human creatures." So if what goes on in our minds is nothing more than the consequence, or expression, of what goes on in our bodies, then we can indeed assume that the way feelings operate in ourselves must be at least roughly similar to the way they operate in other people.

I'm not sure Smith saw this answer in Hume, in part because he may not have attended adequately to the ways in which Hume virtually reduces the mind to the body. Smith seems himself in any case to be considerably less happy than Hume was with a materialistic approach to mind, and more interested in preserving a distinction between mind and body. So the moves I've just attributed to Hume are not open to him.

14 He even uses language that echoes Hume: "a smiling face is, to every body that sees it, a cheerful object; as a sorrowful countenance... is a melancholy one" (TMS I.i.1.6; 11).

15 Hume says that the sympathy in this case is "of a partial kind," arising from a limited view of its object. In general, he says, cases in which we sympathize without actually sharing the other person's feelings constitute "a pretty remarkable phaenomenon" of sympathy (T 370). They are explicable only by appealing to general rules. In this particular case, a general rule that foolish behavior leads people to feel ashamed of themselves has sway over us even when we see no sign of shame in the particular case. We see a person playing the fool; we apply the general rule, "Most people who act this way will feel ashamed of themselves"; and that leads us to think that this person must feel ashamed of himself too, even though he clearly doesn't.

This is a tortuous way of getting to a conclusion that, on Smith's projection theory, is straightforward. Smith alludes directly to Hume's example: "We blush for the impudence and rudeness of another, though he himself appears to have no sense of the impropriety of his own behavior" (I.i.1.10; 12). But for Smith, the explanation of our embarrassment is simple: we blush for such a person "because we cannot help feeling with what confusion we ourselves should be covered, had we behaved in so absurd a manner."

16 E.g., TMS 31–2, 34, 44, 70. A search engine on one online edition turns up 96 occurrences of this phrase.

17 TMS 14, 15, 17.

18 "Original" is a term that Hutcheson uses for the first sources of our ideas of beauty and virtue, and that Hume uses for feelings that arise in us independently of reflection or education (T 275, 295, 438). Smith uses it, as we will see in Chapter 9, for the first or paradigm case of legitimate property ownership.

19 Kate Abramson summarizes the ways in which sympathy must be transformed, for Hume, in order to function as a source of moral judgments in "Sympathy and the Project of Hume's Second Enquiry," *Archiv für die Geschichte der Philosophie*, 83 (2000), note 5 and pp. 53–4. See also Remy Debes, "Has Anything Changed? Hume's Theory of Association and Sympathy after the *Treatise*," *British Journal for the History of Philosophy*, 15 (2007), pp. 317–18, and note 18 to p. 318.

Smith's suggestion that morality and the emotions are intimately interwoven is plausible, I think, and helps Smith explain, more convincingly than Hume, why it is so hard for us to throw off the call of morality. Smith supplements or clarifies Hume's response to the "sensible knave" (EPM 232–3/282–3): he tells us why we will lose "inward peace of mind," etc. and why "these are circumstances very requisite to happiness." We say to the knave: your own emotions are so constituted that you cannot help but make moral judgments, on yourself and on others, and consequently will not even *feel* much (long-lasting) pleasure if you are conscious all the while of having come by that pleasure in a way of which other people disapprove.

20 It is contagious sympathy that can be explained by "mirror neurons." There is no reason to suppose that projective sympathy, when it does not mirror what others feel, will align our neurons with those of our targets.

For doubts about how much mirror neurons can in any case tell us about sympathy, see Remy Debes, "Empathy and Mirror Neurons," in H. Maibom (ed.), *The Routledge Handbook of Philosophy of Empathy* (London: Routledge, 2017).

21 It's worth stressing that I am here exploring simply Hume's account of what he calls *sympathy*, not of moral judgment. There are several steps, for Hume, between our various sympathies with other people, and our willingness to call them or their actions "virtuous" or "vicious." In the first place, sympathy is just a tool for figuring out which traits or actions are useful and/or "agreeable" to other people. In the second place, we need to correct our inclinations to approve or disapprove of others for a variety of biases if we are ever to "converse together on reasonable terms" about morality (T 581). So thoughts about the consequences of actions, and an appeal to a shared moral language, are necessary to moral judgment, for Hume (see T III.iii.i and EPM section V, part ii and section IX, part i). They are not necessary to sympathy, which he construes strictly as a non-reflective transaction, shaped by biological and social forces that we are barely aware of, and cannot control.

22 See T 322–3, 359–62 and "Of National Characters," in David Hume, *Essays: Moral, Political, and Literary*, ed. E. Miller, revised edition (Indianapolis: Liberty Fund, 1987), 202–6.

23 Amy Coplan stresses the fact that in contagious empathy "the transmission of emotion occurs via unconscious processes and is involuntary" while projective empathy "is a motivated and controlled process, which is neither automatic nor involuntary and demands that the observer attend to relevant differences between self and other." (Coplan, "Understanding Empathy: Its Features and Effects," in A. Coplan and P. Goldie (eds.), *Emotions: Philosophical and Psychological Perspectives* (Oxford: Oxford University Press, 2011), 8, 14.

24 Leslie Jamison, *The Empathy Exams* (Minneapolis: Graywolf Press, 2014), 5

25 Charles Griswold, "Smith and Rousseau in Dialogue," in V. Brown and S. Fleischacker (ed.), *The Philosophy of Adam Smith* (Abingdon: Routledge, 2010). But see also Griswold, *Jean-Jacques Rousseau and Adam Smith* (London: Routledge, 2018), chapter 3, which revises his earlier essay and comes closer to the "ends of a spectrum" view I propose in this paragraph.

26 See also Bence Nanay, "Adam Smith's Concept of Sympathy and Its Contemporary Interpretations," in V. Brown and S. Fleischacker (eds.), *The Philosophy of Adam Smith*, 91: "[A] crucial question to ask about Smith's account of sympathy is what we should mean by 'X's situation' when talking about imagining oneself in someone else's situation." Understanding how X might feel when attacked, for instance, will require us to consider such factors as whether "X knows something about the attacker that could be a means of defending herself (say, by blackmailing)." So "X's situation" will include "psychological [and] epistemic" factors as well as physical ones. Moreover, although Nanay does not stress this, "X's situation" will also include *affective* factors. If X, long steeled by military combat, takes physical attacks in stride, she will react very differently than if she

has been sheltered from danger all her life. Her situation will also include cultural factors. An X raised in a culture that valorizes physical combat, and pours shame on anyone who flinches in the face of danger, will react very differently to an attack than an X raised on the motto, "discretion is the better part of valor."

27 An example that Peter Goldie uses: "Centrally imagining *myself* (as an irritable person, I will correctly assume) missing the plane leaves the narrator very cross and frustrated. Successfully empathizing with, say, Mother Theresa … leaves the narrator serene" (Peter Goldie, *The Emotions: A Philosophical Exploration* (Oxford: Oxford University Press, 2000), 201.

28 I elaborate all of these points in *Being Me Being You*, Chapter 2.

Further reading

Stephen Darwall, "Empathy, Sympathy, Care"

Sam Fleischacker, *Being Me Being You*, chapter 2

Charles Griswold, *Adam Smith and the Virtues of Enlightenment*, chapter 2

Charles Griswold, "Smith and Rousseau in Dialogue"

John McHugh, "Ways of Desiring Mutual Sympathy in Adam Smith's Moral Philosophy"

Five
Moral approval and moral judgment

The core of Smith's moral theory is an account of moral approval: of the nature and causes of the feelings that lead us to call some actions and people (morally) "good" and others (morally) "bad." Remember, Smith is a sentimentalist, committed to the idea that it is sentiment, not reason, that provides us with the foundations of moral judgment. He is explicit about this:

> What is agreeable to our moral faculties, is fit, and right, and proper to be done; the contrary wrong, unfit, and improper. The sentiments which they approve of, are graceful and becoming: the contrary, ungraceful and unbecoming. The very words, right, wrong, fit, improper, graceful, unbecoming, mean only what pleases or displeases those faculties.
>
> (TMS 165)

So the objects of moral assessment are sentiments (in the first instance, at least: we of course often assess sentiments insofar as they help motivate an action or constitute a character) and moral assessment itself consists in a set of sentiments: in what is agreeable or disagreeable, pleasing or displeasing, to our moral faculties. No rational procedure comes in here—whether of calculation, in proto-utilitarian mode, or of formal argument, in proto-Kantian mode.

Not all approval is moral approval, however. Nor do our overall moral judgments, for Smith, depend simply on the approving or disapproving feelings we have about an action or character. The device that Smith calls the "impartial spectator" enters the scene to enable us to distinguish between approval in general and the specifically moral kind of approval; general rules, and a consideration of utility, play a role as well when we move from moral approval to overall moral judgments. Smith gives us a somewhat eclectic account of how we make moral judgments, characterizing them, in summary, as follows:

> When we approve of any character or action, the sentiments which we feel, are ... derived from four sources, which are in some respects different from one another. First, we sympathize with the motives of the agent; secondly, we enter into the gratitude of those who receive the benefit of his actions; thirdly, we observe that his conduct has been agreeable to the general rules by which those two sympathies generally act; and, last of all, when we consider such acts as making a part of a system of behaviour which tends to promote the happiness either of the individual or of the society, they appear to derive a beauty from this utility, not unlike that which we ascribe to any well-contrived machine.
>
> (TMS 326)

Smith says, in the first sentence of this passage, that the four "sources" he is about to describe constitute how we "approve" of a character or action, and he identifies that approval with "sentiments which we feel." The latter two of the sources he lists depend on and figure into more a process of reasoning than a sentiment, however, and it will in any case help us to keep in mind the differences among the various components Smith lists here if we use the phrase "moral judgment" for the result we come to when we bring to bear all four of these sources while reserving "moral approval" for what we feel when we employ just the first two. I will lay out these various pieces of Smith's moral theory in this chapter.

5.1 Approval

Approval in general, for Smith, arises directly from sympathy. He defines it as the pleasurable feeling we have upon finding that our sympathetic feelings on another person's behalf mesh with the feelings she has herself. We project ourselves into the other's situation, and the feelings we think we would have in that situation (either as ourselves or as her) seem to be just the feelings that she has. Smith calls this "mutual sympathy," and says that it is always pleasurable.

Hume criticized Smith on this score. Writing to Smith in response to the first edition of TMS, he said,

> I wish you had more particularly and fully prov'd, that all kinds of Sympathy are necessarily Agreeable. ... [I]t would appear that there is a disagreeable Sympathy, as well as an agreeable: And indeed, as the Sympathetic Passion is a reflex image of the principal it must partake of its Qualities, and be painful where that is so. ... An ill-humord Fellow; a man tir'd and disgusted with every thing, always ennuié; sickly, complaining, embarrass'd; such a one throws an evident Damp on Company, which I suppose wou'd be accounted for by Sympathy; and yet is disagreeable. ... [If] all Sympathy was agreeable[, a] Hospital would be a more entertaining Place than a Ball.
>
> (CAS 43)

Smith responded to this critique, in a footnote he added to the second edition of TMS, with an important distinction. While it is indeed painful to share the pains of others, he says—we would hardly be "sharing" them otherwise—the *awareness* that I share another's feelings is always pleasurable. And it is this awareness of shared feelings that constitutes the sentiment of approbation:

> [I]n the sentiment of approbation there are two things to be taken notice of; first, the sympathetic passion of the spectator; and secondly, the emotion which arises from his observing the perfect coincidence between this sympathetic passion in himself, and the original passion in the person principally concerned. This last emotion, in which the sentiment of approbation properly consists, is always agreeable and delightful. The other may be agreeable or disagreeable, according to the nature of the original passion, whose features it must always, in some measure, retain.
>
> (TMS 46n)

Now one might object that Smith is changing the subject. He seems to be granting that sympathy is not always pleasurable, while insisting that a different feeling, approbation, is always pleasurable. For Smith, however, approbation consists in our "observing the perfect coincidence" between our sympathetic passion for a person and "the original passion" in that person herself, and feeling a pleasure in that coincidence. So approbation is itself a kind of shared feeling—a kind of sympathy. And indeed, elsewhere in TMS, Smith speaks as if the pleasurable awareness of shared feeling is what he had in mind by what he calls "sympathy."[1] Strictly speaking, then, Smith here acknowledges that sympathy has several components, which he had not previously distinguished.

One might therefore legitimately complain that Smith's response to Hume shows that his account of sympathy is somewhat muddy. Otherwise, however, the response seems to me an effective one. Other commentators disagree, on the grounds that your bad feelings, and my bad feelings on your behalf, cannot add up to a good feeling.[2] But this misses Smith's point. The awareness of sympathy is not for Smith a matter of adding your feelings to my feelings—it is not a mixture of the two feelings, as jam is a mixture of fruit and sugar.[3] Rather, it is a new feeling, distinct from both your original feeling and my sympathy for you. It is a second-order feeling, we might say, taking as its object the concord between our two first-order feelings, rather than the objects of those feelings themselves.

In addition, for Smith a sympathetic passion is not a mere "reflex image" of the passion in the other person, as it is for Hume. Hume reads his own account of sympathy too much into Smith, as if Smith too were a contagion theorist, assuming that my sympathetic feelings mirror your feelings. For Smith, however, my sympathy arises from thinking myself into your situation and it is an open question whether I will then feel as you do. If you are "ill-humord" and constantly complaining, I may not share your feelings. And if I do feel as you do, there is a new element to the situation—the harmony between us—about which, if I am aware of it, I will also have feelings. The sentiment of approbation emerges from that new element of the situation, not from your feelings alone, nor from my sympathetic feelings for you alone. There is no reason why this new feeling has to have the character of the feelings whose concord gives rise to it. And in cases where the original feelings were painful, says Smith, it does not: it is, rather, "always agreeable and delightful."[4]

The remaining question is whether this point is true. Smith notes that sympathy "alleviates grief by insinuating into the heart almost the only agreeable sensation which it is at that time capable of receiving" (TMS 14). We take comfort from the grief of our friends at funerals, even if we continue to mourn our loss. In addition, whatever Hume may have thought, sometimes a hospital is more entertaining than a ball. Imagine walking through a hospital and feeling very much in synch with the suffering of the patients. Now imagine being at a ball while feeling out of synch with the pleasure that the other people seem to be having. Where would you rather be? Experiencing a ball as an outsider to the fun others are having can be sharply painful, and not a few of us will leave a ball like that for a place where people are suffering. Sometimes, we agree with *Ecclesiastes*: "It is better to go to the house of mourning than to the house of feasting" (*Ecclesiastes* 7:2).

This is especially true where we disapprove of "the house of feasting." Imagine being at a ball in the middle of a world crisis, when you think people should not be celebrating. You might very well prefer to be at a hospital then, or in any case somewhere dominated by the darker-hued sentiments you consider suited to the time. Cheerfulness of which we disapprove tends to be depressing and anger or grief of which we approve tends to instil in us at least a modicum of pleasure—by way of the solidarity we feel with the person experiencing it.[5]

And it is that sense of solidarity, I suggest, that Smith most wants to bring out. The reason why awareness of mutual sympathy is always pleasurable is that in it we are re-assured that we participate in a common humanity. We find that our feelings are characteristic of the human community and experience that as comforting and encouraging. We don't want to be idiosyncratic in our feelings. Sometimes we are regarded that way, and worry about it. A friend or colleague disapproves of my anger, my self-pity, my joy in my accomplishments, even my good cheer, and I fear that I am weird, cut off from other people, emotionally malformed in some way. So it is a relief to find that others *do* share in my feelings.[6] Finding that others feel as I do signals my membership in the general human community. Finding that I feel as another does—that I can enter into the pain or anger of a person before me—signals the same thing: I am re-assured that I belong, emotionally, to the general human community. And this feeling of common humanity is always a pleasure.[7] It is, moreover, precisely the pleasure that constitutes our "approving" of the feelings of others: when I feel it, I think that the other person has commendable feelings about her situation, feelings that I approve of. This point is pretty much definitional. To feel pleased about the feelings a person has is to approve of them; to feel displeased is to disapprove.

5.2 Moral approval

But we have not yet arrived at *moral* approval. Suppose that a co-worker of yours, whom you find pompous and irritating, is treated unfairly by your boss. You are pleased by this (even if you also feel a bit guilty about your pleasure), and I, equally irritated by your co-worker, find your pleasure well suited to your situation, and share it. My awareness of our sympathetic concord surely does amount to my *approving* of your feelings—but both you and I will probably admit, if we are decent people, that this is not moral approval.

Or suppose my son wins a competitive fellowship and is delighted about that. I will probably share his pleasure, and take an additional pleasure in the awareness of our concord of feelings. But insofar as I would not take a similar pleasure in the pleasure of other winners—I would indeed have been displeased by their pleasure had my son lost—my approval of my son's pleasure is not moral approval.

Again, suppose I root for my hometown soccer team, and share in their pleasure when they win and their disappointment when they lose, explicitly and emphatically approving of those who share these feelings, moreover, and disapproving of those who do not. This too would not be moral approval (although there are some people so caught up in sports fanship that they may mistake their feelings, in these cases, for moral ones).

What is missing in all these cases is the impartiality that marks moral approval. My siding with you against your co-worker is a partisan feeling, as are the pleasures I take in the success of my son and my hometown team vis-à-vis their rivals. There need be nothing wrong with such partisan feelings—perhaps there is something wrong with the pleasure I take in my co-worker's ill-treatment, but not with the vicarious pleasure I take in the success of my son or my hometown team—but there is also nothing especially good about them: nothing that merits approval.

Moral feelings are not like this. We should be able to approve of our own moral approval and disapproval, for Smith (TMS 322–3). But that means, he says, that they should be issued from a perspective that we at least aim to render impartial. The pleasure we take in sharing the feelings of another will be a moral pleasure if and only if it is a pleasure that we think an "impartial spectator" would also experience.

The impartial spectator is the most famous element of Smith's moral theory, and it makes good sense of the difference between plain approval and moral approval. If we apply it to the first of the three cases we have considered, we can see immediately that an impartial spectator would approve of the feelings of the co-worker who has been treated unfairly and not the pleasure of those who delight in his ill-treatment. An impartial spectator would not allow him or herself to be biased by the ties of friendship, of course, and would surely consider fairness to all employees to outweigh the pleasure that their co-workers may feel at the comeuppance of someone they find irritating. Smith says explicitly that when it comes to "hatred and resentment, with all their different modifications," our sympathies are "divided between the person who feels them, and the person who is the object of them" (TMS 34)—and is particularly concerned that we moderate these feelings by imagining how an impartial spectator would regard them (38).

The second and third cases are more complicated. An impartial spectator would presumably find pleasure suited to a situation in which a person has won something, and therefore approve to some degree of the pleasure that my child feels in winning a fellowship and that my team feels in winning a game. But given that such success is almost always in part a matter of luck, and given that there are losers in these cases who, quite reasonably, feel disappointment, an impartial spectator is unlikely to find anything to approve of in the winners' delight that luck has favoured them. That reaction is eminently understandable, and an impartial spectator is unlikely to condemn my child or my team for having it, or me for sharing it. But the fact that the impartial spectator would not herself approve of it suggests that the pleasure we take in our own luck is at best morally indifferent: neither good nor bad. And that, I submit, is exactly how most of us do regard these reactions.

"At *best* morally indifferent," because there are cases in which victors crow too much about their victories and losers sulk too much about their losses. There are also cases in which victors take an unusually modest and moderate level of pleasure in their successes, sometimes extending sincere condolences to the losers and praise for their efforts, as well as cases in which losers take a remarkably restrained, stoic approach to their losses. In these cases, moral approval and disapproval seems eminently merited: disapproval of the swaggering victors and self-pitying losers, and approval of the generous victors and stoic losers. But these are also cases in which we think the impartial spectator would disapprove of the former and approve of the latter; an impartial spectator test yields exactly the right results. And I may in some cases take up the impartial spectator stance and add it to my partisan response to the feelings of my child or my home team. I may *morally* approve of my son's or my team's generosity in victory, in addition to the simple pleasure I take in that victory, or morally disapprove of their strutting boastfulness, even as I approve, in a partisan manner, of the pleasure they take in their win. Indeed, sometimes, moral disapproval of a loved one's boastfulness will drown out the partisan approval we feel of his or her success. And sometimes moral approval of a loved one's stoicism will outweigh our partisan disappointment in his or her failure.

The takeaway point is just that moral approval is a sentiment we feel insofar as we take up, or try to take up, the standpoint of an impartial spectator. That is the device Smith uses to distinguish the specifically moral kind of approval from the pleasure we take in shared feelings generally.

5.3 The impartial spectator

It's worth noting that moral approval, so understood, goes out in the first instance to feelings we have both as agents and as people who have been acted upon: a person's emotional *reaction* to winning and losing, or to seeing someone else promoted, will be subject to moral assessment, and not just the actions he or she may take as a result of her feelings. This may sound odd to followers of contemporary moral theories, which tend to be concerned exclusively with actions and their motivations, but I regard it as an advantage of Smith's theory that it allows for the moral assessment of reactions. There is something contemptible about extravagant joy in one's own successes and extravagant misery about one's own defeats, and in our ordinary moral lives we recognize this point. That Smith's theory makes room for this recognition is a mark of its phenomenological acuity.

But before we consider the objects of moral assessment any further, let's examine the impartial spectator. Smith's most extended discussion of how we construct the standpoint of the impartial spectator runs as follows:

> When we first come into the world, from the natural desire to please, we accustom ourselves to consider what behaviour is likely to be agreeable to every person we converse with, to our parents, to our masters, to our companions. We address ourselves to individuals, and for some time fondly pursue the impossible and absurd project of gaining the good-will and approbation of every body. We are soon taught by experience, however, that this universal approbation is altogether unattainable. As soon as we come to have more important interests to manage, we find, that by pleasing one man, we almost certainly disoblige another, and that by humouring an individual, we may often irritate a whole people. … In order to protect ourselves from such partial judgments, we soon learn to set up in our own minds a judge between ourselves and those we live with. We conceive ourselves as acting in the presence of a person quite candid and equitable, of one who has no particular relation either to our selves, or to those whose interests are affected by our conduct, who is neither father, nor brother, nor friend either to them or to us, but is merely a man in general, an impartial spectator who considers our conduct with the same indifference with which we regard that of other people.[8]

So the impartial spectator is (1) something "we … set up in our own minds," (2) in response to the real, partial (partisan) judgments made on our conduct by people around us, (3) who resembles a *real* "person quite candid and equitable" and is distinguished from the real people who judge us in a partisan manner by (4) being "neither father, nor brother, nor friend either to [the people whose lives we affect] or to us." One thing that should be clear from this description is that there is no reason to suppose that this notional spectator is *ideally* rational, ideally just or kind, or indeed uses as criteria for moral judgment anything other than the moral standards we are already familiar with from our fathers, brothers, and friends. Smith does make clear, elsewhere, that the spectator needs to be well-informed as well as impartial (TMS 115–6), but there too he does not suggest that it needs *perfect* information: merely to know the relevant facts about the situations it is brought in to judge. Indeed, an ideally decent or omniscient figure, godlike, could not do the job for which Smith is calling in the impartial spectator: would not be enough like our family and friends—the people from whom we have learned how to approve and disapprove—for us to know what norms it is likely to employ.

It is therefore a mistake to identify Smith's "impartial spectator" with Roderick Firth's "ideal observer,"[9] or any other device introduced into moral theory in order to represent what a perfect view of humanity or the human good, a moral "view from nowhere," might look like.[10] The impartial spectator enters TMS as a bit of common sense, something that we are supposed to recognize ourselves as using in daily life. Unrestrained anger, says Smith early in Book I, is "detestable." What we admire is the person who suffers the greatest injuries while responding to them with only the controlled indignation that "an impartial spectator" would feel towards such injuries (TMS 24). It is perhaps no accident that the phrase appears in the course of a discussion of resentment, a passion of which Smith thinks we need to be especially wary.[11] But Smith invokes the impartial spectator as well, in these early pages, when discussing the need to restrain our selfishness (78, 82–3), and implies that it should govern our grief (24). Whenever we need to control our emotions, we should, and generally do, try to lower them to "that pitch of moderation, in which the impartial spectator can...enter into them" (26).

In these contexts, the impartial spectator is clearly supposed to be a familiar notion. It appears without fanfare, as if it had no technical significance, and appealing to its judgments seems to be of a piece with appealing to the judgments of actual spectators. The phrase first appears in the course of a discussion initiated by the remark that *all* spectators naturally try to enter imaginatively into the circumstances of the people they are trying to sympathize with, while the latter try to "assume [the circumstances] of the spectators" (TMS 22). Nothing about impartial spectators shows up until pretty late in this discussion, and Smith similarly moves from speaking in one sentence of "every impartial spectator" to speaking in the next of "every human heart," as if these were the same thing, at the beginning of Part II (69). The word "impartial" seems in these passages to be thrown in just as a reminder that, when looking to spectators as a guide to how we should feel or act, we of course don't want to rely on a spectator who happens to be our mother, or best friend, or bitter rival in love or business. When we look to the sympathetic feelings of actual spectators as a way of correcting for the excesses or errors in our own feelings, we want impartial spectators rather than partial ones. Again, this is supposed to be a bit of uncontroversial common sense, not something that requires us to engage in abstruse philosophical argument. And the impartial spectators we look to are real people—just not our mothers or hated rivals—with real passions and capacities, not Platonic paragons of virtue or moral judgment.

It is essential to bear in mind these humdrum beginnings when we come to Smith's description of the impartial spectator, in Part III, as a "demigod within the breast," and says that it has a "divine" as well as a human origin (TMS 131). Despite these remarks—to which I'll return—I think Smith's impartial spectator remains throughout an idea culled, if refined a bit, from our experience of the real human beings around us, with nothing of the pure rationality and dispassion to be found in Firth's ideal observer. In the first place, the impartial spectator *enters into our passions* rather than lacking all passions; it also, in Book II, shares some of the "irregularities" of our everyday judgments (97). On the most natural way of reading TMS, moreover, the formal account of the impartial spectator in Book III, which includes the "demigod" remark, is a further development of the eminently human character alluded to casually in Books I and II. As we saw in the long excerpt above, the account in

Book III of how we develop the impartial spectator also draws on the psychology of ordinary people. Smith says that the impartial spectator is "partly of immortal, yet partly too of mortal extraction," and has a "human" as well as a "divine" origin (131): I think he clearly intends it to derive from spectators we have actually known, and to be only a partial, not a full, idealization of these actual spectators.

This reading fits with Smith's philosophical method in general, as I have characterized it in Chapter 2. Smith always tries to draw philosophical systems out of everyday thought, rather than to impose a rational grid on that thought from above, and he is particularly insistent that moral philosophy be conducted that way (313–4). It would therefore be surprising if he called on us to correct our ordinary moral judgments by way of a Platonic ideal. He is far more likely to develop that corrective from within our ordinary forms of moral judgment.

Why, then, the language of "demigods" and a "divine" origin? Well, first we should note that Smith also calls *actual* human beings God's "vicegerent upon earth, [appointed] to superintend the behaviour of [their] brethren" (TMS 130). Nature has set things up so that we constantly "censure" and "applaud" one another: judge one another, and enforce our judgments with favourable or unfavourable attitudes. If nature has been created by a God,[12] then, this process— what our neighbours think of us—should represent a first pass at God's judgment of us. And the judgment of our own consciences— of the "supposed impartial and well-informed spectator" within our breasts—is a second pass at that judgment: a "higher tribunal" that comes closer to how we think God may judge us (131). The impartial spectator thus approximates God's judgment, just as real spectators do, but is not identical with God. It is a "demigod," not a full god, half human and half divine, and when we are unsure which of its aspects we are hearing from, we may appeal, if we are believers, "to a still higher tribunal, ...that of the all-seeing Judge of the world, whose eye can never be deceived, and whose judgments can never be perverted" (131). Smith's introduction of this third, fully divine level of judgment makes clear, I think, that the impartial spectator is *not* divine: merely a pointer towards the divine.

In short, Smith's impartial spectator is much more like the "seemingly impartial [ordinary] guy observing the scene" whom the economist Dan Klein calls "Rick" than like God.[13] Smith's impartial spectator is an *improved* Rick, to be sure: not seemingly impartial but actually so, or as close to that as an ordinary person can come, and as well-informed as an ordinary person can ordinarily be (TMS 131, 294). Smith also presumes that the Rick to whom we are appealing cares about us—is trying to sympathize with us. But the impartial spectator knows only as much, cares only as much, and is only as impartial as a human being can be; it never becomes a god. It is "well-informed" rather than omniscient, and neither its caring nor its impartiality will ever be perfect. A good way to think about its judgments is indeed to imagine what the best-imaginable-Rick you know—a thoughtful and concerned neighbour, or a fair and scrupulous juror[14]—might think of what you or someone else does. If he seems to err because of a gap in information, you will presumably ask him, "But Rick, what about x? Doesn't that change your verdict?" And if he seems to show a bias of some sort in his judgment, you will call that to his attention. You also expect him to change his mind if he finds your corrections reasonable. What a best-imaginable-Rick certainly *wouldn't* say to these questions is "Thanks, but I've got all the information I care to have," or "Thanks, but I've checked all the biases I feel like bothering with." A best-imaginable-Rick will be *concerned to look out for the best information he can gather* about a situation he is judging, and *concerned to be as impartial as he can be* in his judgments. His judgments will always be open to improvement along these dimensions.

This characterization of the impartial spectator fits with the role that that figure is meant to play in Smith's moral philosophy. Smith brings in the impartial spectator to answer a problem in Hume's version of moral sentimentalism. Hume had said that the feelings of approval and disapproval raised in us by the mere "survey or reflexion" of people's motives and characters "constitute our praise or admiration" of those motives and characters (T 471, 575): they *are* our moral judgments. We have a "moral taste" much like our aesthetic taste—a pleasure or disgust that arises "upon the contemplation or view of particular qualities and characters" (581)—and moral judgment is the expression of that taste. Hume recognized, however, that this account of morality seems in some ways ill-suited to our moral practice. We may feel greater love and kindness for "a familiar friend or acquaintance" than for a hero of ancient Greece (581), yet we judge the ancient hero to be far more virtuous than our friend or acquaintance. Hume accounts for this by saying that we take up certain "steady and general points of view" by which we correct our sentiments: "or at least, …our [moral] language" (581–2). Hume seems doubtful about the degree to which we can correct our sentiments, but even if we cannot change them, we will need some shared moral language for many social purposes. And taking up the "steady and general points of view" he mentions will enable us to uphold "some general inalterable standard[s]" for moral approval and disapproval, which "are … sufficient for discourse, and serve all our purposes in company, in the pulpit, on the theatre, and in the schools" (603). "Our passions do not readily follow" these standards, but that doesn't really matter (582). The needs of society and conversation will lead us to correct for the biases of our passions in what we say, and that is enough to enable us to co-ordinate our moral judgments.

This is an uncomfortable halfway house for a sentimentalist theory of morals, Smith thinks. Hume starts by saying that our sentiments are the source of our moral judgments, but then concedes that they are too partial to do that job adequately and brings in standards from outside them to correct them. This is, however, to concede that our sentiments, just as such, are non-moral: bald, non-normative facts about us. Smith argues instead that normativity is built into our sentiments. The idea that we *should have* certain sentiments is built into those sentiments themselves. We want to have the right kind of approving and disapproving sentiments, and are willing and able to change ourselves so that we have these sentiments. Smith tells a developmental story showing how the desire to have the feelings of an impartial spectator arises in us,[15] and he is far more optimistic than Hume about our ability to internalize the judgments of this spectator. The "wise and just man," says Smith, "does not merely affect the sentiments of the impartial spectator. He really adopts them. He almost identifies himself with, he almost becomes himself that impartial spectator, and scarce even feels but as that great arbiter of his conduct directs him to feel" (TMS 146–7). Thus for Smith but not for Hume *we have feelings that seek their own improvement.* We desire to have just those desires that deserve moral approval. And we distinguish between what *actually* wins moral approval and what properly *deserves* approval: we want, not merely to be in fact approved of in "society and conversation," but to be people of which those around us, if they were impartial and well-informed, *should* approve. The idea that we are naturally led to develop the impartial spectator within ourselves, and to shape our feelings to its judgments, amounts to a claim that a desire to have sentiments that are worthy of moral approval, and to change them where they fail of that aspiration, is built into our sentimental structure. It doesn't need to be imposed from outside—much less to take a form that affects our ways of talking about morality without necessarily changing our feelings at all.[16]

I think Smith takes this to be a significant advance on Hume's moral theory, and I think he is right about that. But it is an advance only insofar as it builds normativity into our ordinary moral sentiments. It follows that Smith would be ill-served by an impartial spectator that resembled God, or a Platonic or other rationalist ideal. Such an impartial spectator would be something quite *extra*-ordinary, out of reach for most or all of us. Smith wants to show that our ordinary moral sentiments are richer, more robustly open to normative correction, than Hume had supposed. He does not want to replace these ordinary moral sentiments with a moral standard that only a skilled philosopher might come up with. That is what makes Smith so psychologically plausible, and so appealing to philosophers who want their moral theories to be psychologically plausible.

5.4 Merit

To return now to the other components of our moral judgments, on Smith's eclectic account of how we arrive at them:

When we judge an action or a person, for Smith, the first and most basic constituent of that judgment is whether we think an impartial spectator would approve of the feeling that motivated the action, or that characteristically motivates the person. But that is not the only constituent of our judgments. For all that Smith regards his predecessors as having placed too much emphasis on the effects of actions, he acknowledges that those effects do and should make up some part of our ordinary judgments about morality. When we consider a motive as appropriate or inappropriate to the situation that gave rise to it, we are regarding it under the rubric of propriety or impropriety. When we approve or disapprove of a motive as giving rise to actions that have certain effects, we are regarding it under the rubric of "merit or demerit" (TMS 18; see also 67). Smith notes that in common life we judge of motives under both rubrics, complains that philosophers in recent times have ignored the first of them, and makes a case that propriety is the most important factor in moral judgment. But he does not ignore merit.

Even when he gets around to merit, however, he does not simply treat the effects of an action as good when they bring people happiness and bad when they bring on pain. Instead, he says that we praise an action for its effects (regard it as meritorious) when its intended target would properly feel *grateful* to the agent and we condemn an action for its effects when its intended target would properly feel *resentful* of its agent. We assess effects, that is, *by way of the feelings of the people affected by an action*, which we in turn evaluate with the assistance of an imagined impartial spectator: that is what makes the difference between proper and improper gratitude or resentment. Sympathy and the impartial spectator thus shape how we assess merit as well as propriety. Smith distances himself once again from the proto-utilitarian leanings of both Hutcheson and Hume, refusing to identify all pleasurable effects of action as good and all painful ones as bad, much less to add them up across everyone who experiences those effects, regardless of whether they were intended targets of the action.

What does this mean in practice? Above all, it means that we discount for effects that are not intended by their agents. If your attempt to injure or kill me in fact leads me, by some fluke, to meet the love of my life, I have no reason to be grateful to you. If your attempt to do me a great favour, through no fault on your part, winds up injuring me instead, I have no reason to resent you. Smith adds that gratitude prompts us to reward people and resentment to punish people: systems of justice, he says, are based on the sentiment of resentment (TMS 79). So another way of putting these points is to say that you deserve ("merit") no reward in the first case and no punishment in the second one.

Smith acknowledges that we do in fact sometimes resent people who accidentally harm us and feel grateful to people who accidentally help us. We don't discount entirely for the fact that an effect is unintended, and we blame people far more for harms they actually bring about than for harms they merely intend to bring about. In this connection, Smith develops an interesting, early account of moral luck.[17] He calls our unwillingness to discount entirely for luck an "irregularity" in our moral sentiments, but offers some reasons to think that that irregularity is in some ways useful: it prevents us, above all, from carrying out intrusive interrogations into people's motives (TMS 105). It is not entirely clear how Smith thinks he can square his defence of this tendency with his inclination to call it an "irregularity," but by using the word "irregularity," he at least marks some distance between what he is doing as a theorist of moral judgment and the way we judge in common life.

A larger question looms here: why does Smith take the way we judge in common life as a guide to the way we *should* judge at all? Why did he consider it a sufficient response to his predecessors' emphasis on effects to say that in common life we assess actions under the aspects of both propriety and merit? One answer to that question is that Hume, the predecessor he most had in mind, had himself presented moral philosophy as a sort of mapping and immanent correction of the judgments we make in common life. A deeper answer would need to explore how Smith integrates descriptive and normative elements in moral theory. We will take up that issue in Chapter 6.

5.5 Moral rules

Propriety and merit are not the only elements of moral judgment, for Smith. Moral rules also contribute to those judgments. These are especially important, according to Smith, when we turn from judging others to judging ourselves. Smith treats judging ourselves as significantly different from judging others—so much so that he devoted an entire Part of TMS to the subject (Part III) and added a subtitle to the book in its fourth (1774) edition that ran: "An Essay towards an Analysis of the Principles by which Men naturally judge concerning the Conduct and Character, first of their Neighbours, and afterwards of themselves" (TMS, editors' introduction, 40).

The progression implied in this subtitle is spelled out at the beginning of Part III:

> [O]ur first moral criticisms are exercised upon the characters and conduct of other people … But we soon learn, that other people are equally frank with regard to our own. We become anxious to know how far we deserve their censure or applause, and whether to them we must appear those agreeable or disagreeable creatures which they represent us. We begin, upon this account, to examine our own passions and conduct, and to consider how these must appear to them, by considering how they would appear to us if in their situation. We suppose ourselves the spectators of our own behaviour, and endeavour to imagine what effect it would, in this light, produce upon us.
>
> (TMS 112; see also 129)

We come to judge ourselves as if we were outside ourselves: as if we were "spectators of our own behavior" rather than the agents of it. As this metaphor suggests, there is a bit of a contortion involved here. We have to wrench ourselves out of the passions and interests that govern us as agents and try to see our actions from the perspective of someone who lacked those passions and interests. There may be some strain involved in doing this when we judge our neighbours as well: taking up an impartial spectator's view of another's conduct may require us, as we have seen, to set aside ties of kinship and affection that make us partial to some agents and biased against others. But the degree of effort needed when we judge ourselves is presumably much greater.

Moreover, Smith suggests that the difference is not just a matter of degree. Rather, a threat of gross distortion is built into our judgments of ourselves in a way that is not true of our judgments of others. When moved to action, Smith says, "the eagerness of passion" tends to "discolour our views of things, even when we are endeavouring to place ourselves in the situation of another," and to "call us back" to a position from which all "the objects that interest us … appear magnified and misrepresented by self-love" (TMS 157). This "mysterious veil of self-delusion" pervades our deliberations, is virtually impossible to take off, and is "the source of half the disorders of human life" (158).[18]

The remedy Smith proposes for this problem is to rely on general rules of propriety. Smith says that we form general rules by way of our detestation or admiration of certain particular actions. These feelings lead us to form a resolution never to commit the former or always to seek opportunities for performing the latter. Smith gives the example of the rules we form for ourselves against murder, saying that that rule helps keep even a "man of furious resentment" from inflicting a bloody revenge on someone who has insulted him, although

> the fury of his own temper may be such, that had this been the first time in which he considered such an action, he would … have determined it to be quite just and proper, and what every impartial spectator would approve of.
>
> (TMS 160–1)

In a case like this, we would not accurately ascertain the impartial spectator's view without relying on a rule. By quelling, or forcing us to set aside, our passion, the rule gives us an access to the impartial spectator that we would not otherwise have.

This makes a reliance on rules look like a heuristic, if perhaps a necessary one, in getting at the impartial spectator's particularistic judgments. But elsewhere Smith indicates that relying on rules for certain kinds of virtues—justice especially, but also prudence (TMS 175, 173)—can shape our characters in healthy ways. (He thinks we should *not* rely on rules to determine the offices of friendship or love or generosity: 172, 174.) As regards justice, one of the things that relying on a rule teaches us is "the real littleness of ourselves, and of whatever relates to ourselves"—it teaches us that "we are but one of the multitude in no respect better than any other in it" (83, 137). By prescribing blanket prohibitions against certain kinds of conduct—murder, injury, theft—the rules of justice bring out respects in which all human beings are equal: equally deserving of certain protections. By relying on these rules, then, by giving them priority in our moral judgments, we impress on ourselves a respect for the basic moral equality of human beings. Reliance on rules, at least where justice is concerned, thus goes beyond a heuristic: it expresses and displays to us a central element of morality.[19]

Smith's distinction of self-judgment from other-judgment, and emphasis on the difficulties of the former, marks a significant departure from Hume and Hutcheson, neither of whom takes up the subject in his moral philosophy.[20] Part III of TMS is also the most original and the deepest section of the book, in the opinion of many scholars. In addition to its accounts of self-deceit and justice, it contains a distinction between praise and praise-worthiness and an argument that the truly virtuous person seeks the latter rather than the former (thereby undermining Mandeville's presentation of morality as governed by our desire for praise), as well as a discussion of accountability, reason and conscience, and the nature of the self. All these points are linked. The desire for praise-worthiness rather than praise alone is a desire to live up to our self-judgments, rather than the judgments of others; we see ourselves as accountable for our actions only when we have a notion of our selves and hold our selves up to our own judgments; moral reason, for Smith, consists in the formation and application of moral rules; and conscience, for Smith, consists in the process by which we judge ourselves—making use of rules, among other things, in order to do that honestly. The rules we lay down to ourselves to prevent or overcome self-deceit are thus an essential part of the process by which we develop a sense of self, and make use of it to lift ourselves beyond merely being socialized into morality: into a condition in which we can seek virtue for its own sake rather than its social rewards, and hold ourselves responsible for both our virtues and our vices. It is no wonder that Part III is often quoted by those who see Smith's moral theory as anticipating Kant's.[21]

5.6 Utility

Finally, Smith acknowledges that one component of moral judgment, especially among philosophers, consists in considering acts "as making a part of a system of behaviour which tends to promote the happiness either of the individual or of the society" (TMS 326). Smith spends much of TMS fending off this component. He acknowledges that we do assess acts in accordance with the way they fit or fail to fit with larger social systems, and assess the systems them-selves in accordance with their utility, but he regards this as a very marginal constituent of moral judgment—even something of an after-thought—rather than something essential to it. Acts "appear to derive a beauty from [their] utility, not unlike that which we ascribe to any well-contrived machine," he admits (326), but also says that

> it seems impossible that the approbation of virtue should be a sentiment of the same kind with that by which we approve of a convenient and well-contrived building; or that we should have no other reason for praising a man than that for which we commend a chest of drawers.
>
> (188)

This last remark is a slap at Hume, who had traced the source of our moral judgments *primarily* to a sense that certain qualities "tend to promote the happiness either of the individual or of society." Criticisms of this view appear throughout TMS. "The utility of [the intellectual virtues], it may be thought, is what first recommends them to us," Smith notes in Part I, "and, no doubt, the consider-ation of this, when we come to attend to it, gives them a new value." But "originally ... we approve of another man's judgment, not as something useful, but as right, as accurate, as agreeable to truth and reality." We also "originally approve of" good taste, "not as useful, but as just, as delicate, and as precisely suited to its object." Smith explicitly calls the utility of intellectual and aesthetic virtues "an after-thought" here, denying that it is "what first recommends them to our approbation" (TMS 20; compare 189).

At another point, Smith grants that various unnamed authors who preceded him were right to describe human society as "a great, an immense machine, whose regular and harmonious movements produce a thousand agreeable effects" and to characterize virtue as "the fine polish to the wheels" of this machine. But he notes that such descriptions lead the reader to see "a *new* beauty in virtue, and a *new* deformity in vice, which he had never taken notice of before" (my emphasis). And the very newness of these perceptions, the very fact that this aspect of the virtues had "never occurred to [the reader] in his life" before he read the philosophical works that Smith is discussing, shows that utility "cannot possibly be the ground of that approbation and disapprobation with which [the reader] has always been accustomed to consider those ... qualities" (TMS 316; compare 192).

Elsewhere, Smith describes the pleasure we feel upon seeing how acts fit into a well-run system in a yet harsher light. Rejecting Hume's argument that we see objects as beautiful when we think they conduce to pleasure or convenience, Smith says that we see objects as beautiful when they are *well-suited to conduce* to pleasure or convenience: when they form part of a system, or potential system, that is well "adjust[ed] ... for attaining ... conveniency or pleasure," whether or not those ends are actually achieved. And this "love of system," this "regard to the beauty of order," is often what leads people to "recommend ... institutions which tend to promote the public welfare":

> When a patriot exerts himself for the improvement of any part of the public police, his conduct does not always arise from pure sympathy with the happiness of those who are to reap the benefit of it. It is not commonly from a fellow-feeling with carriers and waggoners that a public-spirited man encourages the mending of high roads. When the legislature establishes premiums and other encouragements to advance the linen or woollen manufactures, its conduct seldom proceeds from pure sympathy with the wearer of cheap or fine cloth, much less from that with the manufacturer or merchant. The perfection of police, the extension of trade and manufactures, are noble and magnificent objects. The contemplation of them pleases us, and we are interested in whatever can tend to advance them. They make part of the great system of government, and the wheels of the political machine seem to move with more harmony and ease by means of them. We take pleasure in beholding the perfection of so grand a system, and we are uneasy till we remove any obstruction that can in the least disturb or encumber the regularity of its motions.
>
> (TMS 185)

But this machine-like construal of society can be harmful, and in the last edition of TMS Smith famously rails against the "man of system" who is "so enamoured with the supposed beauty of his own ideal plan of government, that he cannot suffer the smallest deviation from any part of it." A politician motivated by the love of system will tend to be arrogant, forgetting that "the members of a great society" are not like pieces on a chess board:

> the pieces upon the chess-board have no principle of motion besides that which the hand impresses upon them; but ... in the great chess-board of human society, every single piece has a principle of motion of its own, altogether different from that which the legislator might chuse to impress upon it.
>
> (233–4)

All this being said, Smith concedes that we do in fact assess actions in part according to how they fit in with larger, useful social systems, and that there are some advantages to our doing that. Even the "man of system" passage just quoted goes on to admit that "some general, and even systematical, idea of the perfection of policy and law, may no doubt be necessary for directing the views of the statesman." And even the heavily ironic description of "patriots" who propose public improvements, not because they care about the people who will be affected by those improvements, but because they are entranced by the opportunity to make "the wheels of the political machine ... move with more harmony and ease," grants that the institutions thus established *are* improvements, which will help various members of society.[22] Elsewhere in TMS Smith allows that a sentinel in time of war may rightly be executed for falling asleep on his watch, because "the order of society" requires such a punishment (90–1).[23]

It's worth noting that in the sentinel case, the *survival* of a society, or at least of many of its members, may be at stake. Smith never expresses approval of the sacrifice of an individual's life or liberty for the mere *happiness* of other people. Indeed, his condemnation of "men of system" who ignore "the principle of motion" in each of us suggests strongly that he would disapprove of any such instrumental treatment of an individual. So the utilitarian element in Smith's moral theory may trump the other three elements he lists only when life is at stake. And it is reasonable to suppose that in *such* cases worries about propriety, merit, and general rules need to take a back seat. In any case, there is a utilitarian element to Smith's moral thinking, if a much lesser one than is to be found in Hutcheson and Hume. On the whole, as he says explicitly at one point, the utility of characters and acts is an "after-thought" in our moral considerations, not their primary or original ground.

5.7 Why Smith is not a utilitarian

A further word on utility. James Otteson, a prominent contemporary Smith scholar, has argued that Smith needs to appeal to something like the greatest happiness for the greatest number on a secondary or meta-level of morality in order to select among the many alternative norms for practice that arise in a society.[24] Otteson grants that our moral judgments, for Smith, are in the first instance likely to conform simply to what our peers in a given society consider to be right and wrong. But if we are to regard these judgments as truly of the good, they must over time evolve so as to satisfy a standard of goodness independent of what they themselves proclaim to be good. Moreover, Smith does seem to see morality as evolving in this way, and does seem to see that process of evolution as leading to real improvements in our moral judgments. So he must have a higher, meta-standard of goodness or rightness, beyond the norms actually upheld by societies at any given time, by which to endorse the process of evolution by which these norms change. Otteson thinks that only the utilitarian criterion can serve as this standard.[25]

I agree with every step of this argument except the final one. Smith did think that moral norms must in the first instance fit the circumstances of a society at a particular time, that they tend to evolve, and that this process of evolution is on the whole a good thing.[26] It is also true that he could not hold all of these positions consistently without having some way of evaluating moral norms independent of the impartial-spectator procedures that actually obtain in each society. But the utilitarian principle need not play this role for him, and I do not think that he in fact appealed to anything of the sort.

To begin with, the utilitarian principle is certainly not the only principle that can adjudicate among first-level, culturally entrenched norms. One might instead appeal to a divine law, or to an ideal of the virtuous person, along Platonic or Aristotelian or Stoic lines. Or one might appeal to a principle of liberty, or of natural rights.

Smith does not do the first of these things—he is no divine command theorist—and if he has a universal ideal of what human beings should look like, he does not make that clear. But he does appeal to "natural justice" or "natural equity," as against various features of British law,[27] and expressly says that the rights that make for liberty take priority over, and cannot be reduced to, considerations that make for people's happiness (WN 539). So if Otteson wants a Smithian transcendental principle by which to judge among given moral norms, and show that they are evolving in a positive direction, a libertarian principle of some kind would be a more plausible candidate for that principle than a utilitarian one.

But Smith also engages in various kinds of immanent critique of the moral norms around him, suggesting that they depend on biases, or misinformation, or an inadequate exercise of our imaginations—that they are not what a well-informed and sympathetic impartial spectator would endorse—or using some of our moral norms against others. These procedures allow him to judge the norms that a society upholds at one time as inferior to the norms it upholds at a later time without employing any transcendental moral principle. Otteson's concern about how Smith can endorse a progressive account of moral history can thus be met without bringing in any such principle.

I will return in Chapters 7 and 9 to question about how Smith can make room for a critique of the norms of one's society. For now, let's stick simply to the question of whether he was a utilitarian. There are two reasons for denying that he was. First, he explicitly tells us that "the care of the universal happiness of all rational and sensible beings is the business of God and not of man." "To man is allotted a much humbler department," he says: the care of his own, local social group—"his family, his friends, his country"—by way of the "active dut[ies]" assigned to him by the moral system that proceeds via impartial-spectator judgments of propriety and merit, and the moral rules that prevent us from skewing those judgments so as to gratify our self-deceit (TMS 237). To be sure, this passage does imply that the upshot of everyone carrying out her local and limited duties should be happiness, for the agent and everyone around her. But it also forbids us from explicitly taking the happiness of these people, let alone of everyone, as our aim in lieu of our local and limited duties. It forbids us from seeing those duties as transparent to some grander utilitarian end, and trying to pursue that end directly, or to criticize and revise our duties in its light.

Second, and more deeply, Smith's notion of happiness does not allow for the clear separation between happiness and duty or virtue that utilitarians need in order to hold up the former as a criterion for the value of the latter. Smith doesn't explicitly define happiness anywhere, or discuss its composition in any detail, but his scattered remarks on the subject make living up to the moral standards of one's society essential to it. He tells us for instance that "the chief part of human happiness arises from the consciousness of being beloved" (TMS 41). But we will be "beloved" only when our friends and neighbours approve of us, and they will do that only if we live up to their standards of virtuous conduct. A few pages later Smith asks, rhetorically, "What can be added to the happiness of the man who is in health, who is out of debt, and has a clear conscience?" (45). But to have "a clear conscience" requires one to live up to what one takes to be standards of virtue. And in one of the few other passages in which Smith gives some content to the notion of happiness, he says that it consists in a balance between "tranquillity and enjoyment," with the accent on tranquillity (149). But in the paragraph that immediately follows this line, Smith tells us that it is a virtuous contentment with the station we actually occupy that most preserves our tranquillity and it is the violation of "the rules ... of prudence or of justice" that most "corrupt[s] the ... tranquillity of our minds, either by shame from the remembrance of our own folly [in abandoning prudence], or by remorse from the horror of our own injustice" (149). This theme pervades the whole of the paragraph, and is implicitly present throughout the book; virtue is, for Smith, what most makes for tranquillity and vice is what most readily destroys it. Once again, then, living up to what one takes to be standards of virtue is an essential condition for happiness.

It follows that happiness, for Smith, is so essentially shaped by the possession of what we take to be virtue that it cannot serve as an independent goal by which we might define virtue. It is essential to the hedonic calculus beloved of utilitarians that happiness be defined independently of whatever we take to be morality, so that it can bestow content on moral claims. That is impossible, for Smith. Smith sees meeting the demands of the impartial spectator as intrinsic to happiness; there is no happiness independent of meeting these demands.[28] Consequently, there can be no way of defining moral norms and virtues by appeal to happiness.

Smith's account of moral judgment makes the question of how we can criticize our society's norms very difficult for him—his system has been accused, with reason, of verging on a kind of cultural relativism. That problem cannot be solved, however, in the way that Otteson proposes. It is a mistake, in any case, to suppose that Smith was a utilitarian.

5.8 Culture and morality

The issue of cultural relativism brings us to Part V of TMS. The four components of moral judgment that we have surveyed thus far correspond closely to the major sections of TMS. Part I deals with propriety, Part II with merit, Part III with moral rules, and Part IV with utility. The last section of the book (Part VII, in the 6th edition) provides a history of moral philosophy, bringing out the affinities of Smith's views to themes in Plato, Aristotle, and the Stoics. And what we now know as Part VI, added to the book in its sixth (1790) edition, consists in a theory of virtue.

But what of Part V? At first glance, it looks as though it is meant to offer a fifth component of moral judgment, one that varies with what Smith calls "custom and fashion"—what today we might call "culture."[29] But it turns out that Smith does not think that custom and fashion play much of a role in our moral judgments, and he is uncomfortable about giving them any *legitimate* role in those judgments.

This is quite interesting since Smith's moral system has often been accused, with some reason, of having culturally relativist tendencies. It is unclear how the impartial spectator, as Smith construes that device, can avoid being a mouth-piece for whatever norms happen to be entrenched in the society in which we grow up. Smith says relatively little about how this concern can be overcome. I shall argue later that this is not entirely a disadvantage of his views: Smith's moral system gains in some ways from being more open to cultural difference than the systems of many of his Enlightenment peers.[30]

But Smith himself is concerned in Part V to show that our judgments both of beauty and of morality rest primarily on principles built into human nature, like the ones laid out in Parts I to IV, not on the varying whims of custom and fashion. "I cannot ... be induced to believe that our sense even of external beauty is founded altogether on custom," he says, and he thinks the influence of custom on our moral sentiments is "much less than it is everywhere else" (TMS 199–200).

Which is not to say that he entirely downplays that influence. He grants that custom and fashion, where they coincide with the natural principles of morality, can "heighten the delicacy of our sentiments, and increase our abhorrence for every thing which approaches to evil" (TMS 200). He grants that many of our aesthetic judgments vary with culture, giving as an example the different conceptions of human beauty in Europe and in Africa.[31] He also grants that some moral standards vary across culture. "That degree of politeness, which would be highly esteemed, perhaps would be thought effeminate adulation, in Russia," he says, "would be regarded as rudeness and barbarism at the court of France." And the degree of "order and frugality, which, in a Polish nobleman, would be considered as excessive parsimony, would be regarded as extravagance in a citizen of Amsterdam" (204). Another example comes from a contrast between Europeans and Native Americans:

> The savages in North America, we are told, ... would think themselves degraded if they should ever appear in any respect to be overcome, either by love, or grief or resentment. Their magnanimity and self-command, in this respect, are almost beyond the conception of Europeans.
>
> (205)

He also says that "there is not a negro from the coast of Africa who does not, in [the face of death and torture], possess a degree of magnanimity which the soul of his [European] master is too often scarce capable of conceiving" (206).[32] So Smith's reflections on cultural variation include some of his most vigorous attempts to combat his fellow Europeans' closed-mindedness and bigotry.

But Smith's main point, in his discussion of cultural variation in moral judgments, is that if we enter sympathetically into the circumstances of people in other cultures, we will understand why their judgments differ from ours, and how we in fact share the same basic procedure for judging despite these differences. Why does an aboriginal tribesman in the Americas and Africa put up so nobly with death and suffering? Because he lives "in continual danger"—he is "often exposed to the greatest extremities of hunger, and frequently dies of pure want." As a result,

> his circumstances not only habituate him to every sort of distress, but teach him to give way to none of the passions which that distress is apt to excite. He can expect from his countrymen no sympathy or indulgence for such weakness. Before we can feel much for others, we must in some measure be at ease ourselves.
>
> (TMS 205)

By contrast, "humane and polished people[s]," like the French and the Italians, can openly express emotions: can even weep in public (207). Similarly, "the different situations of different ages and countries" explain the differences between politeness at the courts of Russia and France, and "order and frugality" among Polish aristocrats and Amsterdam merchants.[33]

Even quite extreme moral differences across cultures can be explained in this circumstantial way. Smith accounts for infanticide in ancient Greece as originally practiced out of "extreme indigence," then maintained out of the unfortunate tendency of all human beings to be "led away by ... established custom" (TMS 210). Elsewhere, he criticizes his own society for maintaining customs that have outgrown their original value (LJ 41, 296–7). Without justifying the fact that "the polite and civilized Athenians" exposed infants, then—on the contrary, he calls this practice "a dreadful violation of humanity" (TMS 210)—Smith explains that practice on the basis of the same drive to win the approval of other people by which he accounts for the rise and maintenance of our own norms.

Smith adds that "the general style and character of conduct and behaviour" in a society can never deviate as widely from the norms we live by in our own society as "a particular usage" like infanticide. "No society could subsist a moment," he says, "in which the usual strain of men's conduct and behaviour were of a piece with [that] horrible practice" (TMS 211). Moral notions, it seems, are determined in good part by what is necessary to enable societies to survive. So in general societies will agree to a large extent in these notions. And when they differ sharply, that will be because the circumstances in which they live dictate different conditions for survival. The "natural principles" of morality that Smith develops in Parts I through IV of TMS should thus largely converge on a single conception of virtue and vice.

The upshot of all this is that Smith does not give culture or history, in Part V, an independent role in the formation of our moral judgments. Cultural and historical variation function as something like the "irregularities" he describes in Part II: they have some good effects—ensuring that each society winds up with norms suited to its particular circumstances—but are not intrinsically part of the process of moral judgment. At least in Smith's own view, then, his moral theory is not vulnerable to the charge of relativism.

But Part V of Smith's book does give us grounds to return to a worry we have raised earlier: that it is not entirely clear whether Smith is giving us a descriptive or a normative account of morality. Smith devotes an entire section to the influence of "custom and fashion" on our judgments because he recognizes that these factors in fact lead people to uphold different norms in different places and times. But why should he do that if his book is meant to tell us simply how we *ought to* judge? That question can also be put to his discussion of moral luck. Surely the fact that we give disproportionate weight to what actually happens as a result of an action, rather than what the agent intends, and that we judge actions differently in different places and times, are things that we do but should not do, on Smith's own view—features of moral judgment that we should overcome, and need not include, except perhaps with a recipe for how to overcome them, in a normative book on morality. Smith however seems to feel compelled to discuss these things. And far from giving us a recipe for how to overcome them, he treats them as inevitable. So it looks very much as if Smith is more interested in describing how we actually make moral judgments than in prescribing how we ought to make them.

I think this is incorrect, or at least that the relationship between the descriptive and the prescriptive in moral theory is much more complicated, for Smith, than this sketch suggests. We will take up that relationship in the next chapter, after first considering the account of virtue that Smith added to the final edition of TMS.

5.9 Summary

Smith maintains that our judgment of actions depends on four factors: their propriety, their merit, their conformity with certain rules, and the degree to which they contribute to a system which promotes the happiness either of the agent or of her society. He places greatest emphasis on propriety, which he says figures into our judgments by way of a feeling of approval ("approbation") or disapproval, as long as we think an "impartial spectator" would share that feeling; his most distinctive contribution to moral philosophy comes in his account of this approval and of the impartial spectator. The other three factors play roles of varying significance in moral judgment, he thinks, and it is important, especially, not to exaggerate the last of these factors: the one that conduces to a utilitarian view of morality. Smith also acknowledges that cultural influence can affect our moral judgments, but sees that influence as fairly insignificant.

Notes

1 See for instance TMS 14: "Sympathy ... enlivens joy and alleviates grief. It enlivens joy by presenting another source of satisfaction; and it alleviates grief by insinuating into the heart almost the only agreeable sensation which it is a that time capable of receiving." Compare also 22–3.

It's worth noting that in these passages the awareness of shared feeling is mutual: not only do I share your feelings, and know that I do, but you know that I do and I know that you know. All of these things are needed if I am to comfort you, which seems to be what Smith has in mind by "alleviating grief." But there are other cases where I share your grief or anger or joy but you don't know that, or you know that I share your feelings but I am unaware that you know that (you see me nodding my head when you speak up in righteous indignation, but I don't realize that you saw that). Is the shared feeling here also pleasurable, for Smith? I think so, since it clearly amounts to approbation. And the account I offer below of the pleasure in approbation—as a pleasure in human solidarity—will fit these cases well. But they are not the cases Smith generally has in mind, when he talks of our attempt to reach a "unison" in feeling with others: mutual awareness of one another's feelings seems clearly to be his paradigm. So there is a further distinction he could have drawn. Since it doesn't affect his main line of argument, however, I leave it aside in what follows.

2 David Raynor, "Adam Smith and the Virtues." See my response to Raynor in the same issue of the *Adam Smith Review*.

3 In the footnote with which he responds to Hume, Smith makes exactly this point, albeit with a different metaphor: "Two sounds, I suppose, may, each of them taken singly, be austere, and yet, if they are perfect concords, the perception of their harmony and coincidence may be agreeable" (TMS 9n, 46).

4 Which is not to deny that this "agreeable and delightful" feeling may be faint, and over-ridden by the painful first-order feelings to which it responds. This is presumably what happens at funerals, and other tragic occasions. We take some pleasure in our mutual harmony of feelings but that pleasure is over-ridden by our mourning.

5 To be sure, this modicum of pleasure in the concord of our feelings may be over-ridden by the anger or grief with which we feel that concord. But that is just what Smith himself says (sympathy "alleviates" grief, in the sentence just quoted, but does not remove it), and he goes on to stress that we much prefer to sympathize with joy than with grief: hence, among other things, our baleful tendency to sympathize more with the rich than the poor (TMS 61–6).

6 John Steinbeck writes:

> We are lonesome animals. We spend all life trying to be less lonesome. One of our ancient methods is to tell a story begging the listener to say — and to feel — 'Yes, that's the way it is, or at least that's the way I feel it. You're not as alone as you thought.'

—Quoted in George Plimpton, *Writers at Work: The Paris Review Interviews*, Fourth Series (New York: Viking, 1976), 183.

7 Smith does not explicitly say that the reason empathy is always pleasurable is that in it we experience our shared humanity: I am reconstructing Smith's view here, rather than simply reporting it.

8 TMS 129, from editions 2–5; this passage was not in edition 6, but compare 135–6, which presents a condensed version of it.

9 Roderick Firth, "Ethical Absolutism and the Ideal Observer," *Philosophy and Phenomenological Research* 12/3 (1952). Firth cites Smith as an inspiration for his device.

10 See Thomas Nagel, *The View from Nowhere* (Oxford: Oxford University Press, 1986), chapters VII–IX, for arguments in favour of grounding morality (and knowledge) in principles constructed from such an ideal standpoint.

11 Its third appearance in the book also concerns resentment: TMS 38.

12 As Smith seems to assume in TMS and in any case grants to his theistic readers: see further discussion in Chapter 8.

13 Daniel Klein, "My Understanding of Adam Smith's Impartial Spectator: A Symposium Prologue," *Econ Journal Watch*, 13/2 (2016). The account I give of the impartial spectator in this paragraph accords well with the account in D.D. Raphael, *The Impartial Spectator* (Oxford: Clarendon Press, 2007), chapter 6, although I do not agree with Raphael that Smith's moral theory is meant to be descriptive rather than normative.

14 Something we may presume that Smith, trained in law as he was, had in mind. He indeed occasionally uses "impartial judge" or "equitable judge" instead of "impartial spectator" for his device (TMS 85, 110, 228).

15 For more on this developmental story, see Nir Ben Moshe, "An Adam Smithian Account of Moral Reasons," *European Journal of Philosophy* (2019), and "Making sense of Smith on sympathy and approbation: other-oriented sympathy as a psychological and normative achievement," *British Journal for the History of Philosophy* (forthcoming).

16 Several Hume scholars have protested to me that Hume has more of a place for moral self-correction, and for an internalist account of moral motivation, than I allow here. And Hume certainly does seem to think that "what is fair, what is becoming, what is noble, what is generous takes possession of the heart, and animates us to embrace and maintain it" (EPM 136/172) and that "an antipathy to treachery and roguery" is built into "all ingenuous natures" (EPM 233/283). But he treats this taste for virtue and distaste for vice, insofar as we have it, as a brute fact about us, rather than something intrinsic to the way our selves develop, as Smith suggests in TMS III.1–2 (see my *Being Me Being You*, chapter 2). Correspondingly, Hume never suggests that we are driven to improve ourselves by a desire for self-approval—a desire to be able to see ourselves as "praise-worthy," as Smith puts it. He does suggest, in "Of the Delicacy of Taste and Passion" and "The Stoic," that moral improvement can calm our passions, and thereby help us achieve a more stable happiness. But the motivation for moral improvement here is once again independent of the parts of ourselves that need improving, not built within them.

   I am grateful to discussions with Geoffrey Sayre-McCord and Kate Abramson on this issue, although I suspect they will still disagree with my take on it.

17 See Aaron Garrett, "Adam Smith über den Zufall als moralische Problem," in C. Fricke and H-P. Schütt (eds.), *Adam Smith als Moralphilosoph* (Berlin: de Gruyter, 2005) and Keith Hankins, "Adam Smith's Intriguing Solution to the Problem of Moral Luck," *Ethics* 126/3 (2016).

18 See my "Adam Smith on Self-Deceit," *Adam Smith Review* 7 (2011), for a more detailed treatment of this aspect of Smith's thought.

19 We'll return to this aspect of the rules of justice in Section 9.4.

20 Hume does have insightful accounts of self-deceit in his *History of England*—see his accounts of Thomas à Becket, Oliver Cromwell, and Joan of Arc, especially—but

does not talk about it in his moral theory. Shaftesbury and Bishop Butler discuss the subject in some depth (see Butler, "Upon the Character of Balaam" and "Upon Self-Deceit," in Butler, The Analogy of Religion to the Constitution and Course of Nature; also, Fifteen Sermons, ed. J. Angus (London: The Religious Tract Society, 1855) and Shaftesbury, "Soliloquy," Part I, sections 1–2, in his Characteristics). Smith may have been influenced by Butler's discussion; Butler's influence in any case shows up fairly clearly in TMS III.5. See 164–5, and the editors' note thereto.

21 See for instance my "Philosophy in Moral Practice," Stephen Darwall, "Sympathetic Liberalism," Philosophy & Public Affairs, 28/2 (1999), or Maria Alejandra Carrasco, "Adam Smith's Reconstruction of Practical Reason," Review of Metaphysics, 58/1 (2004).

22 This last passage comes from the first edition of TMS and Smith would later change his mind about the value of "premiums and other encouragements"— bounties—for manufactures.

23 See note 35 to Chapter 9 for more on this case.

24 James Otteson, Adam Smith's Marketplace of Life (Cambridge: Cambridge University Press, 2002), 249–52.

25 Otteson, Marketplace of Life, 249.

26 These last two points come out especially in his lectures on jurisprudence: see Chapter 9, below.

27 See LJ 100, 104, 130 for instance.

28 Compare John McDowell, Mind, Value and Reality, 13–9, 168–9.

29 The word "culture" was not used for modes of living that can vary from place to place until the early nineteenth century. One might speak of a mind having or lacking culture, but not of multiple cultures. Even writers who defended views that anticipate modern cultural relativism described the bearers of different modes of living as "peoples" or "nations" rather than cultures. Gustav Klemm coined the modern anthropological sense of culture in 1843; it was introduced into English by the British anthropologist E.B. Tylor, in his 1871 book, Primitive Culture. See my Ethics of Culture (Ithaca: Cornell University Press, 1994), chapter 5.

30 I've discussed this issue in detail in "Smith und der Kulturrelativismus," in Adam Smith als Moral Philosoph, and published in English as "Adam Smith and Cultural Relativism" in the online Erasmus Journal for Philosophy and Economics, 4/2 (2011).

31 He notes, interestingly, that while Europeans disapprove of North American tribes for their attempts to re-shape the bodies of their children, they themselves maintain very similar practices (TMS 199).

32 This passage continues:

> Fortune never exerted more cruelly her empire over mankind, than when she subjected those nations of heroes to the refuse of the jails of Europe, to wretches who possess the virtues neither of the countries which they come from, nor of those which they go to, and whose levity, brutality, and baseness, so justly expose them to the contempt of the vanquished.

33 Smith stresses elsewhere that commercial economies bring about an increase
   in order and frugality, and often uses Amsterdam as a model of a commercial
   economy: see LJ 504–5; WN 209, 454, 479–87.

Further reading

Fonna Forman-Barzilai, *Adam Smith and the Circles of Sympathy*
Charles Griswold, *Adam Smith and the Virtues of Enlightenment*, chapter 5
James Otteson, *Adam Smith's Marketplace of Life*, chapters 1 and 2
DD Raphael, *The Impartial Spectator*
Eric Schliesser, *Adam Smith: Systematic Philosopher and Public Thinker*, chapters 4 and 5

Six

The character of virtue; description and normativity

In March 1789, Smith told his publisher Thomas Cadell that he had written "a compleat new sixth part containing a practical system of morality" for TMS, "under the title of the Character of Virtue" (CAS 320). Clearly, Smith seemed to think of his new Part VI as a contribution to moral practice. And he carried out this contribution by portraying character traits, rather than offering guides to particular actions—by sketching what he regarded as the major human virtues and vices. Part VI explores the nature of prudence and benevolence, of self-command, of pride and vanity; it also includes detailed and striking sketches of the prudent man and of the wise and virtuous man. More than any other part of the book, moreover, it presents some character traits as admirable, and others as contemptible. If one function of moral philosophy—the primary function, according to Smith's teacher Hutcheson—is to recommend some kinds of conduct and character to us, and steer us away from other kinds, then Book VI is the part of the book that most seems to accomplish that task. "The question concerning the nature of virtue" is important in practice, Smith says: it "necessarily has some influence upon our notions of right and wrong in many particular cases." The question concerning "the principle of approbation" has no such importance—it is "a mere matter of philosophical curiosity" (TMS 315). But the first five parts of TMS—the whole of that book in its first five editions, except for its section on the history of moral philosophy—would seem to deal just with the principle of approbation, not with the nature of virtue. Consequently, it would seem to be a mere matter of philosophical curiosity, the work of a philosopher who wants just to describe how our practices of moral judgment work, not to prescribe how they should work.

That is in fact the view that many Smith scholars take of TMS. They therefore regard Part VI as a surprising addition to the book's final edition, and one that alters the book considerably. These scholars also point to a line in a footnote to Part II of TMS, where Smith says that "the present inquiry is not concerning a matter of right, ... but concerning a matter of fact" (TMS 77). This shows decisively, they say, that Smith originally regarded TMS as a purely descriptive inquiry, not a normative one.[1]

I disagree both with the novelty that these scholars attribute to Part VI of TMS and with the idea that the rest of the book is devoted purely to a descriptive rather than a normative account of our moral faculties and practices. These questions are vexed, however: there are deep reasons, built into Smith's entire methodology, why it is not easy to disentangle the normative from the descriptive in Smith. For this reason, one's view of Part VI of TMS and one's view of whether TMS as a whole is an exercise in descriptive or normative moral philosophy are likely to be connected. Hence the juxtaposition of these questions in this chapter. I shall proceed by first laying out the contents of Part VI in some detail. Then I'll make a case for the implicit presence of much of its normative contents in the earlier parts of TMS. After that, I'll turn to the footnote in Part II mentioned above, arguing that it should not be taken as an interpretive clue to the entire book. Finally, I'll address the question of why the normative and the descriptive elements of Smith are hard to disentangle.

6.1 The virtues, in Part VI of TMS

Part VI of TMS is divided into three sections: a short one on prudence, a longer one on benevolence, and a longer one yet on self-command. In each case, Smith devotes most of his attention to what it is like to possess these virtues and what factors enable us to develop them. This brings his virtue theory closer to Aristotle's than to Hume's. Jacqueline Taylor writes:

> Aristotelian virtue ethics focuses on the perspective of the virtuous agent, examining how one becomes virtuous, and the role

of virtue in practical deliberation and living a good life. In contrast, Hume is much more interested in how we recognize and evaluate traits of character than in how we become virtuous, or in how virtue relates to deliberation and living well.[2]

Like Aristotle and unlike Hume, Smith presents the virtues largely from the perspective of how we might achieve them, rather than how we might recognize them in others. His sketches of virtuous characters are written so that we can see why we might want to aspire to resemble them, and when he is not sketching virtuous characters, he directs his attention largely to the circumstances that enable us to develop benevolence or self-command.

Taylor also says that for Aristotle, "The virtuous agent sets the standard for moral knowledge, and is a model for others to imitate as they cultivate their own virtuous character," while for Hume, "The identification and valuation of character traits is a social process, requiring conversation, and at times, negotiation and debate. On this view, moral knowledge about which characters are praiseworthy or blameworthy is a collectively established resource." Smith stands between Hume and Aristotle in this respect. As we saw in Chapter 5, he agrees with Hume that "the identification and valuation of character traits is a social process," but he also thinks we should ultimately judge of good and bad by way of the impartial spectator, which transcends, and can correct for, the norms of our society. In Part VI, he frequently appeals to the impartial spectator to set the standard for what should count as virtue (see for instance 215, 228, 244–8). He also sets up an ideally virtuous agent as "a model for others to imitate as they cultivate their own virtuous character": an "idea of exact propriety and perfection" that the "wise and virtuous man" always seeks to emulate (247–8).[3] Throughout Part VI, Smith seems especially close to ancient schools of ethics.[4]

Smith differs sharply from Aristotle and other ancient ethicists in two respects, however. First, ancient ethicists, and especially Aristotle, tended to treat virtue as something that only a small elite will ever achieve, while Smith generally presents virtue as something that most people can achieve. There is a moment in Part I of TMS in which he contrasts virtue with "mere propriety," reserves the latter term for what most of us achieve, and says that "Virtue is excellence, something uncommonly great and beautiful, which rises far above what is vulgar and ordinary" (TMS 25). But in the rest of the book, and especially in Part VI, he seems content to use the word "virtue" for quite modest achievements—even the judicious self-care of the prudent man (213).[5]

Second, Smith does not share Aristotle's belief in the unity of the virtues. Aristotle says that it is impossible to be morally good in some respects but not others, "for with the presence of the one quality, practical wisdom, will be given all the excellences."[6] This claim has been well glossed as a conceptual one.[7] Acting in accordance with temperance, but in a way that compromises on courage or magnanimity, does not count as truly acting temperately for Aristotle: temperance, as a virtue, must be guided by practical wisdom, which is always concerned to pick actions in accordance with all of our virtues, not just one of them. By contrast, Smith presents virtues—in Part VI as well as other Parts of TMS[8]—as existing in some tension with one another, such that developing one may come at the cost of letting others atrophy.[9] There is not just *one* model of the virtuous man, for Smith; there are many. Accordingly, he accounts for the virtues in Part VI in good part by sketching the different types of character who exemplify each trait.

This is especially true of the section on prudence. Smith says that the prudent person takes good care of his own "health, ... fortune, ... rank and reputation" (TMS 213), pointing out that such a person will need to be honest, sincere and inoffensive in his everyday conduct, "very capable of friendship," cautious in business enterprises, and disinclined to get involved in political disputes or to interfere in other people's affairs (213–6). Since this sort of prudence is both fostered by and essential to success in a market economy, according to Smith, it is interesting to note how very far it is from the dishonesty, ambition, and thorough-going egoism attributed to market actors by other commentators on capitalism (even some of its advocates: Smith's prudent man looks nothing like the arrogant heroes of Ayn Rand's novels). Market economies, for Smith, rest on and nurture what Deirdre McCloskey has called "the bourgeois virtues"—the modest kinds of virtue most of us expect of one another—even if they do little to promote the high levels of courage, caring, and integrity that we most admire.[10]

But Smith also describes a higher level of prudence—"wise and judicious conduct, when directed to greater and nobler purposes" than one's own well-being—and says that this is a quality we admire in civic leaders: great generals, statesmen, or legislators, for instance. "Prudence is, in all these cases," says Smith, "combined with many greater and more splendid virtues, with valour, with extensive and strong benevolence, with a sacred regard to the rules of justice, and all these supported by a proper degree of self-command" (TMS 216). But a person with all these qualities may sacrifice his or her well-being for the good of others—her "valour" may lead her to death on the battlefield or her "strong benevolence" to death in caring for Ebola victims. So this is not prudence at all, in the sense that is tied to egoism. It is prudence, rather, in the sense of "good judgment": wisdom about the *means* one uses, to whatever ends one has. And Smith's point is that even people whose primary ends are the good of their neighbours or country rather than their own well-being need to pay judicious attention to the means they use. At the same time he warns darkly against over-rating the importance of prudence in great leaders, and under-rating the need for them to be just and humane. People regard brutal and unjust conquerors "with foolish wonder and admiration," he says, and wrongly rank them above leaders who are decent but imprudent (217). Political prudence needs to go with other virtues; there is nothing admirable about it on its own.

Smith now turns to benevolence. The section on this virtue is mostly concerned with what has come to be known as "the circles of sympathy."[11] Smith cites the Stoics at the beginning of this section and picks up throughout on an old Stoic theme: that by nature we care most for ourselves and our families, somewhat less but still a good deal for our neighbours and co-workers, less again for our countries, and very weakly for sentient beings across the universe. Smith does not think these limitations on our concern can easily be overcome. Affection arises from "habitual sympathy," he says, but the very nature of sympathy, as he has described it—putting ourselves in detail into the situation of others—entails that we will experience it most strongly with people with whom we come into regular face-to-face contact. Notably, this suggests that even family ties are based on social relationships rather than biology—a point

Smith makes explicitly: TMS 223—and that our feeling for people beyond our national borders can be increased if we have opportunities to interact with them. (This is one of the benefits that Smith thinks can come of international trade: WN 493.) Smith also thinks there are some advantages to the limits on our benevolence. Nature has wisely ensured that our efforts at caring for others go out most readily to those around us, since these are likely to be the people whose needs we know best and whom we can most easily help.

But Smith also mentions the limits on our benevolence as part of a sharp critique of "national prejudices and hatreds" (TMS 228–30). And he concludes this section by affirming that we are capable of universal benevolence, and in principle can and should care for the well-being of "any innocent and sensible being" (235). It is God's job, not ours, actually to bring about the happiness of all such beings—our duties are much narrower in scope, focused on those around us—but the fact that we can and should care about that happiness serves as a warning against resting satisfied with a narrow patriotism, or a narrow loyalty to our family or clan.

Finally, Smith turns to self-command, which he describes as the foundation of all other virtues: without it, we will often not be able to do our duty, and "from it all the other virtues seem to derive their principle lustre" (TMS 227, 241). Self-command seems to be similar to Kantian freedom—an ability to rise above all passions that tempt us away from morality. Smith does not give this virtue an *a priori* cast, however, instead treating it as on a continuum with "magnanimity": the courage and self-control that allows even some criminals to brave dangers and face death unflinchingly (239). Accordingly, Smith acknowledges that war can be a great arena for developing self-command, although he warns against the license for injustice that comes with war, and notes that a person who becomes inured to his own suffering may also become inured to the suffering of others (244–5). Ideally, self-command consists, not just in the control over fear that we learn in wartime, but in a control of all our passions, to the degree necessary for us to develop prudence, justice, benevolence, and all the other virtues, in the manner laid down to us by the impartial spectator (262–3).

Since self-command is so much the virtue of heeding the impartial spectator, Smith is led by his discussion of it to consider how "the wise and virtuous man" operates in general—how, especially this man makes use of the "idea" (the Platonic connotations of this word are surely intended here) of "exact propriety and perfection" (TMS 247–8). Such a paragon of virtue will "study this idea" constantly, and try every day to improve some feature of his character in its light. He will "imitate the work of a divine artist," constantly looking up to the idea of perfect virtue for guidance rather than down at other people, no matter how much further they are than he is from that idea. This means that the wise and virtuous person will among other things be humble—the section concludes with a critique of pride and vanity—but it also means simply that such a person will no longer look outwards for approval and instead hold him or herself up to standards (s)he has internalized.

Ryan Hanley, who has written an entire book on Part VI of TMS, argues ingeniously that Smith here brings classical notions of virtue together with Christian ones and uses these sources implicitly to answer the great critiques that have been made, in his day and since, of capitalist society (what Smith would call "commercial" society): that it renders people consumerist and frivolous, robbing them of noble virtues like courage; that it leads people to become egoists, caring about no-one except themselves; and that it fosters inequality, with a rich elite looking down on the poor. Each section of Part VI answers one of these critiques, says Hanley. Smith's prudent merchant delays gratification and seeks modest amounts of material goods: is not, therefore, the frivolous lover of luxury or vain seeker of social status that Mandeville and Rousseau took him to be.[12] The citizens in Smith's commercial society are benevolent, caring for one another—sometimes even risking their lives for one another. Some of those citizens, at least, are also "wise and virtuous," aspiring to a degree of perfection that instils in them something like Christian humility, rather than a contempt for those beneath them.

But Smith does not present his points in this Part as responses to critiques of commercial society.[13] And even if Hanley is right to read Smith this way, we are offered no argument in Part VI to show that the classical and Christian virtues can in fact survive so easily in the commercial age. What we are given instead is an inspiring portrait of what people with various virtues might be like: models which may move us to improve ourselves. We are also given reasons to think that prudence, much despised by many moralists, has some worthwhile features, and that it is fine for us to practice a limited beneficence most of the time, even if in principle we should be able to care for any innocent and sensible being. So Part VI works as a whole to encourage us to cultivate virtue in ourselves and to remove certain psychological obstacles that may get in the way of that cultivation. It is very much a fulfilment of Hutcheson's admonition that moral philosophy should help people become more moral, and it makes no bones about praising some kinds of people (patriots, wise and virtuous men) and casting aspersions on others (vain people, men of system). It is unquestionably a contribution to normative rather than purely descriptive philosophy.

6.2 Normative language in Parts I–V of TMS

It would be a mistake, however, to think that the first five Parts of TMS are devoid of normative elements—to regard them as a forerunner of modern positivist social science, abjuring normativity in favour of a neutral description of our moral practices.

Explicitly normative language pervades TMS. "To feel much for others and little for ourselves … constitutes the perfection of human nature," Smith tells us early in Part I (TMS 25). "There is … something disagreeable" in resentment and indignation, he says a bit later (35), but a resentment that is "guarded and qualified" by attention to the judgment of the impartial spectator, "may be admitted to be … generous and noble" (38). Smith calls people who enjoy causing trouble between friends "detestable" (39) and laments that "to the disgrace of human nature," we seldom "cordially congratulate our friends" (47). He tells us that "the present misery and depravity of the world" is "justly lamented" (45), and describes our admiration for the wealthy and powerful as a product of "vanity" and "delusi[on]" (50–1). In the sixth edition, he devotes an entire chapter to "the corruption of the moral sentiments" that he regards as arising from this admiration (61–6).

All of the above lines appear in Part I, but there are normative judgments in the other parts as well. In Part II, Smith says that governments that neglect the enforcement of some beneficent duties will "expose the commonwealth to many gross disorders and shocking enormities," but to push the enforcement of these sorts of virtues too far "is destructive of liberty, security, and justice" (TMS 81). In Part III, he says that self-deceit "is the source of half the disorders of human life" (158). Part IV includes a thoroughly moralistic fable about a "poor man's son whom heaven in its anger has visited with ambition" (181–2) and Part V ends with a discussion of "the horrible practice" of infanticide in ancient Greece (209–10; quotation from 211).

I have picked out places where it is hard to see how any reader could deny the normative import of Smith's claims. Talk of "perfection" and "corruption" and "disorder," of "proper" objects of various sentiments and of what is "justly lamented," is all clearly normative, an explicit appeal to moral standards that cannot be translated into positivistic terms. But Smith more commonly talks of what "we admire," "we detest," "we are concerned for," etc. (e.g., 24, 34): language that is ambiguous between the normative and the descriptive.[14] It may be just a fact about our psychology that "we admire" or "we detest" certain things. But most of the time it seems clear that Smith *shares* the judgments that he describes in this fashion. (Occasionally, he uses this language for a judgment he regards as corrupt or deluded—as in our admiration for the rich—but then he signals his disapproval explicitly.) I think he also expects the reader both to see these sorts of claims as accurately capturing the moral judgments we make and to endorse those judgments. A certain conflation between the descriptive and the normative thus runs through the entire way he carries out his investigation of morality. More on that anon.

Before we get there, note that the implications of both the clearly and the more ambiguously normative claims that Smith makes are such as to commend a certain sort of *character* to us, not just a certain form of moral judgment. If unqualified resentment is "detestable," then we should work on ourselves so as to tamp down or eliminate our tendency to such resentment. If "generosity, humanity, kindness, compassion, mutual friendship and esteem … please the indifferent spectator upon almost every occasion" (TMS 38–9), then we should strive to cultivate such virtues in ourselves. If "mere wealth and greatness" does not deserve our respect (62), and their trappings are "follies" (64), then we should not pursue them. Smith tells us explicitly that we should "feel much for others and little for ourselves" (I25). He also devotes an extended section of Part III to an examination of ways that we might achieve this "perfection of human nature." That section concludes with two paragraphs of explicit moral advice:

> Are you in adversity? Do not mourn in the darkness of solitude, do not regulate your sorrow according to the indulgent sympathy of your intimate friends; return, as soon as possible, to the day-light of the world and of society. Live with strangers, with those who know nothing, or care nothing about your misfortune; do not even shun the company of enemies; but give yourself the pleasure of mortifying their malignant joy, by making them feel how little you are affected by your calamity, and how much you are above it.
>
> Are you in prosperity? Do not confine the enjoyment of your good fortune to your own house, to the company of your own friends, perhaps of your flatterers, of those who build upon your fortune the hopes of mending their own; frequent those who are independent of you, who can value you only for your character and conduct, and not for your fortune. Neither seek nor shun, neither intrude yourself into nor run away from the society of those who were once your superiors, and who may be hurt at finding you their equal, or, perhaps, even their superior. The impertinence of their pride may, perhaps, render their company too disagreeable: but if it should not, be assured that it is the best company you can possibly keep; and if, by the simplicity of your unassuming demeanour, you can gain their favour and kindness, you may rest satisfied that you are modest enough, and that your head has been in no respect turned by your good fortune.
>
> (154)

This may well be the stretch of TMS that most looks like a handbook in practical morality; very little else comes so close to preaching (if restrained, and nonsectarian, preaching). But the very fact that Smith includes such a passage at all—and in Part III, not Part VI[15]—makes clear that he did not conceive his treatise in a purely descriptive light. Nor, clearly, did he see it as focused just on moral judgment, as opposed to the character traits that such judgments track, and foster.

6.3　Concerning matters of right, and of fact

How, now, should we interpret Smith's remark, in the long footnote to Part II, chapter i, that "the present inquiry is not concerning a matter of right, ... but ... a matter of fact" (TMS 77)? Well, one thing to note is that in its immediate context, "the present inquiry" seems to refer just to the principles upon which we approve of *punishment*, not to TMS as a whole.[16] The sentence right after the one about "the present inquiry" reads: "We are not at present examining upon what principles a perfect being would approve of the punishment of bad actions; but upon what principles so weak and imperfect a creature as man actually and in fact approves of it." And since Smith is explaining his view that our inclination to punish arises out of resentment, which he himself describes as generally "the most odious ... of all the passions" (76), it is not hard to see why he might want to add the qualifier that he is describing the actual, rather than the ideal, genealogy of punishment.

But it is hard to limit Smith's point here to the genealogy of punishment. For the entirety of TMS, not just this chapter, deals with the principles upon which "so weak and imperfect a creature as man actually and in fact" approves of things, rather than the principles upon which "a perfect being" would approve of them. So if that is what it takes to show that an inquiry concerns matters of fact rather than matters of right, then the whole of TMS is indeed restricted to matters of fact. There is thus a straightforward case for the claim that TMS is by Smith's own account an exercise in the sociology of morals rather than in normative moral philosophy.[17]

This case faces a number of difficulties, however. In the first place, there is the large body of explicitly or implicitly normative content to be found in TMS, as described above. In the second place, given this normative content, one would expect a Smith committed to a purely descriptive enterprise to make that clear, and a single sentence buried in a footnote on punishment is not a good way of doing that. Finally, it would be very surprising if Smith, who tells us expressly that the whole point of systems of moral philosophy is to "direct" our moral judgments (TMS 293), would write a system of moral philosophy that refrains from doing that.

These considerations are I think enough to scuttle the grand interpretive claims that have been made on the basis of the line in this footnote, but there is an additional point to be made, of greater philosophical significance: that it is far from obvious that an inquiry that examines the basis of human, rather than divine, moral judgment must by virtue of that fact be a descriptive rather than a prescriptive enterprise. The seventeenth and eighteenth centuries were awash in attempts to find a purely humanistic basis for morality. Hobbes and Locke offered reasons why human beings do and should enter into a social contract with one another. Shaftesbury, Hutcheson, and Hume rooted the moral norms we accept and the ideals we aspire to in a sense or set of sentiments by which we love or admire certain types of conduct and character; they urged us also to endorse that sense or set of sentiments. None of these people made any claims to the effect that the principles they were delineating would be used by a perfect being as well as such imperfect beings as ourselves. Hobbes' and Locke's normative principles would be pointless for perfect beings, and Hume stresses the non-ideal nature of the foundations for morality that he proposes.[18] Even if there are problems with their conceptions of normativity, moreover, those problems have little or nothing to do with the fact that they are attempting to make sense of normativity from a purely human rather than a divine standpoint.

So Smith, in the footnote with which we have been wrestling, is running very much against the grain of the moral philosophy of his day if he is proposing a view by which morality cannot be normative unless it is rooted in the reason or will of God. That's a view that had a good deal of purchase in medieval philosophy, and has had defenders again over the past half century. But it was strongly *rejected* by the naturalistic moral philosophers of the Enlightenment to which Smith belonged. And nowhere else does Smith himself show any fondness for a theocentric morality. Nowhere else, certainly, does he suggest that, without God, we would have no properly moral principles at all.[19]

I am therefore inclined to regard the footnoted passage we have been considering as ill-expressed, and in any case ill-suited to provide a basis for understanding Smith's moral thought as a whole. It makes best sense when limited to a comment on the tendencies that make for punishment, and would have been better put had Smith simply said that in *describing resentment as the basis for punishment*, he was recounting a matter of fact rather than a matter of right (without making any reference to the judgments of God). His point then would have clearly been just that the fact that resentment moves us to punish people needs to be separated from the proper justification for punishment, and that only the resentment of the impartial spectator is an appropriate source for judgments about rightful punishment. That is in fact Smith's position in the rest of Part II of TMS, and it would nicely distinguish the facts about human nature that actually lead us to develop penal practices from the moral considerations that legitimize (some of) those practices. It would also give us reason to criticize some actual penal practices as falling short of justice, a point of considerable importance to Smith in LJ. At the same time, putting things this way would have acknowledged that all of our moral practices arise in the first instance from the facts of human nature—a point of importance to Smith throughout his writings. And if Smith had put things this way it would be clear, as it is not in the footnote Smith actually wrote, that Smith is engaged in *both* a descriptive *and* a normative project, but that the facts about the sentiments we act on, and practices we engage in, do not by themselves dictate the normatively correct form of those sentiments and practices. That I think is Smith's real point, and it has nothing to do with the judgments of God, or the relationship that those judgments might have to the judgments we imperfect beings make.

Smith never puts the relationship between the descriptive and the normative in his work in quite this fashion. I don't think that relationship was clear to him. There are deep reasons for that, which affected his friend Hume as well. I'll close this chapter with a few words on those reasons.

6.4 The painter and the anatomist; theory and common life

Upon receiving a copy of Hume's *Treatise* from its author, Hutcheson apparently wrote Hume a letter complaining that his book lacked "a certain warmth in the cause of virtue."[20] To which Hume responded, in a return letter, with a comparison between an anatomist and a painter. The work of the anatomist is unappealing, but without it, the painter would not be able to represent the human body beautifully. Similarly, the moral philosopher—the "metaphysician," Hume calls him—may provide a dry and unappealing diagnosis of how morality works, but that diagnosis is necessary to the moralist, who presents virtue with "warmth" and beauty. Hume repeats this comparison in both his *Treatise* and his *Enquiry Concerning Human Understanding* (T 620–1; EHU 5/10).

It's therefore tempting to say that Hume sees his work on morality as descriptive rather than normative, but as having implications for those who do normative work. What implications? Perhaps that it makes no sense to urge moral norms or ideals on people unless those norms and ideals can get a grip on our sentiments, and serve the purposes for which human beings need morality; perhaps that understanding the naturalistic basis for morality will make it easier for us to see why we should be moral; perhaps that understanding the naturalistic basis for morality will enable us to distinguish between properly moral norms and the manipulative urgings of political and religious leaders.[21] In any case, the anatomist's work would seem to set constraints on the sort of virtue for which the painter should express warmth.

But the attentive reader will have noticed that there is an implicit normative dimension to even the anatomist's work, as I have characterized it: there are *properly* moral norms, norms that *ought* to be regarded as such—the naturalistic ones—and *improperly* moral norms, norms that are wrongly regarded as such. And I don't think any scholar of Hume's moral philosophy would deny that one of its points is to bring out the errors and confusions underlying certain sorts of moral claims.[22] In addition, Hume engages openly in the "painter's" work, expressing warmth in the cause of virtue, in his *Enquiry Concerning the Principles of Morals*.[23]

So I am inclined to offer a more complicated reading of the relationship between the descriptive and the normative in Hume. This time let's consider, not the anatomist/painter comparison, but the passage at the end of Book I of the *Treatise* in which Hume offers a rationale for turning away from epistemology and metaphysics to "the principles of moral good and evil," the "nature and foundation of government," and the causes of our passions (T 271). Hume has just concluded that he cannot settle such basic questions as what counts as his own identity, and whether he can trust his own reason. His response to this radical scepticism is despair, a condition in which he has begun to "fancy [him]self in the most deplorable condition imaginable, inviron'd with the deepest darkness, and utterly depriv'd of the use of every member and faculty." "Nature herself" breaks him of this mood, however—cures him of "this philosophical melancholy and delirium"—and he becomes willing to grant that he "must yield to the current of nature, in submitting to [his] senses and understanding." And when he returns to "a serious good-humour'd disposition," and decides that he may as well use his reason, despite his doubts about it, whenever it "mixes itself" with some inclination to do so, the subjects that he finds himself most inclined to explore are those that crop up often in "reading and conversation"—which turn out to be the principles of moral good and evil, the nature and foundation of government, etc. These Hume also calls the subjects of "common life," and he recommends philosophy, as opposed to "superstition," as the safest, because least dogmatic, guide to thinking about them.[24]

This parable, unlike the one about the anatomist and the painter, suggests that the philosopher moves around in the sphere of common life without being able to establish foundations for it—without being able to ground it in some deeper order, even a natural order like the anatomical science that undergirds the painter's work. The philosopher *clarifies* what we already do, but does not ground it. But if so, then the philosopher presumably clarifies, among other things, how we make normative moral judgments without giving them a deeper grounding. Moral practices are among the most common and most important practices of common life—Hume himself picks them out as his prime examples of that sphere—and Hume sets out to explore them as they present themselves to him rather than to discover a grounding principle for them.

But exploring them as they present themselves means accepting their normativity at face value. The Humean philosopher, on this view, is one among the rest of us in common life, vested with the same normative commitments that we all have; he cannot pretend to divest himself from them without pretending to be looking down at our practices from a standpoint that transcends them. Philosophers can offer us a clearer, less prejudiced eye on these practices, can free themselves from the prejudices of "superstition" especially, but only from a position *within* them, not a position beyond them. The philosopher is a participant in the practices she examines, not an observer from afar.

It follows that Hume cannot draw any sharp line between the normative and the descriptive. Moral practices can be adequately described from a participant position only if their normativity has some grip on the describer, and that can have any number of effects on what they prescribe. When Hume says, "we blame equally a bad action, which we read of in history, with one perform'd in our neighbourhood t'other day" or "When a person is possess'd of a character, that in its natural character is beneficial to society, we esteem him virtuous, … even tho' particular accidents prevent [the] operation [of that character]" (T 584), he is simultaneously *reporting* on how we judge of vice and virtue and *endorsing* that report. He can do no other, as a philosopher of common life. That doesn't mean he must accept every particular judgment that his neighbours make. Often they are misinformed or misapply their own standards; sometimes there may be a deep incoherence between what they are trying to accomplish and what a particular practice actually achieves. There is therefore room for an immanent critique of common-life practices. It is indeed essential to many of our practices—to our normative practices, certainly—that they make room for such criticism. But that criticism must take place from within common life itself. So getting the facts right about the nature of how we judge, within our common-life practices, is a necessary preliminary, if we are to turn these modes of judgment on themselves.

Now if my argument in Chapter 2 is correct, Smith very much follows Hume in pursuing a common-life mode of philosophizing, rather than trying to uncover foundational principles for common life. Indeed, Smith may be more thorough-going than Hume is, in setting foundational questions aside—he may think that the very exploration of such questions is just a path to scepticism, and find both scepticism and the denial of scepticism to be indefensible. That at least is the proto-Wittgensteinian reading of Smith I proposed in Section 2.8. But even if this reading goes too far, and we cannot attribute quite such a meta-philosophical view to him, it is clear that what Smith actually does throughout his writing is map our common-life scientific and moral and economic practices from within, without reaching for *a priori* principles by which to justify them. He criticizes particular applications of them, moreover, only in terms with which they themselves provide him. So regardless of what justification he may think he has for his philosophical method, in fact Smith is as whole-hearted a follower of "the true old Humean philosophy," in his determination to stay within the terms of common life, as Hume himself was.[25] It follows that Smith is saddled with exactly the same intertwining of the normative and the descriptive that marks Hume's moral and political writings, along with the difficulties that may attend that combination. Certainly, whenever Smith says "we admire," "we detest," "we are concerned for," etc., it makes best sense to understand him to be simultaneously reporting and endorsing these judgments: to be a participant observer, sharing the judgments he describes—their overall contours, at least—even while distancing himself enough from them to be able to assess them critically.

The basic idea underlying this approach to moral philosophy[26] is that we simply *do* judge morally and cannot expect any philosophical reasoning either to justify or to undermine our doing that.[27] There is no space outside our moral discourse from which either to give it foundations or to show that it has no foundations. But it does not follow from this that we cannot correct particular moral judgments. It is of the nature of normative practices that they involve a constant appeal to standards (norms) to which particular actions may or may not live up. Indeed, a practice as a whole may not live up to its own purported standard. A practice of hazing in a boys school or military unit may for instance breed cowardly bullying rather than the courage or stoic endurance it is said to build up. In that case, the practice may be corrected in its own terms. More generally, the fact that we constantly make judgments in the course of carrying out normative practices entails that we constantly present ourselves as meeting the appropriate conditions for rendering a moral judgment, and open ourselves to the possibility that we are wrong about that. It is central to Smith's views that we can at any point be too partial or too poorly informed to render a proper moral judgment, and can be corrected (by others or by ourselves, in a calmer or better-informed condition) if we render an improper one. Smith also explicitly says that we must be able to judge our basic moral faculties themselves as morally wanting, disagreeing in this respect with Hutcheson, who thought that it was absurd to call our moral faculties themselves virtuous or vicious. We would condemn a person so constituted as to applaud "a barbarous and unmerited execution," Smith says, and regard the sentiments of such a person as "depraved" (TMS 323). But in the course of saying this, he again uses the sort of ambiguous language I drew attention to above. He says that we *would* "abominate" such a person and that "we admire" a person whose moral sentiments display an "uncommon and surprising justness" (23). He again, that is, positions himself as a participant observer within our moral practices, drawing out their implications while simultaneously embracing those implications. Which is to say that he sees our moral practices as having a place for self-correction built into them. Their normativity entails that we need not, and sometimes should not, accept them at face value: that we can, and sometimes should, correct them by their own means.[28]

Thus Smith himself will go on in LJ and WN to criticize primogeniture, entail, slavery, imperialism, and laws that oppress the poor by appealing to facts about these practices that his readers may not know, or may not fully appreciate, or to standards of impartiality that he takes to be fundamental to all moral practice (perhaps to a commitment to human equality that he takes to be entailed by the impartial-spectator standpoint). And since his criticisms are immanent to the practices he is criticizing, they should get a grip on anyone participating in them. Criticizing these practices is indeed a mode of participating in them. Morality is and must be constantly open to self-critique, for Smith.

6.5 Reflective endorsement

The view I am proposing of what Hume and Smith are doing is close to Christine Korsgaard's theory that they employ a "reflective endorsement" criterion for the legitimacy of moral practices.[29] Korsgaard argues that Hume (following Hutcheson) proposed to defend our moral sensibilities by showing that when we reflect on them, we find that they live up to their own standards, as well as to the standards of the other sensibilities (prudential or aesthetic, especially) by which we judge things to be good and bad. "Reflection on the origin of our moral sentiments ... serves to strengthen those sentiments" for Hume, says Korsgaard, citing a passage at the end of the *Treatise* in which Hume says that our "sense of morals ... must certainly acquire new force, when reflecting on itself, it approves of those principles, from whence it is deriv'd."[30] Our *understanding* does not survive this reflective test for Hume, Korsgaard points out: it undermines its own principles. So it is an achievement, not something to be taken for granted, that our moral faculties do survive the test. Indeed, if we determined that our moral faculties were a product of social indoctrination and gave rise to nothing but hypocrisy, as Mandeville suggested, or if we determined that they arose from hatred and cowardice, as Nietzsche was to suggest, we would not conclude that they lived up to their own standards. But on Hume's and Hutcheson's view, in which our moral faculties are an outgrowth of our sociability—our sympathy with and care for one another—we have every reason to endorse them. And if this is right, it applies just as much to Smith's view as to Hume's and Hutcheson's.

Korsgaard's textual basis for attributing the reflective endorsement view to Hume is rather shaky. The sentence she quotes from the *Treatise* reads in context as an afterthought, adding to reasons Hume thinks he has already given for accepting his account of the origin of morals rather than serving as a methodological guide to that account. Indeed, it is prefaced by a coy hypothetical, warning the reader not to take it too seriously. "Were it proper in such a subject to bribe the readers assent, or employ any thing but solid argument," Hume says, he could point out that "all lovers of virtue ... must certainly be pleas'd to see moral distinctions deriv'ed from so noble a source." So the appeal to our feeling of approval for the moral faculties that he goes on to give is supposed to be not quite a "proper" way of approaching readers. It is indeed a "bribe" that they should ideally resist, if they are not convinced by the rest of the argument.

Nevertheless, I think it fair to say that Hume justifies morality, to the extent that he does that, in part by showing that our endorsement of it survives reflection. As Korsgaard says, his account of morality is meant to help us see its merits in its own lights, rather than to reject it. This is even more true of Smith, who explicitly raises the issue that our moral faculties are themselves open to moral scrutiny, who at several points says that reflection on our moral impulses can help entrench them (TMS 115, 160, 170, 192), and who presents us with a more attractive picture of the sources of morality than Hume does. For Smith, our sympathies track a real fittedness of feelings to situations, rather than arising out of a bald, incorrigible instinct to share feelings; we institute systems of punishment out of an immediate sense that certain actions are wrong, rather than just because such systems are useful to society; and we seek praise-worthiness rather than mere praise—we hold ourselves up, ultimately, to our own standards rather than seeking simply to conform to what others expect of us. In all these respects, Smith's reflections on the basic principles of morality vindicate more of what we actually think and do in everyday moral practice than Hume's do, and in all these respects, Smith therefore gives us a better basis for a whole-hearted reflective endorsement of morality than does Hume. He fits Korsgaard's account of a reflective endorsement theorist, in any case, at least as well as Hume does.

Still, there is a difference between Korsgaard's reading of these philosophers and mine. For Korsgaard neatly separates the levels of description and normativity in Hume. Hume simply describes our moral practices in the first instance, on her view, and then urges us to see how attractive they are: their normativity thus derives only from the feeling of (second-order) approval we experience when we understand their (first-order) workings. On my view, Hume instead mingles the descriptive and the normative throughout his account of morality, adding in something like Korsgaard's reflective endorsement test for normativity only as an afterthought at the end. The idea, then, is that making sense of morality from within the common-life standpoint in which it appears does not allow for any neat distinction between describing and prescribing. We cannot describe our moral practices adequately without endorsing at least their basic normative shape and we cannot issue moral prescriptions except in accordance with the types of norms that our practices already license. Korsgaard's account makes for a clearer analysis of Hume than mine does, but I think mine is closer to what Hume is actually doing.

As I've indicated, I think that Smith's way of engaging in moral philosophy follows Hume's closely. I therefore take it to arise more out of a belief that normative practices cannot be given metaphysical foundations, and that describing how they work is therefore our best guide to figuring out how they ought to work (and, if necessary, change), than in an effort to arouse the reader's approving sentiments in favour of the approving sentiments that he is describing. Neither Hume nor Smith write encomiums to virtue, most of the time; both seem instead to think that laying out our modes of moral approval—giving a phenomenology of them, as we might say today—will itself help us embrace them and deploy them. The conflation of the descriptive and the normative is thus central to their project.[31]

6.6 Summary

Smith offers an account of the virtues in the new Part VI that he added to TMS in 1790 which brings his view of the good human life more explicitly close to the views of ancient moral philosophers like Plato and Aristotle than it had been before. But this explicitly normative addition should not occlude the normative language that runs through the rest of the book, from its first edition onwards. Normative claims are closely interwoven with descriptive ones, for both Hume and Smith.

Notes

1 See especially T.D. Campbell, *Adam Smith's Science of Morals* (London: George Allen & Unwin, 1971), 19–22, 46–52. D.D. Raphael does not rely on the line in TMS II, but comes to similar conclusions about TMS: *The Impartial Spectator*, 10–11, 47–8, 65–72.

2 Jacqueline Taylor, "Virtue and the Evaluation of Character," in S. Traiger (ed.), *The Blackwell Guide to Hume's Treatise* (Oxford: Blackwell Publishing, 2006), 276.

3 See Hanley, *Character of Virtue*, 195–202 for a rich and beautiful reading of this passage, placing it in relationship to the ancient schools of ethics that it evokes.

4 Part VI is replete with classical references: see for instance 210, 214, 216, 233–4, 238, 240, 241, 251–3, 258. Of course, this is not unusual for TMS. See Gloria Vivenza, *Adam Smith and the Classics* (Oxford: Oxford University Press, 2001).

5 My thanks to Zac Harmon for urging me to comment on this issue. For contrasting views of the tension between the more and less demanding views of virtue in TMS, see Ryan Hanley, "Adam Smith and Virtue," in Berry et al., *Oxford Handbook of Adam Smith*, 222–30 and Schliesser, *Adam Smith*, 225–9.

6 Aristotle, *Nicomachean Ethics*, 1145a2, in J. Barnes (ed.), *The Complete Works of Aristotle* (Princeton: Princeton University Press, 1984).
7 John McDowell, "Virtue and Reason," in *Mind, Value and Reality*.
8 Part V, especially, when he talks of certain virtues as characteristic of Russia and Poland, while others dominate in France and Amsterdam. See also TMS 152–3, which argues for a tension between the acquisition of self-command and the acquisition of humanity, WN 349, which suggests that a "liberal or generous spirit" that prevailed in pastoral and feudal times has been fading in favour of "private frugality" alongside "base and selfish disposition[s]" in commercial society, and WN V.i.g, which describes the decline of courage and political judgement as costs that come along with the advantages of commerce.

Smith does present a portrait of the "wise and virtuous" person at one point in Part VI (247–8), but the discipline he ascribes to that person is precisely one of recognizing the ways in which he or she fails to live up to an ideal of excellence and trying every day to correct for those failings. So the ideal itself is clearly unrealizable in practice—and one reason for that unrealizability may well be that the pursuit of virtue requires an attempt to balance conflicting factors built into the nature of the virtues. That reading fits at any rate with Smith's characterization of virtues elsewhere in the chapter.

Of course, one could save the unity of the virtues thesis, in the face of this conflict among the virtues, by saying that no-one is ever virtuous. But Smith does not say that—he instead characterizes people as virtuous when they have developed some among the virtues to a high degree, and avoided the worst of the failings that characteristically come along with those virtues. That seems very different from Aristotle's understanding of virtue.

I take the uneasy, inharmonious account of virtue in Smith to be an important mark of the way he adapts ancient ideas to a modern, liberal outlook: an important mark of the way he does not simply take over Plato, Aristotle, Stoicism, or medieval Christian thought.

9 He says this explicitly in his lectures on rhetoric and belles-lettres: "Other characters all very commendable can not be blamed because they want some perfections we are apt to admire, for these perhaps are not at all consistent with them, and can hardly meet in the same person" (LRBL 34). This pluralist conception of good character also leads him to reject Aristotle's doctrine of the mean:

> Extreme moroseness and gravity … would not be admired: neither would one of such levity that the smallest incident would make lose himself. But it is not in the middle point betwixt these two characters that an agreable one is to be found, many others that partake more or less of the two extremes are equally the objects of our affection. In the same way it is with regard to a spirited and silly behavior, and every other two other opposite extremes in the Characters of men.

(LRBL 40)

10 See Christopher Berry, "Smith and the Virtues of Commerce," in NOMOS XXXIV: *Virtue* (New York: New York University Press, 1992), Deirdre McCloskey, *The Bourgeois Virtues* (Chicago: University of Chicago Press, 2006), and Hanley, *Character of Virtue*, chapter 4.

11 See Fonna Forman-Barzilai, *Adam Smith and the Circles of Sympathy* (Cambridge: Cambridge University Press, 2010).

12 "Smith's conception of prudence … offers an alternative to Mandeville's complacent acceptance of commercial society in its viciousness as well as to Rousseau's enthusiastic rejection of commercial society for its viciousness."— Hanley, *Character of Virtue*, 103.

13 As Hanley has pointed out to me, however (personal communication), Smith does present some of his most powerful critiques of commercial society in terms of virtue (e.g., WN 787–8 or TMS 61–6). So he may well have had concerns about commerce in mind when writing up his account of virtue in Part VI.

14 "Arguably [Smith's] own seemingly descriptive statements are normatively laden, as his appeals to what 'we' observe to be the case might suggest."— Griswold, *Jean-Jacques Rousseau and Adam Smith*, 85.

15 Albeit in a section of Part III that was written for the final edition. But compare TMS 22–3, which contains much the same idea.

16 Compare Otteson:

> The scope of the phrase 'the present inquiry' is not clear. … Does it mean all of TMS? The context of the passage seems to suggest that Smith means to confine his remark to a narrower range than the whole of TMS; it suggests I would say, that it applies only to the discussion in this chapter.
>
> (*Marketplace of Life*, 224)

17 As Campbell explicitly proposes: "Purely as an aid to enlightened interpretation, it is better to regard Smith as presenting a sociological and psychological but not a philosophical theory of morals and law" (*Science of Morals*, 19).

18 See Geoffrey Sayre-McCord, "On Why Hume's 'General Point of View' Isn't Ideal–and Shouldn't Be," *Social Philosophy and Policy*, 11/1 (1994).

19 There would in addition be a certain incoherence in the way Smith puts his point in the footnote, if he were proposing a theocentric morality. For he tells us not only that he is examining the principles upon which imperfect beings like us approve of punishment, but also that "the Author of nature" has entrusted that approval to a feeling like resentment rather than our reason because punishment is necessary to "the welfare and preservation of society" and resentment is more likely to lead us, effectively and reliably, to carry out punishment than reason would do. This way of putting the point presumes that we *can* grasp the principles upon which a perfect being—the Author of nature—would act, however. So we *can* know the "matter of right" as well as "the matter of fact," as regards punishment. Smith takes for granted a normative perspective even as he

judges the way we actually approve of punishment to fall short of the demands of that perspective. This incoherence reinforces my inclination to read Smith as not at his best in this footnote and to seek an alternative way of putting his point.

20 Hume, letter to Hutcheson on September 17, 1739 (summarizing a letter, now lost, that Hutcheson had apparently sent to him), in J.Y.T. Greig (ed.), *The Letters of David Hume*, 2 vols (Oxford, 1932), 1, 32.

21 See Hume's critique of the "monkish virtues": EPM 219/270.

22 Religious ones, especially, but also claims to the effect that such legal principles as "accession" or "prescription" can be derived from reason: see T 506–8n1, 509nn1–2.

23 See, especially, the dialogue about Cleanthes in EPM, chapter 9.

24 Quotations in this paragraph from T 269–71 (¶s 12, 8, 9, 10, 13, respectively). I am summarizing the stages of the complex dialectic in this chapter very roughly; I think and hope the summary is nevertheless adequate for the point I am trying to make. For a more nuanced reading of the chapter, see Annette Baier, *A Progress of Sentiments* (Cambridge: Harvard University Press, 1991), chapter 1.

25 Smith's friend and colleague John Millar described Smith's essays in EPS as following "the true old Humean philosophy" (see editor's introduction to EPS 16).

26 Naturalized moral philosophy, we might call it, on a continuum with everyday moral judgment just as Quine's naturalized epistemology is supposed to be on a continuum with the science whose methods it explores.

27 Compare Korsgaard, expounding Hutcheson:

> Hutcheson's point is that goodness of a sense must be assessed from some point of view from which we judge things to be good or bad, and that we have a limited number of such points of view to which we can appeal. We can judge the moral sense from the point of view of the moral sense itself; we can judge it from the point of view of benevolence towards others; or we can judge it from the point of view of our own self-interest. What we cannot do is get outside of all of the points of view from which we judge things to be good or bad and still coherently ask whether something is good or bad. There is no place outside of our normative points of view from which normative questions can be asked.
>
> (Korsgaard, *Sources of Normativity*
> [Cambridge: Cambridge University Press, 1996], 64–5)

There is a subtle but important respect in which Smith does not hold quite this view, however: see the rest of the paragraph to which this note is appended.

28 Geoffrey Sayre-McCord lays great stress on Smith's argument, against Hutcheson, that our modes of approval must themselves meet with our approval, and has been building a theory of normativity himself around the idea that it is criterial of normative practices that to be constantly susceptible to further evaluation.

See his "Sentiments and Spectators: Adam Smith's Theory of Moral Judgment," "Hume and Smith on Sympathy, Approbation, and Moral Judgment," "On a Theory of a Better Morality" (unpublished), and "Rational Agency and the Nature of Normative Concepts" (unpublished).

29 And is vulnerable to the same kind of Kantian critique of that procedure, if one is inclined to think that normativity requires an *a priori* foundation. Korsgaard of course does think this, and I agree with her on that.

30 Korsgaard, *Sources of Normativity*, 63, citing T 619.

31 I use the word "conflation" here advisedly—I share the Kantian view that they should have distinguished the descriptive from the normative. It is also hard to get away from the impression, at many points in Hume's writings, that he himself wants to say that various people—religious people, especially—should not believe what they seem to believe, and it is very unclear how his method allows him to do this. The doubts many philosophers have had about the very idea of a fully "naturalized" epistemology are I believe warranted, and the same goes for a fully naturalized moral theory, whether in Hume's hands or in Smith's.

Further reading

T.D. Campbell, *Adam Smith's Science of Morals*
Ryan Hanley, *Adam Smith and the Character of Virtue*
D.D. Raphael, *The Impartial Spectator*
Eric Schliesser, *Adam Smith: Systematic Philosopher and Public Thinker*, chapter 9

Seven
Advantages and disadvantages of Smith's moral philosophy

How should we assess Smith's moral philosophy? Does it represent a significant contribution to the field, or is it mostly a re-hash of what Hume and Hutcheson had already done? In its day, TMS was widely acclaimed; it made Smith's reputation, long before WN came out. Indeed, one likely reason why WN became well-known so quickly is that it was written by the author of TMS.[1] By the beginning of the nineteenth century, however, its fame had declined, and it received little attention for most of the next two centuries. WN has certainly far eclipsed it in reputation.

I don't want to make excessive claims for TMS's importance, but I am among the growing number of philosophers who regard Smith as having made significant contributions to moral philosophy that cannot be found in Hume or Hutcheson. I will try to lay out these contributions in this chapter, to some extent bringing together points I have already made over the course of the past few chapters. After that, I will address some of the limitations of TMS, which may help explain why its reputation went into decline.

7.1 Advantages

Smith's approach to moral philosophy has a number of advantages over those of his fellow moral sentimentalists. By way of his eclectic criteria for moral judgment, Smith vindicates more of the judgments we ordinarily make than do Hume or Hutcheson, and makes better sense than most of his contemporaries do of the complexity that we ordinarily attribute to both virtue and the judgment of virtue.

(Smith is expressly concerned to do justice to this complexity, criticizing Hutcheson for reducing virtue too single-mindedly to benevolence, and Hume for putting too much emphasis on utility.) So if the work of moral philosophers should be assessed, even in part, by the degree to which they explain what we actually do when we make moral judgments, then Smith's theory is an improvement over the theories of his predecessors. Its phenomenological accuracy is also, of course, supremely well-suited to the "common life" approach to doing philosophy that I attributed to Smith in Section 2.4.

In addition, none of Smith's predecessors developed such an essentially social conception of the self. Hutcheson and Hume both see human beings as having a natural disposition to *care* about the good of their society, but for Smith, all our feelings, whether self-interested or benevolent, are *constituted by* a process of socialization. Smith says that we do not so much as become aware that we *have* a self until we see it in the mirror of society (TMS 110–1; see above, Section 4.7), and that when we do come to self-awareness, we also come to shape our emotions and our desires in accordance with how others around us are likely to regard them. Winning the approval of others is thus essential to who we are, for Smith. Accordingly, he conceives of humanity as less capable of solipsism than Hume does—less capable of the thoroughgoing egoism that Hume, in his famous discussion of the sensible knave, finds it so difficult to refute (EPM 232–3/282–3). At the same time, Smith reconciles his social conception of the self with a deep respect for the importance of each individual and the capacity of each individual for independent choice. Ethical development, for Smith, is inspired and guided by social pressures but ultimately carried out by each individual for him or herself. The "impartial spectator" begins as a product and expression of society, but becomes, once internalized, a source of moral evaluation that enables the individual to stand apart from—and, if necessary, criticize—his or her society. Individually free action and the social construction of the self are compatible, for Smith, even dependent on one another.

Smith also gives the imagination a greater role to play in morality than his predecessors do, and sees moral judgments as more aimed at a reality outside of ourselves than other sentimentalists do. As always, we can sharpen these points by comparing Smith with

Hume. Smith's thought circles around Hume's: there is virtually nothing in either TMS or WN without some sort of source or anticipation in Hume, although there is also almost no respect in which Smith entirely agrees with Hume. One place where this comes out, as we've seen, is in their respective accounts of sympathy. When Hume describes the workings of sympathy, he says that emotions "readily pass from one person to another," just as the motion of a string equally wound up with other strings "communicates itself to the rest" (T 576; see also 317, 605). He then explains that we obtain our idea of other people's feelings by inference from the effects or causes of those feelings. In either case, the other's feeling, once inferred, communicates itself directly to us, and our imaginations just intensify our idea of that feeling so as to raise it to the level of an impression (T 576, 319–20). For Smith, by contrast, we place ourselves in the other's situation and imagine what we would feel if we were there. Imagination is essential to the production even of the "idea" of another's feelings, for him, and sympathetic feelings need not be ones that the other person actually has. This allows for us to judge other people's feelings against the background of our sympathetic feelings for them. Smithean sympathy is not just a way of *sharing* feelings with others—it also opens a *gap* between their feelings and ours. And that gap gives us a grip on the notion that certain feelings are appropriate to a situation, while others are not.

These seemingly slight shifts from Hume—understanding sympathy as (1) produced by imaginative projection and (2) a response to situations rather than to what others are actually feeling—have immense implications for the shape of Smith's thought. The first of them leads him to give a central place to works of the imagination in moral development. He frequently brings in examples from poetry and drama to explain or give evidence for his points (e.g., TMS 30, 32–3, 34, 177, 227), twice recommends fiction writers as "instructors" in certain virtues (TMS 143, 177),[2] and seems to see moral philosophy itself as a work of the imagination, a project that ought to draw on our imaginative resources and aim at extending and enriching our imaginations (compare AVE, chapter 1). It is therefore for him a project to which clarity, vivacity, and elegance are as important as good argument. And Smith was in fact very concerned with finding the appropriate rhetoric—the appropriate appeal to the imagination—for his works.[3] Both TMS and WN are beautifully written, and filled with vivid, memorable examples.

The second of the shifts enables Smith to be more of a moral realist than Hume. Smith finds an ingenious way of importing Samuel Clarke's concern with "fitnesses" into moral sentimentalism.[4] On Smith's view, we aim to have, and to act on, just those feelings of which an impartial spectator would approve in our situations; the feelings that pass this spectator test are then the ones fitted to those situations. So our feelings have something to aim at, something by which they can be judged or measured. This allows Smith to talk of "fitness" (e.g., TMS 149, 159, 165, 305, 311), of feelings being "suitable to their objects" (16–20, 40, 70, 73, 102), and, by extension, of people being the "proper objects" (fitted or suitable objects) of the approval or disapproval bestowed upon them (58, 114, 118, 126). He thereby restores a meaning to our ordinary view of value judgments as capable of being correct or incorrect, and not merely of encouraging or discouraging useful actions and qualities.[5] Relatedly, he sees our sentiments as more flexible than Hume does, and more responsive to criticism. As socialized human beings, we do not simply desire certain objects but desire to *have* just those desires of which an impartial spectator would approve: what today we would call "second-order desires" accompany and shape all our first-order desires.[6] "To a man who from his birth was a stranger to society," he says, "the objects of his passions, the external bodies which either pleased or hurt him, would occupy his whole attention." But once we come into society, "the passions themselves, the desires or aversions, the joys or sorrows, which those objects excite[…] become the causes of new passions." The approval and disapproval of others breeds in us "new desires and new aversions, new joys and new sorrows"—second-order emotions whose objects are the having of appropriate first-order emotions. This gives our emotions the internal structure they need, if they are to be capable of changing in response to norms.

Accordingly, it makes much more sense for Smith than for Hume that we ought to assess our sentiments critically.[7] Hume grants that, once we become concerned to make moral judgments, we correct the sympathies we feel for partiality in accordance with certain "steady and general points of view" (T 581–2), but for Smith this concession comes too late. Smith sees our desire for mutual sympathy as building an aspiration to make one's sentiments harmonize with the sentiments of others into those sentiments themselves. If they did not already have such an aspiration, we would have neither motivation nor reason to take up any "steady and general point of view." It makes little sense to treat our sentiments as naturally impervious to reason, but then add that they need correction. If sentiments are impervious to reason, they can be neither correct nor incorrect, and we have reason, at most, to *appear* to have sentiments other than the ones we happen to have, not truly to *have* those sentiments. For Smith, the aspiration to be worthy of approval belongs to our sentiments themselves. And we have both motivation and reason to change our sentiments if they obstruct this aspiration.

Relatedly, for Smith but not for Hume there is a lot to learn about what sentiments we should have. In neither the *Treatise* nor the second *Enquiry* does Hume spend any significant time on how we might learn to acquire new sentiments or alter the ones we have. By contrast, the first five parts of TMS—almost two-thirds of the text—are devoted to a delineation of the various ways in which we learn to assess our sentiments, and in which learning to assess them enables us both to express them with propriety and to change them. Smith also offers numerous accounts of the social conditions that make for moral improvement (see TMS 145–6, 152–4, 239–50, 327–40; WN 773–9). Hume, as far as I am aware, never does this.

There is also for Smith, far more than for Hume, a place for moral history. Smith's deep interweaving of individuals with their society, and of socialization with moral development, alerts him to the many ways in which moral norms and ideals are indexed to historical circumstances.[8] This will inform the detailed accounts he gives, in his lectures on jurisprudence, of how notions of property, contract, marriage, and punishment have arisen and changed in various societies. He thus opens up a place for a history of morals. And in fact his lectures on jurisprudence—via his student John Millar, who attended those lectures—were an important source of later sociological and anthropological accounts of normative change.

Finally, Smith provides us with a robust alternative to utilitarianism: a great advantage of his views, for those of us who consider utilitarianism to be a shallow and dangerous approach to morality.[9]

Both in Smith's day and later on, moral sentimentalists have had a tendency to slide towards utilitarianism.[10] Smith resists this slide, objecting to it in Hutcheson and Hume. Hutcheson coined the phrase "the greatest happiness for the greatest number" and set it up as the goal at which a benevolent human being should aim. Hume defined virtues as those qualities that are agreeable or useful, either to the agent or to other people. Neither of these views is identical with utilitarianism as Bentham and his followers conceived it,[11] but both are much closer to it than Smith is.

Smith explicitly criticizes Epicurus, the great classical ancestor of utilitarianism, for trying "to account for all appearances from as few principles as possible" (TMS 299). He criticizes the proto-utilitarian strands of Hutcheson and Hume for much the same reason. Right in the beginning of TMS, Smith sets himself against those "philosophers, of late years"—Hume is clearly one intended target—who have considered simply the consequences of our sentiments, and not their intrinsic propriety (18). Both the notion of sentiments as having or lacking an intrinsic propriety independently of their effects, and the arguments, in Books II and IV of TMS, against reducing our interest in justice and beauty to our interest in their useful effects, are meant to counteract the utilitarian tendencies in Hume and Hutcheson. Smith's particularist conception of moral judgment also distances him from utilitarianism. He believes that our faculties of moral evaluation are directed towards the motivations and well-being of particular individuals in particular situations, not to goods that might be possessed jointly by groups of human beings. "The concern which we take in the fortune and happiness of individuals does not, in common cases, arise from that which we take in the fortune and happiness of society," he says. Our regard for individuals does not arise from our regard for the multitude. On the contrary, our regard for the multitude is "compounded and made up of the particular regards which we feel for the different individuals of which it is compounded" (89–90).

Smith explicitly rejects the idea that our assessments or decisions should aim at the greatest happiness for the greatest number of people. "The care of the universal happiness of all rational and sensible beings is the business of God and not of man," he says; our job is rather to fulfil our various duties to our families, friends, and country (TMS 237). To be sure, by fulfilling these duties he thinks we will *contribute* to the universal happiness of all rational and sensible beings. But this is a different position from that of any utilitarian. Universal happiness figures, in this passage, just as the frame of a system of duties, not as something at which we should intentionally aim, even indirectly.[12]

Moreover, as we saw in Section 5.7, Smith sees happiness as so essentially shaped by the possession of morally appropriate dispositions that it cannot serve as a non-moral goal that could help us define those dispositions. Happiness depends essentially on morality, for Smith: we cannot be happy unless we live up to the demands of the impartial spectator. But there is then no non-moral condition from which we can derive morality: the hedonic calculus becomes useless, even meaningless.

7.2 Three disadvantages

I turn now to the disadvantages of Smith's moral philosophy.

Smith's moral theory has been accused of three major failings. First, it offers us no clear procedure for deciding which actions we should take in specific circumstances—no guidelines for how we can tell, in specific cases, what the impartial spectator has to say. Second, the impartial spectator seems too enmeshed in the attitudes and interests of the society in which it develops to be free of that society's biases, or to help us care impartially for all human beings. And third, even if Smith's analysis of moral claims is correct, even if it is true that moral judgments in ordinary life consist in attempts to express how an impartial spectator would feel about our conduct, it remains unclear what *justifies* these judgments. Why should we heed the demands of the impartial spectator?

Smith would probably dismiss the first of these objections, as based on an erroneous notion of what moral philosophy ought to do. Moral philosophy can deepen our love for virtue, refine our understanding of the virtues, and enrich our understanding of ourselves, all of which can conduce to a firmer moral disposition and to a wiser, more careful approach to our moral decisions. But it cannot and should not replace the common-life processes by which we actually make those decisions. Philosophy is an abstract, intellectual, and solitary activity, while moral decision-making is and should be concrete, driven by emotion as much as by the intellect, and shaped by our interactions with the people who will be affected by our decisions.

The second and third objections constitute what we might call a relativist and a sceptical challenge. The relativist sees no reason to extend moral sentiments or modes of judgment to people outside his society, and no reason to criticize the basic structures of moral sentiment in his society. He thereby seems to miss a central feature of moral demands. But where is the room for a universalist morality in Smith's account? We construct the impartial spectator within us out of attitudes in the society around us. So how can that spectator reach beyond our society sufficiently to achieve a sensitive and impartial concern for members of other societies, and to recognize where our own society's sentiments are biased or corrupt?

The sceptic represents a yet deeper problem. Smith says that when we issue a moral judgment, of others or of ourselves, we express the relationship of one set of sentiments—the cooler, more reflective sentiments characteristic of a spectator—to another. This seems a plausible account of what we actually do, when judging morally; it captures nicely the "feel" of ordinary moral judgments. But how can it give us reason to heed such judgments? How can it explain the normativity of moral judgments, our sense that we ought to listen to them?

We'll explore what can be said in response to the relativist and sceptical challenges in the next two sections.

7.3 The relativist challenge

Smith clearly rejects any local limit to the reach of moral demands. He adopts the Stoic view that each person is "first and principally recommended [by nature] to his own care" (TMS 219), and that we care more about members of our own society than about people far from us (139–40, 227–8). At the same time, however—again like the Stoics—he conjoins these limitations on our ability to take care of others with the view that our moral feelings extend, if in diminishing degrees, to all rational and sensible beings: "our good-will is circumscribed by no boundary, but may embrace the immensity of the universe" (235). Indeed, he regards accepting harm to one's local community, if that is necessary for the good of the universe, as a mark of the highest wisdom and virtue (235–6). Amartya Sen has argued that Smith also wants us to evaluate our conduct from the perspective of any human being anywhere, not just a member of our own society. Sen quotes a passage in TMS in which Smith says that we "endeavour to examine our own conduct as we imagine any other fair and impartial spectator would imagine it" (TMS 110), and takes the "any other" in this passage to imply that we should seek to be informed by the views of people far outside our cultural communities. "The need to invoke how things would look to 'any other fair and impartial spectator,'" says Sen, "is a requirement that can bring in judgments that would be made by disinterested people from other societies as well."[13] I have doubts about whether Smith himself intended for us actually to consult people outside our culture when making moral decisions, but there is no question that he aspired to provide a universal framework for making moral judgments, a structure for morality that could be shared by all human beings, regardless of national and cultural borders.

But is Smith's impartial spectator *capable* of coming up with concrete norms that transcend such borders? Consider two of its features. First, it uses sentiments rather than reason as the basis of its judgments. It is not like Firth's ideal observer, dispassionately watching people from above the emotional fray. Rather, Smith follows Hutcheson and Hume in tracing moral judgment, ultimately, to feelings. The impartial spectator is supposed to be free of *partisan* feelings—feelings that depend on a stake it might have in a dispute, or on blind favouritism or dislike for one party or the other—but it is not supposed to be free of feelings altogether, nor to reach for a principle derived from reason alone, independent of feeling.[14] But our feelings are notoriously shaped by our societies, and it is not clear how a device that depends on feelings could correct for the biases built into them.

Second, the impartial spectator develops within us as part of our efforts to align our feelings with those of the people around us. The "chief part of human happiness," for Smith, comes from the consciousness that we are "beloved" by other people (TMS 41). But that is impossible unless our feelings, and the actions that those feelings prompt us to take, meet with other people's approval. The struggle to have feelings that we can share is a basic human drive, for Smith, and it leads among other things to the rise of morality. He does of course insist that we need to correct the modes of approval used by the people around us for bias and misinformation, that we seek the judgment of an impartial spectator within ourselves rather than of the partial spectators who surround us. But he never suggests that the impartial spectator uses different *methods* of judging, appeals to different sorts of norms, than our neighbours do. It arises out of the actual process of moral judgment around us, and we heed it as part of our drive to achieve a harmony of feelings with our actual neighbours. The impartial spectator is thus unlikely to use a method of judging radically different from those of our neighbours, or to perceive, let alone correct for, a systematic bias in their sentiments. If sentiments of condescension or dislike towards poor or black or gay people pervade our society, there is every reason to expect that the impartial spectator we build within us will share those biases rather than rising above them.

These are the sorts of considerations that led Smith himself to worry about the danger that "established custom" can distort moral judgment (TMS 210), and that nature may lead people, foolishly and unjustly, to admire the rich and despise the poor (50–62). Smith also worried that political faction and religious fanaticism can "pervert" our moral feelings (155–6, 176–7), offering no suggestions as to how we might correct for that danger. He may have been unable to come up with any such suggestions—his moral theory has no clear way of correcting for deeply-entrenched biases.

Moreover, much that is attractive about Smith's theory is bound up with this limitation. The fact that he eschews transcendental principles in favour of judgments rooted in our everyday sentiments, the fact that he sees morality as enabling us to achieve an emotional harmony with our neighbours, the astute psychological insights he offers into moral development—all these things go together with a picture on which our modes of moral judgment are deeply shaped by our local society. But it follows that we can turn those modes of judging on that society only with difficulty.

Smith does have some resources to deal with this problem. I've argued elsewhere that Smith thought that better information about the lives of poor people, along with a greater effort to imagine oneself into those lives, could help well-off people judge the poor more favourably.[15] When Smith points out that "great labour ... continued for several days together" normally leads people to a need for relaxation without which they may endanger their health, and uses this point to explain why British workers often take a three-day weekend (WN 100), he brings his well-off readers, in imagination, into the condition of the poor and thereby tries to arouse sympathy for them. There is a great deal of detail about the circumstances of poor people in WN, and, given his account of sympathy in TMS, Smith may have intended this detail as a way of arousing his readers' sympathy for the poor. Perhaps he thought that slavery could also be overturned by better information, and a use of that information to project oneself into the lives of slaves. History, and other social sciences, could thereby contribute to morality.

It is also possible, on Smith's account of morality, to shift people's emotional attitudes by using one societal norm against another. When Smith says that "there is not a negro from the coast of Africa who does not ... possess a degree of magnanimity which the soul of his sordid master is ... scarce capable of conceiving" (TMS 206), he employs his British readers' admiration for magnanimity to shake up the contempt most of them felt for a group of people who displayed that virtue. When he notes that "the property which every man has in his own labour ... is the original foundation of all other property," and uses this familiar Lockean ground for property rights to criticize laws that require people to undergo unpaid apprenticeships (WN 138), he is appealing to one set of entrenched British norms in order to undermine other British norms. The same strategy is at work, more explicitly, when he says that the British laws of settlement, in "remov[ing people] who [have] committed no misdemeanour from the parish where [they] chuse to reside," are committing "an evident violation of natural liberty and justice" (WN 157). Smith frequently engages in this sort of immanent criticism of his society's moral and legal principles.

But there can of course be no *guarantee* that an increase in people's factual knowledge, a set of imaginative exercises, or an appeal from one set of norms to another, will bring about fundamental moral change. It is not hard to think of deeply rooted forms of racism, sexism, or homophobia, for instance, that may resist all of these manoeuvres. Modern moral philosophers have for that reason generally sought a ground for morality that would show *in principle* why merely local codes of conduct are inadequate, and local views that license disrespectful or callous behaviour towards certain groups of human beings are wrong. Both utilitarianism and Kantianism get their strength from this impulse.

Now it should be noted that many utilitarians and Kantians have produced arguments in favour of racist, sexist, and other grossly inegalitarian norms and institutions. Kant himself, notoriously, maintained racist, sexist, and anti-Semitic views long after coming up with his arguments for equal worth.[16] But one might think there is something to be gained by having a general principle upholding the equal worth of every human being, whether or not one applies it appropriately. If so, Smith will disappoint. He distances himself firmly from utilitarianism, and never enunciates anything like Kant's categorical imperative. Some philosophers have seen an *a priori* basis for moral criticism implicit in the foundations of Smith's moral theory. Smith drops proto-Kantian hints that a concern for the equal worth of each and every human being is built into all moral sentiments (TMS 90, 107, 137), and Stephen Darwall and Remy Debes have brought out a latent egalitarianism in the structure of Smith's moral theory that can be turned against inegalitarian social institutions.[17] But even if this is Smith's intent—and the arguments he launches on behalf of the poor suggest that he has a strong egalitarian bent—he never states it clearly. Nor does he say much, explicitly, to justify his egalitarian tendencies. Once again, these silences are of a piece with some of the strengths of his moral philosophy: its particularism, and its attempt to work out from norms that people actually accept, rather than trying to impose norms on them from some imagined theoretical height. But this approach does make moral critique difficult, and has a tendency to vindicate our local biases.

So it must be admitted that the relativist challenge brings out weaknesses in Smith's theory, and cannot easily be answered without sacrificing some of its central elements.[18]

7.4 The sceptical challenge

Smith does better with the sceptical challenge. As we saw in the previous chapter, Smith can be seen as offering what Christine Korsgaard calls a "reflective endorsement" argument to the person who asks, "why be moral?"[19] Reflective endorsement theorists substitute the question, "are the claims of our moral nature good for human life?" for the question, "are moral claims true?" They identify a certain faculty for approval or disapproval as giving force to moral claims, and then ask whether, on reflection, we can approve of that faculty itself. This test requires in the first instance that the faculty of moral approval approve of its own workings. It then looks to whether our other faculties of approval can endorse the moral one: we seek a comprehensive endorsement, by all our modes of approval, of moral approval in particular. The second part of the test asks above all whether the faculty for prudential approval—the faculty by which we applaud or condemn things in accordance with our self-interest—can applaud the moral faculty, since the latter often requires us to override our self-interest.

We should not assume that the first part of the test is trivial. Korsgaard quotes Hume's declaration that our "sense [of morals] must certainly acquire new force, when reflecting on itself, it approves of those principles, from whence it is deriv'd, and finds nothing but what is great and good in its rise and origin" (T 619), and contrasts this with Hume's earlier demonstration that the understanding, when reflecting on its own procedures, undermines itself.[20] So a faculty can fail to live up to its own standards for evaluation. But the sense of morals, for Hume, and the impartial spectator, for Smith, pass their own tests. Indeed, a good way to read TMS is to see Smith as demonstrating, to an impartial spectator in a moment of reflection, that the impartial spectator we use in the course of action operates in a reasonable and noble way—that, in particular, it is not just a tool of our self-interest.

At the same time, to meet the full reflective endorsement test, Smith needs to show that heeding the impartial spectator does not, overall, conflict with our self-interest. He does this by trying, like many ancient ethicists, to get us to re-think the nature of self-interest. If we consider our real interests, Smith maintains, we will see that the very question, "why should I be moral?," with its implicit supposition that being moral is something I might want to avoid, is based on a misconception of self-interest. If "the chief part of human happiness arises from the consciousness of being beloved" (TMS 41), then I will need to be lovable, and being lovable normally entails being morally decent, acting in accordance with the demands of the impartial spectator. Violating those demands will also normally bring on internal unease—fear of discovery, pangs of conscience, and the like—making it difficult to achieve the tranquillity that Smith takes to be a prime component of happiness (149). Moreover, if one fully incorporates the impartial spectator into oneself, one will discover that moral self-approbation is itself a great source of happiness (129, 147–8). But if happiness consists so centrally in the approbation of others, and in self-approbation, there can be no general conflict between pursuing happiness and pursuing morality. So the demands of our moral sentiments are justified, capable both of endorsing themselves and of being endorsed by our non-moral sentiments.

It should be clear that this argument does not involve any *reduction* of morality to self-interest. For Smith, the agent who supposes that self-interest can be defined independently of morality, and morality then reduced to it, misunderstands the nature of self-interest. Such an agent lacks a well-developed impartial spectator within herself, and therefore fails to realize that acting in accordance with moral demands is essential to her own happiness. She will gain a better understanding of happiness only once she starts to engage in the pursuit of virtue. Smith explicitly says that the virtuous agent sees things that others do not (TMS 115–7, 146–8). Like the contemporary philosopher John McDowell, he thus suggests that the virtuous agent can properly see the point of virtue, and how virtue helps constitute happiness, only from a perspective shaped by the actual practice of virtue. But, as McDowell says, there is no reason to think one can find better arguments, or indeed any arguments, for seeking virtue from a perspective independent of such practice.[21] There may therefore be a certain circularity to Smith's defence of morality, as some of his critics have alleged, but the circularity is not a vicious one, and an entirely non-moral defence of morality, which the critics seem to want, may be impossible.

7.5 Conclusion and summary

Smith himself does not clearly spell out the responses I have proposed to the relativist and sceptical challenges, or offer a clear grounding for morality from which those responses might flow. Moral philosophers need not be concerned solely with the grounds of morality, however. Displaying and clarifying the internal connections in the way we think about virtue is already a philosophical task, even if we set aside the question of whether that way of thinking is justified. There are indeed philosophers who reject the very idea that philosophy is well-suited to offer justifications. Smith's work fits in with a view propounded by Iris Murdoch: that moral philosophy consists in the attempt "to fill in a systematic explanatory background to our ordinary moral life."[22] His astute and nuanced analysis of what goes into moral approval— of the sorts of factors that the impartial spectator considers, of how it can deceive itself or otherwise go wrong, of how it develops and how it judges different virtues in different ways—is accomplishment enough, regardless of whether he adequately justifies the fact that we engage in such approval at all. And it is a properly philosophical accomplishment, at least if philosophy can consist in tracing out and linking up the kinds of claims we make in common life, while bracketing the question of whether those claims are, at bottom or overall, justified. Smith was a moral phenomenologist, and at that he was as good as any philosopher before him or since.

Notes

1 Certainly, that seems to have been the hope of Smith's publisher Strahan, who put an advertisement for TMS immediately after the title page of the first edition of WN (LAS 270). Adam Ferguson also announced to readers of his 1767 *Essay on Civil Society* that "Mr Smith, author of the Theory of Moral Sentiment" was probably going to furnish the public soon with a great theory of national economy.—Ferguson, *An Essay on the History of Civil Society*, ed. F. Oz-Salzberger (Cambridge: Cambridge University Press, 1995), 140n.

2 See also LRBL 51: "[Swift and Lucian] form a System of morality from whence more sound and just rules of life for all the various characters of men may be drawn than from most set systems of Morality."

3 A point discussed in depth by Griswold in AVE, Jerry Z. Muller, *Adam Smith in His Time and Ours* (New York: The Free Press, 1993) and Vivienne Brown, *Adam Smith's Discourse*, (London: Routledge 1994).

4 See Clarke, *A Discourse ... of Natural Religion* (1705). A kind of fittedness relationship—using the words "suited" and "suitable": style should be "suited" to the author's intentions and character, Smith says—appears prominently in Smith's lectures on belles-lettres as well (LRBL, lectures, 7, 9–11). I don't know quite what to make of this parallel between his aesthetic and moral theories. A thorough study of the way Smith incorporates Clarke's fitness relation into his sentimentalism would be very welcome.

5 This subject has come back into contemporary value theory largely in response to an essay by Justin d'Arms and Daniel Jacobson: "The Moralistic Fallacy: On the 'Appropriateness' of Emotions," *Philosophy and Phenomenological Research* 61/1 (2000).

6 TMS 110–1; compare Harry Frankfurt, "Freedom of the Will and the Concept of a Person," *The Journal of Philosophy.* 68/1 (1971).

7 But see chapter five, note 16.

8 On this subject, see Schliesser, *Adam Smith*, 33–8 and chapter 7.

9 For critiques of utilitarianism today, see *Being Me Being You*, chapter 8.

10 This is true of both Hutcheson and Hume, as I go on to note here; in later years, sentimentalism and utilitarianism come together in the writings of Mill, JJC Smart and Joshua Greene.

11 The *fundamental* criterion for the virtue of an action is the degree to which it reflects the agent's benevolence, for Hutcheson, not its felicific consequences. And Hume both makes traits of character rather than actions central to morality and evaluates those traits in terms of agreeableness as well as utility. So neither of them regards the utility principle, as Bentham does, as the sole touchstone of ethics.

12 That the duties with which we find ourselves, as a result of our sympathetic interactions with our friends and neighbours, fail to promote universal happiness is for instance not necessarily a reason to revise them, for Smith.

13 Amartya Sen, *The Idea of Justice* (Cambridge: Belknap Press, 2009), 125.

14 See Raphael, *Impartial Spectator*, chapter 6.

15 See my *On Adam Smith's Wealth of Nations*, chapter 10 and *Short History of Distributive Justice*, chapter 2.

16 See Charles Mills, "Kant's *Untermenschen*," in his *Black Rights/White Wrongs* (New York: Oxford University Press, 2017), and my review of that book, "Charles Mills on Deracializing Liberalism," *Journal of World Philosophies* (Summer, 2020).

17 Darwall, "Sympathetic Liberalism"; Remy Debes, "Adam Smith on Dignity and Equality," *British Journal for the History of Philosophy*, 20/1 (2012).

18 For more on these issues, see Forman-Barzilai, *Circles of Sympathy* and my "Adam Smith and Cultural Relativism."

19 Christine Korsgaard, *Sources of Normativity* (Cambridge: Cambridge University Press, 1996), 19, 49–89.

20 Korsgaard, *Sources of Normativity*, 62.

21 John McDowell, "The Role of *Eudaimonia* in Aristotle's Ethics" and "Virtue and Reason," in *Mind, Value and Reality*.

22 Iris Murdoch, *The Sovereignty of Good* (London: Routledge, 1971), 43.

Further reading

Fonna Forman-Barzilai, *Adam Smith and the Circles of Sympathy*
Christine Korsgaard, *Sources of Normativity*, chapter 2
D.D. Raphael, *The Impartial Spectator*

Eight
Religion

Before leaving Smith's moral philosophy, we should say a few words about his view of religion. Insofar as Smith maintained religious views at all, he did so for moral reasons. He indeed affirms God's existence in his own voice only in TMS; elsewhere, he at most attributes belief in God to other people he is discussing. There is also controversy among scholars about whether Smith's affirmations of God's existence in TMS are to be taken at face value or not. I think they are, for reasons I will explain shortly, but we should be careful not to exaggerate the importance of religious faith to his theories. We should be even more careful not to attribute to Smith a specifically Christian belief in God. He seems rather to have believed in what the eighteenth century called "natural religion": a roughly Stoic theism that comports with the "pure and rational religion" that, he claims, "wise men in all ages" have "wished to see established" (WN 793).[1] I'll begin this chapter by surveying some of the controversy over Smith's religious beliefs, then attempt to bring together the various things he says about religion into a coherent whole.

8.1 Scholarly debate over Smith on religion

The Enlightenment inaugurated a bitter debate over the proper place of religion in human life that has still not subsided. Popular debate over that issue has indeed intensified in recent years, and many academics, in various disciplines, have felt compelled to weigh in on it: mostly in defence of atheism but sometimes of Christianity, or of the importance of religious faith, of whatever kind, to a stable social and political order. And a number of scholars have brought in Smith, as a prominent and widely respected Enlightenment figure, in support of their view on these issues. The elusiveness of Smith's views on religion makes him a potential ally for people on both sides of our contemporary controversies, however.[2] He was cagey about religion in conversation,[3] and much of what he wrote on the subject began as lectures given in his capacity as a Professor at the University of Glasgow, which required its faculty to sign an avowal of faith and expected that faith to be manifest in what students were taught.[4] These factors make it hard to pin down exactly what he believed when it comes to religion.

Take this as a framework for understanding the surprisingly sharp scholarly disagreements over Smith's religious views.[5] Peter Minowitz has insisted that Smith is an atheist, subtly undermining Christianity in particular at every turn in WN, and making use of apparently religious language in TMS merely as "a rhetorical boost" for his moral claims.[6] Minowitz is not alone in thinking this. As early as 1777, in response to Smith's encomium to Hume upon the latter's death, George Horne accused Smith of wanting to "persuade us, by the example of DAVID HUME Esq, that atheism is the only cordial for low spirits, and the proper antidote against the fear of death."[7] (It should however be noted that the term "atheist," in the eighteenth century, was often used for anyone who did not affirm traditional Christianity.) Emma Rothschild quotes this and other animadversions on Smith's religious commitments in his lifetime. While she does not entirely endorse them, she does see Smith's religious opinions as "quite close" to Hume's (ES 130), arguing that Smith largely rejected even a Stoic faith (ES 131–4). "It is most unlikely that he believed ... in the existence of an all-ordering providence," she says, and she takes his mention in the last edition of TMS of a person who suspects that we live in "a fatherless world" to be a self-description (ES 130, 135).

Charles Griswold says, contra Minowitz, that "nothing in Smith's scheme assumes atheism." (AVE 280n40) But he joins Rothschild in taking Smith's remark about "a fatherless world" to reflect Smith's own views, and presents a similar passage about the tragic features of our world (TMS 169) as showing Smith's doubts about the existence of God (AVE 169, 220, 325–7).

Dennis Rasmussen holds a view close to Griswold's. He too agrees with Rothschild that Smith was sceptical about the existence of God, and that his views on religion were similar to Hume's (IP 44,195) although he is more circumspect than Rothschild about exactly what Smith believed. Rasmussen takes Smith to differ from Hume primarily over whether or not "bold criticisms of religion [are suitable for] the public eye." As we saw in Section 2.9, he also reads Smith's "History of Ancient Physics" as implying that monotheistic religions, just like polytheistic ones, are a product of the human imagination, invented to allay non-rational hopes and fears (IP 43–4, 196).

On the other side of the spectrum we have D.D. Raphael, who says that "Smith ... certainly believed in the existence of God," and that "although he abandoned Christian doctrine in his maturity, he seems to have retained a belief in natural religion."[8] Paul Oslington goes further. He notes that Smith signed the Westminster Confession of faith upon taking up his initial position at the University of Glasgow, remarks that Smith's general integrity suggests that he could not have done that in bad faith, and maintains that "[there is no] evidence of Smith's holding unorthodox religious views."[9] He then spends several pages downplaying the plentiful evidence that Smith did hold unorthodox views. Anthony Waterman similarly reads Smith as defending Christian ideas, although he does not think Smith necessarily intended to do that. Ryan Hanley describes the highest category of virtue for Smith as drawing on Christian ethical traditions, but takes pains not to imply that Smith was a Christian in any ordinary sense of that term.[10]

The great differences among these views of Smith may in part reflect the religious or anti-religious commitments of the scholars who hold them. But it also reflects real difficulties in how to read Smith. We should not expect much progress on this issue to come of a tit-for-tat debate over particular texts or incidents in Smith's life—the texts are too ambiguous, and the incidents too little attested, for that. I will instead present an overall proposal for how to understand Smith's religious views, which I think fits most of the texts and incidents that people wrangle over.

That said, some of the scholarly readings I've mentioned seriously misconstrue Smith, and bringing that out will help lay the groundwork for my alternative proposal. I'll examine a few of these views in some detail, therefore, before laying out my own proposal.

8.2 Against sceptical readings of Smith (I)

Griswold takes a passage that Smith quotes from a sermon by the bishop of Clermont to show that Smith could not accept the idea that a good God is the author of our world. Here is the passage:

> Does it suit the greatness of God to leave the world which he has created in so universal a disorder? To see the wicked prevail almost always over the just …? From the height of his greatness ought God to behold those melancholy events as a fantastical amusement, without taking any share in them? Because he is great, should he be weak, or unjust, or barbarous? … O God! If this is the character of your Supreme Being, … I can no longer acknowledge you for my father. You would then be no more than an indolent and fantastical tyrant.
>
> (TMS 169, as quoted by Griswold in AVE 325)

This outburst "disrupt[s]" the comforts of natural religion, says Griswold, and "Smith neither prepares us for [it] nor has a word to say in response to it." Griswold dwells on the latter point, saying that the paragraph immediately preceding the quotation from the bishop urges us to "turn to God for comfort in the face of the injustices of 'the natural course of things,'" and the paragraphs that immediately follow that quotation "simply reassert the importance, for a coherent moral life, of trust in an 'All-powerful Being.'" But nowhere does Smith give us reason to maintain that trust, says Griswold, given the evils that the bishop has pointed out (AVE 325–6).

What goes missing in Griswold's discussion is any mention of an afterlife. One would never know by reading Griswold that Smith says explicitly, in the paragraph before the quotation from the bishop, that we need to "hope that the great Author of our nature … will, in a life to come, render to every one according to the works which he has performed in this world" and affirms again, in the paragraph immediately after the bishop's sermon, that we learn from it to regard our moral rules "as the laws of an All-powerful Being, … who, in a life to come, will reward the observance, and punish the breach of them" (TMS 169–70). That is also the import of the bishop's own words. "If this is the character of your Supreme Being," says the bishop—if you let the innocent suffer without recourse and the wicked triumph—then "I can no longer acknowledge you for my father." Further down in the passage, the bishop again uses a conditional tense: "You *would* then be no more than an indolent and fantastical tyrant" (my emphasis, in all three cases). So the bishop, and Smith, are arguing for the need to believe in an afterlife, if one is going to believe in God, and the importance of a belief in both God and an afterlife to a whole-hearted pursuit of justice. Given that Smith argues this, it is simply not true that he has "[not] a word to say in response" to the bishop's litany of natural injustices.

I don't know why Griswold overlooks the centrality of belief in an afterlife to this passage. Perhaps he simply finds it hard to credit Smith with such a belief. Either that, or he takes the "natural religion" with which Smith is generally associated to be a faith that nature *as it stands* is good, without needing to be complemented by super-natural conditions like an afterlife. But in fact natural religion in the eighteenth century standardly did include belief in an afterlife; it did not follow Spinoza in identifying God simply with the nature we experience in our lifetimes. Samuel Clarke and William Wollaston offered proofs of the immortality of the soul; Lessing, Mendelssohn, and Kant agreed that reason (if just *practical* reason, for Kant) can underwrite a belief in immortality.

In any case, it should be clear that the bishop's speech, when read in context, does not in the least challenge the possibility of faith in a providential God. On the contrary, it helps make the case for belief in a more robustly providential God than one might have expected Smith to affirm: a God who will suspend or extend the natural order sufficiently to make sure, in a life to come, that the injustices of this world are righted. The passage that Griswold cites is thus a poor prooftext for the claim that Smith was a sceptic about traditional religion; it is indeed one of Smith's most traditionally religious moments.

8.3 Against sceptical readings of Smith (II)

Something similar can be said of the way Rothschild understands Smith's remark that "the very suspicion of a fatherless world must be the most melancholy of all reflections" to a person of universal benevolence (TMS 235). This remark occurs in a context in which Smith's point is precisely that a belief in God helps underwrite our aspiration to maintain a universal benevolence. The sentence immediately preceding it says that

> universal benevolence, how noble and generous soever, can be the source of no solid happiness to any man who is not thoroughly convinced that all the inhabitants of the universe … are under the immediate care and protection of that great, benevolent, and all-wise Being … who is determined to maintain in [the universe], at all times, the greatest possible quantity of happiness.

And the point of this remark, and the rest of the chapter in which it appears, is to encourage us to maintain a faith in that Being. To take the bit about "a fatherless world" out of context, and suggest that that is Smith's own view, is to distort the chapter entirely.

Now Rothschild is aware of the context of the "fatherless world" remark, and indeed quotes the sentence preceding it in a footnote. But she takes Smith to be setting up a "tragic choice" here, a pair of difficult options: "the tragic choice of the person who is without faith: to believe in something (some providence) which one knows to be unbelievable, or to believe in the frightening eternity of a 'fatherless world'" (ES 130). This "dilemma" is "characteristically Humean," Rothschild says:

> One possibility is to be convinced of something quite unconvincing, that is to say, of the existence of a super-natural and super-utilitarian God. The other possibility is to be endlessly gloomy, unconsoled by the sort of conviction which almost everyone, ever, has held.
>
> (ES 300n79)

But Rothschild is importing her dilemma into Smith. Far from finding it "quite unconvincing," Smith himself shows no doubt whatever about "the existence of a super-natural and super-utilitarian God" in the chapter she cites. Instead, he relies on the existence of such a God to support its two main conclusions: that "the wise and virtuous man" should be willing to put up with losses to his local interests, trusting that those losses will serve a "great society" of which God is "the immediate administrator and director," and that we should fulfil our local duties rather than trying to maximize happiness for everyone, since it is God's role, not ours, to carry out the latter task (TMS 235–7). The resignation in the face of suffering, and the focus on local duties, that Smith is promoting here make no sense unless there is a benevolent God ruling the universe, and Smith accordingly urges wise and virtuous people not to entertain "the suspicion of a fatherless world." They should rather maintain a faith that our world is governed and cared for by God.

Once again, it is hard to understand how a scholar as careful as Rothschild could so misread a text—unless she simply finds it hard to attribute a belief to Smith that she herself regards as "unbelievable."

8.4 Against traditionally Christian readings of Smith (I)

It is however equally difficult to see how Paul Oslington can say that "[there is no] evidence of Smith's holding unorthodox religious views" and attribute to him a sincere faith in the Westminster Confession. Smith's encomium to Hume alone—"I have always considered him … as approaching as nearly to the idea of a perfectly wise and virtuous man, as perhaps the nature of human frailty will permit"—is about as unorthodox a comment, for an eighteenth-century Christian, as one could possibly find. An out-and-out agnostic, renowned for his mockery of Christians and Christianity, approaches more closely to "the idea of a perfectly wise and virtuous man" than any faithful Christian Smith has ever known? Smith's teacher Hutcheson was accused of heresy by the Presbytery of Glasgow for "teaching to his students in contravention of his subscription to the Westminster Confession … that we could have a knowledge of good and evil, without, and prior to a knowledge of God."[11] How on earth could Smith not be at least equally heretical if he regarded a thoroughly secular figure like Hume as a model of virtue? And Smith was in fact accused by many of his contemporaries of undermining Christianity by praising Hume in this way.[12] It is baffling, in the face of this incident, how Oslington can describe Smith as an orthodox Christian.

Moreover, the incident by no means stands alone. We might consider Smith's reference to "whining Christian[s]" in his private correspondence,[13] or his treatment of religion, throughout his work, as useful at best for moral purposes, ignoring or dismissing the doctrines of salvation central to Christianity. Or we might attend to his harsh criticisms of Christian clerics in both TMS and WN (e.g., TMS 132–4; WN 802–4, 808–9) and the hope he expresses in WN that all religions will eventually be reduced to a "pure and rational religion."[14] Smith also sided with Hume against an Anglican bishop when the latter ranted at Hume for his levity about religion ("the Bishop is a brute and a beast"—CAS 131), was regarded by his students as a deist at best,[15] and was thought by many people who knew him well, like his student James Boswell, to be a sceptic or an infidel (ES 130; IP 156). Perhaps any one of these facts might be explained away, but together they give us strong reason to deny that Smith was a faithful Christian. Oslington too seems inclined to read his own religious predilections into Smith rather than letting him speak for himself.[16]

8.5 Against traditionally Christian readings of Smith (II)

Finally, to Anthony Waterman's ingenious reading of Smith as representing a deeply Christian worldview. Waterman sees WN as a sort of theodicy, explaining how God turns even human vices like greed, pride, or sloth to good purposes; he also sees hints of a doctrine of original sin in the book, and maintains that Smith "concludes his remarkable, Providentialist account" of the workings of the social world with a "ringing tribute to his own national church" (ET 918).

Now Waterman tells us right from the beginning of his article that he is "not trying to discover what Adam Smith actually believed in 1776." But he does think it makes sense to see the book, whatever Smith himself intended in writing it, as in good part an exercise in natural theology parallel to Newton's *Principia*, which he says "was read [throughout the eighteenth century] by Cambridge men preparing for Holy Orders in the Church of England as part of their theological training" (ET 919). And he gets some interesting results by applying this framework to WN. He points, for instance, to a moment in Book III in which Smith says that the "natural order of things" is for capital to be directed to agriculture before manufacturing, and to manufacturing before commerce, but then adds that this natural order has been inverted in every modern European country (WN 380). What is this but an indication that human beings corrupt their own nature, suggests Waterman—that they fall inevitably into sin?[17] Waterman also draws attention to the fact that Smith sees the "original principles in human nature" (WN 25) as good, but later describes these principles as deformed or undermined by tendencies to "levity," "folly," "sloth," and "avidity" (ET 911; all of these are Smith's own terms). Overall, Waterman sees Smith as working with two notions of "nature," one which comprises what does happen and one which prescribes what should happen, and presenting a view on which over the long haul the first kind of nature, because guided by a benevolent and Creator, will lead us to develop institutions that bring our societies into line with the second kind of nature: in spite of, indeed by making use of, our sinful intentions and tendencies. This is an intriguing reading of WN, which draws useful attention to the loaded normative terminology that Smith sometimes employs.

But the reading is marred by several deep flaws. First, Waterman sometimes simply misunderstands or distorts the text. He describes justice as a "sentiment" for Smith (ET 911), but it is not that.[18] His claim that Smith offers "a ringing tribute" to the Scottish Presbyterian church mangles the argument of the chapter in which the supposed tribute appears.[19] More seriously, Waterman says that in a series of cases the word "nature" is "nearly synonymous with the God referred to in [WN] as 'the Deity'" (ET 909). This implies that Smith identifies nature with "the Deity" on the pages that Waterman cites in support of his claim (WN 770, 772). But in fact the references to "the Deity" on these pages do no such thing: Smith is merely noting that the nature of the Deity was a subject of study in ancient and medieval universities. These are also the only two pages in WN that use the phrase "the Deity," or in any other way refer to God. Contrast Newton, to whom Waterman compares Smith. The *Principia* famously ends with a "General Scholium" declaring that the solar system "could only proceed from the counsel and dominion of an intelligent Being," Who "governs all things" and Whose existence, inferred from the "appearances of things" described in the rest of the book, "does certainly belong to Natural Philosophy."[20] Nothing remotely like these claims appears anywhere in WN.

This textual distortion of Smith reflects a fundamental historical distortion. What Waterman wholly ignores, throughout his essay, is the fact that Hume intervenes between Newton and Smith. Hume's influence on Smith has several crucial implications for the case Waterman is trying to make. First, to read Smith as a latter-day Newton, intent on presenting the workings of the social world as guided by a Providentialist God, is to ignore the powerful critique, with which Smith was well acquainted, that Hume had launched of natural theology. Second, Smith seems to take over Hume's analysis of causality; at least, he treats causal relationships as connections drawn in our imaginations throughout his "History of Astronomy." But if so, it is a mistake to attribute to Smith a belief in laws of nature that "operate of necessity," as Waterman does (ET 910), or, thereby, to find a paradox in the fact that Smith will describe certain economic processes as "natural," yet still maintain that they can be diverted or overturned. Smith uses "natural" in WN to describe patterns that hold *generally*, not exceptionlessly: he has a Humean rather than a Newtonian conception of nature. Finally, Hume suggests that it is a mistake to contrast the "natural" with the "artifactual": it comes naturally to human beings, after all, to produce artefacts, to control and shape our environments (T 473–5). If this Humean idea also influenced Smith, as there is every reason to think that it did, then there is no paradox involved in Smith's claim that we sometimes "by nature" overturn what nature alone would otherwise do. There is no need, then, to import views about original sin in order to make sense of Smith's view of nature. Smith, like Hume and unlike Newton, carries out his economic analysis with a wholly secular conception of nature.

8.6 Natural theology

Let's turn now to what Smith actually said on the subject of religion. To begin with, we should note the absence of any attempt to prove that God exists in his work. While we know that Smith taught a course on natural theology at Glasgow, no record of those lectures has survived and Smith seems never to have tried to turn any part of them into a publication. This last point is itself significant. Every other subject Smith taught, from logic and belles-lettres to morality, jurisprudence, and political economy, became the subject of a manuscript that Smith at least planned to publish. Natural theology alone seems not to have interested him enough to want to write about it, and there are only a handful of passages in his published writings that so much as allude to it.[21] In that handful of passages, moreover, Smith restricts himself to describing ideas of the divine in the thought of ancient peoples or the curriculum of medieval universities, without endorsing any of the beliefs he describes. He never even mentions the ontological or "first cause" arguments for God's existence, and although he alludes to the design argument at various points, he never explicitly endorses it.

We might add that when Smith does talk about how human beings came to believe in divinities, in his "History of Astronomy," he attributes the origin of such beliefs to "cowardice and pusillanimity," or at most to a crude first attempt to explain "irregular" features of nature (EPS 48–9; see also WN 767). As we've seen, Rasmussen takes Smith also to believe that monotheism is a product merely of the human imagination, designed to still various fears and provide us with "mental comfort."[22] But, as Rasmussen himself acknowledges, Smith in these early essays takes *all* scientific theories, even Newton's, to be "invention[s] of the imagination, driven by human desires" (IP 43). I argued in Chapter 2 of this book that that is not meant to impugn the truth of some of these theories—Newton's, especially. Smith is a realist, and he indicates that the process by which scientific theories progressively explain more and more of the irregularities that disturb our imaginations is a process by which they also come closer and closer to the truth. So to put monotheism on the same level as science is a mark of deep respect, for Smith—even if he takes the imagination to play a crucial role in our acceptance of both of these things. The paragraph that Rasmussen cites from "Ancient Physics" goes on to describe the way that ancient Greek sages, unlike their polytheistic ancestors, came to believe in a unified designer of the universe as a presupposition for the unified order they saw in it, concluding that "as ignorance begot superstition, science gave birth to the first theism" (EPS 9, 114). Smith is clearly *contrasting* polytheism and (mono-)theism here, not putting them in the same category. And theism comes off well in the contrast.

That is not to say that Smith endorses the argument for God that he sees in these ancient Greek philosophers. He does not, any more than he endorses their scientific systems. Nor does he ever provide an argument of his own for God's existence.

He does at various points in TMS seem to *pre-suppose* the design argument for God, however. He tells us, among other things, that the fact that we treat violations of justice as so much more serious than violations of beneficence reflects "the wisdom of God" rather than the wisdom of man (TMS 87); that the fact that we are naturally inclined to punish one another only for actions, not for unfulfilled intentions, "demonstrates the providential care of [nature's] author" (105); that "the all-wise Author of nature has ... taught" us to respect the moral judgments that other people make upon us (I128–30); that that same "Author of nature" brought us into existence for us to be happy (166); that "Providence" intended our sentiment of approval "to be the governing principle of human nature" (326); and, famously, that "When Providence divided the earth among a few lordly masters, it neither forgot nor abandoned those who seemed to have been left out in the partition" (185): that the rich are led by natural forces to distribute much of their wealth to the poor, and that we can see the workings of Providence in this fact. All of these claims, at least on their face, pre-suppose that we can see signs of God's existence in the design of nature. And Smith occasionally says things along these lines. "In every part of the universe we observe means adjusted with the nicest artifice to the ends which they are intended to produce," he tells us, and a few sentences down he identifies this adjustment to "ends" with "the wisdom of God" (87). A bit later, he says explicitly that "every part of nature, when attentively surveyed, equally demonstrates the providential care of its Author, and we may admire the wisdom and goodness of God even in the weakness and folly of man" (105–6).

These remarks certainly lend credence to the idea that Smith was a theist. We could perhaps put some of them down to the boilerplate religious language expected of a professor at Glasgow[23]—all the passages that refer to "providence," in particular, come from the period in which Smith held that position—but others were written after Smith had quit his professorship. A more important caveat is that Smith's *avowal* of design in features of nature, in passages of this sort, is not the same as an *argument* for design. And in fact nothing Smith says about these features depends on a belief that an intelligent and benevolent Being has designed nature. Instead, every time Smith speaks of God or Providence as the Author of nature, he also provides a wholly unmysterious, secular account of the particular feature of nature he is discussing. If we did not give justice priority over beneficence, our societies would not survive, Smith argues (TMS 86–8). He also gives good naturalistic reasons for why we do not punish unfulfilled intentions (106), how the sentiment of approval comes to be the governing principle of our behaviour (110–3), and why the rich need to distribute much of their wealth to the poor (184). He takes it to be obvious that happiness is our ultimate natural goal (hence God's goal in creating us, if God did create us), and that we naturally look to one another to be judges of the moral quality of our behaviour (127–31). Never does he hold up a feature of nature and say that it could not possibly have come into existence unless an intelligent being designed it.

That, however, is the characteristic move of those who try to *argue* to God's existence from some feature of nature.[24] Hutcheson had done that, devoting an extended section of his *Inquiry into the Original of Our Idea of Beauty* to an attempt to show that it is "next to an absolute strict Impossibility" that beings as complex as plants and animals could come about without a designer.[25] Nothing remotely like this argument appears anywhere in Smith. Never does Smith say, "Look at the intricacy or perfect fittedness of means to ends in this flower or aspect of human nature—surely that means that an omniscient and benevolent Being designed it." Instead, writing for an audience that for the most part accepted the argument from design, Smith uses that belief to help underwrite his claim that various features of human nature must have some good purpose. At the same time, he explains the apparent purposiveness of these features on the basis of empirical facts that believers and unbelievers alike can readily recognize. So nothing he says in this regard requires his reader to believe in a benevolent Designer of nature, nor does he say anything that would convince readers to believe in such a designer, if they did not already accept that idea.[26] To this extent, then, Rothschild is right: whatever Smith himself may have believed, what he says about nature allows for it to "be orderly without having been ordered"

(ES 135). In fact, Smith far more often speaks of "Nature," rather than "the Author of Nature," as doing something purposive—as in, "Nature has, for the wisest purposes, implanted [fellow-feeling] in man" (EPS 7, 136).[27] That does not mean that he rejects the idea that nature has an author, but it indicates that he is inclined to find order in nature without worrying overmuch about whether that order comes from an intelligent orderer or not.

Indeed, many of the passages in which Smith speaks of purposes in nature can be read as proto-Darwinian. Smith, along with Hume, has long been regarded as anticipating Darwin, someone to whom Darwin may have looked for a source of his idea that order could come about without anyone planning it.[28] And there are elements in Smith's account of the apparent purposiveness of natural phenomena that fit well with Darwinian modes of explanation. To begin with, Smith tells us at several points that societies would not survive without this or that feature of human nature.[29] That is significantly different from saying, as would a Christian influenced by Aristotelian teleology, that we would not reach our highest moral or intellectual perfection, the final cause to which we aspire, without the feature of human nature in question. It also opens the door to the possibility that some human societies, or individuals, lacked that feature but then died out. These two points are crucial components of Darwinian explanations of the apparent teleology in nature. Teleology is only apparent, for Darwin, and a feature of an organism appears suited for its survival just because organisms with that feature have happened, in fact, to survive.

Smith thus maintains several of the premises by which to build evolutionary explanations of the features of human nature that appear to be designed. And it is easy to construct such explanations for the features that he describes in this way. What would happen if resentment against gross injuries did not lead us to punish people for those injuries? Well, the violent among us would probably run rampant and our societies would quickly die out—just as Smith says. What would happen if we were not "endowed with an original desire to please" our fellow human beings (TMS 116)? Or if we simply pleased one another—won each other's praise—but were not truly "praise-worthy": if we seemed to be but were not really fit for society (117)? Again, we would die out: in either of these scenarios, people would not co-operate with one another enough to sustain a society, and human beings cannot live long on their own. I suspect that every feature of human nature that Smith presents as intended by Nature for a certain purpose can be similarly explained as something without which human beings would fail to survive, and which may have in fact evolved, in Darwinian fashion, because people without those traits died out. That is not to say that Smith was insincere in his teleological language. But Smith's views do not depend on a teleological framework, and he goes to some lengths to show how one can accept his accounts of human nature without endorsing that framework.[30]

The framework disappears altogether in WN, where there is not a single reference to an "Author of nature" nor a single case in which purposes or intentions are attributed to nature. The word "God" does not even appear in the singular (Smith does talk twice about ancient beliefs in "the gods"), and the word "Deity" appears only in a discussion of the place of theology in university curricula. Some scholars have used this fact as evidence that even if Smith believed in a designing God when he wrote TMS, he abandoned that belief as he got older.[31] I don't think this inference goes through. When revising TMS for what was to be its final edition, a dozen years after publishing WN, not only does Smith keep almost all of the teleological language of the early editions, but he adds two new passages using that language.[32] It is nevertheless notable that Smith gives only secular, naturalistic explanations of the social structures he describes in WN, even when they might appear designed.[33] That adds force to the hypothesis that he is reluctant in general, even in the passages in TMS that use teleological language, to explain features of nature by appeal to God's designing benevolence alone.

To sum up, Smith avoids natural theology and shows no interest in the logical and metaphysical and empirical proofs that his predecessors and peers had given for the existence of God. At the same time, he speaks as if he believes that nature has a designer throughout TMS and never betrays any sign of insincerity or ambivalence in that belief: never winks or nods at sceptical readers to indicate that he shares their doubts. So there are no grounds for saying, as Rothschild does, that "it is most unlikely that [Smith] believed ... in the existence of an all-ordering providence." But she is right that his accounts of the world enable his readers to see how it could "be orderly without having been ordered" (ES 135). Whether this was intentional on Smith's part or not, every bit of his social science can be accepted by theists, agnostics, and atheists alike. It is written so as to finesse theological debates rather than enter into them.

8.7 Revelation

But to say that Smith provides us with no logical or metaphysical or scientific reasons to underwrite religion is not to say that he provides us with no reason of *any* kind to underwrite religion. Logical and metaphysical and scientific reasons—arguments produced by what Immanuel Kant was to call our "speculative" or "theoretical" reason—are not the only possible kinds of reasons. One alternative to a reliance on science or metaphysics as a basis for a belief in God is to appeal to revelation as a *sui generis* cognitive authority. Some say that the Bible, or a direct word of God to the believer, can teach us things that we could not learn in any other way: that faith in this word of God is itself a cognitive organ of some sort. Versions of this idea were made famous by Søren Kierkegaard in the nineteenth century, and have been promoted by Alvin Plantinga in recent decades.[34] And Blaise Pascal, writing a century before Smith, as well as Smith's German contemporaries Johann Georg Hamann and Friedrich Jacobi, were founders of this sort of view.

Smith had little regard for Pascal, however,[35] and is unlikely even to have heard of Hamann or Jacobi. There are two explicit references to revelation in his published works. One occurs in a paragraph on atonement in TMS, removed from the final edition of that book (TMS 91–2); the other occurs in the "History of Ancient Physics." Neither reference gives us much reason to think Smith believed that revelation provided an alternative source of knowledge to reason and experience.

The passage in "Ancient Physics" consists of the laconic remark that "science gave birth to the first theism that arouse among those nations, who were not enlightened by divine Revelation" (EPS 114). Smith's point here is that a secular science can give rise to the same doctrines that revelation teaches (monotheism, in this case). Revelation seems wholly unnecessary here, and the word "enlightened" even has a bit of an ironic connotation: it implies, after all, that revelation came just to nations whose scientific skills were inadequate to lead them towards monotheism on their own.

The atonement paragraph seems at first sight a more promising place to look for a robust affirmation of revelation, as a distinctive source of truth. That paragraph is indeed the most explicit affirmation of a distinctively Christian doctrine anywhere in Smith's writings, private or public. He says in it that our moral sentiments lead us to feel that we cannot expect our "infinite Creator" to approve of us, imperfect as we are, even if we repent for our wrongdoings: "some other intercession, some other sacrifice, some other atonement," we imagine, must be made for us "before the purity of the divine justice can be reconciled to [our] manifold offences." And he follows up this remark by saying that "the doctrines of revelation coincide, in every respect, with th[e]se original anticipations of nature."

But this last comment shows that revelation functions even here only as a confirmation of what we already learn by nature: what our natural moral sentiments already teach us. In addition, this paragraph was withdrawn from the final edition of TMS. I am in this case inclined moreover to agree with the prevailing scholarly view that that withdrawal is a sign that Smith no longer affirmed the doctrine of vicarious atonement in the 1780s.[36] There is, for one thing, no other ready explanation of why Smith would withdraw the passage. In addition, the idea that we need vicarious atonement to compensate for our sins comports ill with Smith's otherwise quite relaxed attitude towards most wrongdoing, as well as his express view that our guilt over grave crimes can be overcome only if we are forgiven by those we have wronged (TMS 84–5).

Smith does quote or allude to passages from the Bible elsewhere, discussing them in a respectful and thoughtful way. In the course of arguing that we do and should take the judgments upon us of our fellow human beings as the initial source of our moral opinions of ourselves, Smith says that God has "made man ... the immediate judge of mankind" and "has, in this respect, as in many others, created [man] after his own image" (TMS 130). In the course of arguing that religious motives should not be the sole guide of our conduct, Smith notes that the second of the two precepts Jesus cited as the core of religious commitment was to love our neighbour as we love ourselves. But since "we love ourselves ... for our own sakes, ... not merely because we are commanded to do so," we should love our neighbours for their own sakes and not merely because God has commanded us to do that (171). The first of these allusions understands the "image of God" implanted in us according to Genesis 1:27 as our capacity for moral judgment, which of course arises out of our sympathetic sentiments for Smith. This is a clever re-working of a long tradition that had linked the divine image to moral judgment via our capacity for reason. The second passage uses Jesus's invocation of the second love commandment against religious figures who believe that we should act on the love of God alone. Both of these examples show that Smith was capable of astute readings of Biblical texts. But both also invoke the Bible only to support points (one of them directed *against* making morality too dependent on religion!) that Smith wants to make anyway.

These mentions of revelation thus give us no reason to suppose that Smith regarded it as an alternative source of truth, alongside logic and science. And Smith's expressed hope, in WN, that all faiths will eventually be "reduce[d] ... to that pure and rational religion, ... such as wise men have in all ages of the world wished to see established" (WN 793) suggests that he held no very high opinion of revealed teachings. I think we can clearly rule out revelation as an independent basis for religious belief, for Smith.

8.8 Moral faith

Which leaves us with moral reasons for believing in God. Smith could say that we have no logical or scientific reasons for believing in God but that people should nonetheless maintain such a belief because the promise of divine reward and threat of divine punishment is important to keeping them virtuous.[37] Or he could say that morality needs no religious belief to sustain itself but that it leads us to a belief in God, or makes best sense within a religious framework. Smith nowhere makes the first of these moves,[38] but there are several places where he makes the second.

In doing this, Smith anticipates Kant.[39] Smith was almost certainly unaware of Kant's existence. Kant began to become famous only in the 1780s, and was little read in Britain for several decades after that. Kant did know of Smith's existence, and was quite interested in his work.[40] But there is little reason to think that his view of the relationship between morality and religion owes anything much to Smith. So I don't mean to suggest any historical connection between Smith and Kant on this score. The link between morality and religion that I believe we can see in Smith is however clearer in Kant. I will therefore turn to him to explain the point and then return to Smith.

Kant's views on religion are complicated, and changed somewhat over time, but they can be summarized, broadly speaking, as follows:

In the *Critique of Pure Reason*, Kant examined the standard philosophical proofs of God—the ontological proof, the "first cause" proof, and the design proof—bringing out devastating flaws in each. He also provided general reasons to suppose that there can be no logical or empirical proof of God: no logical proof, because logic can never show the existence of anything, and no empirical proof because God lies beyond all possible experience. This was indeed a major thrust of the first *Critique*, one of the main things Kant meant by saying that he was laying out the limits of all possible experience. And one consequence of the success of that book was that arguments for God's existence more or less went out of business, in mainstream philosophy.[41] Kant also argued, however, that there could be no *disproof* of God's existence, for more or less the same reasons that there could be no proof of it: because logic cannot show the existence or non-existence of any thing (it abstracts from the existence of things) while if God is beyond all possible experience, no experience can tell against His existence.

With these points in the background, Kant defended a moral faith in God. Morality does not require a God for its content or its incentives, for Kant.[42] Our reason alone is perfectly capable both of enabling us to figure out what we ought to do and of motivating us to do it. But there is something pointless, something absurd, about acting morally in a world in which terrible things happen to good people, the best things we do often fail to achieve their ends, and beings like us, who yearn to exist eternally, instead have short, often drab and painful, lives. It would make much more sense to devote ourselves to moral goodness if there were a God who cares about our actions, ensures that good actions in the long run have good effects, and grants us an afterlife in which the injustices of this world can be corrected, and our minds or souls can persist eternally. A world without such a God is a world that is inhospitable to morality. So we are justified in positing that there is such a God—indeed, our practical or moral reason *demands* that we posit such a Being. At the same time, as we have seen, our speculative reason—the kind of reason that carries out logic and science—can say nothing against that posit. Moreover, practical reason takes priority over speculative reason, for Kant. We are all practical beings, engaged in action, first and foremost: even carrying out a stretch of speculative reasoning is an act. So if practical reason posits a God, and speculative reason cannot undermine that posit, speculative reason should go along with practical reason. It is therefore reasonable overall to believe in God, Kant says. It's just that our moral reason, rather than the reason with which we do logic or science, drives us in this respect. Insofar as we act morally, we implicitly commit ourselves to a world that is hospitable to morality. This commitment is what Kant calls "moral faith." Since he thinks it is reasonable to have this moral faith, he also calls it "rational faith" (*Vernunftglaube*). Morality does not depend on religion, Kant says, but it "inevitably *leads to* religion."[43]

One consequence of this view is that it entails that only morally good actions can please God. We come to our belief in God as part of our commitment to morality, which we define and ground independently of religion. So the only kind of God we can believe in is a God who upholds our idea of moral goodness. It makes no sense that such a God would command us to do something morally bad. It does not make sense even that such a God would be angry at us for failing to carry out morally *indifferent* things—rituals, or the upholding of metaphysical doctrines like the Trinity—and certainly not that such indifferent things would take priority, in God's eyes, over our moral duties. Kant therefore argued that the legitimate core of every religion is a commitment to the moral duties that our reason teaches us, and that the particular dogmas and rituals that each faith adds to this core have a value, if they do, only insofar as they help us be moral.

Now Smith does not share the complex epistemology on the basis of which Kant argued that speculative reason cannot prove the existence of God, and he held a sentimentalist rather than a rationalist view of how we determine the content of morality, and are motivated to live up to its demands. That said, in its broad contours, his view of the relationship between morality and religion is very similar to Kant's. The workings of our sentiments—the way by which we share sentiments with one another, in particular—lead us to develop moral standards and try to live up to them whether or not we believe in a God; no religious source is needed for us to learn morality nor is any religious sanction needed for us to heed it. But in "the natural course of things," unjust and indecent people win out over just and decent ones. So our moral impulses lead us to believe that "the great Author of our nature ... will complete the plan which he himself has taught us to begin" and establish for us "a future state" in which justice and decency are rewarded (TMS 168–9). People who lack such a belief need not be immoral— they may indeed, like David Hume, be models of virtue—but they will be prone to the "melancholy ... reflection" that they live in "a fatherless world." People who instead believe that God administers and directs the "great society of all sensible and intelligent beings" can see themselves, when they act morally, as foot-soldiers in God's army, carrying out God's will "upon the forlorn station of the universe" (235–6): they can see themselves as "co-operat[ing] with the Deity" (166). These reflections make overall sense of the project of being moral: they represent the universe as hospitable to morality. Religion is thus not necessary to morality, but religious reflections are a natural outgrowth of carrying out a moral life, and they help support our moral commitments. "Religion enforces the natural sense of duty," says Smith; those who believe in it "act under an additional tie, besides those which regulate the conduct of other men" (170).[44] For Smith, as for Kant, a moral faith in God is a reasonable consequence of a commitment to virtue, and a laudable addition to the other, purely secular reasons sustaining that commitment.

Note that in the passages I've just been discussing, references to God are not pleonastic. Elsewhere, when Smith says that "Nature" or "the Author of Nature" intends such-and-such an end by way of a certain moral sentiment, he also gives us a naturalistic case for endorsing that sentiment which readers can accept even if they do not believe in God. In the chapters I have just cited, by contrast, Smith's whole point is to show the importance of belief in God to our moral lives. Belief in God is crucial to our ability to see the natural order as potentially just and decent, Smith argues here; only if the natural order is nested in and complemented by a supernatural one do our moral actions contribute to a good universe. There is no way of re-stating this point without mentioning God. In these sections of TMS, Smith is arguing for religion, not merely using religious terms or images to present a point that he could put just as well without religious colouring.

Note also that the reasons Smith gives us for belief in God support only a religion in which worship consists in moral action. If morality is something we can determine and follow for purely secular, naturalistic reasons, and if we come to a faith in God only because we think that being moral is somehow absurd unless we live in a universe governed by a moral God, then there can be no reason to suppose that God would demand of us non-moral rituals, or a belief in doctrines that are unnecessary for morality. And Smith, like Kant, in fact sees such rituals and doctrines as distracting people from the moral core of religion. He says that "the first duty" of religion should be "to fulfil all the obligations of morality," and that "the natural principles of religion are … corrupted by the factious and party zeal of some worthless cabal" where people are taught instead "to regard frivolous observances, as more immediate duties of religion, than acts of justice and beneficence" (TMS 170).[45,46] He rails against anyone who represents "the public and private worship of the Deity … as the sole virtues which can either entitle to reward or exempt from punishment in the life to come" (132). He notes that religion can be used to invert the notions of duty that ought to guide us—giving, as an example, people who are told to kill a virtuous man as an "enemy of their religion"—and says that "false notions of religions are almost the only causes that can occasion any very gross perversion of our natural sentiments in this way" (176–7). As we have seen, he also looks forward to a day when all religions will be reduced "to that pure and rational religion, free from every mixture of absurdity, imposture, or fanaticism, such as wise men have in all ages of the world wished to see established" (WN 793).

These views help support Smith's harsh critique of clericalism in WN. The medieval Catholic church constituted, he says, "the most formidable constitution that ever was formed against the authority and security of civil government, as well as against the liberty, reason, and happiness of mankind" (WN 802–3). Catholics are, however, not his only target. Pastors elected by their parish in Calvinist churches tend to be "the most factious and fanatical of [their] order" (WN 808)[47]: the democratic qualities of the Presbyterian church foster factionalism. At the same time, Smith tells us that the poor pay that Presbyterian clerics receive leads them in general to be "learned, decent, independent and respectable." Why? Because "nothing but the most exemplary morals can give dignity to a man of small fortune" (WN 810). So clerics win Smith's respect only when they represent a general human morality; any distinctively Christian rituals and doctrines that they teach tend more to obstruct than to promote the true, moral religion. The less they represent Christianity's distinctive rituals and doctrines, the more they represent just "the natural principles of religion," the more, for Smith, they are to be praised. These views, too, are exactly in line with Kant's moral faith.

8.9 Moral faith in TMS

The moral faith reading I am proposing of Smith can I think account for everything he says about religion. Ryan Hanley is right to say that Smith incorporates Christian elements into his conception of virtue. Smith cites "the great law of Christianity" approvingly when discussing love of neighbour (TMS 25, 171), and Hanley draws out astutely the ways in which a version of Christian *caritas* figures in the portrayal of virtue in Part VI of TMS.[48] But *caritas* is by no means regarded as a virtue only by Christians, as Hanley concedes, and Smith brings the idea into his moral philosophy because he thinks the moral views we come to naturally will also support it. The same is true of the passage on atonement in the first five editions of TMS. Smith says there that the idea that we may need some vicarious "intercession, … sacrifice, … atonement" to compensate for our wrongdoing in the eyes of a supremely good Being arises from our "natural sentiments" even without revelation: he endorses "the doctrines of revelation," here, because they "coincide, in every respect, with those original anticipations of nature." (TMS 92) Perhaps he no longer thought that our natural sentiments support such a doctrine by the time he came to revise TMS for its final edition; perhaps he continued to think that but had other reasons to omit the passage. Either way, he appealed to revelation only when he thought the ideas he found in it could also be endorsed by a purely naturalistic moral faith.[49] That fits perfectly with a view, like Kant's, by which supposedly revealed texts are actually human attempts to approximate the teachings that a moral God would want us to believe: and by which all such texts, including the Christian Bible, should be re-interpreted in a naturalistic moral light if they seem to teach anything else.[50]

As for the passages in TMS that talk of an "Author of nature," or impute benevolent and intelligent intentions to nature, they too can be fitted in nicely with a moral faith. Once we have moral reasons to believe that an intelligent and benevolent Being has structured the universe, it is perfectly reasonable to look for signs of that Being's designs in the natural world. We have no guarantee that we will find them, and even when we do find them, they do not prove that God exists. But a moral faith provides us with an outlook that *allows* for any and every part of nature to be given a teleological reading.[51] Thus when Smith says that "in every part of the universe we observe means adjusted with the nicest artifice to the ends which they are intended to produce" (TMS 87), I propose that we read him as saying that in every part of the universe we *can* "observe means adjusted ... to ... ends": if we look at it from the perspective of a moral faith. That is almost exactly what he does say a bit later. "[E]very part of nature, when attentively surveyed," he tells us, "equally demonstrates the providential care of its Author, and we may admire the wisdom and goodness of God even in the weakness and folly of man" (105–6). We *may* admire the wisdom and goodness of God even in folly: if we approach "every part of nature" from the perspective of a moral faith. Even then, the part of nature before us will yield up its appearance of design only "when attentively surveyed"—when surveyed, I suggest, with a *moral* attention. Science alone will not force us to take up a teleological approach to nature. There are always nonteleological alternative explanations available to us, like the evolutionary ones that Smith himself hints at. Nor can teleological explanations of natural phenomena count as evidence for God's existence—they are plausible only if we already assume that God exists. But if we do already assume that God exists, for moral reasons, then it makes good sense to seek out ways in which God's designing hand may be manifested in natural phenomena. It makes especially good sense to seek out signs of divine intent in aspects of human nature that otherwise disturb us, like our tendency to resentment, or to value praise over praise-worthiness—two contexts in with Smith is especially prone to using teleological language (see TMS 77, 86–8, 105, 128–30, 298). For these are aspects of ourselves that can lead us to doubt whether we are capable of virtue. Explanations that show something good about them—something that God might have intended—help relieve us of such doubts, and restore our confidence in our moral capacities. Natural teleology can thus support our moral faith, and is justifiable when it does that.

A moral faith reading of Smith on religion also makes good sense of his comments about "whining Christians" and his encomium to Hume on the latter's death. For if religion is justifiable only when it supports views and actions to which our natural moral sentiments also lead us, and actively corrupts morality when it represents non-moral doctrines and rituals as more important than virtue,[52] then there is no reason to respect people who trumpet their Christian piety (let alone people who believe that only Christians can be decent human beings), and every reason to respect someone who manages to be virtuous without religious faith. If Smith held the moral faith I am attributing to him, he may have felt pity for Hume for not sharing that faith[53]—thinking that at some level Hume must have suffered from the "melancholy" that comes with "the ... suspicion of a fatherless world" (TMS 235)—but he had no reason to criticize him for a lack of virtue. Instead, Hume was the supreme example, for Smith, of how one can be virtuous without religion. Hume was indeed worthy of "admiration," in the technical sense in which Smith used that word. "Admiration" is "approbation mixed and animated by wonder and surprise," says Smith, and it goes out—as "wonder and surprise" always do, for him—only to something rare, something strikingly above the ordinary (TMS 31; see also 20, 48 and EPS 33–4). But by being virtuous without faith, and especially by being cheerful, without faith, in the face of death, Hume accomplished a rare feat, displayed an extraordinary fortitude.

8.10 Conclusion and summary

On my reading of him, Smith endorses a moral faith in God while rejecting all other grounds for religious belief. I venture to say that this reading of Smith fits with every remark that Smith ever made about religion, in private or in public, and every act he took with religious import. That is not true of more sceptical readings of Smith on religion—ones that make him out to be an agnostic or atheist. They need to distort the chapters of TMS in which Smith argues for a belief in God, and to discount the many references to God that appear elsewhere in the book. It is also not true of readings of Smith that make him out to be an orthodox Christian. They need to distort or discount Smith's irritation with "whining Christians," encomium to Hume, and harsh critiques of Christian churches. Only the moral faith reading enables us to avoid dismissing anything Smith said, or taking things he said to mean the opposite of what they seem to mean. It is also a coherent position, held by no less respectable a philosopher than Kant. And it makes for a fulsome explanation of Smith's thought about religion as a whole. All of these are strong reasons to uphold it against its competitors.

Notes

1 Even Paul Oslington, who tries to read Smith as a traditional Christian rather than a Stoic, acknowledges that "there is no denying Stoic influences on Smith." (Oslington, Introduction to *Adam Smith as Theologian*, [New York: Routledge, 2011], 6) He adds, however, that since Stoicism played such an important role in shaping both early Christianity and eighteenth-century Scottish Calvinism, we should not treat Stoicism and Christianity as "mutually exclusive categories" (6). This is a good point, which should be borne in mind by those of us who believe, as I do, that Smith distanced himself from the more distinctive doctrines of Christianity.

2 He is also a useful enemy for those who want to attack the Enlightenment (or, like Jonathan Israel, the "moderate" element within it: see Section 1.10, above).

3 "Contemporaries frequently noted that Smith was 'very guarded in conversation' when the topic of religion came up," says Rasmussen (IP 15).

4 I am grateful to Dennis Rasmussen for pointing out the relevance of Smith's official position to some of what he wrote about religion.

5 As will become clear, my view of Smith's religious commitments is closest to those advocated by Dennis Rasmussen and DD Raphael (who do not entirely

agree with one another). Other writings on Smith's religious beliefs that I admire include Benjamin Friedman, "The Influence of Religious Thinking on the Smithian Revolution," and John Haldane, "Adam Smith, Theology, and Natural Law Ethics," both in Oslington (ed.), *Adam Smith as Theologian*.

6 Peter Minowitz, *Profits, Priests, and Princes* (Stanford: Stanford University Press, 1993), chapters 7–10; quotation from p. 219. Minowitz proceeds by way of a great deal of speculation and innuendo. Many points are made with leading questions—"is the biblical God, from Smith's point of view, just one among a collection of 'mysterious beings... which happen... to be the objects of religious fear'?" (197)—or formulations like "one wonders if" or "one suspects": e.g., "One suspects... that [Smith praises those who treat] 'the philosophy of law... by itself' because [that] entails treating it as free of God and revelation, free of divine law" (*Profits, Priests, and Princes*, 217. See also 167–8, 175–6, 179–80, 203, 204, 210, 214, 215, 230). Elsewhere, he relies heavily on arguments from silence (142–3, 150–1, 156–9, 167, 193, 207, 229). (He takes the fact that the *Wealth of Nations* fails to mention Jesus, for instance, to suggest that Smith "rejected all forms of Christianity" (143): but why should a book on political economy mention Jesus?) And sometimes he reads anti-religious overtones into passages that say nothing explicitly about religion (185–6, 215). The book is very much a product of the Straussian school of interpretation in which Minowitz was trained, and partakes of its dubious tendency to read its favoured doctrines (including atheism) into texts however much stretching of their literal content that might take. The Straussians also have their virtues, however—they certainly pay close attention to the details of a text!—and some of Minowitz's readings are astute and insightful.

7 [George Horne, Vice-Chancellor of Oxford, President of Magdalen College, and a chaplain to King George III] "A Letter to Adam Smith LL.D. on the Life, Death and Philosophy of his Friend David Hume Esq., *By One of the People Called Christians*," in D. Rasmussen (ed.), *Adam Smith and the Death of David Hume* (Lanham: Lexington Books, 2018), 68.

8 Raphael, *Impartial Spectator*, 63; see also 98, 101.

9 Oslington, *Adam Smith as Theologian*, 4.

10 Hanley, *Character of Virtue*, 175–7 and n4 to 176. Brendan Long makes a point like Hanley's but without Hanley's caution. "The strongest basis for the interpretation that Smith's theism is genuinely Christian is the emphasis he places on Christianity's Golden Rule: to love others as we love ourselves" (Long, "Adam Smith's Theodicy," in Oslington (ed.), *Adam Smith as Theologian*, 99). But even if we set aside the fact that Smith makes eccentric use of the Golden Rule—drawing from it the very Stoic point that we should love ourselves only as much as we love our neighbour (TMS 25), rather than emphasizing its implications for benevolence—there is nothing distinctively Christian about the Golden Rule. Versions of it exist in cultures across the world (among other things, the Christian version originated in Judaism, of course, and there are close parallels

to it in Confucian texts). See Jeffrey Wattles, *The Golden Rule* (New York: Oxford University Press, 1996).

Long is the scholar who tries hardest in general to make Smith out to be a faithful Christian. He says that Smith "had religious duties at Glasgow which he seemed to take seriously" (98), that he was a supporter of the Sunday School movement, and that he prayed at his mother's deathbed (99). But all three of these claims are problematic. The evidence for the first of them is a letter Smith wrote to William Johnstone, urging the latter to delay a visit because it was "sacrament week" (Easter week, apparently) and Smith would be busy with his duties at the university. The next sentence of that letter adds however that once the holidays are over Johnstone "will find everything ten times more joyful on account of the melancholy of the foregoing week" (CAS 326). Ian Ross, reasonably I think, says that this line shows "Smith's distaste for the compulsory religious duties of his professorial days," rather than his commitment to them (LAS 118).

As for the "Sunday School movement," one might think from that name that Smith supported what we *today* call "Sunday School": classes on religious subjects at a church or synagogue, designed to supplement the secular education one gets on weekdays. But that is not at all what Robert Raikes was promoting with his Sunday School movement (Rae, on p. 407 of his *Life of Adam Smith*, mistakenly calls him "Thomas" Raikes: that was Robert's brother). The Sunday Schools were the only schools that working class children attended—they were held on Sundays because the children worked during the week—and they primarily taught reading, writing, and arithmetic, even if they also taught the Bible. Given Smith's strong commitment to the education of the working classes (see LJ 540; WN 784–8), it is no wonder he approved of these schools, quite independently of any religious function they may have played. (He is reputed to have said that they would "effect a change of manners" [Rae, *Life of Adam Smith*, 407], but in LJ (*loc. cit.*) he suggests that that would be due less to religion than to the fact that workers who can read have "ideas with which [they] can amuse [themselves]" and are therefore less likely to devote their leisure time to "riot and debauchery.")

Finally, to the point about Smith praying at his mother's deathbed. It is worth quoting at some length the passage in Rae on which Long relies:

> According to Ramsay of Ochtertyre, Smith was so disconsolate [after his mother's death] that people in general could find no explanation except in his supposed unbelief in the resurrection. He sorrowed, they said, as those who have no hope. People in general would seem to have little belief in the natural affections; but while they extracted from Smith's filial love a proof of his infidelity, Archdeacon John Sinclair seeks to extract from it a demonstration of his religious faith. It appears that when Mrs. Smith was visited on her deathbed by her minister, her famous son

always remained in the room and joined in the prayers, though they were made in the name and for the sake of Christ; and the worthy Archdeacon thinks no infidel would have done that.

(Rae, *Life of Adam Smith*, re-print of 1895 edition
[London: Augustus Kelley, 1965], 393)

So Rae himself embeds this claim in a passage which primarily recounts the general view that Smith was an *unbeliever*, unable to accept the resurrection in particular, and when he does get to the bit about Smith, possibly, praying at his mother's deathbed, he holds that report at arm's length, stressing that we know of it only from the Archdeacon, and that the idea that it speaks to Smith's faith is just the Archdeacon's interpretation of the matter. There are, it should be clear, alternative interpretations (even supposing that the report is true): that Smith didn't want to upset or offend the minister or his mother; that Smith thought prayer in these circumstances to some sort of God was appropriate, and was willing to put up with references to Christ just as part of that prayer; or that Smith was overcome so deeply by grief and anxiety by the prospect of losing the person he loved most in the world that he yielded to religious impulses that he would normally have resisted. Certainly, this passage alone would be a very weak reed on which to hang an attribution to Smith of traditional Christian faith. It might contribute to a case for that attribution if it were supported by a lot of other evidence of a similar kind. But in fact there is a mountain of evidence (including the initial lines of the very passage I have quoted) going in the opposite direction.

I think that the idea that Smith was either an atheist or an orthodox Christian is a false choice. If these were our only options, however, the evidence we have, both in Smith's texts and in what we know of Smith's life, favours the former more than the latter.

11 Rae, *Life of Adam Smith*, 12–3.

12 See IP 206–7 and Rasmussen (ed.), *Adam Smith and the Death of David Hume*, 59–80. See also Haldane, "Adam Smith, Theology, and Natural Law Ethics," 28.

13 CAS 203. See also CAS 67–8, 73, 131 (with 126–7), 181–2, for other mocking comments about Christianity or its defenders.

Oslington mentions the "whining Christian" remark but says that it "seems to have been provoked by Boswell's insensitive visit seeking Hume's deathbed conversion"; he therefore considers it "a mistake to read much into [it]." (5) But the idea that the remark was prompted by Boswell's deathbed visit seems to be Oslington's invention—Smith certainly does not suggest this, nor, as far as I know, did any of his friends. What does seem to have prompted the remark, and Smith's writing of a formal encomium to Hume, is the set of exchanges that Hume had imagined having with Charon, the boatman to the underworld (see CAS 204, 206, as well as the encomium itself, in CAS 217–21), which includes the fantasy of "seeing the churches shut up, and the Clergy sent about their business" (CAS 204)—a slightly toned-down version of which appears in Smith's encomium. That Smith delighted in this comment gives us very good reason indeed to "read much into" his remark about whining Christians!

14 Admittedly, his targets are mostly Catholic clerics, as Oslington stresses. But Smith describes the targets of his critique, at one point, as all those who think "the duties of devotion, the public and private worship of the Deity" are "the sole virtues" which God expects of us (TMS 132): hardly a description that applies to Catholic clerics alone. Minowitz also suggests, not implausibly, that the fact that Smith "freely appl[ies] the terms 'Christian' and 'Christianity' to Catholic phenomena" implies that he doesn't mean to limit his critique of these phenomena to Catholics alone (Minowitz, *Profits, Priests*, 143, 297n12).

15 Relying on a report by John Ramsay of Ochtertyre, John Rae says that Smith was regarded with suspicion because

> he was a friend of "Hume the atheist"; he was himself ominously reti-
> cent on religious subjects; he did not conduct a Sunday class on Chris-
> tian evidence like Hutcheson;... and it is even stated by Ramsay that he
> petitioned the Senatus on his first appointment in Glasgow to be relieved
> of the duty of opening his class with prayer, that his opening prayers
> were always thought to "savour strongly of natural religion"; [and] that
> his lectures on natural theology were too flattering to human pride, and
> induced "presumptuous striplings to draw an unwarranted conclusion,
> viz. that the great truths of theology, together with the duties which man
> owes to God and his neighbours, may be discovered by the light of nature
> without any special revelation."
>
> (Rae, *Life of Adam Smith*, 60)

Oslington mentions the petition to dispense with opening prayers—a point of which Rae himself is dubious (he says that there is no record in the College minutes of any such petition, and "the story is probably nothing but a morsel of idle gossip")—but says that "we have to be careful not to read too much into [it], for it probably tells us more about Smith's views on the appropriateness of the lecture hall as a place for prayer than it does about his views on the legit-imacy of prayer, or the existence of God." (4) Oslington does not tell us why he thinks this is probable, however, and as there is no discussion anywhere in Smith's writings, public or private, of what locations are appropriate for prayer, I can't imagine what evidence he has in mind. The passage in Rae certainly suggests no such reason for the supposed petition.

Oslington passes over in silence all the other evidence, in the passage from Rae, that Smith was at best unorthodox.

16 Long makes much of Smith's refusal to help publish Hume's *Dialogues on Natural Religion*, saying that this shows that Smith "rejects [Hume's] view" that the exist-ence of evil is a challenge to those who believe in God (Long, "Adam Smith's Theodicy," 102; see also 99). But Smith never mentions any objection to the

content of the *Dialogues* as a reason for not wanting to see them published. He says instead just that he "could have wished that [they] had remained in Manuscript to be communicated only to a few people," and expresses a concern about what the "clamour against" them may do to Hume's reputation (CAS 211, 216–7)—a concern that fits well, as Rasmussen has pointed out, with Smith's general allergy to arousing public anger (IP 145, 196). Moreover, practically all the views in the *Dialogues* had appeared, if less sharply put, in Hume's earlier writings; the use of the existence of evil as an argument against the design argument for God, in particular, makes an important part of Hume's argument in chapter XI of EHU.

17 ET 911, quoting WN 92–3, 378, 563, 567, 674.

18 Sometimes it refers to an institutional framework, sometimes to the end that that framework is supposed to achieve, and sometimes to an individual virtue. Even in the last of these cases, while it may be *driven* by certain sentiments, it *consists* in a disposition to behave in certain ways.

19 Smith's point, when he praises the Presbyterian church in Scotland (and in Holland, Geneva, and Switzerland: 810), is simply that the relative poverty of that church prevents it from doing as much social damage as other established churches do. And the argument of the chapter as a whole is that, if a state is to have an established church at all, it should pay the clergy of that church poorly, so that they can achieve respectability in the eyes of those they serve only by acting decently. Which is to say—as Smith makes quite clear—that clergymen should focus on being moral role models, not on spreading Christian doctrine. He also makes clear that ideally there would be no established churches at all, and religious establishments everywhere would wither to the point at which "the doctrine of the greater part of [religious sects would reduce] to that pure and rational religion... such as wise men in all ages of the world wished to see established" (WN 793). A "ringing tribute" to the Scottish Presbyterian church this is emphatically not.

20 Isaac Newton, *Principia*, trans. A Motte, ed. F. Cajori (Berkeley: University of California Press, 1962), 544, 546.

21 I think the following is a complete list: EPS 49, 112–6; TMS 36, 300–301; and WN 767–7. All five of these passages merely describe what certain ancient or medieval groups believed or taught, and the last of them contains a denigration of theology in favour of physics: in medieval universities, says Smith, "the doctrine of spirits, of which so little can be known, came to take up as much room in the system of philosophy as the doctrine of bodies, of which so much can be known" (WN 770).

22 IP 44, internal quotation from EPS 9, 113.

23 I'm grateful to Dennis Rasmussen for suggesting this point to me.

24 See, for instance, the second of Berkeley's *Three Dialogues Between Hylas and Philonous*; Part II, section 4 of Shaftesbury's *The Moralists*; or Samuel Clarke, *A Demonstration of the Being and Attributes of God*, ed. E. Vailati, (Cambridge: Cambridge University Press, 1998), 43–4.

25 Frances Hutcheson, *An Inquiry into the Original of Our Ideas of Beauty and Virtue*, ed. W. Leidhold, revised edition (Indianapolis: Liberty Fund, 2008), Treatise I, section V (46–60).

26 We might add that Smith sometimes presents nature as at least appearing to work at cross-purposes to our ends, rather than serving them (see, for example, TMS 34, 53) and that the two explicit references cited above to nature as manifesting "the wisdom of God" appear in contexts in which Smith is urging his reader to see something good in aspects of human nature that do not seem to be good at first sight (the rootedness of punishment in resentment, and the fact that we do not punish people with evil intentions, respectively). The function of his appeal to a view of the universe as designed is thus to encourage pious readers to take seriously a naturalistic account of the good that can come of some morally unattractive features of human nature; what Smith says is not something likely to help a person who already has doubts about the goodness of the universe to overcome those doubts.

27 Far more often, in fact. If we restrict ourselves to passages where "Nature" is clearly presented as purposive (generally passages in which the word is also capitalized), and set aside discussions of the Stoics and other authors who took up a teleological approach to nature, I find at least 36 places in which Smith talks of "Nature" as doing something for an end but only nine in which he talks of an "Author" or "Director" of nature. Examples can be found on TMS 11, 37, 85, 86, 116, 142.

28 See Friedrich Hayek, *Law, Legislation and Liberty* (London: Routledge, 1998), 22–3 and David Levy and Sandra Peart, "Adam Smith and the State: Language and Reform," in Berry et al., *The Oxford Handbook of Adam Smith*, 373.

29 He says this explicitly about systems of justice and about moral systems not being "of a piece" with practices like infanticide (TMS 211); he implies this about our desire for praise-worthiness rather than praise alone on TMS 117.

30 Compare Knud Haakonssen: "Nothing hinges on teleological explanations" in Smith, he says: "wherever a piece of teleology turns up in Smith, it is fairly clear where we have to look in order to find a 'real' explanation in terms of … efficient causes" (SL 77).

31 ES 129–31. Minowitz suggests that Smith expressed his doubts about religion "more frankly as death approached," but acknowledges that if he really rejected religion altogether, "the alterations in the 1790 edition of *The Theory of Moral Sentiments* should have been more radical" (*Profits, Priests*, 189).

32 TMS 128 (which echoes a passage in the 1759 edition but adds the qualifier "all-wise" to the phrase "Author of Nature") and 235. See also the whole of chapter VI.ii.3.

33 He certainly does not say, as some have supposed, that the invisible hand that guides the market to socially beneficial outcomes is an expression of providence: see below, Section 11.6.

34 Kierkegaard calls faith a cognitive "organ" in his Philosophical Fragments, but probably means the term in something of a metaphorical sense (Kierkegaard does not believe we gain knowledge of God in any way). Plantinga treats the "sensus divinitatis" as more literally a cognitive organ in his Warranted Christian Belief (New York: Oxford University Press, 2000).

35 He calls him a "whining and melancholy moralist" in a note to TMS 139.

36 For discussion, see the editors' Appendix II to TMS (383–401), Hanley, Adam Smith and the Character of Virtue, 197–8n, and Gavin Kennedy, "Adam Smith on Religion," in Berry et al., Oxford Handbook of Adam Smith, 474–5.

37 A voice in one of Hume's discussions of religion offers such a view (EHU 114/147) and some scholars have supposed that Hume himself held it (see for instance, Gertrude Himmelfarb, The Roads to Modernity [New York: Vintage Books, 2004], 40). This is a mistake: Hume in fact argues elsewhere in the same book that we should never maintain beliefs for their social utility if we do not think they are true (EHU 75/96). He also maintains throughout his writings that there are perfectly good naturalistic reasons to be moral regardless of whether there is a God and that religiously-based moralities tend to be baleful rather than healthy.

38 Which was discouraged already by Hutcheson: Inquiry into the Original ..., Treatise II, chapter II, section vii.

39 Ryan Hanley similarly compares Smith's views on religion with Kant's, in "Adam Smith on the 'Natural Principles of Religion,'" The Journal of Scottish Philosophy 13/1 (2015).

40 See my "Philosophy in Moral Practice."

41 Some modern-day analytic philosophers have brought back versions of those arguments. See for instance Norman Malcolm, "Anselm's Ontological Arguments", Philosophical Review 69 (1960) and Alvin Plantinga, The Nature of Necessity (Oxford: Oxford University Press, 1974).

42 This is his view, at least, from the Groundwork onwards. Before that, he seems to have thought that belief in God and an afterlife was necessary if we were to have an incentive to be moral. See for instance Critique of Pure Reason A811–14/ B839–41. I discuss this change in Kant's views in my Divine Teaching and the Way of the World (Oxford: Oxford University Press, 2011), 497–8n24.

43 Immanuel Kant, Religion within the Boundaries of Mere Reason, trans. A. Wood and G. di Giovanni, (Cambridge: Cambridge University Press, 1998), 35 (Ak 6:6), my emphasis.

44 As this quotation indicates, Smith links religion in particular to duty: obligatory actions, rather than supererogatory ones, and especially obligations that can be defined by a strict rule: he thinks moral rules are appropriately seen as "laws of the deity" (TMS 161).

45 It's worth noting that the "frivolous observances" here pretty obviously will include prayer and baptism and communion in any church, not just the sorts of fasting and scourging that Smith and Hume regularly criticize in the Catholic tradition. So much for Oslington's and Waterman's insistence that Smith's attack on clericalism was directed at Catholics alone.

We should also emphasize that the worry here is about God demanding rituals or non-moral doctrinal commitments of us, or allowing such rituals and doctrinal commitments to replace our moral obligations. There can be quite innocuous religious rituals—a religious wedding can be a beautiful thing—and the idea that God suffers with humanity, say, can be given an attractive moral interpretation. For both Smith and Kant, problems only arise if one considers it a grave sin to have a non-religious wedding or to reject the idea that God suffers with humanity: or if one thinks that going through religious ceremonies, and accepting religious dogmas, can compensate for wrongdoing.

46 Compare also WN 771:

[W]hen moral, as well as natural philosophy, came to be taught only as subservient to theology, the duties of human life were treated of as chiefly subservient to the happiness of a life to come. In the antient philosophy the perfection of virtue was represented as necessarily productive, to the person who possessed it, of the most perfect happiness in this life. In the modern philosophy it was frequently represented as generally or rather as almost always inconsistent with any degree of happiness in this life; and heaven was to be earned only by penance and mortification, by the austerities and abasement of a monk; not by the liberal, generous, and spirited conduct of a man.

I am grateful to Dennis Rasmussen for pointing out to me the relevance of this passage to my argument.

47 The language here echoes the "factiousness" Smith imputes to those who emphasize "frivolous observances" in the passage from TMS 170 quoted above.

48 Hanley, *Character of Virtue*, chapter 6.

49 And he implies strongly that any element of the Christian revealed text that a naturalistic moral faith could not support—ones that insist, or seem to insist, that a faith in non-moral doctrines (e.g., that no-one can be saved without believing that Christ is their saviour) is more important to God than moral action—count as the sort of "absurdity, imposture, or fanaticism" that should not be mixed into religion.

50 Kant, *Religion*, 115–6, 118–22 (Ak 6:106–7, 109–14) and *Conflict of the Faculties*, trans. M. Gregor (Lincoln: University of Nebraska Press, 1979), 60–85 (Ak 7:36–48).

51 This is the import, I take it, of Kant's claim that "moral teleology makes good the defect of physical teleology" in his third Critique: *Critique of the Power of Judgment*, trans. P. Guyer and E. Matthews (Cambridge: Cambridge University Press, 2000), 310 (Ak 5:444).

52 It should, I imagine, be obvious now why Smith would have not wanted to lead his class in prayer, and had no problem mocking doctrines like that of "sins against the Holy Ghost" (see Section 1.7).

53 This seems to have been Kant's attitude towards Spinoza: *Critique of the Power of Judgment*, 317–8 (Ak 5:452).

Further reading

Eric Schliesser, *Adam Smith*, chapter 14
Ryan Hanley, "Adam Smith on the 'Natural Principles of Religion'"
Peter Minowitz, *Profits, Priests, and Princes*, chapters 7–10
Paul Oslington (ed.), *Adam Smith as Theologian*
Emma Rothschild, *Economic Sentiments*, chapter 5

Nine
Justice

Smith ends TMS by promising to follow it up with a book on justice. Justice is the only virtue that can and should be expressed in precise rules, he believes, and he believes also that a set of these rules, or principles for generating such rules, should provide "the foundation of the laws of all nations." This "natural jurisprudence" would then let us know whether the positive laws of each state are just or not. Indeed, he says that "every system of positive law may be regarded as a more or less imperfect attempt towards a system of natural jurisprudence." The laws actually instituted in each state, to the extent that they are intended to be just, represent that state's interpretation of universal or natural justice, its understanding of the basic rules that ought to govern all human beings. And, following a long tradition in natural law theory, Smith regards laws that do not aim at justice as not properly laws at all: merely modes of wielding power on the part of "orders of men who tyrannize the government" (TMS 340–1).

But if there is a natural justice, then it should be possible to come up with some theoretical—philosophical—account of what that natural justice looks like. And since this account will presumably draw on the principles of morals more generally, it makes sense for an inquiry into moral philosophy to be followed by an inquiry into "the natural rules of justice independent of all positive institution." Accordingly, Smith promises to produce such an inquiry: "a discourse [that will] give an account of the general principles of law and government, and of the different revolutions they have undergone in the different ages and periods of society." Indeed, he promises that

that discourse will cover not only justice, but also "police, revenue and arms, and whatever else is the object of law."[1]

Smith never did produce his book on natural jurisprudence, but there is good reason to think that it would have contained much that was in his lectures on jurisprudence, which he gave as a sequel to the class on moral philosophy that became TMS.[2] He did produce a book on what he calls "police" in the last paragraph of TMS—"policy," which he says is primarily concerned with "cheapness or plenty" (LJ 486). That was WN, which Smith regarded as also containing some of what he had planned to say, in his jurisprudential book, on "revenue and arms."[3] It is just the section on the natural rules of justice—by far the largest part of the lecture course on jurisprudence[4]—that never found its way into a published book.

The theory of natural justice is clearly the main link between moral philosophy and political philosophy, for Smith. It's tempting to say that this shows that Smith regarded justice as a condition for the legitimacy of any government action, including government action designed to manage the economy. And in fact Smith does believe that justice is a condition on any decent economic order—that free markets neither can nor should flourish unless they come along with firm government protections of our basic rights, including our right to own property. But the priority of justice in Smith's jurisprudential lectures is not, I think, driven by his view of justice as the first task of governments. It has to do rather with the fact that Smith saw justice as the most philosophically interesting of the tasks of government, and the one most closely tied to an account of moral philosophy. When beginning the section of his lectures on "police," Smith says that that heading properly covers cleanliness, security, and cheapness or plenty, but the first two of these topics are "too mean and trifling a subject" to be covered in a course on jurisprudence (LJ 5; see also 331, 486). It's not entirely clear what he means by this, but I presume he thinks that solutions to problems of cleanliness and security are too pragmatic, or too dependent on varying empirical details, to be put into general principles.

Which implies that justice, revenue, and arms, as well as the economic aspects of "police," do lend themselves to such principled treatment. And indeed in LJ and WN Smith proposes, not only principles of justice, but rules for taxation ("revenue"), and a review of the "laws of nations" (see LJ 545–54): a central component of any theory of "arms." So it seems clear that Smith took his primary task, in the law book that was to follow on his moral philosophy, to be the laying out of *principles* to guide what governments should do: principles to structure what he called "the science of a legislator" (WN 468). These principles are of very different kinds, however. Only the principles of justice, according to Smith, can be rendered fully precise. The other tasks of government will always depend to some extent on a grasp of changing empirical details: on the skills, therefore, not just of "the legislator," but of "that insidious and crafty animal, vulgarly called a statesman or politician" (468).

We'll focus in this chapter on what Smith means by justice.

9.1 Justice in TMS

In Part II of TMS, Smith singles out justice as a virtue that is essential to the maintenance of society. Beneficence, he says, "is the orna-ment which embellishes the building [of human society]," while justice is "the main pillar that upholds the whole edifice." If justice is removed, "the great, the immense fabric of society … must in a moment crumble into atoms." Without justice, people "would, like wild beasts, be at all times ready to fly upon [one another]," and "a man would enter an assembly of men as he enters a den of lions" (TMS 86). Such a war of all against all would destroy everything we hold dear—destroy the conditions necessary for developing benefi-cence, among other things. Virtues are possible only in society, so if justice is necessary to society, it is necessary to all virtue. There is an asymmetry, then, between justice and all other virtues: we must enforce justice, even if we do not enforce any other virtue. Smith calls this asymmetry the basis of "that remarkable distinction between justice and all the other social virtues" (80), which he says has recently been insisted upon by "an author of very great and ori-ginal genius" (presumably Hume, but he may mean Lord Kames).[5]

Justice is so important because it is the virtue that prevents us from inflicting "real and positive hurt" on one another (TMS 79). We can survive in a society in which there is an abundance of greed or laziness or intemperance, or a dearth of kindness and gratitude. A society like this would be unpleasant, and were we to live in one, or were the society we presently live in begin to deteriorate into such a condition, we would surely rebuke our neighbours for their selfishness or nastiness, and perhaps form groups to counteract the vice around us. But we could do such things only as long as there remained a social framework—a "fabric of society"—in which rebuke, and group formation, could go on. Were we all constantly inflicting "real and positive hurt" on one another, were it as dangerous to meet fellow human beings as to walk into a lions' den, we could not rebuke anyone, much less organize social groups to combat vice. Fortunately, Smith says, nature has outfitted us with a tool to prevent us from constantly inflicting harm on one another: resentment, which we feel both on our own behalf when we are injured and on other people's behalf when they are injured (79–80). Resentment is a sentiment that leads us to take revenge for injuries. So if you commit an injury, you can expect that everyone who learns of the injury (not just the injured person him or herself) will seek to inflict a similar pain on you. This is the origin of the idea of punishment. Smith takes justice to be a virtue that regularizes punishment, striving to ensure both that every injurer is punished, and that punishment is inflicted only upon injurers, and only in accordance with the degree of injury inflicted. Justice thereby prevents us both from inflicting unprovoked harm on one another, and from inflicting undeserved or excessive punishment on those whom we suspect of having inflicted unprovoked harm.[6] Justice thereby reduces, and ideally eliminates, the violence that could destroy society.

Four things to note about this account of justice. First, it presupposes that all human beings have a notion of "real and positive hurt." Second, it presupposes that the alternative to systems of justice is a Hobbesian state of war. Third, it presents justice as dealing only with violence and its prevention. Finally, it implicitly presents justice as a virtue that reflects human equality: everyone equally resents, and is equally worthy of protection from, real and positive hurt.

Each of these points requires some elaboration. I'll set the first of them aside for a while—it is the most problematic feature of Smith's account of justice and will occupy us for much of this chapter—but take up the others in order.

9.2 Smith and Hobbes

Smith's language for a world without justice readily evokes Hobbes. When he tells us that without justice we "would, like wild beasts, be at all times ready to fly upon [one another]," it is hard not to be put in mind of the war of all against all that Hobbes says we would be in if it were not for government. But there are crucial differences between Smith and Hobbes on this topic.

In the first place, for Hobbes the only way of ending our natural state of war is to set up a government, which can use its powers to prevent us from harming each other. For Smith, what stops us from killing each other is a natural tendency to feel vicarious resentment on behalf of any innocent person who is injured, which results in our ganging together to prevent such violence, or to punish those who inflict it:

> When one man attacks, or robs, or attempts to murder another, all the neighbours take the alarm, and think that they do right when they run, either to revenge the person who has been injured, or to defend him who is in danger of being so.
>
> (TMS 81)

This is more like Locke's view of the state of nature than Hobbes's— much more like Locke's, as we'll see shortly—although the natural principle that limits violence, for Smith, is a set of sentiments rather than Locke's rational law of nature.[7] What Smith wants to stress is just that beneficence is not the right sentiment to do the job of preventing violence. Our feelings of beneficence, especially to anonymous strangers, are not strong enough to keep us from inflicting harm on one another:

> Men, although naturally sympathetic, feel so little for another, with whom they have no particular connexion, in comparison of what they feel for themselves; ... they have it so much in their power to hurt [each other] and may have so many temptations to do so, that if [the terror of punishment] did not stand up within them in [every individual's] defence, ... they would, like wild beasts, be at all times ready to fly upon him.
>
> (TMS 86)

Unlike Hobbes, Smith allows that we feel some basic inclination to help one another, and that our feelings for those with whom we have a "particular connexion" may well be stronger than the selfish interests that would lead us to harm them, but he thinks these feelings are not enough to prevent harm in any society that extends beyond a close-knit kin group. What does keep us from destroying each other, even in large societies, is "those terrors of merited punishment which attend upon [the] violation [of justice]" (86). So we don't need *government* to maintain a basic societal peace—we don't need a formal system, with a monopoly on the legitimate use of violence. We just need to act on our natural sense that innocent people should not be subjected to real and positive hurt, and that those who inflict such hurt should be punished.

The major political implication of this difference between Smith and Hobbes is that for Smith, as for Locke, attempts to bring down a government need not be a disaster. Societies need some way of punishing people for inflicting harm on others, but there are ways of doing this without government. It is therefore not true that any government is better than none; a harshly oppressive government can be worse than none at all. Smith's support for the rebellious American colonists—who appealed in part to Locke to justify their rebellion—should not be surprising.

But the most interesting philosophical difference between Smith and both Hobbes and Locke[8] on the subject of justice is that Smith sees justice as directed first to the protection of each *individual* and only secondarily to the protection of *society*. For Smith, the sentiment that grounds justice is vicarious resentment at injuries done to innocent individuals, and it is only because we are inclined to act on that sentiment—only because "the neighbours [will] take the alarm and ... run to revenge the person who has been injured, or to defend him who is in danger of being so"—that society can be kept from falling into Hobbes's war of all against all. And the laws and institutions that arise from this feature of our nature are also designed in the first instance to protect individuals and only indirectly to protect society. Smith's anti-utilitarian streak appears again here. He notes that his predecessors had, with some reason, understood the purpose of justice to be the good of society as a whole: "As society cannot subsist unless the laws of justice are tolerably observed," he says, "… the consideration of this necessity, it has been thought, was the ground upon which we approved of the enforcement of the laws of justice by the punishment of those who violated them." This thought is mistaken, however:

> [I]t is not a regard to the preservation of society, which originally interests us in the punishment of crimes committed against individuals … The concern which we take in the fortune and happiness of individuals does not, in common cases, arise from that which we take in the fortune and happiness of society.
>
> (TMS 86–9)

From the perspective of theorists of justice, and perhaps from God's perspective, the purpose ("final cause") of systems of justice is the preservation of society (87–8). But from the perspective of each of us in ordinary life, these systems, and the sentiments that underpin them, aim at protecting individuals. It's just that protecting individuals from harming each other will itself prevent the random violence, and/or constant feuds, that would otherwise tear societies apart.

9.3 Distributive justice

The third point we noted above was that Smith seems to regard justice as a virtue whose sole job is to protect us from injury by the others. But is justice so limited? Are there not also aspects of justice that require governments to provide certain goods to all: distributive or social justice, as we call these requirements today?

It is tempting to return a simple "no" to these questions, as far as Smith is concerned. Smith tells us explicitly that only "commutative justice"—the kind of justice that protects us from violence—"may be extorted by force." By contrast, "distributive justice" belongs "to a system of moralls" that does "not fall under the jurisdiction of the laws" (LJ 9; see also TMS 269). Several scholars have used this passage to show that Smith "excluded" the aspects of justice that involve helping poor people from the proper mandate of government.[9] But these scholarly claims rest on two misunderstandings.

In the first place, Smith does not use the phrase "distributive justice" in our modern sense, which has to do with government responsibilities to the poor. That sense did not exist in his day.[10] Instead, he takes over the phrase from a tradition, rooted in Aristotle and passed down via figures like Grotius, Pufendorf, and Hutcheson, in which it meant "charity" or "generosity," as he explicitly tells us (TMS 270; LJ 9). To say that "distributive justice" in this sense should not be enforced is then just to say that people should not be forced to give charity, or to treat their friends and family generously. The very essence of these virtues, Pufendorf and Hutcheson and Smith believed, depends on the kind intentions behind them. So carrying out their offices out of compulsion would nullify what is good about them. It by no means follows that governments must never force us to pay taxes that will be used for the benefit of the poor. It follows only that paying those taxes will not demonstrate our charity or generosity: our "distributive justice" in the sense that Smith uses that phrase.

And in the second place, to say that Smith "excludes" what today we call distributive justice from the virtue that must be enforced by governments is to imply that earlier thinkers had included this category in their political thought. But that is not true. There were few provisions to help the poor in pre-modern legal systems—the welfare state is a development of the nineteenth and twentieth centuries—and what provisions there were tended to be justified either by considerations of utility (giving the poor food and shelter would keep them from turning to crime) or by what Smith calls commutative justice, not distributive justice. Thomas Aquinas formulated a "right of necessity" by which the poor were conceived to have a property right in whatever they needed to survive. A failure to provide them with these basic needs was therefore a violation of their property rights: an "injury" or "real and positive hurt" in the sense that Smith regards as relevant to commutative justice. This idea was carried over in the political philosophies of Grotius, Pufendorf, and Hutcheson and widely used to justify the appropriation of granaries by poor people in times of famine.[11] Smith shares the belief of his predecessors in the "right of necessity." He talks about it rarely, but when he does, he agrees that there is such a right and that it is rightly invoked by poor people who take over granaries in a famine.[12] He therefore sees some provision for the needs of the poor as a matter of commutative justice.

In addition, Smith allows for the enforcement of even what he calls "distributive justice"—duties of beneficence—to some degree:

> The civil magistrate is entrusted with the power not only of preserving the public peace by restraining injustice, but of promoting the prosperity of the commonwealth, by establishing good discipline, and by discouraging every sort of vice and impropriety; he may prescribe rules, therefore, which not only prohibit mutual injuries among fellow-citizens, but command mutual good offices to a certain degree.
>
> (TMS 81)

It is unclear what the scope of these "mutual good offices" might be, but one example Smith gives is the duty of "parents to maintain their children, and children to maintain their parents."[13] Smith says that a failure to enforce some of these good offices "exposes the commonwealth to many gross disorders and shocking enormities." And it is readily imaginable that the neglect of young children and elderly parents, in societies that have few welfare protections, might count as a "gross disorder" or "shocking enormity."

But whatever the exact range of examples Smith might have in mind, the fact that he is talking about one-on-one acts of kindness should help clarify the much quoted but much misunderstood end of the paragraph I have been quoting. Its final sentences read:

> Of all the duties of a law-giver, however, [the enforcement of duties of beneficence], perhaps, is that which it requires the greatest delicacy and reserve to execute with propriety and judgment. To neglect it altogether exposes the commonwealth to many gross disorders and shocking enormities, and to push it too far is destructive of all liberty, security, and justice.
>
> (TMS 81)

Opponents of activist government seize on this passage with delight, as proof that Smith thought that anything more than minimal government aid to the poor "is destructive of all liberty, security, and justice." But Smith is not here talking about government programmes that help the poor, or the taxes that may support those programmes.[14] He is talking about using government power to compel citizens to express a virtue—to compel them to perform acts that should properly come from character traits that they develop freely. Smith speaks a few paragraphs earlier of "that remarkable difference between justice and all the other *social virtues*" (80, my emphasis)—the difference being that only (commutative) justice should be enforced—and identifies "distributive justice" with these other "social virtues" (270). A virtue, however, for Smith as for every virtue theorist before him, is an excellence of an individual that is expressed primarily in that person's intentions and only derivatively in his or her acts. So the observance of most virtues should be "left to the freedom of our own wills" (79). To enforce virtues other than commutative justice will be a serious threat to our liberty, which itself would constitute an injustice. Only commutative justice, because it is necessary for society to survive (which in turn is a condition for our being able to act freely), should be enforced. The point here has to do with governments trying to take charge of the kind of people we become, not with the institutions they may set up and run.

Once we see that Smith is talking about virtues rather than institutions in the chapter of TMS we have been discussing, the argument of that chapter as a whole becomes clear. A violation of "proper beneficence" is blamable, Smith says in its opening paragraphs, but should not be punished; a violation of (commutative) justice—an act of violence—is by contrast punishable. He then develops this point as follows:

> Even the most ordinary degree of kindness or beneficence … cannot, among equals be extorted by force. Among equals each individual is naturally, and antecedent to the institution of civil government, regarded as having a right both to defend himself from injuries, and to exact a certain degree of punishment for those which have been done to him. Every generous spectator not only approves of his conduct when he does this, but he enters so far into his sentiments as often to be willing to assist him. When one man attacks, or robs, or attempts to murder

another, all the neighbours take the alarm, and think they do right when they run, either to revenge the person who has been injured, or to defend him who is in danger of being so.

(TMS 80, my emphasis)

Smith identifies living "among equals," here, with a condition "antecedent to the institution of civil government." So although Smith (like and probably following Hume) does not believe that a "state of nature" of the sort that Hobbes and Locke describe ever existed, he uses the idea of a state of nature to conduct a thought experiment: he asks us to think about whether we would regard one another as having a right to enforce various virtues if we were all equal in authority and power to one another, if we had no "civil government" above us. And he says that we would, even in this condition, grant one another the right to enforce justice. Not only would "every generous spectator" approve of the use of force to prevent or punish injuries, but all our neighbours would "take the alarm" and join us in that use of force. This is a very Lockean point. Locke makes much of the fact that "everyone has the executive power of the law of nature": that in the state of nature—which he also calls a "state of perfect equality"—everyone can use force to prevent or punish violence, whether or not he or she is a victim of that violence. Locke says that "this will seem a very strange doctrine to some men," but argues that such a general right to prevent violence both makes sense in itself and explains why legal systems, the world over, take themselves to apply even to "strangers" who act violently in their jurisdictions.[15] So in granting that our neighbours will join us in protecting ourselves against violence, even without civil government, Smith is accepting Locke's "very strange doctrine": he is probably alluding to it. The one difference between Smith and Locke in this regard is that Locke attributes the "law of nature" that forbids us from injuring one another to our reason, while Smith regards our feeling of resentment, not our reason, as the basis of our granting one another rights against injury.

Now when we bear in mind this Lockean background to the paragraph about enforcing justice "among equals," it should be clear that when Smith begins the next paragraph by talking about "a superior," who is also described a few lines later as "the civil magistrate" and a few lines after that as "the sovereign" (TMS 81), he is simply following Locke in moving from the state of nature to a condition in which there is civil government. The "superior" in question is superior over us just as regards authority and power. And where there is such a superior, Smith says, it is no longer true that only justice can be enforced. On the contrary, once a government has been established, it can "with universal approbation" require us "to behave ... with a certain degree of propriety to one another." The legal systems of "all civilized governments" require parents to take care of their young children and children to take care of their elderly parents. And they *should* do this, Smith thinks. Once power comes to be used to enforce justice, it can be used to enforce other social virtues as well. It is "blamable" to disobey sovereigns in general, even when what they command is morally indifferent, so of course it is blamable to disobey them when they command us to do things that we should do, morally, in any case. It is just that this enforcement of morality, if "push[ed] too far," may become "destructive of all liberty, security and justice." Smith is concerned about the surveillance and moral corruption, on the part of the government, and fear and resentment on the part of their subjects, that come of political regimes that try to make their citizens virtuous (think of Savonarola, or of oppressive Puritan communities in early America). He is not talking about governments setting up institutions that help provide their poorer citizens with shelter, food, or other items of welfare.

9.4 Equality

Smith's treatment of justice as an individual virtue does have some implications for how we think about what we call "social justice," however. That is because it presupposes that all human beings are fundamentally equal, and that that equality should be enshrined in law. This is the fourth of the points mentioned above that I wanted to discuss.

Some recent commentators have argued that there is a notion of fundamental human equality built into Smith's entire approach to morality.[16] By taking up your perspective in sympathy, they say, and assuming that you can take up mine, I presuppose that we are fundamentally the same kind of being, and by caring for you on the basis of that sympathy, I presuppose that we are equally worthy of being cared for. Human equality is thus built into Smith's methodology.

This is a clever and appealing reading of Smith, but it is not an obvious one and Smith does not explicitly lay out his account of sympathy, or care, in this way.[17] He does, however, twice insist on a basic human equality when discussing justice. "In the race for wealth, and honours, and preferments," he says, a person "may run as hard as he can, and strain every nerve and every muscle, in order to outstrip his competitors." But "if he should justle, or throw down any of them, the indulgence of the spectators is entirely at an end. It is a violation of fair play, which they cannot admit of." Why not? Because "This man is to them, in every respect, as good as he; they do not enter into that self-love by which he prefers himself so much to this other." A similar phrase occurs in a later chapter, in which Smith is speculating on why, since we would lose little sleep over the deaths of a hundred million people in a far-off land (China, in his example), we would nevertheless be horrified at the idea of actually bringing about those deaths ourselves. What makes our "active principles" so much more generous to others than our "passive feelings"? The answer is not "that feeble spark of benevolence that Nature has lighted up in the human heart," says Smith, but "reason, principle, conscience," which call to us "that we are but one of the multitude, in no respect better than any other in it." And when we ignore this basic equality between ourselves and everyone else, "we become the proper objects of resentment." But "proper resentment" is the response called up in us by injustice. Smith goes on, a few lines later, to describe what "reason, principle, conscience" shows us, when it reminds us that we are "in no respect better than any other" in the multitude: "the deformity of injustice," he says, "the deformity of doing ... injury to another" (TMS 83). So the paradigmatic violation of fundamental human equality, for Smith, would seem to be injustice.[18]

This makes good sense, given what else Smith says about justice. Human beings are not equal in talents and virtues—the things that make for "wealth and honour and preferments"—or in the expensiveness of their tastes or their capacity to enjoy various goods. But we are equal in our susceptibility to "real and positive hurt." And the rules that forbid inflicting such hurt are rules that we normally formulate in a universal manner, applying indifferently to everyone. Since reason, for Smith, is the faculty that comes up with and applies rules (TMS 319), it also makes sense that reason is the faculty that prevents us from inflicting harm on distant others, in the passage on deaths in China. The rules forbidding harm to anyone are rules that implicitly represent everyone as equal: equally worthy of the respect, at least, that forbids us from harming them.

But it is this insight that proponents of social justice invoke when they call for laws and institutions ensuring that poor people have equal access to housing and education and health care, or an equal starting point in the socio-economic realm. (Smith's metaphor of a "race" for wealth and social status, in the passage quoted above, readily calls up the notion of equal starting points.) We might say that these activists regard poverty itself, or some of its appurtenances, as a "harm," a "real and positive hurt," that no-one should have to undergo. Or we could say that they extend the idea of equality such that what human beings equally deserve is not just protection from harm but the enjoyment of certain basic goods: a certain level of well-being.

Smith himself does not say either of these things, but at several points in WN he does indicate that societies are fairer when they ensure the well-being of the poor. "It is but equity," he says, "that they who feed, cloath and lodge the whole body of the people, should have such a share of the produce of their own labour as to be themselves tolerably well fed, cloathed and lodged" (WN 96). He also suggests that luxury vehicles should pay a higher road toll than freight vehicles so that "the indolence and vanity of the rich [can be] made to contribute to the relief of the poor" (725). And he says it is reasonable for rich people to pay proportionally higher taxes than the poor (842).

We should bear in mind that there were no proponents of social justice in Smith's day; the very notion was to be developed after he died. Instead, the vast majority of writers on poverty, among Smith's predecessors and contemporaries, maintained that poor people needed to be kept poor: either because they would not work other-wise, or because a division of ranks, in which poor people can look up to the wealthy as guides and role models, is divinely or naturally ordained. I have argued elsewhere that Smith is one of the first writers on poverty to argue against these views. In WN, Smith presents poor people both as naturally inclined to be hard-working and as virtuous, without any need for guidance from the rich.[19] This image of the poor was a startling novelty in Smith's day, and did much to pave the way, I believe, for the later rise of the notion of social or distributive justice.[20]

It should in any case be clear that nothing in Smith's account of justice rules out government aid for poor people, and even more clear that justice is for Smith, as for modern proponents of social justice, rooted in the basic equality in worth of all human beings. It is justice that expresses our belief that we are "in no respect better than any other" human being.

9.5 "Real and positive hurt"

Let's turn now to the question I have thus far set aside: what exactly does "injury" mean? What does Smith mean by "real and positive hurt"?

This question is both extremely difficult to resolve and crucial to Smith's account of justice. For only if we can delineate quite precisely what belongs under "real and positive hurt" can we come up with strict, exceptionless laws to prohibit it, and only if we can carry out this delineation without adverting to local history and customs can we come up with universal principles of justice: principles that hold across all nations. Coming up with such strict and universal principles is however the core of Smith's ambition, when he sets out to develop what he calls a "natural jurisprudence."

A number of philosophers have suggested that human beings do universally share a notion of harm, and that that notion can be sharply delineated.[21] Surely everyone, everywhere, recognizes murder and battery and torture to be grave harms? Even if we disagree vigorously over what makes for a good human life, surely we can agree that these things are bad.

But it is not altogether clear that we agree, universally, over what counts as murder or battery or torture. (Is it murder if I kill you in a duel? how about if you were in bed with my spouse?) And even if we grant that there is a large degree of overlap in the definition of these things across cultures and times, we will have a lot more trouble finding cross-cultural agreement about harms that go beyond our bodies. But Smith, like most jurisprudential theorists, explicitly regards harm to property and reputation, as well as harms to the body, to be "real and positive hurt"—violations of justice (LJ 8, 399). It is however clearly not the case that all human beings, everywhere, agree even roughly on what counts as a harm to a person's property or reputation.

Smith's moral philosophy is also particularly ill-suited to the idea that there can be universally recognizable harms, especially as regards property and reputation. As we have seen, the process of moral judgment begins for Smith with our internalizing the norms and attitudes of our loved ones and neighbours, while trying to apply them in an impartial and well-informed manner. It is possible that we can show some of these norms and attitudes to be based on bad information or bias, but it is not easy to see how we would discern that: our paradigmatic moral judgments, on Smith's model, will be heavily shaped by our cultural and historical context. If harsh coming of age rituals, or gladiatorial contests, are an everyday part of life in our tribe or town, we will have a hard time perceiving them as "injurious," in the justiciable sense. And even if some baseline of bodily harm might horrify the impartial spectator in every society, it is hard to imagine how a Smithian impartial spectator, working out from the occurrent norms in his or her society, could determine the point at which one product amounts to the theft of intellectual property from the makers of another product, or decide whether beaches can be private property or not. The same goes for the many fine questions that can be raised about offenses to reputation. Is calling someone gay or a Jew insulting, if they are not? How about saying, incorrectly, that an unmarried woman has lost her virginity? (This was a grave insult to a woman's reputation, in Smith's time). It seems unlikely that there are universal answers to questions like these, and even if there are, it is hard to see how one could generate them from Smith's impartial-spectator procedure.[22]

Nevertheless, a number of commentators have suggested that Smith has a notion of real and positive hurt that is meant to transcend cultural boundaries. Knud Haakonssen says that "some situations involving injury are so basic to human life that the spectator's verdicts will always be recognizably similar" (SL 148). Fonna Forman is less confident of this, but she does explore the possibility that, for Smith, "harm ... is universalizable."[23]

Haakonssen's interpretation of Smithian justice depends heavily on Smith's repeated description of pain as more "pungent" than pleasure, and of our sympathy with pain as correspondingly more pungent than our sympathy with pleasure (TMS 44, 45, 121–2, 296). This accounts for both the precision and the universality of rules of justice, says Haakonssen: "The rules of justice are precise because they are derived from spectator reactions which are unusually 'universal' and 'distinct,' namely the 'pungent' feeling of sympathetic resentment occasioned by 'real and positive hurt'" (SL 86; see also 83–7). But one feeling can be more pungent than another without being either more universal or more distinct. I can feel an intense anguish upon hearing a story that recalls a lost love to me, without that reaction being either something that other people are likely to share or something whose causes, contours, and duration is entirely clear to me. I can also feel a mild, not at all pungent, pleasure in seeing the sun come out that is both perfectly "distinct" to me—I know exactly what I am feeling and why—and, possibly, universalizable. The same goes for my sympathetic pleasures and pains. I may feel a strong sympathy with a pain you are experiencing even though that pain, and my sympathy with it, is inchoate and depends on quirky, non-universalizable circumstances that you and I happen to share. And I may feel a clear and readily universalizable sympathy with a pleasure that you are experiencing (perhaps in the sun coming out) even though that pleasure is not at all pungent. Pungency does not vary with either distinctness or universality, and there is no obvious reason, of either a philosophical or a textual kind, to attribute a belief that these things are linked to Smith.[24] Indeed, Haakonssen admits that Smith himself "never spells out his explanation" of the precision and universality that he attributes to rules of justice. The idea that the "pungency" of pain explains these features is Haakonssen's own proposal (SL 86).

I think that Smith makes an interesting attempt to bring the universality of rules of justice together with their cultural and historical situatedness in LJ that does not rely on any appeal to pungency.

He also offers suggestions there, which do not draw on pungency, about why the laws of justice need to be precise. I don't think his arguments in these regards entirely work, but they are worth exploring. And they are more nuanced, and better integrated with his overall moral views, than the argument from pungency that Haakonssen proposes.

9.6 The precision of justice

To begin with precision:

Smith tells us in LJ that clear and precise laws of justice protect people against the potential arbitrariness of judges. He sees a regularized system of punishment, with courts determining guilt and meting out punishment, as fairer and more effective than the gangs of "neighbours" that, following Locke, he imagines as performing this function "antecedent to the institution of civil government."[25] But he also thinks that judges or courts unrestrained by clear and precise laws can be very unfair. "Courts at their first institution have allways taken great liberties," says Smith, and to "a rude people" their authority appears "altogether insufferable": "the judge is necessary and yet is of all things the most terrible" (LJ 287, 314). "At the first establishment of judges," Smith thinks, "... every one trusts to the naturall feeling of justice he has in his own breast and expects to find in others." But this feeling varies greatly from person to person, and people live in "terror" of how their judges might rule. The only cure for this situation is "to establish laws and rules which may ascertain [the judge's] conduct ... for when it is known in what manner he is to proceed the terror will be in a great measure removed" (LJ 314). These laws and rules may be established either by a legislature or by a history of precedents (see LJ 287), but in order to ensure that someone subject to them can "ascertain" what she will be held liable for in advance, they need to be clear and exact. Only then can people subject to those laws plan their actions freely, tailoring their behaviour in advance to the contours of what is permitted to them. The precision of a legal system thus secures liberty to its subjects. Smith praises the English legal system, after it had evolved from its initial form, for this reason: "[T]he liberty of the subjects was secured in England by the great accuracy and precision of the law and decisions given upon it" (LJ 282). And he says expressly that the importance of this accuracy and precision lies in the restraint it puts upon the power of judges:

> [A]n other thing which greatly confirms the liberty of the subjects in England … was the little power of the judges in explaining, altering or extending or correcting the meaning of the laws, and the great exactness with which they must be observed according to the literall meaning of the words.[26]
>
> (LJ 275)

So the most explicit argument that Smith makes for the need for law to be precise depends on the need for those subject to the law to be able to predict how it will be applied. This is an argument that resonates with old and deeply entrenched intuitions about justice: it has long seemed unfair and oppressive, to natural law theorists in the West as well as their counterparts in other legal traditions, for people to be punished for actions they did not know were punishable in advance.[27] We can also integrate Smith's point here with his belief that justice expresses the fundamental equality we attribute to human beings, the sense in which we are "in no respect better" than anyone else. A legal system in which each judge makes up her own mind about how to interpret "the naturall feeling of justice" is one in which friends and close kin of the judge are likely to be favoured over others—are likely, even if the judge strives for impartiality, to "ascertain" better what her "naturall feeling" will lead her to decide. Equality requires that everyone have the same ability to figure out what they are likely to be punished for, however, so a system run by "accurate and precise" laws will satisfy this feature of justice better than one that puts it into the hands of individual judges.[28]

Note that these grounds for demanding accuracy and precision of laws of justice do not also give us reason to expect a single set of laws, or even a single way of generating laws, for all nations. If the precision of justice is a formal constraint on whatever laws happen to be enforced in a society, then the content of those laws can vary widely. A particular act (e.g., distributing one's wealth equally to one's children, instead of favouring one's oldest son) may be counted as a harm in one set of laws while the opposite of that act is counted as a harm in another set of laws. Yet so long as both laws are equally precise, they could be equally just.

This point has vast implications, both philosophically and practically. Philosophically, it matters greatly for the shape of Smith's jurisprudence whether the universal features of justice are formal ones, like the exactitude in formulating laws that he stresses in the passages I have cited from LJ, or substantive ones, like the restrictions on a particular set of harms that Haakonssen thinks we can derive from TMS. Practically, Smith's usefulness to a hard-libertarian view of property depends in good part on whether he can be read as a defender of the view that depriving people of their private property is always a harm. If Smith means to rule out a particular list of harms as unjust, and if depriving me of my ownership of a type or amount of property is included on that list, then laws mandating that I give up that property will be universally unjust, for him. If *any* clearly formulated and promulgated law will meet Smith's "precision" requirement, by contrast, then even a law confiscating all capital property could be just, and certainly many lesser modes of transferring property from the rich to the poor will pass muster.

I think it is clear that Smith is insisting on the second of these things, not the first, when he argues that laws of justice need to be precise. Insofar as he would object to laws re-distributing property—and he probably would object to a confiscation of all capital goods, although not to every form of re-distribution from rich to poor—it would not be on grounds of justice, and certainly not on the grounds of the precision of justice.[29] But I am not going to deal further with this practical point. The more important takeaway, for our purposes, is that the "universal" features of justice that Smith draws out in LJ, if his account of precision is any guide, seem to be formal ones, not substantive ones.

9.7 The universality of justice

With that thought in mind, let's turn to how Smith moves, more generally, between the universal and the variable features of justice in LJ. We will see again and again that the universal principles that

Smith proposes are formal ones, the content of which he expects to be filled in differently, in different cultural and historical settings. Smith's emphasis in these lectures is indeed on the cultural and historical aspects of law. Much of LJ consists of a quick sketch of what Smith calls the "originall or foundation from which [rights] arise" (LJ 13)—the purportedly universal basis of concepts like property, contract, punishment, or marriage—followed by an extensive survey of how these principles have played out in various historical contexts, with little further mention of the "originall."

In justifying the "originall" of property, Smith largely re-works an argument to be found in Locke, with the help of his own impartial-spectator theory of morality. He attempts to justify the basic ways in which people claim property, for example, by saying that an impartial spectator would agree with Locke that an apple becomes my property once I pull it from a hitherto unowned tree:

> The first thing to be attended to is how ... it is that a man by pulling an apple should be imagined to have a right to that apple and a power of excluding all others from it — and that an injury should be conceived to be done when such a subject is taken for the possessor. From the system I have already explain'd [in the lecture course that provided the basis for TMS, which students in the jurisprudence course would have attended], you will remember that I told you we may conceive an injury was done one when an impartial spectator would be of opinion that he was injured, would join with him in his concern and go along with him when he defend[ed] the subject in his possession against any violent attack, or used force to recover what had been thus wrongfully wrested out of his hands. This would be the case in the abovementioned circumstances. The spectator would justify the first possessor in defending and even in avenging himself when injured ... The cause of this sympathy or concurrence betwixt the spectator and the possessor is, that he enters into his thoughts and concurrs in his opinion that he may form a reasonable expectation of using the fruit or whatever it is in what manner he pleases. ... The spectator goes along with him in this expectation, but he can not enter into the designs of him who would take the goods from the 1st

possessor. The reasonable expectation therefore which the first possessor furnishes is the ground on which the right of property is acquired by occupation.

(LJ 16–7)

Note that there is no appeal here to Locke's notorious idea that I somehow mix my labour with the apple by pulling it off the tree, nor to the law of nature that, for Locke, vindicates his labour-mixing theory. Instead, all the work in Smith's account is done by appeal to how an impartial spectator would react to a scenario in which one person comes into first physical possession of an object, and another tries to take it from him. Smith proposes that the impartial spectator will enter sympathetically into the thoughts, opinions, and expectations of the first possessor—that *we*, imagining this scene impartially, will enter into these thoughts and expectations—but not into the "designs" of one who would take the apple away from that possessor. There is not much argument here, but the proposal does seem intuitively plausible. Barring an elaborate twist on the facts as Smith describes them,[30] most people will probably agree with him.

But the scenario described here justifies property only in previously unowned things that are now physically in someone's possession. This is a minuscule subset of what we generally think of as property.[31] In addition, the aspect of the scenario that interests Smith, as the lectures go on, is simply the link between property and "reasonable expectations." Property in general, for Smith, depends on whether we can reasonably expect exclusive rights to use a thing or not. After treating of first possession, he goes on to invoke reasonable expectation—defined, again, as the expectation of an impartial spectator—as the basis of our right to property by way of prescription (long possession):

[I]n the same manner as the spectator can enter into the expectations of the 1st occupant that he will have the use of the thing occupied, and think he is injured by those who would wrest it from him ..., the right of prescription is derived from the opinion of the spectator that the possessor of a long standing has a just expectation that he may use what has been possessed,

and that the form<er> proprietor ... has so far lost all right
to it, has no expectation of using it, as that it would appear
injurious in him to deprive the present possessor.

(LJ 32)

Smith invokes reasonable expectation yet again when he comes to the
foundation of contract law. A mere declaration of intention cannot
establish a contract, says Smith. Only an express promise, uttered
with the intention that the hearer will depend on that promise, can
do that: "The expectation and dependence of the promittee that he
shall obtain what was promised is hear [sic] altogether reasonable,
and such as an impartial spectator would readily go along with."[32]

Now what exactly makes an expectation "reasonable" Smith does
not say, other than that it is what the impartial spectator would take
to be reasonable, and one might protest that both what counts as
reasonable and the reactions of an impartial spectator are likely to
vary across cultural contexts. I don't see how Smith can deny that,
but his point seems to be just that a legitimate claim on property
must depend on whatever each culture, in each historical period,
counts as a "reasonable expectation," or the expectation of an impartial spectator, to the exclusive use of a thing. This formal point is
then the element of universal justice that cuts across cultures and
time periods, not the specific content that a reliance on reasonable
expectations, in each society, might yield.

Reading Smith this way enables us to make sense of why he
devotes the bulk of his discussion in LJ to the differences between
modes of property acquisition across cultures and time periods,
rather than to the "originalls" that ground the claim of each of these
modes to moral legitimacy. For in fact Smith grants all the variability
in regimes of property rights that a historian or cultural anthropologist might insist on. Indeed, his jurisprudence is one of the
sources of the so-called "stadial theory of history," by which the
legal structure of a society, as regards property rights, familial rights
and governance, inevitably varies with its socio-economic system.
Hunter-gatherer societies recognize individual property rights in
very few things, for Smith, require parents to do much less for their
children than later societies do, and have fairly egalitarian systems
of governance (LJ 107, 172; WN 709, 712–3). Pastoral societies are

far more hierarchical, and grant extensive property rights to their chieftains, while abjuring property in land. Property in land comes on the scene only with agricultural societies: Smith calls this mode of property "the greatest extention it has undergone" (LJ 23). And agricultural societies develop feudal hierarchies, in which vassals owe economic goods to their lords in return for military protection, which commercial societies tend to dissolve.

There is a lot more to be said about the interlocking legal, socio-economic and political differences between these societal stages, and the very idea that societies go through these stages. The stadial theory was to become very influential, and Smith played a major role in its development.[33] The merits and demerits of the stadial theory as an account of history do not matter much, however, for the purposes of a book on Smith as a philosopher. What does matter for our purposes is that Smith recognizes that property rights are not simply derived from an *a priori* "originall," but are "extended" to cover whatever practices each society finds it reasonable to recognize, as establishing exclusive use to things, given its historical and socio-economic context. Abstract and universalizable moral concerns thus do not do the bulk of the work in determining property rights, for Smith; they are, and must be, supplemented by historical factors. To be sure, Smith will sometimes say that "there can be no reason in equity" (LJ 24) for a particular legal enactment (here, a law forbidding people from hunting on their own grounds unless they have a certain amount of wealth) or describe a mode of inheritance as not being "founded in the nature of things" (LJ 42). He also decries primogeniture, in both LJ and WN, as "contrary to nature, to reason, and to justice" (LJ 49; see also LJ 69–70; WN 383–5). But on the whole he seems to accept the customs and laws that societies actually give rise to as not just the actual but the proper standard by which to adjudicate disputes over what should count as property. For Smith, as later for Hegel, right works primarily through history, not through *a priori* reasoning.

9.8 Principles and history

Smith's treatment of other aspects of justice in LJ follows much the same pattern as his treatment of property. He deals with punishment too, for instance, by way of a brief discussion of its moral basis followed by an extended treatment of its history. "[T]he measure of the punishment to be inflicted on the delinquent," Smith tells us, "is the concurrence of the impartial spectator with the resentment of the injured." Only a punishment that "the spectator would concur with the offended person in exacting" will "appear[...] equitable in the eyes of the rest of mankind" (LJ 104).[34] Smith proposes this standard for just punishment as an alternative to the utilitarian one put forward by Grotius and his followers, saying that "consideration of the publick good" can justify punishments that most of humankind will regard as grossly unjust. He gives the example of a seventeenth-century British law establishing the death penalty for exporting wool. Even on the assumption, which he does not accept but grants to make his point, that "the wealth and strength of the nation" might depend on its woollen trade, and that the flourishing of that trade could be hurt by exporting wool, such a penalty was so clearly unjust in the eyes of the British people that the government "could get neither jury nor informers" to enforce the law (LJ 105). Smith takes this as evidence that utilitarian considerations cannot vindicate the punishment of a crime unless that punishment also matches up with the resentment an impartial spectator would feel on behalf of the crime's victims. He does allow, briefly and uncomfortably, that there may be some exceptions to this rule, but he gives only one such exception—the sentinel who falls asleep on his watch—and stresses that the principle of impartial resentment that normally guides just punishment tracks the injury done to individuals, not to society as a whole.[35]

Once again Smith's principle for just punishment is a formal one, which is open to widely varying implementation in varying cultural and historical contexts. Indeed, after the short consideration of the "originall" of punishment, Smith spends the rest of this and the following lecture on punishment (34 pages in the student notes, as opposed to 2 pages on the "originall") going through the history of punishment in various nations. In the course of this history, he does at several points advert to the basic principle he has established, suggesting in particular that capital punishment for theft (common in Britain, at Smith's time) is unjust: "The punishment which is commonly inflicted on theft is certainly not at all proportionable to the crime. It is greatly too severe, and such as the resentment of the injured person would not require" (LJ 128). He also indicates that societies often start by inflicting either too mild or too harsh a punishment on a particular crime, but that their modes of punishment adjust over time to the standard of the impartial spectator's resentment (see LJ 106–9, 121, 129–31). But on the whole he not merely accepts but stresses the fact that societies in different historical circumstances, with different power structures and different economies, will develop different systems of punishment.[36] The "natural jurisprudence" of punishment can provide us only with a thin principle to guide us through the historical thickets that determine punishment in each nation and time.

Smith divides his jurisprudential lectures into a consideration of three issues—the rights we have (1) as human beings (the rights "which belong to a man as a man" (LJ 3, 7, 141), (2) as family members, and (3) as members of a state—and his treatment of the second two headings similarly begins with a few remarks on general principles, rooted in "nature" or "reason," followed by a lengthy account of how these principles have played out in various legal systems. Under the heading of familial rights, we get an account of the natural basis for marriage and child-raising,[37] and of the circumstances that have tended to turn household servants into slaves—which Smith thinks has no basis in justice and is a source of grievous injustices (LJ 176 ff)—followed by lengthy histories of household structures in a variety of societies. Under the heading of our rights as "citizens or members of states" (LJ 7), we get an account of the "originall" of government, which turns out in this case to be not a moral principle attributed to the impartial spectator, but a theory of how, historically, governments evolved: once property holdings grew large enough, and hence disputes over property grew frequent enough, there came to be a need for a "supreme power" to settle these disputes (LJ 203).[38] Again, this is followed by a lengthy history of how governments have arisen, changed, and fallen in a variety of societies—how, in particular, the governments of pastoral societies differ from the governments of agricultural and commercial societies. It's harder to separate the "originall" from the history this time, since the originall is itself historical, but the notes on Smith's 1762–3 lectures contain roughly 5–10 pages on the former and 120 pages on the second.

So Smith's jurisprudential lectures are far more concerned with the history of legal and political institutions than with their moral foundations. And frequently Smith seems to regard the fact that historical circumstances lead a practice to be approved of, in a certain place or time, as itself a way of legitimating that practice. He says explicitly, for instance, that

> it is not any superiority of humanity or refinement of manners above the antients which has made tyrannicide be abhorred amongst us, when at the same time it was rewarded amongst them, but merely the different state and circumstances of the times.
>
> (LJ 292)

That is not to say that Smith recounts the cultural or historical factors he describes in a wholly uncritical fashion, or that he thinks we should accept whatever laws and political institutions we happen to have. He explicitly defends resistance to government, although he rejects Locke's arguments for it (LJ 320, 323). He is unequivocally opposed to slavery (LJ 176–92), attributing it to "the love of domination and authority over others," which he regards as a natural but baleful human inclination (LJ 192). He objects sharply to primogeniture and entail, and to certain kinds of punishment, and he presents laws promoting "the liberty of the subject" in a favourable light (e.g., LJ 284).

But he rarely offers us much moral argument for these points. Sometimes he suggests that understanding how a law or policy arose historically will help us see that and why it should no longer apply. He warns that many customs "continue after the reason of [them] is at an end" (LJ 41; cf. TMS 210). But once we know "the reason of" a custom or law that has come to an end, we should be able to see that it is unreasonable for that custom or law to continue. And indeed Smith says exactly this about Elizabeth I's harsh strictures against Catholics: they were "alltogether reasonable at [the] time" that they were implemented, given the "the vast disturbances and danger [that] the bigotry of the papists exposed [people] to," but "it were proper they were repealed" once those circumstances came to an end (LJ 296–7). He may similarly hope that giving the historical reason why primogeniture and entail arose—Smith explains in great detail how they made sense in their original historical context (49, 55–61)—will help people see why they are no longer reasonable in his own day. Smith is well aware that "everything by custom appears to be right" (322), but he seems to think that understanding the circumstances that gave rise to a custom can help break that custom's hold over us.

It seems unlikely that this historical mode of critique will work in every case, however—the hold of custom may just incline us to find rationalizations for policies that have passed their expiration date. It seems especially unlikely that this mode of critique will bring down forms of injustice deeply rooted in basic human inclinations: like slavery, on Smith's own account of that institution. One might well, for that reason, prefer to have a rule, like the utilitarian one, that could show us that certain laws and practices are wrong even if they seem reasonable to most of us. Smith does not appeal to any such rule, even though the motivation for his work on jurisprudence, by his own admission, was to find principles of "natural justice" by which all laws and policies could be judged. He does not even make much use of his impartial-spectator procedure to criticize laws or policies.

Smith does tell us with some confidence, as we have seen, what the impartial spectator has to say when it comes to the death penalty that Britain tried to impose for exporting wool. But there he can cite the fact that British subjects in fact refused to enable the government to carry out that penalty in support of his view of the impartial spectator's verdict. That suggests that he is most comfortable offering *immanent* criticism of laws and policies—criticisms that he thinks the vast bulk of the society to which those laws and policies are supposed to apply would themselves accept. Sometimes he seems to want to open his audience's eyes to the harms inflicted by various practices, as when he relates details about the lives of slaves that seem designed to arouse sympathy for them (LJ 177, 179, 180–1). But once he has given us the information we need to see a set of harms, and prodded us to engage in imaginative exercises that can help us appreciate that these things *are* harms, he seems to expect our moral condemnation of the laws and policies giving rise to those harms to follow automatically. Nothing more than clearly seeing an injury, and sympathizing with its victims, seems on his view necessary for us to condemn it as an injustice. At any rate, he gives us little else: no *a priori* way of telling what is just and unjust, certainly.

9.9 Relativism again

So LJ brings us back to the question we asked earlier about whether Smith's moral philosophy is vulnerable to a charge of moral relativism. Smith talks openly in the lectures about the danger that customs will live on after the reason for them has lapsed, and he seems well aware, throughout, of the degree to which we regard what is, in the realm of law, as what ought to be. He does model an immanent critique of our legal practices in some places, and offers us some hope that history leads societies to improve themselves: establishing fairer punishments, for instance, as governments grow stronger. And as we might expect, when he criticizes occurrent practices he abjures utilitarian arguments—explicitly rejecting them when it comes to punishment—in favour of what the impartial spectator would consider to be the "reasonable expectations," or justifiable "resentment," of an individual. Justice protects the liberty and rights of individuals, first and foremost, and makes for the peace and happiness of a society only as a consequence of this concern for individuals. But Smith no more offers us a clear libertarian principle to ground universal justice than he offers us a clear utilitarian ground for it: just some formal procedures for thinking about justice that are themselves susceptible of being variously interpreted in various societies. What counts as a "reasonable expectation" or a justifiable resentment in one place and time may be regarded very differently in another.

My overall takeaway from Smith's jurisprudence lectures is thus that Smith tried to show us, but did not fully succeed in showing us, how universal principles of justice could be brought together with the thought that laws need to be suited to each society's structure and history. I don't think Smith's failure in this endeavour is surprising—reconciling these two things is enormously difficult. One of Smith's main heirs in the project was Hegel,[39] who developed a conception of right that was vastly better suited than Smith's to being shaped by historical circumstances, and who did a far more thorough-going job of showing how that conception was realized in various cultures and historical periods. Yet Hegel's version of this project has not convinced many people either. We are strongly gripped both by the intuition that some notion of right or justice must transcend all cultures and time periods and by the intuition that what people are held accountable for by legal and political systems must be suited to the expectations, beliefs, and circumstances of their societies in their time and place. How exactly to reconcile these two intuitions has eluded all philosophers and political theorists thus far.

9.10 Conclusion and summary

On the whole, I think that Smith's attempt to develop principles of natural justice must be adjudged inadequate. It is not a total failure by any means. One can see why Smith thought there must be such principles; he provides intriguing sketches, which fit in with his moral philosophy in TMS, of what the moral principles underlying property and punishment might look like; and the historical materials he brings to fill out these sketches are rich and plausible. But we are not really shown how moral principle gets a grip on history, or how history might supplement moral principle. If Smith integrated these elements of his jurisprudential theory more deeply in the manuscript for his book on jurisprudence, then that book must have looked quite different from the lecture notes that we have now. But I suspect he did not succeed in doing that, and asked for the manuscript to be burned because he did not think he had carried out his aims successfully.[40]

In any case, when we turn to WN we do not see the attempts at providing an "originall" for property or punishment that are so striking in LJ. There are references to justice throughout WN, but no definition of it nor any mention of the idea that there might be universal principles of natural justice.[41] There are references also to property, but no attempt to provide a moral basis for our right to it. Smith does say at one point that "the property which every man has in his own labour, as it is the original foundation of all other property, so it is the most sacred and inviolable" (WN 138). This line is fascinating in the way it reverses Locke's famous argument for property—arguing from our right to material possessions to a more basic right to control our own labour—and thereby supports the polemic Smith carries out throughout WN on behalf of workers, as against the claims made by their masters. But on a theoretical level, the line represents a disappointing abandonment of the attempt Smith had made, in his jurisprudential lectures, to re-work Locke's argument for property in terms of his own impartial-spectator procedure. Smith must either have given up on such an argument or considered it not worthwhile to introduce it into WN.

There is one mention of punishment in WN that makes some allusion to its moral grounds. But it too fails to spell out those grounds. Speaking of an "injudicious tax" that tempts people into smuggling, Smith says that such a law,

> contrary to all the ordinary principles of justice, first creates the temptation, and then punishes those who yield to it; and it commonly enhances the punishment, too, in proportion to the very circumstance which ought certainly to alleviate it, the temptation to commit the crime.

> (WN 826)

The idea, central to Smith's discussion of punishment in LJ, that punishments need first and foremost to be "in proportion" to the wrong involved in a crime, rather than imposed for utilitarian ends, appears clearly here, but without any mention of the resentment of an impartial spectator. Again, Smith seems not to have thought it worthwhile to introduce the apparatus of his jurisprudential thought into his book on political economy.

We cannot say that Smith left these things out of WN because he believed that justice is irrelevant to political economy. Again and again in WN he condemns policies as unjust or insists that justice forbids or requires a policy of some sort. He simply does not provide us with a philosophical discussion of what justice is. Presumably he thinks our common sense idea of justice, or the idea we can glean from our country's laws and political traditions, will suffice for his purposes. Whether he also thought that the view of justice he had tried to develop in his jurisprudential lectures was insufficiently worked out, or whether he simply decided that it would clutter up his book on political economy, is impossible to determine. He did not, in any case, provide us in WN with a clear picture of what the "natural jurisprudence" he had mentioned in TMS was supposed to look like. If Smith had a well worked-out theory of justice, we do not know what it was.

Notes

1 All quotations in this paragraph from TMS 340–2.
2 Charles Griswold denies that the book on jurisprudence was likely to resemble what we have in LJ. Given the closeness of WN to what the notes in LJ have to say on "police, revenue and arms," however, I see no reason to think that the manuscript on jurisprudence would be any further removed from what Smith said about jurisprudence in his lectures.
3 TMS, "Advertisement," 3.
4 Measured both by number of pages and by the weeks spent on the material, if the dates in LJA are anything to go on. Even assuming that the notes break off significantly before the point at which the course ended—assuming, that is, that there were one or two more sessions, thus bringing the class to the end of April or beginning of May 1763—the class would have spent three months on jurisprudence (end of December through the end of March) and just one month on police, revenue and arms.
5 D.D. Raphael and A.L. Macfie have a footnote to their edition of TMS insisting that the author must be Kames (note 1 to TMS 80), but—as they admit—it is hard to imagine that Smith would call Kames "an author of very great and original genius." That distinction much more readily fits Hume. (Haakonssen also takes the reference to be to Hume: SL 203n20.) Hume did distinguish sharply between justice and the other virtues, but Raphael and Macfie say that Hume's distinction is "drawn quite differently." Hume does make the point about the necessity of justice to any social peace that most concerns Smith, however. Moreover, as Raphael and Macfie themselves acknowledge, Smith seems clearly to refer to Hume later in his discussion of justice: see TMS 87 and note 1 thereto.
6 Smith makes this last point most explicitly in a manuscript that pre-dates TMS:

> Improper punishment, punishment which is either not due at all or which exceeds the demerit of the Crime, is an injury to the Criminal, may and ought to be opposed by force, and if inflicted, exposes the person who inflicts it to punishment in his turn.
>
> (TMS 390)

7 Compare Locke, *Second Treatise of Government*, chapter 2, sections 4–12.
8 As well as Hume and Kames.
9 Istvan Hont and Michael Ignatieff, "Needs and Justice in the *Wealth of Nations*," in Hont and Ignatieff (eds.), *Wealth and Virtue* (Cambridge: Cambridge University Press, 1983), 24; see also AVE 250 and Donald Winch, *Riches and Poverty* (Cambridge: Cambridge University Press, 1996), 100.

10 I've argued for this point elsewhere: see Samuel Fleischacker, *A Short History of Distributive Justice* (Cambridge: Harvard University Press, 2004) and "A Right to Welfare: Historical and Philosophical Reflections," in C. Boisen and M. Murray (eds.), *Distributive Justice Debates in Political and Social Thought* (London: Routledge, 2016).

11 See my *Short History* and E.P. Thompson, "The Moral Economy of the English Crowd in the Eighteenth Century," *Past and Present* 50/1 (1971).

12 See LJ 197. For an extended discussion of the history of the idea of distributive justice before Smith, and Smith's relationship to the natural law tradition's way of thinking about the poor, see my *Short History of Distributive Justice*.

13 An example he also alludes to in the two paragraphs preceding this one.

14 He also does not present taxes as any sort of infringement on property rights. On the contrary, he says that "the subjects of every state" should see themselves "joint tenants of a great estate, who are all obliged to contribute" to its upkeep (WN 825).

15 Locke, *Second Treatise*, chapter 2, sections 8–13.

16 Darwall, "Sympathetic Liberalism" and Remy Debes, "Adam Smith on Dignity and Equality."

17 He does come close at one point, however:

> Though it may be true... that every individual, in his own breast, natur-ally prefers himself to all mankind, yet he dares not look mankind in the face, and avow that he acts according to this principle.... When he views himself in the light in which he is conscious that others will view him, he sees that to them he is but one of the multitude in no respect better than any other in it.
>
> (TMS 83)

Perhaps unsurprisingly, these lines occur in the chapter on justice from which I am about to quote.

18 Another passage that supports this reading is TMS 90, where Smith says that our concern for individuals who have been injured "is no more than the general fellow-feeling which we have with every man merely because he is our fellow-creature," and stresses that we feel this concern even for "an odious person, when he is injured by those to whom he has given no provocation."

19 If anything, the poor, throughout Smith's work, come off as *more* virtuous than the rich.

20 See my *On Adam Smith's Wealth of Nations*, chapter 10 and *A Short History of Distributive Justice*.

21 See, for instance, Karl Popper, *The Open Society and Its Enemies* (London: Routledge & Kegan Paul, 1966), vol. 1, 284–5, Judith Shklar, "Liberalism of Fear," in S. Hoffman (ed.), *Political Thought and Political Thinkers* (Chicago: University of Chicago Press, 1998) and Forman-Barzilai, *Adam Smith and the Circles of Sympathy*, 231–7.

22 Smith attends to the cultural and historical variability of offenses to reputation at LJ 122–4.

23 Forman-Barzilai, *Adam Smith and the Circles of Sympathy*, 237.

24 I elaborate the points in this section in *On Adam Smith's Wealth of Nations*, chapter 8, especially 155–61.

25 Locke himself argued for civil government on the grounds that the law of nature will often be unfairly and ineffectively enforced in the state of nature: see *Second Treatise*, chapter 7, sections 87 and 90, and chapter 9.

26 In addition to the passages cited in this paragraph, see LJ 280, 423, 426 for discussions of the "accuracy" or "precision" that law needs.

27 On promulgation in the natural law tradition, see Aquinas, *Summa Theologica* I-II, Q90A4, in D. Bigongiari (ed.), *The Political Ideas of St. Thomas Aquinas* (New York: Hafner Press, 1953), 9–10. Rulers in ancient China and India displayed the importance of promulgation to them, in practice, by making sure that their laws were well publicized throughout their realms.

28 Smith suggests other arguments for the exactitude of laws of justice—for instance, that only exact laws will keep us from self-deceit when we are tempted to violate them (TMS 175)—in various places, but the one I have sketched here seems to be his main one (and is the only one that is laid out explicitly). For further discussion, see my *On Adam Smith's Wealth of Nations*, chapter 8.

29 Except perhaps if those laws worked via a bureaucratic agency, with discretion to favour some individuals over others, rather than through a general law. But here the objection would be to the *means* of re-distribution, not to the re-distribution itself.

30 Suppose, for instance, that there is a convention in the world of these apple-pickers, flouted by this first occupant, according to which those with damaged arms or legs should have first crack at virgin apples. Pufendorf considers a scenario along these lines: see my *On Adam Smith's Wealth of Nations*, 302n12.

31 Smith says explicitly that "the notion of property seems at first to have been confined to what was about ones person, his cloaths and any instruments he might have occasion for" (LJ 20).

32 LJ 87. See also LJ 400—"The foundation of contract is the reasonable expectation which the person who promises raises in the person to whom he binds himself."—and LJ 88.

33 That is partly through its appearance in sections of WN, but Smith's more extensive treatment of it in LJ seems to have also had a great influence on his student John Millar, whose *Origin of the Distinction of Ranks* bears striking resemblances to Smith's lectures.

34 Compare LJ 475, from Smith's 1766 jurisprudence course: "Injury naturaly excites the resentment of a spectator, and the punishment of the offender is reasonable as far as the indifferent spectator can go along with it. This is the natural measure of punishment." Again, Smith goes on to contrast this "measure" of punishment with a utilitarian one, and denies that utility can be the foundation of just punishment.

35 Both in TMS and in LJ, Smith does call the punishment of the sentinel "just": "When the preservation of an individual is inconsistent with the safety of a multitude, nothing can be more just than that the many should be preferred to the one" (TMS 90; see also LJ 475–6). But he also stresses that we feel very uncomfortable about this sort of case. Not only do we not feel resentment toward the sentinel, he says, but

> a man of humanity must recollect himself, must make an effort and exert his whole firmness and resolution, before he can bring himself either to inflict [the death penalty on the sentinel], or to go along with it when it is inflicted by others.

He adds that such a punishment "is far from being founded upon the same principles" as the sort of punishment that is founded upon the resentment of the impartial spectator (TMS 91). It instead arises "merely from a view to the general interest of society, which, we imagine, cannot otherwise be secured" (TMS 90); in one of the parallel passages in LJ, he says that the punishment of the sentinel "is intirely founded on the consideration of the publick good" (LJ 105).

This last claim in LJ appears, however, almost immediately after Smith's *rejection* of appeals to "the publick good" as an adequate basis for punishment, and conflicts with the principle he enunciates, a bit earlier, that "in all cases the measure of the punishment to be inflicted on the delinquent is the concurrence of the impartial spectator with the resentment of the injured" (LJ 104). Smith also tends to couple the sentinel example, in which he accepts a public good justification for punishment, with the example of a death penalty for wool exportation, discussed above, in which he rejects that justification (LJ 105, 475–6). The sentinel example thus seems to be, for Smith, a rare exception to the rule that the public good alone can never justify a punishment. And it is reasonable to suppose that it is only the great stakes involved in this example that gives force to the public good argument.

Commentators have not known quite what to make of Smith's sentinel example (compare for instance Raphael and Macfie's discussion of the passage in Appendix II to their edition of TMS 394–5, with Haakonssen's in SL 120–3). I think Smith himself did not quite know what to make of it. In an early manuscript, and again in one of his jurisprudential lectures, he describes the sentinel as being "sacrificed" to the security of many (TMS 389; LJ 105), and in TMS he calls him an "unfortunate victim" of the army's needs. This sort of language takes the case out of the realm of punishment altogether, assimilating it instead to cases in which some innocent people, in a natural disaster or wartime situation, need to be "sacrificed" if a larger number is to survive. I think we can safely say that the sentinel example is an anomaly for Smith, a concession to utilitarianism that he feels forced to make, because no lesser good than life is at stake—and the lives of many people at that.

I am grateful to Tony Hernandez and Olivia Bailey for pressing me to discuss the sentinel case.

36 Smith especially discusses British law, of course, but he talks also a great deal about ancient Greek and Roman law, sometimes about French or German laws, and occasionally mentions China, Africa, or aboriginal tribes in the Americas.

37 Which among other things leads Smith to say that "there is not any reall injustice in voluntary divorce or in polygamy" (LJ 150) although he does not in the end approve of them.

38 Smith presents this account explicitly in counterpoise to a social contract theory of government, denying, as Hume had before him, that the authority of any government comes from anything like a formal agreement among those subject to the government (LJ 207, 316–7)—even if he believes, as he does, that that authority depends on the continuing assent of those subjects (LJ 318–22).

39 Largely an unwitting heir, I think, but see Angelica Nuzzo, "The Standpoint of Morality in Adam Smith and Hegel," in Brown and Fleischacker (eds), The Philosophy of Adam Smith, and Lisa Herzog, Inventing the Market: Smith, Hegel, and Political Theory (Oxford: Oxford University Press, 2013).

40 Haakonssen argues in SL for a deep and subtle reconciliation, in Smith's writings, between the natural basis of justice and its historical incarnations; Griswold suggests in AVE that Smith's entire project of natural jurisprudence conflicted so deeply with other elements of his thought that it "perhaps … could not be written." (AVE 37n61) I agree with Griswold on this rather than Haakonssen.

41 The phrase "natural justice" does appear at one point in WN (898), but without definition. The reader is presumably supposed to know what it means.

Further reading

Sam Fleischacker, On Adam Smith's Wealth of Nations, Part IV
Charles Griswold, Adam Smith and the Virtues of Enlightenment, chapter 6
Knud Haakonssen, The Science of the Legislator

Ten
Police

By "police" Smith means policy. Towards the end of his jurisprudential lectures, Smith took up questions of governmental policy, especially as regards "cheapness or plenty" (LJ 331, 487); his treatment
of these questions would later form the basis of WN.[1] I will postpone
consideration of Smith's economic views until the next chapter, but
his remarks on police in LJ provide us with a good opportunity to
examine his view of governmental activity in general, aside from
the provision of justice. I'll make some remarks about how Smith
conceives the purposes of government overall, then turn to the
reasons why he thinks governments should be concerned about economic well-being, in particular. That will serve as a transition to our
consideration of WN.

10.1 Purposes of government

Smith lays out four purposes for government in both TMS and LJ:
justice, police, revenue, and arms (TMS 342; LJ 5–7, 331, 398,
541). In WN, this list is transformed into three tasks for which government is necessary—protecting the society from attack by other
societies; protecting each member of the society from "injustice or
oppression" by other members of it; and setting up "certain publick
works and… publick institutions" that promote the good of society
as a whole but that it would never be worthwhile for individuals
to set up on their own (WN 687–9, 708, 723)—plus the raising
of the revenue needed in order to carry out these three tasks. So
"police" gets translated into "certain publick works and… publick

institutions," and "revenue" gets separated off from the other three tasks as the condition for carrying them out. WN thus makes the list of tasks a little more precise, and makes more sense of it, but the contents remain the same.[2]

At first glance, at least, Smith's list of tasks for government is unremarkable. Locke had essentially presented "the true... end of civil government" in the same way, although without translating it into a list of tasks.[3] The American *Declaration of Independence*—written in the same year that WN was published—ends by saying that the 13 new states, now that they are independent, "have the full power to levy war, conclude peace, contract alliances, [and] establish commerce."[4] Eleven years later, the American Constitution would describe the purposes of the government it established as to "establish justice, insure domestic tranquillity, provide for the common defence, promote the general welfare, and secure the blessings of liberty to ourselves and our posterity." These lists of governmental purposes do not differ in any significant respect from Smith's.[5]

But in comparing Smith's writings with other Enlightenment documents like Locke's *Second Treatise* and the American Constitution, we may overlook one striking respect in which all of these texts differ radically from the way in which government had been conceived in earlier times: there is no reference in any of them to the idea that governments might be tasked with the promotion of *virtue*, and of religious virtue in particular. For Aquinas, law was supposed to habituate us in virtue—albeit gradually, and primarily by proscribing "the more grievous vices from which it is possible for the majority to abstain"[6]—and most Christian kings took on this responsibility, prohibiting many things in the name of Christianity and encouraging the spread of Christian teachings in their realm. Even in the Enlightenment, versions of this idea remained common. Until the very end of the eighteenth century, most people thought that an elite of the wise and virtuous should rule,[7] and that governments should underwrite religion. Smith's teacher Hutcheson wrote that

> the civil power should take care that the people be well instructed in [the importance of belief and piety towards God to the achievement of happiness and virtue], and have all arguments presented to their understandings... which can raise these

persuasions, and confirm these dispositions…. The magistrate should therefore provide proper instruction for all, especially for young minds, about the existence, goodness, and providence of God, and all the social duties of life, and the motives to them.[8]

Smith wholly omits religious and moral instruction from his list of the proper tasks of government, and the omission is not an accident. Smith seems not to believe either that there are good arguments for the existence of God or that virtue depends on belief in God. And he certainly doesn't think that government officials are in a good position to figure out how virtue and religion should be taught:

> Articles of faith, as well as all other spiritual matters, it is evident enough, are not within the proper department of a temporal sovereign, who, though he may be very well qualified for protecting, is seldom supposed to be so for instructing the people.
>
> (WN 798)

Moreover, Smith believes that virtue is inculcated by the sympathetic interactions among friends and neighbours that lead us to set up, and attend to, an impartial spectator within ourselves. The conversation of friends, and even better of strangers, composes us and breaks us of our self-absorption (TMS 153–4). The "great school of self-command" begins with the child's discovery that it needs to moderate its anger and self-pity to win the approval of its "play-fellows and companions" (145). These small-scale social interactions are for Smith the key to moral development; there is no need for, and nothing to be gained by, the example set by powerful people,[9] let alone laws that attempt to instil virtue by force. Smith's views on the role of government in the inculcation of virtue parallel his view of government intervention in the economy: governments do most to promote virtue where they refrain from doing things to promote virtue. Writing of sumptuary laws, which were defended as ways of instilling prudence in the poor, Smith says,

> It is the highest impertinence… in kings and ministers, to pretend to watch over the private oeconomy of private people…. They are themselves always, and without any exception, the

> greatest spendthrifts in the society. Let them look well after their
> own expence, and they may safely trust private people with
> theirs.
>
> (WN 346)

Needless to say, Smith is no more enthusiastic about having kings
and ministers watch over the piety of private people.

Smith is thus very much in line with the secular, pragmatic view
of government purposes that arose in the Enlightenment. He is
indeed one of its most thorough-going proponents. That is probably one reason why he has come to be seen as not caring, in WN,
about whether people develop virtue or not: as encouraging them
to pursue their self-interest instead. That view is mistaken, I believe,
and a contributor to deep misconceptions about Smith's political
philosophy. What is true is that Smith thought governments should
allow people to pursue virtue, and come to religious views, on their
own: in liberty, rather than by way of legal incentives or threats.

10.2 Principles

As we have seen, Smith ends TMS by telling us that he wants to
develop a system of "the general principles which ought to run
through and be the foundation of the laws of all nations" (TMS
341). In LJ we learn that those laws will pertain to justice, police,
revenue, and arms. But we are also told that two aspects of police—
cleanliness and security—are too "trifling" a subject to be treated
of in a system of jurisprudence (LJ 5; see also 331, 486). I think it
is fair to infer that he regards these subjects as having no "general
principles." In any case, the fact that Smith does treat of revenue,
arms, and the economic component of police implies that he thinks
these subjects *can* be guided by general principles. What does he
mean by "principles" here?

Well, one thing he means is moral principles. Under the heading
of "arms," he includes "the laws of peace <and> war, the jura belli et
pacis" (LJ 7). The first set of lecture notes we have breaks off before
it gets to that part of Smith's course, but the second set includes a
substantial discussion of them (545–54). Smith follows Grotius in
many ways, but he also attempts to derive the just causes of war (ius

ad bellum) from the resentment theory he had used to ground punishment (546). In addition, he makes mention of the evolutionary idea he had discussed in connection with punishment: that the laws of war become more humane over time (548; see also 7).

Smith also gives us moral principles to guide the raising of revenue. The discussion of taxation in WN begins with four "maxims" (WN 825–7):

1 Everyone ought to contribute to the state "in proportion to their respective abilities."
2 Taxes should be "certain, and not arbitrary."
3 Taxes should be imposed "at the time, or in the manner in which it is most likely to be convenient for the contributor to pay it."
4 Taxes should "take out and keep out of the pockets of the people as little as possible, over and above what it brings into the publick treasury of the state."

With the possible exception of the fourth maxim, these are moral principles, not principles of efficiency, concerned with treating tax payers fairly rather than assuring the state's fiscal health. That is not to say that they are likely to be *bad* for the state's fiscal health—Smith attributes "justice *and* utility" to them (WN 827; emphasis added)—just to stress that here, as in Smith's account of the laws of war, the "general principles" running through and founding law are first and foremost moral ones.

I stress this because *most* of what Smith has to say about arms, revenue, and police does not consist of moral principles. Even LJ includes an account of "the various species of armed forces" that different states have used under the heading of "arms" (LJ 7), and the discussion of arms in WN is devoted entirely to that subject. The discussion of "revenue" in both LJ and WN, aside from the paragraphs on the four maxims of taxation, is overwhelmingly concerned with the effectiveness of various taxes, not their justice.[10] And what Smith has to say about political economy is almost entirely non-moral; he certainly does not devote himself to drawing out moral principles that should guide economic policy.

So we need to take the word "principles" in a broad enough sense to encompass non-moral as well as moral ideas. The second chapter of WN is entitled, "Of the Principle which gives occasion to the Division of Labor." Here "principle" refers to the feature of human nature underlying the division of labour: "the propensity to truck, barter, and exchange one thing for another" (WN 25). Smith leaves open whether this propensity is "one of those original principles of human nature of which no further account can be given" or something based on a deeper principle, like our ability to reason and speak (WN 25). In either case, the principle involved is a non-moral feature of human nature, a tendency that governs how we in fact behave, not necessarily how we should behave. It is one of the main "causes" of the wealth of nations that Smith promises to investigate in the title of his book, and the simplest way of describing what Smith means by calling it a "principle" is that it is something that lends itself to a causal generalization,[11] a feature of humanity that obtains widely enough to form a good basis for explanation and prediction.

Accordingly, when Smith says that a system of jurisprudence should display the general principles that ground and "run through" laws, we should take him to be looking for descriptive as well as moral generalizations that legislators in all nations can use to guide their decisions. Law varies, and should vary, with cultural and historical circumstance, for Smith, but there are some general ideas, of descriptive as well as normative varieties, that properly shape how every state adapts to its cultural and historical circumstances. These general ideas are what a "system" or "theory" of jurisprudence can and should address. When it comes to justice, they will take a mostly normative form. When it comes to revenue, arms, and police, they will take a mostly descriptive form: they will be principles of social science rather than morality. Only under this umbrella can we make sense of why Smith included the science of political economy—the generalizations over human nature that explain how wealth is produced—under jurisprudence.

10.3 Moral principles of political economy

That is not to say that there are *no* moral principles of political economy. We might ask why states should be concerned with wealth in the first place, for instance. To what larger goals, what overarching human goods, does the wealth of a nation contribute?

Smith never directly raises this question. Perhaps for that reason, his readers in later generations have attributed all sorts of different views on it to him. I'll propose two answers to it that I think fit with his moral philosophy in a moment. But first, let's canvas a variety of unsatisfactory answers to the question, from a Smithian point of view.

One might in the first place value national wealth because one values national glory, and supposes that nations filled with palaces and museums, or nations that rule over vast territories and populations, are better off than nations that make do with a simpler public space and more modest dominions. Smith opposes colonial projects and the wars that are needed to maintain them, however. He gives Versailles and the "noble palaces" of England and Italy but a passing compliment (WN 347), and he devotes just a dismissive half page to the expenses that rulers use to enhance their homes and courts (814). So he seems clearly not to care about wealth as a means for glorifying nations.

An alternative is to suppose that wealth is good because people gain pleasure from the things they use it for, happiness consists in an aggregate of pleasures, and the happier the people in a nation are, the better off that nation is. This kind of utilitarian thinking is often attributed to Smith. But we have seen that Smith's moral philosophy is quite opposed to utilitarianism. He also does not think of happiness as a sum of pleasures.[12] And he rejects any correlation between wealth and pleasure. Smith thinks that the "trinkets" and "gewgaws" on which rich people spend money are signs of their shallowness (WN 349), and don't bring them much pleasure (TMS 181–2). He certainly did not develop his political economy to help anyone accumulate such things.

A third possibility, subtly different from the second one, is that wealth enables people to satisfy their preferences—whether for pleasure or for anything else—and that states should help their citizens live out their preferred conception of life, whatever it may be. This is called "preference utilitarianism," and while it is also often attributed to Smith, the fact that Smith praises quite specific ways of living, in TMS, and condemns others as vain or lacking in self-command, suggests that he would not endorse the relativism about goods implicit in this view.

With these possibilities cleared away, here are two conceptions of why wealth is valuable that there is reason to attribute to Smith. First of all, in both LJ and WN there are certain basic goods that Smith thinks all people should have. Over and over he talks about the "three great wants of mankind": "food, cloaths, and lodging" (LJ 340; compare 337–8; WN 178). Indeed, he mentions them so often that the student writing up the first set of notes we have on his lectures at one point refers to them simply as "f., c., l" (378). And in WN Smith says, right after declaring that "no society can... be flourishing and happy, of which the far greater part of the members are poor and miserable," that "they who feed, cloath and lodge the whole body of the people should have such a share of the produce of their own labour as to be themselves tolerably well fed, cloathed and lodged" (WN 96). So it is not unreasonable to suggest that the overriding reason for increasing the wealth of a nation, for Smith, is to enable everyone in it, and especially those who would otherwise be "poor and miserable," to be well supplied with food, clothes, and lodging. Even if Smith does not consider it important that we achieve every pleasure we seek, he does seem to think that everyone needs these three goods. "What can be added to the happiness of the man who is in health, who is out of debt, and has a clear conscience?" he asks (TMS 45). But to be "in health" one needs an adequate amount of food, clothing and shelter; one is moreover likely to go into debt, or do things that will cloud one's conscience, if one is desperate for these things. Smith also tells us that "the chief part of human happiness arises from the consciousness of being beloved" (41). But it is hard to maintain the composure and decency needed to win other people's respect, let alone to be "beloved" by anyone, without having adequate food, clothing, and shelter. And indeed, prominent Smith scholars have argued that Smith wrote WN above all to show nations how they could increase their food production and keep their populations from starving.[13]

I think this is in fact a major reason why Smith thinks states need to attend to economic policy, and why he devoted so much of his career to laying out its principles. While he does not think that policy makers should seek to maximize everyone's happiness (he regards that as the job of God, remember, not of human beings: TMS 237), he does seem to think that they should maximize everyone's chances of having their basic needs met.[14] And it is very plausible that his contribution to political economy was aimed in large part at helping them accomplish this.[15]

But that is not his only purpose. In what Dennis Rasmussen has called "the single most important passage in *The Wealth of Nations*" (IP 162), Smith writes that "commerce and manufactures gradually introduced order and good government, and with them, the liberty and security of individuals, among the inhabitants of [Europe], who had before been almost in a continual state of war with their neighbours, and of servile dependency upon their superiors," going on to describe this as both "the least observed" and "by far the most important" of all the effects of commerce (WN 412). He also points to the value of commerce in preventing dependency in LJ, adding that "nothing tends to corrupt and enervate and debase the mind as dependency, and nothing gives such noble and generous notions of probity as freedom and independency" (LJ 333). In addition, he praises commerce for bringing "probity, liberality,… and amiable qualities" to people (333; compare 528, 538–9). So he seems clearly to think that commercial societies foster freedom and independence, which in turn helps people develop and maintain important virtues.

To be sure, Smith also notes ways in which commerce has a deleterious impact on virtue. The advanced division of labour that comes with commerce "confines the views of men," especially of poor workers in manufacturing, who spend all their time carrying out a small monotonous task. Given that the poor also have very little education, they come to have "no ideas with which [they] can amuse [themselves]" and consequently "betake [themselves] to drunkenness and riot." In addition, commerce "sinks the courage of mankind" (LJ 539–40). Smith recommends state-run remedies for these problems in WN, however (WN 781–8), and his overall view is clearly that a commercial society that takes care to compensate for its own limitations can nurture some important virtues in its citizenry. Free markets are thus for Smith not just a means of increasing consumer goods, even the consumer goods that enable everyone to satisfy their basic needs. They are also a training ground for virtue. By breaking down feudal structures, and then leaving people alone to take "care of their own interest" (WN 531), legislators can serve both the material and the moral well-being of their people.

I think this last point is crucial to Smith's brand of liberalism. He does not promote liberty because he wants everyone to have their preferences satisfied but because he thinks moral qualities are best developed in freedom. Liberty is not a political good because it allows us to live out our selfish desires, for him, but because it is an arena for the flourishing of moral qualities. Liberalism—the promotion of liberty—is thus not a morally neutral political philosophy; it is, rather, morally good.

10.4 Why self-interest is not a basic economic principle for Smith

This view of Smith's liberalism is not a standard one. It flies in the face of the popular view that Smith praises selfishness in WN, or at least sees it as inevitable, even if he bases his moral system in TMS on benevolence. It also differs sharply from the view of the prominent Smith scholar Charles Griswold, according to whom Smith sees vanity—a deeply corrupting vice—as the engine of commerce, but praises commercial society anyway, because of the material good it does for the poor (AVE 259–66). Elsewhere, I have dealt in depth with what I consider the flaws in these views;[16] I will summarize the main points of those discussions here.

In the first place, it is simply a mistake to see Smith as praising selfishness, or even regarding self-interest as the inevitable driver of human action, in WN. The main prooftext cited in support of this idea has been badly misunderstood. In perhaps the most famous lines of his book (the only lines, often, that people read in introductory economics classes), Smith says:

> It is not from the benevolence of the butcher, the brewer, or the baker, that we expect our dinner, but from their regard to their own interest. We address ourselves, not to their humanity but to their self-love, and never talk to them of our own necessities but of their advantages. Nobody but a beggar chuses to depend chiefly upon the benevolence of his fellow-citizens.
>
> (WN 27)

But if Smith wanted to show that people are motivated exclusively by self-interest, he would not have picked such a humdrum example.

Of course we address our butcher and the baker in terms of what they can get from us! Who would ever think otherwise? If Smith's point were that people are always motivated by self-interest he should have used a less obvious example—shown us, like Mandeville, perhaps, that charitable actions are really motivated by self-interest.[17] No self-respecting person, in ordinary circumstances, would dream of going into a butcher shop and begging for a cut of sirloin. Nor does Smith deny that in extraordinary circumstances people do beg. "Nobody but a beggar chuses to depend chiefly upon... benevolence": but a beggar does so choose.

So these lines cannot possibly make the point that people are motivated exclusively by self-interest. And Smith's overall point in the paragraph from which the lines come is quite a different one: that human beings, unlike other animals, *know* what is in one another's interests and can therefore pursue their self-interests together—can "*address* [themselves]... to [one another's] self-love." That is why market exchange exists among human beings but not among dogs (to deploy a contrast that Smith explicitly draws on, in this passage). Smith roots economic exchange in a cognitive feature of human beings, not a motivational one.

The main text used to support the self-interest view of WN has therefore been misread. And the broader idea that WN reverses course from the critique of selfishness in TMS is an artefact of certain late nineteenth-century scholars in Germany. Noting that TMS talks throughout of "sympathy" while WN almost always refers to an agent's "interests," they maintained that there was an unbridgeable gap between the two books. Thus was born *das Adam Smith Problem*.[18] Contemporary Smith scholars tend to deny that there is any such problem, stressing the implausibility of such a large gap, on such a central issue, in the work of an author who was busily revising his earlier book even as, and after, he wrote the later one. They also point out that the German scholars misunderstood what Smith meant by "sympathy," that selfish pursuits are constrained by justice in WN, that self-interest is given a respectable place in human motivation even in TMS, and that WN is concerned simply with economic activity, not with human behaviour as a whole. To these points, one might add that if there were such a large gap between the two books, it would be odd that none of Smith's contemporaries noticed it.

To be sure, some non-altruistic motivational assumptions are necessary to Smith's account of how markets work. If people produced and exchanged goods largely out of a love for their society, or a belief that the gods or spirits require them to produce those goods, their exchanges would fail to constitute the signal system that Smith sees in the market. If people bought more or less corn than they need out of a love for their society, or a traditional taboo, then the depth and extent of a famine would not show up properly in the prices of foodstuffs, pace Smith's analysis at WN 524–34. For markets to provide that kind of information, the agents in those markets must be (a) rationally pursuing some interest, rather than blindly following a ritual or taboo, and (b) mutually disinterested—uninterested in the projects of the people with whom they are exchanging. But it does not follow that these agents need to be self-interested. They may care about their families and friends, their religious communities, or any of a variety of political and social projects. It is just that, if they live in a large society, they will not normally be making economic exchanges with family members, friends, fellow environmentalists, and the like. If I buy bread from you because I care about you, or because I believe that supporting your bakery is good for our society, then the price I pay will not reflect how much I, or my family and friends, want your bread. So it is important to an argument that the market gives information about supply and demand that the participants in the market not be interested, qua market participants, in each other's well-being; it is entirely unnecessary for such an argument that they be interested only in their own well-being. And Smith in fact makes the former but not the latter assumption. All of Smith's analyses of economic phenomena rely on an assumption of mutual disinterest; nothing he says requires the assumption that people are self-interested. In the words of the modern economist Lionel Robbins, Smith thinks that economic actors are "non-tuists," not that they are (necessarily) self-interested.[19]

Of course, even non-tuism suggests that the economic realm is not particularly conducive to the display or development of benevolence. And Smith did not think that it was. There is nothing surprising about that—practically no-one has ever thought that we produce and exchange goods out of the goodness of our hearts. Certainly, no major figure thought that in Smith's day. Even Hutcheson, the most uncompromising promoter of benevolence in the entire eighteenth century, remarks that "general benevolence alone, is not a Motive strong enough to Industry, to bear Labour and Toil, and many other Difficultys which we are averse to from Self-love."[20] The virtue that commerce can foster, for Smith, is not benevolence but self-command. In refraining from speaking constantly of our own needs to those with whom we exchange goods, and making an effort, instead, to understand and address the needs of others, we learn to control our desires and emotions. And this training, especially if we work in conditions of some "independence"—if we do not constantly have to pay "servile and fawning attention" to a lord and master (see WN I.ii.2; 26)—helps us to develop the "probity" that Smith sees as coming with commercial society. The fact that our economic activity does not directly encourage us in benevolence, therefore, is no barrier to its contributing to our capacity for virtue.

10.5 Why vanity is not a basic economic principle for Smith

Griswold's challenge to the "liberalism-for-virtue" view of Smith takes a very different form. Griswold emphasizes the famous parable about the vanity of the pursuit of wealth in TMS—the passage that begins, "The poor man's son, whom heaven in its anger has visited with ambition,... admires the condition of the rich..." (TMS 181–5)—saying that "*The Wealth of Nations*, and so the world of wealth getting it promotes, is painted within [the] frame" of this passage (AVE 222). In the parable, the poor man's son struggles all his life to attain great wealth and then realizes, when he does achieve it, that "the palaces, the gardens, the equipage, the retinue of the great" do not make anyone truly happier, and that he is "always as much, and sometimes more exposed than before, to anxiety, to fear, and to sorrow; to diseases, to danger, and to death" (TMS 182–3). Nature works a "deception" on us when it leads us to think we would be happier if we were rich, Smith says here, but only that deception "rouses and keeps in continual motion the industry of mankind" (183). The pursuit of wealth is thus based on an illusion, which detracts both from the pursuit of virtue and from the real happiness we could achieve by being content to pursue virtue alone.

The takeaway message, for Griswold, is that Smith accepts the fact that increasing the wealth of nations comes at a cost to the pursuit of virtue and true happiness, but considers it worthwhile anyway because of the material goods it brings to society, especially the goods it brings to the poor. We set out after the "baubles and trinkets" that wealth can procure for us, but then, if we succeed, wind up having to pay our servants to "keep in order" all those baubles and trinkets; they get their needs met because of our vanity. The legislator thus does us no moral favours in promoting the wealth of our nation— there is no gain in virtue in any mode of pursuing wealth—but nevertheless does well to promote it.

My response to this argument is that it is a grave error to rest too much on the parable about the poor man's son in TMS, and WN is certainly not "painted within [its] frame." The chapter in TMS in which that parable appears is Smith's earliest published reflection on economic matters—it appears in the first edition of the book, in 1759, and seems to have received little attention from Smith after that (he barely revised it in subsequent editions)—and a number of its features conflict sharply with things that he says later on.[21] For one thing, Smith speaks there of "premiums and other encouragements" for various industries in approving terms (TMS 185), while he later sharply criticizes all such bounties (see, for instance, LJ 382, 525–6; WN 505–24). For another, Smith's paradigm example of the socio-economic advantages of wealth getting in the parable is that poor people can become servants in the homes of the rich. In WN, however, Smith portrays servile work as breeding dependency and leading to idleness and poverty (WN 335–6). He sees the fondness of rich people for "baubles and trinkets" as doing good for society, in WN, only when it gives employment to independent artisans and shopkeepers who make and sell these items (419–20), not when it leads the rich to maintain servants who "keep [them] in order".

Finally, the main driver of economic growth in WN is savings, not consumer spending (WN 339–46); the desire for luxury goods is emphatically not, as it is in TMS, what most "rouses and keeps in motion the continual industry of mankind." But the desire that motivates people to save, to be parsimonious or frugal, is not based on any sort of illusion. We save out of a "calm and dispassionate" desire to improve our condition in a constant, but gradual, way (341–3) and because we want to provide for our children (917). In the final, 1790 edition of TMS, Smith describes this disposition in warmly approving terms:

> The man who lives within his income, is naturally contented with his situation, which, by continual, though small accumulations, is growing better and better every day. He is enabled gradually to relax... in the rigour of his parsimony... He has no anxiety to change so comfortable a situation, and does not go in quest of new enterprises and adventures, which might endanger, but could not well increase, the secure tranquillity which he actually enjoys.
>
> (TMS 215)

This is the disposition of what Smith calls "the prudent man," and there is nothing foolish or confused about it. Small and gradual improvements in one's material circumstances really can bring us some pleasures, for Smith, and can certainly help our children. Seeking them also does not threaten the "tranquillity" that is essential to happiness, for Smith, nor is it incompatible with the acquisition of other virtues.[22] The pursuit of economic improvement is thus no barrier to virtue or true happiness, even if the pursuit of great wealth is. This point may even be implicit in the parable of the poor man's son. In the parable, the poor man's son wants to be rich, not merely better off than he or his father has been hitherto. That is a foolish and corrupting desire—it is "vanity," in every sense of that term. But the same is not true of the desire, gradually, to better one's condition. And it is the latter desire, not the former, that drives economic activity in WN. Once Smith begins to think deeply and seriously about economics, he comes to see prudence rather than vanity as essential to economic growth. WN re-writes the parable of the poor man's son; it does not fit within the frame of that parable. In his mature writings on political economy, Smith does not oppose economic striving to the cultivation of virtue. He can consequently allow, as he does, for certain kinds of economic formations—the world of independent agents that he identifies with commerce—to help us cultivate certain virtues.

10.6 Conclusion and summary

The moral principles guiding politics, for Smith, stem primarily from the importance of liberty and independence. Governments need to protect us from outside attack ("arms"), keep each of us from defrauding or inflicting violence on the others ("justice"), and nurture an economic realm that simultaneously provides us with the material goods to meet our basic needs and enables us to make independent choices about how we work and sell our products ("police"). At the same time, they must raise the money to accomplish these goals ("revenue"), and they should do that in ways that burden people in proportion to their ability to pay, and that maximally respect their freedom and dignity. As a whole this vision of government nicely encapsulates the political philosophy that has come to be known as "liberalism." But Smith's liberalism is concerned above all with the freedom and well-being of the poor, and is not hostile to government institutions furthering that goal, where it cannot be achieved by private efforts alone. Smith therefore does not fit neatly into either the libertarian or the welfare-state camp that mark liberal politics today.[23]

One distinctive feature of Smith's liberalism is that he thinks governments should attend to economic policy in part to help people develop elements of virtue. It is just that he thinks that governments can best foster virtue—foster the independence needed to achieve virtue—by not doing anything: by not interfering with people's lives. He does not think they should enact sumptuary laws, to encourage parsimony; he does not think they should limit the alcohol consumption of the poor (LJ 497); he does not think they should even teach doctrines that encourage virtue. Here and there, Smith thinks the state may do things to promote some attitudes and discourage others, as when he suggests that it combat religious fanaticism by making "the study of science and philosophy" a pre-requisite for entering "any liberal profession" (WN 796; it is fascinating, of course, that the virtue Smith wants to encourage here is meant to counter certain kinds of religious ones). But on the whole, he thinks the state best fosters virtue when it abstains from fostering virtue.

The same ironic teaching lies at the core of Smith's theory of how to foster wealth. One can imagine politicians or political activists agreeing fully with Smith that states should not directly promote virtue or religion, but finding it hard to imagine how a state could possibly promote its nation's economy without, say, supporting or protecting its manufacturing or agricultural sector. "We abandon our responsibilities if we do not put tariffs on cheap foreign goods that undercut our domestic companies," they may say, "or if we fail to subsidize our infant industries, or limit the price of basic foodstuffs." WN is directed at these sorts of claims. Smith regards the thinking behind them as misguided, and reflective of a deep failure to grasp the basic principles of economics. He wrote WN to lay out those principles.

Notes

1 This is true of all three versions of his jurisprudential courses for which we have notes—the two in LJ as well as the so-called "Anderson Notes" published by Ronald Meek in 1976. In the "Anderson Notes," however, economic issues are discussed under headings other than "police"—and indeed there are only a few lines under that heading. For the notes, and discussion of the placement of the section on economics, see Ronald Meek, "New Light on Adam Smith's Glasgow Lectures on Jurisprudence," *History of Political Economy* 8/4 (1976).
2 Smith reverts to his prior formulation in the "Advertisement" added to the 1790 edition of TMS, and describes WN as dealing with "police, revenue and arms" (TMS, Advertisement, ¶ 2).
3 Locke, *Second Treatise*, chapter VII, sections 87–8.
4 It does add that the new states may do "all other acts and things which independent states may of right do": a broad category that could allow for many other tasks.
5 That may not be pure coincidence: Jefferson had read TMS by the time he wrote the *Declaration of Independence*, and many of the framers of the Constitution had read both TMS and WN. See my "Adam Smith and the American Founding," *William and Mary Quarterly* (2002). Smith's influence on American thought more generally is the subject of Glory Liu's book, *Inventing the Invisible Hand: Adam Smith in American Thought and Politics, 1776–Present* (Princeton: Princeton University Press, forthcoming).
6 Aquinas, Summa Theologica I-II, Q96A2 (see also Q95A1, A2), in *The Political Ideas of St. Thomas Aquinas*.
7 See Gordon Wood, *The Radicalism of the American Revolution* (New York: Random House, 1991), 32, 235–41.
8 Frances Hutcheson, *A System of Moral Philosophy* (London: A. Millar, 1755), 3:ix, 1, 2:310.

9 Not the people most inclined to be virtuous in the first place, for Smith: TMS 61–6.

10 Although he does condemn certain taxes in moral terms: see, for instance, WN 846, 853–4, 859.

11 I am inclined to say "causal rule," but Smith—writing in the wake of Hume's critique of causality—does not see causes as having to hold with strict universality, as the word "rule" might imply. See Schliesser, *Adam Smith*, 62.

12 See Section 5.7, above.

13 See Hont and Ignatieff, "Needs and Justice in the *Wealth of Nations*."

14 Importantly, this does not just mean the goods they need for survival: Smith says explicitly that the clothing one needs to be respected by others is also a necessity (WN 870). That reinforces the reading I have proposed in this paragraph, by which a basic level of food, clothes, and lodging subserves our ability to be (and appear) virtuous, not just our health or comfort.

15 Ironically, of course, that will turn out to mean that they should mostly not do anything at all, of course—their nation will become wealthier, making all sorts of goods including food, clothing and lodging cheaper (more "comeattible": LJ 344) for everyone, if they refrain from promoting any particular company or economic sector—but when Smith does allow for government intervention in the economy, it is often to support the basic needs of the poor (see, for instance, WN 158).

16 See Chapters 5 and 6 of my *On Adam Smith's Wealth of Nations.*

17 "When a Man acts in behalf of Nephews or Neices, and says they are my Brother's Children, I do it out of Charity; he deceives you: for if he is capable, it is expected from him, and he does it partly for his own Sake: If he values the Esteem of the world, and is nice as to Honour and Reputation, he is obliged to have a greater Regard to them than for Strangers …." Mandeville, "An Essay on Charity, and Charity Schools," in F.B. Kaye (ed.), *The Fable of the Bees* (Oxford: Clarendon, 1924), 253.

18 See the editors' introduction to TMS 20–5 and Leonidas Montes, *Adam Smith in Context* (London: Palgrave Macmillan, 2004), chapter 2.

19 "The important aspect of Adam Smith's emphasis on self-love, as he calls it, is non-tuism of the person with whom he bargains. He doesn't interest himself — he may, but he doesn't necessarily, interest himself — in what the person with whom he's bargaining is doing with his family. He may be interested in all sorts of things with which he favours his family and wider circles in society." Lionel Robbins, *A History of Economic Thought*, ed. SG Medema and Warren Samuels (Princeton: Princeton University Press, 1998), 132.

20 Hutcheson, *An Inquiry into the Original …*, Treatise II, chapter VII, section viii.

21 D.D. Raphael, who also finds aspects of the passage remarkably out of synch with Smith's later views, remarks that it

> was written for the first edition of 1759, when the young professor in his thirties may well have entertained some romantic notions and thought them suitable for students mostly destined for the ministry. Yet he left it

unaltered when he revised the book in 1789, long after he had written the *Wealth of Nations*. Perhaps he thought it too fine a flourish to be lost, or perhaps he remained genuinely ambivalent [about its teachings].

(*The Impartial Spectator*, 90)

22 Indeed, in another passage added to the final edition of *Theory*, Smith says that "in the middling and inferior stations of life"—the stations in which prudence is necessary and which (therefore) tend to give rise to prudence—"the road to virtue and that to fortune … are … very nearly the same" (TMS 63).

23 I have dealt with the question of whether Smith is properly an ancestor of "leftwing" or "rightwing" liberalism in many places. In "Smith and the Left," in Ryan Hanley (ed.), *Adam Smith: A Princeton Guide* (Princeton: Princeton University Press, 2016), I suggest that, as an historical matter, the question is not really answerable. Elsewhere, I draw on arguments in Smith to support leftwing (welfare statist, and sometimes social democratic) policies: see my *Third Concept of Liberty* and the Epilogue to my *On Adam Smith's Wealth of Nations*. For a critique of such uses of Smith, see Craig Smith, "Adam Smith: Left or Right?" *Political Studies* 61/4 (2013).

Further reading

Sam Fleischacker, *On Adam Smith's Wealth of Nations*, Part V
Charles Griswold, *Adam Smith and the Virtues of Enlightenment*, chapters 6 and 7
Knud Haakonssen, *The Science of the Legislator*, chapters 4 and 5

Eleven
Economic principles

I begin this chapter by briefly canvassing the overall story line, and major principles of economics, to be found in WN. In so doing, I of course mention the division of labour, the tendency to exchange that it depends on, and Smith's views on wages, profit, rent, and interest. But I do not examine them in any detail: these are topics properly explored by economists rather than philosophers. It would also be worthwhile to examine closely Smith's stadial theory of history, on which he relies extensively in WN, by which human beings move from a hunter-gatherer to a pastoral way of life, from there to agriculture, and only then develop commercial societies. But the proper place to explore this theory would be a book on Smith as a historian or a theorist of history. I focus instead in this chapter on assumptions and methodological tools of philosophical interest in WN, especially ones that have, in my opinion, been misunderstood in the secondary literature. In particular, I follow up my initial survey of WN by considering four much controverted analytic tools: the distinction between real and nominal price, the distinction between natural and market price, the idea that some kinds of labour are productive while others are unproductive, and the notion that an "invisible hand" guides economic activity towards the wealth of the nation in which it is conducted, without government help.

11.1 The contents of WN

WN is both a systematic explanation of the basic principles underlying economics and a polemical attack on mercantilism and

Physiocracy, the dominant theories of political economy in Smith's day. We might say: the book is both a "treatise" and a "tract," an heir to Montesquieu's *Spirit of the Laws* or Hutcheson's *System* as well as to the many little pamphlets on corn or money by now-forgotten writers like John Law or Thomas Mun, which it often quotes. A.J. Simmons has pointed out that Locke took his *Second Treatise on Government* to be not merely "an occasional tract in favor of the Glorious Revolution," but a general theory of politics comparable in scope to Aristotle's *Politics* or the jurisprudential systems of Grotius and Pufendorf.[1] Nonetheless, Locke's book has often been read as either a tract or a treatise. It is hard to hold the two things together, after all. The fact that Locke is trying to justify the actions of one side in a particular political struggle provokes doubts about just how general his principles can possibly be, whereas if his principles really are so general, one wonders whether they can really be used to support only one side in that political struggle. The common scholarly verdict at the moment seems to be that Locke's work is supremely successful as a tract, and somewhat less so as a treatise. With Smith, the judgment tends to be reversed. The length and comprehensiveness of WN makes it read most obviously as a treatise. It has also been set aside summarily as too theoretical by many politicians,[2] whenever its conclusions do not fit their current projects. Nevertheless, the enormous WN is as much a polemical tract as Locke's little book is a treatise. They are, indeed, quite similar in this respect (as in the fact that they look back to Aristotle, Grotius, and Pufendorf); they both try, uneasily, to straddle the gap between polemics and philosophy.

WN's polemical thrust provides us with an illuminating key to its overall structure. The very first chapter of the book signals that Smith is going to reject the idea that the wealth of a nation consists either in its reserves of precious metals, as the mercantilists claimed, or in the extent or fertility of its land, as the Physiocrats maintained. What makes nations wealthy, for Smith, is instead the degree to which the division of labour has advanced in them. And the division of labour, we learn in Chapter 2, in turn, depends on the human tendency to exchange goods. A person in a hunter-gatherer tribe begins to specialize as an arrow-maker once he realizes that he can exchange his extra arrows for other goods that he needs. In the third chapter, Smith adds that the extent of the division of labour, in any country, depends on the extent of its trading relationships: its markets. So a case for the supreme importance of free trade to economic well-being has already been made in WN's first three chapters.

The rest of Book I includes a number of arguments against trade restrictions[3] but is mostly devoted to laying out the role of money, the components of price, and the differences among wages, profit, and rent. Book II details how stock is accumulated, the ways in which the growth of stock can be affected by banking policies, the degree to which that growth depends on "productive" rather than "unproductive" labour, and the ways in which it can be used for, and enhanced by, different kinds of enterprise—agriculture, manufacturing, and commerce of various kinds. Together, Books I and II contain the core of Smith's analysis of political economy.

Book III sets out on a different tack. After arguing that by nature, a nation's agriculture will develop before its manufacturing sector, and its domestic trade before its foreign trade, Smith asks why this "natural order of things" has been "entirely inverted" throughout "the modern states of Europe" (WN 380). The answer to this question is meant to imply, contra both the mercantilists and the Physiocrats, that it is unnecessary for governments to promote either manufacturing or agriculture: that if it were not for certain politically unhealthy conditions under which Europe suffered for much of the previous millennium, both its agricultural and its manufacturing sectors would have developed very well on their own. The very long Book IV then explicitly makes the case against the mercantilists and the Physiocrats. It shows how government attempts to direct capital into particular sectors, and to restrict or underwrite exports and imports, almost always undermine their own intended effects, and includes a particularly searing indictment of the colonialist adventures that mercantilist policy had led European nations to embark on; as recent commentators have pointed out, Smith is an early and vigorous critic of colonialism.[4] Smith's economic liberalism is meant to fall out from these critiques. Once the directive programmes of both mercantilism and Physiocracy—"all systems either of preference or restraint"—are taken away, he says, the "obvious and simple system of natural liberty establishes itself of its own accord" (687).[5] Smith concludes, in Book V, by explaining what governments *should* spend money

on—infrastructure, schools: yes; commercial enterprises like the
East India Company: no—and how they should raise money.

A critique of alternative systems of political economy, and a political proposal for how to replace them, is thus integral to the entire
structure of WN. Analysis serves a polemical aim, even while the
polemics provide an opportunity for a vast and deep analysis of economic structures. WN is not an exercise in economic theory for its
own sake alone; it is, throughout, also a contribution to debates in
Smith's day over the proper role of government in economic policy.
Smith's goal seems to be to make his political recommendations
plausible by presenting elements of economic theory as clearly as
possible and in as impartial a light as possible: the "impartial spectator" position from which he writes the book contributes to an
attempt to win readers of various parties and interests over to his
political proposals. That is not to say, of course, that he is insincere in
his economic analysis or his recounting of economic facts. It is just
that these descriptive points are nested within a normative framework, which affects how they are organized and the overall point
they are marshalled to make.

That said, the main analytic tools that Smith develops for himself
in WN are designed primarily to further his descriptive goals, not
to promote a normative agenda. This point has often been missed,
especially as regards what he calls "natural price," "real price,"
"productive" labour, and the "invisible hand." We'll examine these
concepts in the remainder of this chapter.

11.2 Natural price

Smith sets up two dichotomies of price, in Book I of WN: nominal
price vs. real price, and market price vs. natural price.[6] Both have
been criticized by later economists for seeming to hold onto notions
of absolute value that, it is maintained, have no place in a properly
empirical theory. Medieval economic theories relied on a notion of
the "just price" of commodities—the price each commodity *should*
have as opposed to the price that merchants might actually charge
for it—and the great seventeenth- and eighteenth-century advance
that is supposed to have made modern economics possible is the recognition that no commodity has any absolute, true price, that prices

are always relative to the scarcity of and need for each good at a particular time and place. If one wants to talk in terms of justice, one might say that just prices—prices that everyone would freely agree to if they knew the consequences of the entire price-structure—are in fact those prices that result from free bargaining between buyers and sellers. Or one might set aside all talk of justice and simply say that prices can never be determined by moral considerations, that they will reflect only the amoral contingencies that make a market in a particular good possible. Smith's talk of a "real" and a "natural" price might then seem to slip back towards the medieval view. When he says, for instance, that to sell a commodity at its natural price is to sell it "precisely for what it is worth" (WN 72), the phrase "natural price" seems very much a normative rather than a descriptive notion. As one commentator writes, "[t]he natural price is that price a commodity ought to be."[7]

But there is nothing particularly normative, if that means "moral," about what Smith says on either real price or natural price. To begin with the second of these notions: natural price is simply the price to which a commodity will fall where a free market in that commodity operates over any considerable time. Today we would call it "equilibrium price." Smith uses the adjective "natural" because it results where there are no "artificial" constraints on the market for a commodity— laws mandating that that commodity have a certain price, or legal or other forces maintaining a group of sellers in a monopoly over the commodity. Unlike the medieval just price, moreover, it includes the "ordinary rate of profit" that a merchant can expect to make in the neighbourhood in which the commodity is being sold (WN 73). Smith recognizes that if merchants cannot make this profit, they will have reason to move into some other line of work; a merchant who regularly makes less profit than his competitors do will eventually be outbid so badly in the capital and labour markets that he will have to leave the business. There is an element of thought experiment about this—conditions of sale are frequently constrained, so to get at the natural price of commodities involves abstracting from these constraints in much the way that Galileo needed to abstract from friction to get at inertia—but the notion is nothing if not empirical. It provides a measure that can readily be approximated by surveying "ordinary rates" of rent, wages, and profit for a particular good in a particular neighbour-hood, and it plays an essential role in the hypothesis, introduced in the chapter in which it gets explained, that market prices are not arbitrary but will adjust themselves, over "any considerable time," to a level that reflects the supply and effectual demand for each commodity. The hypothesis that markets will clear when left alone depends on the possibility of a gap between actual prices and a price that truly reflects supply and demand. Natural price is Smith's way of ensuring such a gap. It is, therefore, as essential to his empirical theory as motion in a vacuum is to Newtonian physics, and Smith's use of the word "gravitating," to express the relationship between market and natural prices, suggests that he had just such a com-parison in mind.[8]

11.3 Real price

The empirical status of "real price" is somewhat harder to see. "The real price of everything," says Smith, "what every thing really costs to the man who wants to acquire it, is the toil and trouble of acquiring it" (WN 47). "Real price," in short, is labour price, an amount of labour that is somehow equivalent to each thing.[9] This notion has been used by many readers to find a labour theory of value in WN— some of whom applaud Smith for having such a theory, while others condemn him for it—which, in turn, is said to have roots in a nor-mative belief that people should work for their living.

Whether Smith holds a labour theory of value, and, if so, why he does, is a difficult question, but before we come to it, let's note that Smith needs the notion of real prices above all because he wants to compare economic conditions across great stretches of time, and he realizes that the value of any means of currency will fluctuate widely across such time-spans. He contrasts "real price" with "nom-inal price," and stresses how unreliable comparisons of nominal prices—money prices—are over time. By identifying "real price" with the amount of labour needed to acquire a good, and approxi-mating the price of labour by way of the amount of basic foodstuffs ("corn": by which Smith means grain) that a labourer consumes, Smith is able to make empirical claims about shifts in the value of currency. Corn prices approximate labour prices, says Smith, since corn[10] pays "the subsistence of the laborer" (53). And corn prices, "though they have in few places been regularly recorded, are in general better known" than the price of labour "at distant times and places." We may therefore "content ourselves with [corn prices], not as being always exactly in the same proportion as the current prices of labor, but as being the nearest approximation which can commonly be had to that proportion" (WN 56).

On the assumption that labour value remains constant across centuries, and that a substance like corn, which pays the subsistence of labourers, will set the lowest price that labour can bear, corn prices should enable us to measure changes in the real value of money over centuries. From year to year, both the real and the nominal price of a bushel of grain may vary widely, in accordance with the goodness of the harvest. But across centuries, Smith believes, both the average supply and the average demand for grain should remain fairly constant. So the nominal price of grain should give us a good idea of the value of a particular currency. Where the average price in silver of a bushel of grain is high, that reflects a low value of silver rather than a high value for grain; where the average price for grain is low, that reflects a high value for silver.

This point enables Smith to carry out an investigation of supreme importance to his critique of mercantilism. One prominent mercantilist claim was that the value of gold and silver is constantly declining, and that countries need therefore constantly to increase their holdings of these precious metals, by finding new mines or investing in manufacturing goods, which can be readily exchanged for hard currency. To refute this claim, Smith devotes a justly renowned "digression" at the end of Book I to tracing the value of silver over the four centuries preceding his writing, measuring it by way of the price of grain. He concludes that, aside from a sharp but relatively short decline when the gold and silver mines in the Americas were discovered, precious metals more or less maintained their value over that time period—their value may even have increased a bit, given the decay of some coins, and the withdrawal, here and there, of silver and gold from circulation in favour of other uses (melting them down in order to make ornaments or plateware, for instance). Real price, and its association with what it costs to maintain a labourer, thus serves Smith's empirical purposes insofar as he wants to compare economic facts across large swathes of historical time. It is not there in order to make moral points about the superiority of labour over idleness.

But what empirical sense does it make for Smith to understand real price in terms of the labour needed to acquire goods? Insofar as this amounts to a labour theory of value—a theory that all value ultimately reduces to labour and that labour itself has the same value across all societies and times—it raises enormous difficulties, both in relation to the rest of Smith's system and in itself. In relation to the rest of Smith's system, there would seem to be great tension between his analysis of income into the three distinct categories of rent, labour, and profit and his claim that labour ultimately provides the standard by which to measure all three categories (67–8). There is also tension between the claim that labour provides a universal, fixed standard of value (50, 54) and Smith's recognition, in the chapter on real price as well as elsewhere, that the compensation of labour can vary widely (53, 116–35). And in itself, the problems with the labour theory seem insurmountable. How could it be true that labour "never var[ies] in its own value" and provides the sole, "ultimate and real standard" by which to measure the value of all other commodities (51)? Will the amount of labour needed to produce a particular commodity not vary, for one thing, in accordance with the kind of technology available in each society for producing that commodity? A woollen coat may take a year or more to produce in a hunting society, but just a few weeks, or even days, in a society with sophisticated machinery for making coats. Does not the labour of different people vary in its value to others, moreover, even where equally difficult? How about the value of the same person's labour in different circumstances? It certainly seems to me that my labour has varied in its value across my lifetime. When I had no academic degree, and few marketable skills, I found it difficult to get work at more than around $4.00 an hour (minimum wage in those days), and therefore considered it a bargain if I could make on my own an object that required an hour or two's labour. Today, the same object would impose an opportunity cost of many times that amount, so it certainly is not true that I would "lay down the same portion of [my] ease, [my] liberty, and [my] happiness" (50) now, as then, if I devoted an hour to making the object rather than buying it. On Smith's terms, I am to regard the good as cheaper to me now and dearer to me in the past, rather than regarding my labour as having increased in value. But that seems a strange and arbitrary inversion of the way we normally regard these things.

We also have reason to deny that labour alone sets the value of everything else. Surely both scarcity and the need for a particular commodity play independent roles in determining value. We don't value diamonds more than water just because diamonds are hard to find, and we value oil today more than we valued oil in the nineteenth century, even if it was just as hard to find then, because we have more uses for it. If I pick up a diamond in a field, moreover, I will be able to bring in great riches despite my lack of work, while if I labour long and hard to desalinate sea-water, I am unlikely to get much for my pains. One might say that locating diamonds *normally* takes great labour while locating water normally does not, but the effort involved in locating diamonds underdetermines their value, and certainly underdetermines the *difference* in value between diamonds and water. For reasons like this, economists have tended to find the labour theory of value perplexing if not useless, and to suggest that Smith intended it to serve normative rather than descriptive purposes.

What Smith means is, I think, this:

Labour is indeed rewarded differentially in accordance with the difficulty of the task involved, as well as in accordance with "the degree of dexterity and ingenuity" it requires (65). Differences in the honour or shame attached to a type of employment, the risk involved in it, the "constancy or inconstancy of employment" in it, and the degree of trust which "must be reposed in those who exercise in [it]" also make for higher or lower wages (116–7). That said, an hour of labour in any of these different types of employment will buy very different amounts of goods in one condition of society than in another. In a society where there are plenty of goods, a street porter might give up an hour of his time for nothing less than the equivalent of a pint of beer or four loaves of bread, while a master tailor might expect the equivalent of 3 pints or 12 loaves, and a lawyer might refuse to take out his pen and notepad for anything less than the equivalent of 50 pints or 200 loaves. In a society of hunter-gatherers, or one that has been hit by some natural or man-made disaster, the street porter might be happy to work for half a loaf of bread, the tailor for a loaf and a half, and there probably would be no lawyers, but if there were, they might find their services enough in demand that they could afford to ask for 25 loaves. Smith says, about these two conditions of society, that we have to call the goods cheap in the first one and dear in the second one, rather than calling labour dear in the first case and cheap in the second. It is in this sense that an hour's "toil and trouble" (controlling for the amount and kind of toil and trouble) is an hour's toil and trouble across centuries and vastly different conditions of society, and that it can serve as an absolute measure, "never varying in its own value," against which all other values can be determined.

Why *should* it serve as such a measure, however? Could we not say, contrary to Smith, that labour is more expensive in the first of the two social conditions I have just imagined and cheaper in the second one, rather than saying that the goods are cheaper in the first case and more expensive in the second one? To some economists, it might seem that we can say this, that the price of labour is just as relative to the price of goods as the price of goods is to the price of labour. But this misses the order of explanation in any reasonable account we are likely to give of *why* the two conditions of society differ so radically. Unless we assume vast changes in human nature (which are of course possible, but for which, as regards work capacity at least, there is little evidence in the historical record), we are unlikely to suppose that the porter in the second society accepts so much less for his work because he finds carrying things easier than does the porter in the first society. Rather, the best explanation of the difference will be that goods are more *plentiful* and thus easier to come at in the first society and less plentiful, and harder to come at, in the second one. But "cheap" simply *means* "plentiful and easy to come at," while "dear" means "difficult to come at" (50–1). So it is the goods that are cheap, not the labour that is dear, in the first society, and the goods that are dear, not the labour that is cheap, in the second one.[11]

11.4 Comparing commerce to its predecessors

Measuring goods by labour rather than labour by goods also enables Smith to sharpen a general question he has been implicitly raising, throughout the opening of WN, about the value of an advanced division of labour. Chapter i of the book ends by comparing the standard of living of the poorest worker in an advanced economy with that of "an African king"—a king, in Smith's typology, of a hunter-gatherer society. (Smith, famously, has worries about the condition of the poorest workers in advanced economies which will come to the fore in Book V, so the comparison here is not unimportant to him.) And the notion of labour value as real value helps him to sharpen that comparison. Consider the fact that in chapter vi, Smith points out that "rent" and "profit," while *commanding* labour, are not themselves *based* on labour. This point will help set up Smith's sectoral analysis of the economy, and his claim that some kinds of income (rent and wages) rise with the growth of the whole economy while others (profit) do not.[12] Smith does not say, as he would if he held the normative labour theory of value sometimes attributed to him, that rent and profit, since they do not derive from labour, are illegitimate forms of income.[13] But, by reducing all prices to command over labour, he sets things up so that we can ask the question, "is the labor price of most commodities higher or lower in an economy that allows for both rent and profit, than it would be if we all labored for our goods directly?" That is, labour price—real price—enables us to ask the most basic question about commercial society: do we all gain, even those of us who live by labour alone, by having a rentier and a profit-making class?

It is in good part to pose this question, I suggest, that Smith wants the notion of labour price. Chapter v opens by defining "rich or poor" in terms of one's ability to acquire commodities—"the necessaries, conveniencies, and amusements of human life." In the next sentence, it talks about the effect of the division of labour on richness and poverty, in accordance with this definition. Here we are told that after the division of labour each person can supply himself with only "a very small part" of his necessaries, conveniences and amusements by his own labour. For the "far greater part" of those goods, he must rely on the labour of other people, and he can only do that by having commodities of his own to offer in exchange. The world of exchange thus replaces what we originally accomplished by means of our own labour, and the commodities we own represent the ticket each of us has to participate in that world of exchange. It is in this context that labour is said to be "the real measure of the exchangeable value of all commodities."

Set this paragraph, now, in the context of the whole argument of Book I. The word "exchangeable" ties the opening paragraph of chapter v to the chapter that precedes it, which ended with a distinction between "value in use" and "value in exchange." Water has great use value, a diamond little use value, but a diamond, and not water, has great value in exchange. Smith gets to this point after talking about money, which has value only in exchange, and promises at the end of chapter iv to "investigate the principles which regulate" exchangeable value, implicitly setting value in use aside as irrelevant to economics. If we back up yet farther, we find that the entire book thus far has concerned the importance of exchange. After an initial chapter telling us that the division of labour is far and away the most important factor in the expansion of production, we got a chapter explaining how the division of labour is itself made possible by the propensity of human beings to exchange with one another, followed by a third chapter maintaining that the division of labour increases in proportion to the extent of the market. Finally, Chapter 4 tells us how the development of money allows for an increase in the extent of markets: which, by a sequence that should now begin to be familiar, in turn encourages an increase in the division of labour, which, in turn, makes possible an expansion in the production of goods. So by the time we reach the opening of chapter v, we have been led through a series of greater and greater elaborations on the thought that exchange fosters an increase in the production of goods, and that it therefore plays a larger and larger role in human life as society progresses.

When the beginning of chapter v tells us that labour is the real measure of exchange value, then, we are given a measure by which to assess the *entire realm of exchange*, rather than a measure that is supposed to function *within* any particular exchange or system of exchange. We are thereby encouraged to step back and assess the entire economic world in which we participate, measuring it against the world that might once have existed, and now exists only in our imaginations, in which everyone makes all her "necessaries, conveniencies, and amusements" by herself. We are asked to think of what it would take out of our lives to make by ourselves all the material things we use, rather than acquiring them via exchange and a division of labour. This may mean that we should imagine making our food, clothes, and shelter from scratch, in a pre-social world that had never seen humans other than ourselves, or it may mean that we should imagine making things in our current world, with all its machinery, but in which the other people had mysteriously disappeared. We may picture making a coat by slaughtering a sheep, skinning it, cleaning and drying the skin, etc., or by going to a warehouse, selecting some cloth, bringing it to the relevant machines, etc. By comparing what we actually do to acquire goods with the first of these scenarios, we see quickly how much we have gained by the development of technology over the ages,[14] such that each coat can be prepared with so much less labour as to cost, in "real" terms, far less than the coat of a lone hunter. By comparing what we actually do with the second of these scenarios, we see what we gain, even given advances in technology, by continuing to participate in a division of labour rather than trying to produce everything we need by ourselves.

So real or labour price, in this sense, is a tool for thinking *about* economic systems rather than a measure to be used within them. Indeed, Smith sometimes presents "real" or "labor" price as something that *cannot* express the actual exchange value of any good. "[A] commodity which is itself continually varying in its own value can never be an accurate measure of the quantity of other things," he says, and labour alone gives the real price of every commodity because it "never var[ies] in its own value" (50–1). But within a network of exchange *every* commodity, necessarily, varies in its own value, depending upon the supply of and demand for the other commodities available to exchange with it; exchange value is, essentially, something relative. So labour, when Smith calls it "the ultimate and real standard" of all value, must stand beyond all exchanges. According to an argument that goes back at least to Plato, the standard by which to judge any set of objects that change in relation to one another must lie beyond those objects. Accordingly, labour can be "the real measure of the exchangeable value of all commodities" only if it is not itself an exchangeable value. It can measure exchangeable value only because it does not itself participate in exchange. It can help us assess the overall effect of markets only because it is itself not a market entity. It can be a measure of economics only because it is not an economic measure.

But that means that the labour in question cannot be the labour that people put on the market and sell at varying prices in societies where a division of labour and system of exchange has been established. Smith says that labour was "the first price," the "original" price of things (WN 48). His point is that labour *would be* the real price of things in a world without exchange, and that it *was* the price of things before things were exchanged—when "price" was a cost to oneself, not something established in relation to others—not that it remains such a measure in our world. And the labour that we may once have carried out before we had systems of exchange, or that we might carry out if we ceased to have such systems, would indeed be a labour in which equal quantities would be "at all times and places" of equal value—in which all we would have to consider, in assessing the value of an hour's labour, would be the "portion of … ease, liberty, and happiness" it cost us. When we are told that labour gives the real value of commodities, we are being asked to think of labour outside of a context of exchange, outside of economic relationships. We are being asked to participate in a thought experiment, and a thought experiment rather more removed from ordinary empirical testing than the experiment that gives meaning, in chapter vii, to "natural prices."

A thought experiment can serve descriptive rather than normative purposes, however, and Smith's thought experiment here helps make the descriptive point that the broadening of exchange relationships lowers the price of goods, not a normative point about the intrinsic goodness of working for a living. If we accept the notion that labour is the "real price" of goods while "money is their nominal price only," then we can see how very much cheaper goods become, regardless of their money price, where a little labour can enable us to purchase many of them. "At all times and places that is dear which it is difficult to come at, or which it costs much labour to acquire; and that cheap which is to be had easily, or with very little labour" (WN 50–1). It is not hard to imagine that in a world without a division of labour, or with a very limited one, it would take a great deal of labour to acquire even basic food, shelter, and clothing. By contrast, in the commercial world in which Smith's readers live, even a poor worker can quite easily "come at" more than adequate food, shelter, and clothing. So Smith holds at least; one might quarrel with this by contrasting life in certain miserable urban conditions with life in certain hunter-gatherer tribes. But if one quarrels, one quarrels about a fact, not a normative principle, and that is all that matters for present purposes. Smith introduces "labor value" as a tool by which to make broad comparisons of economic conditions across time; the notion functions as part of an historical investigation, not to express a moral sentiment.

11.5 Productive and unproductive labour

Smith's dichotomy between productive and unproductive labour has been dismissed just as uncomprehendingly as his dichotomies between natural and market prices, and between real and nominal prices. Once again, moralistic overtones have also been attributed to it, obscuring the plausible, if in some ways problematic, role it plays in Smith's economic analysis.

Imagine that, for a year, politicians, servants, everyone in the entertainment industry, and "churchmen, lawyers, physicians, [and] men of letters of all kinds" (331) continued to work on their regular schedule, while all farms, manufacturers, freight transport, and sales outlets shut down. What would happen? Well, the scenario is only barely imaginable, because short of some miraculous profusion of fruit on trees in public parks, the politicians, churchmen, lawyers, etc., could not continue to work. Within a very short time, everyone would run out of provisions at home and begin to starve, freeze, and have no means of getting around except their feet.

By contrast, if all the politicians, entertainers, churchmen, etc. went on strike for a year, while the farms and manufacturers and transporters and retailers kept to their regular schedule, the quality of life in our society might be diminished but life itself could go on (as lockdowns during the recent coronavirus pandemic demonstrated). There are indeed whole societies without entertainers, men of letters, and the like, but none without some way to produce and distribute food, clothing, and shelter.

This is all that Smith means by distinguishing between productive and unproductive labourers and saying that the productive ones maintain both themselves and the unproductive ones (332). Unproductive labourers are a luxury, productive ones a necessity. Smith says that unproductive labourers include "some ... of the gravest and most important" professions, and we know from elsewhere that he has great respect for poets and philosophers.[15] So he does not mean to equate "unproductive" with "lazy" or "wasteful." His point is just that a country can afford to enlarge its unproductive sphere, however worthwhile it may be, only in proportion to the extent of its productive sphere.

Smith also wants to make two other points, one of which should be welcome to modern economists while the other is troublesome. The welcome point is directed against the Physiocrats, who had originally introduced the distinction between productive and unproductive labour. For the Physiocrats, only agriculture could be productive. All production must be rooted in "nature" (*physis*), they felt—in the end, all other production depends on those who gather or increase the resources of nature. Smith responds by recognizing not only that manufacturing can give farmers an incentive to produce more than they would otherwise do, and that the manufacturing goods of a country can be exchanged for agricultural produce from elsewhere, but also that the work of merchants, by transporting goods from one market where they are in abundance to another where they are scarce, enhances the produce of a nation. "Unless a capital was employed in transporting, either the rude or manufactured produce, from the places where it abounds to those where it is wanted," he says, "no more of either could be produced than was necessary for the neighborhood" (361). So the merchant, too, is a productive labourer. To return to the imaginary scenario we sketched above, suppose that all retailers (whether online or brick and mortar) were to close for a year, while everything else remained as it is. Only those who lived on or near a farm could survive for long in such a situation, and very soon all manufacturing would close along with the stores. So commercial activity is very much a part of productive labour in any economy with an advanced division of labour. Commercial activity is indeed very much a part of what *nature* produces—as long as we are willing to include under that term the proclivity, in *human* nature, to increase production by dividing up labour and then exchanging the results. Smith is to be commended for deepening what should count as "nature" for economic purposes: for including the work of merchants in the *physis* that determines the degree to which nations can allow for "unproductive" activity.

What is more troublesome is Smith's attempt to link "productive" labour to something that "lasts for some time at least after that labour is past" (WN 330). Using menial service as a model, Smith says that unproductive labour does not "fix or realize itself" in a vendible commodity. Your valet lays out the perfect suit for you to wear. You enjoy the convenience, as well as the respect you get later in the day because you are so well turned out. But what the valet did cannot be re-sold, or "stocked and stored up" to add value to something that will later be re-sold. It "adds to the value of nothing."[16] The acts for which menial servants get paid "generally perish in the very instant of their performance, and seldom leave any trace or value behind them, for which an equal quantity of service could afterwards be procured." The service can be sold just once, to the person who first enjoys it. After he or she enjoys it, it disappears. So it cannot be re-sold—cannot be exchanged for anything else. For the same reason, it cannot be added to the general produce of a nation. It cannot contribute to the plenty of the nation and the consequent cheapness of its goods.

There are two problems with this analysis. First, unproductive labour is not generally as ephemeral as menial service. Second, even ephemeral goods can "leave a trace … behind them," to be sold in a future exchange. The first problem may strike us immediately in a way that it did not strike Smith because we now have ways of preserving what were in Smith's day necessarily ephemeral events. Smith could compare the performance of a play to the work of a menial servant because the play, like the valet's laying out of a suit, gave satisfaction only to those who actually attended it. By way of film and sound recordings, however, practically all art and entertainment can be turned into a "vendible commodity" today, and sold and re-sold many times in return for other goods. The work of an actor very much "fixes and realizes itself in some particular subject" when that work is captured on film. That was not so in Smith's time, which helps explain why he saw artists and entertainers as producing nothing that could, for instance, be sold to other countries in return for food. Yet even in his own day, the work of "men of letters" was not ephemeral, nor was the work of a lawyer or physician, which could permanently change a person's legal condition or state of health. An enhanced state of health might help a person work better, however, and an enhanced legal condition might enable a person to attract investment loans more easily. So it is not at all clear why work that leads to these results should count as "unproductive."

In addition, ephemeral goods *can* leave an economic "trace" behind them. Smith seems to believe that there can never be a regular market for something ephemeral. But that is not true. Consider a nation that has a highly developed tourist industry. Perhaps it has a lively theatre district, or hotels with wonderful service, and these draw in consumers on a regular basis, offering their goods in return for the repetition of an event that, in itself, is ephemeral. Then the theatrical event or hotel service does "leave a trace or value behind it," for which an equal quantity of another good can be procured: in the reputation of the event or hotel, which can draw in ever new customers. We might say that a proper understanding of the good produced is that it consists in a repetition of certain events across time—that the actor and the chef sell, not this particular performance or fine meal, but a series of performances or meals. In this way, services can be sold in a regular market just like any palpable good, and can form a part of a nation's stock. There are nations today that draw most of their goods from other countries in return for tourist services.

Of course that was not true in Smith's day. But it is unclear that he should be excused on this count. One would expect that his sound inclusion of commercial activity within the class of productive labour would have prevented him from assuming that the ephemeral cannot make a regular contribution to market value. For the merchant, too, does not leave a *literal* trace on the goods he moves and sells. The merchant buys corn wholesale from the farmer and then sells it to a retailer, at a considerable markup. Nothing changes in the corn as a result of this; the corn does not get any value added. Or rather: the corn gets no value added unless we count the very movement from one locale where it commands a lower value to another where it commands a higher one as an increase in value. Smith clearly does seem to do that, else he would not include merchants among productive labourers. But the same logic entails that the actor "adds value" to his theatre and the waiter "adds value" to his hotel. If "value added" can consist in anything that enhances the demand for a good, then unproductive as well as productive labourers should be able to add value to a nation's goods.

So there are problems with Smith's dichotomy between productive and unproductive labour, even once it is stripped of all moral connotations, and put to work in economic analysis. But its role as an analytic tool needs to be appreciated. Perhaps it is of little use to modern economists,[17] but it should be clear that and why Smith thought it could illuminate an important factor in how nations amass wealth.[18]

11.6 The invisible hand

We need finally to examine Smith's notorious appeal to an "invisible hand" in the middle of WN, and the reasons why he seems to think, more generally, that markets are guided by such a hand to deliver wealth to nations.[19]

WN is filled with explanations of social institutions in which a result beneficial to society is reached without any agent directly intending that result. In the second chapter of Book IV, this mode of explanation is used to argue that merchants will naturally tend to direct their investments towards domestic industry, even without government regulations to that effect, and even though they are interested in their own gain rather than the good of their societies. About that tendency, Smith says that each merchant is "in this, as in many other cases, led by an invisible hand to promote an end which was no part of his intention" (WN 456). The vivid phrase he uses here has been lifted from the passage to characterize Smith's view of economic activity in general.[20] Whenever people are left alone to pursue their own interests, Smith is said to believe, an invisible hand ensures that they will benefit society as a whole. Which raises the question: does Smith have some sort of empirical or mathematical proof to show that this must be the case, or is he tacitly relying, as the metaphor of an "invisible hand" might suggest, on some notion of Providence, beneficently guiding human activity behind the scenes?[21]

The first thing to say about the interpretation of Smith that prompts this question is that, insofar as it relies on the famous sentence in WN IV.ii, it misreads that sentence. The phrase "in this, *as in many other* cases" has been overlooked, for one thing. Smith provides us elsewhere with a number of cases in which an individual's unconstrained pursuit of his or her interest does *not* benefit the society. In WN II.ii he talks of "projectors" who developed irresponsible ways of raising money that brought on a crisis in British and Scottish banking. In V.i.g, he says that only when a church offers modest pay to its clergy, and pays them equally so as to *remove* any inclination they may otherwise have to "better their condition" materially, will the clergy be appropriately learned, decent, and independent.[22] Here individual self-interest and the well-being of society are in potential conflict, and self-interest must be guided in a certain way if it is to serve society. More generally, as Anthony Waterman puts it, Smith does not see actions on private interest as benefiting society where they are taken "within the wrong sort of institutional framework" (ET 915).[23]

So Smith is by no means propounding a universal rule in WN IV.ii. It would be odd, moreover, if such a rule appeared in this context. Smith is making a relatively small point (that merchants tend to base even their "carrying trade" in their home ports), and has adduced a few plausible but weak generalizations about merchant behaviour in support of that point. If he wanted to proclaim that an invisible hand *always* guides individual economic decisions towards the good of society, whether or not the individual intends that good, we would expect that proclamation at the opening of the book, as part of his grounding theory of economic activity. The theory Smith gives us there does support the claim that people *generally* wind up promoting the social good in their economic behaviour, but there is no hint that this holds in all cases, much less that it is guaranteed to hold by either empirical or metaphysical laws.

Nevertheless, several recent scholars have suggested that Smith's invisible hand claims rest on a belief in a benevolent deity who governs nature for our benefit.[24] If so, Smith's views on economic policy would be far less interesting than they have seemed to his many non-religious readers. Fortunately, religious readings of WN's invisible hand are demonstrably wrong. It is true that the two other occurrences of the phrase "invisible hand" in Smith's work have religious overtones. In the early "History of Astronomy," Smith says that ancient religions attributed certain sorts of events to "the invisible hand of Jupiter" (EPS 49). In TMS, Smith maintains that the rich are "led by an invisible hand" to share most of their wealth with the poor, and follows up this claim by saying that "[w]hen Providence divided the earth among a few lordly masters," it did not forget the poor (TMS 184–5). But in WN the mention of an invisible hand is not conjoined with any reference to Providence, and there is no invocation of that term or any related notion in the entire book.[25] Indeed, WN does not share the optimism that Smith expresses in TMS's "invisible hand" passage about economic relationships always benefiting the poor as well as the rich.[26] The blanket optimism of TMS would in any case render pointless Smith's efforts to demonstrate that free commercial economies promote a great expansion of material wealth. If people are happy regardless of their economic condition, then whether their society has a greater or smaller stock of material goods, and whether they themselves are employed or not, should be irrelevant to them. Smith's views on economic policy should then be that a mercantilist or Physiocratic or indeed a feudal economy is just as good as a free trading economy, since Providence will take care of everyone under every economy. He does not say that, of course. So the central "invisible hand" argument of WN, the argument for the greater beneficent tendencies of unguided than mercantilist or Physiocratic economies, cannot be construed to depend on a general, metaphysical optimism according to which Providence will make sure that everything turns out for the best in all economies.

What does the argument depend on? Simply, I think, on the empirical premise that, normally, *society as a whole makes possible the opportunities for any individual in it to gain.* More precisely, if inelegantly:

> (IH:) Where people act freely rather than under threats of violence, long-term opportunities for any individual to better herself are made possible by the needs and wants of her society.

Like ants or bees and unlike bears or tigers, human beings acquire material goods only in society, which means that an opportunity for one person to gain will normally so much as exist only if the needs or desires of other people make it possible. In general, people will pay you for something only if they need or want that thing. The "invisible hand" thus represents social forces, not Providential ones. An individual may think he is pursuing only his own interest by making or selling a certain good, but it is the needs of society that create the niche within which he can gain. His gains, therefore, will serve the good of society whether he intends to do that or not.

If this seems disappointingly obvious, that is because we expect too much of the invisible hand passage. Smith himself does not write the passage as if it offered particularly striking news. Rather, here and throughout WN, he treats the fact that society shapes the opportunities for each of us to gain as something that ought to be uncontroversial, once one reflects on how the division of labour comes about. That the role to which self-interest draws the merchant is normally one that maximizes the economic gain he can provide for the whole society follows trivially from the account Smith has been giving of economic roles since the beginning of the book. It is no wonder that, two paragraphs after invoking the "invisible hand," Smith recalls the description of the division of labour he gave in Book I, chapter ii:

> The taylor does not attempt to make his own shoes, but buys them of the shoemaker. The shoemaker does not attempt to make his own cloaths, but employs a taylor. The farmer attempts to make neither the one nor the other, but employs those different artificers. All of them find it for their interest to employ their whole industry in a way in which they have some advantage over their neighbors.
>
> (WN 456–7; compare 27–8)

The invisible hand sentence thus depends on the fundamental economic principle of WN: that human beings, alone among animals, have the understanding to realize they can get more for themselves by making goods that satisfy the needs and wants of others.

Neither the invisible hand sentence nor its underlying principle is really trivial, moreover. In the first place, as the principle (IH) we have drawn out of that sentence makes clear, it is true only on condition that people are not threatened by violence. That is where the advantage of commercial economies over feudal economies, and free commercial economies over mercantilist or Physiocratic ones, comes in. In a feudal economy, lords hold threats of violence over their serfs, and in protectionist commercial economies, governments use their threat of violence to prevent some kinds of trades from taking place. It is crucial, for Smith, that trade benefits everyone who participates in it only where governments protect individuals against threats of force by other individuals, and refrain from using their own threat of force to interfere with exchanges unless absolutely necessary.

In the second place, there are a number of empirical, eminently defeasible assumptions built into the claim that people unconstrained by violence will trade for mutual benefit. One might deny that claim by saying that people don't generally know what they need or want, and can therefore be fooled by clever merchants— and there is a long-standing tradition that criticizes free market economies in just this way. Or one might consider differentials in wealth to constitute something like a threat of force, such that wealthy merchants can compel poorer people to buy things at prices much higher than they want to pay; this too is a claim put forward by a long line of critics of the free market. Smith rejects the first of these claims, insisting repeatedly that ordinary people, in general, know very well what they need to know to make their economic choices (WN 138, 346, 362, 456, 531). To the second, he says that any sort of force a particular merchant might have over a particular market at a particular time will normally be dissipated by competition from other merchants who hope to gain by undercutting the first one (77, 329, 361–2). Here competition thrives on the needs of the people oppressed by the would-be monopolist. Once again, social needs structure the opportunities for gain, and gain entails the satisfaction of otherwise unmet needs.

On the deepest level, the point of Smith's invisible hand accounts of social phenomena is that society structures both the means available for any individual to attain his ends and his very conception of those ends. The opening chapters of WN show that opportunities for an individual to better himself are normally made possible by the needs of his society, and chapters I.iii and III.1–3 of TMS make clear that what he will *count* as "bettering" himself normally arises out of the influences upon him, via sympathy, of his friends and neighbours. In WN, the stress is on the fact that we are animals who need the assistance of others like ourselves, a point made as early as the second chapter:

> In almost every other race of animals each individual, when it is grown up to maturity, is intirely independent, and in its natural state has occasion for the assistance of no other living creature. But man has almost constant occasion for the help of his brethren.
>
> (26)

We are structured to help each other, regardless of our intentions; we would not survive otherwise. The would-be arrow-maker in WN I.ii finds that he can make a living off of arrows only because many of his fellow tribespeople want arrows, and this example is supposed to encapsulate the way that the needs of other people, and the trade motivated by those needs, determine the range of things each of us can do to increase our possessions. In WN IV.ii we learn in addition that the way that trust and mutual understanding work leads us to favour our own society over its rivals. The merchant naturally knows his fellow citizens better than he knows foreigners, and trusts them more; that is why he favours trade at home over trade abroad (454).[27] And in TMS, we learn that our desires themselves are shaped by our attempt to have just those feelings that our friends and neighbours can sympathize with.[28] Consequently, as Smith stresses in TMS IV.i, even when social forces lead us into a false conception of our ends, what we do to pursue these illusory goods will benefit the society that has misled us.

It follows from this highly socialized conception of the self that individuals will generally promote the public good regardless of whether their own interest is furthered, harmed, or left alone by their actions. In TMS IV.i, the agents led by the "invisible hand" contribute to the public good without particularly advancing their own good, and in Book III of WN, feudal lords promote the good of society even as they *destroy* their own favourite good (power over their vassals). What powers Smith's invisible hand are the forces by which societies shape individuals, and lead them generally to serve each other's ends. If societies did not do this, they would not survive; Darwinian evolution is an excellent tool for explaining the processes that Smith describes. There is nothing mysterious about them, nothing unnatural, nor need they be rooted in the will of any divine Author of nature.[29]

Of course, Smith's general view of the power society has over individuals, no less than his specific claims about how this power works towards mutual benefit, is open to controversy. What matters for our purposes is not the truth of these claims but their empirical status, however, and their defeasibility testifies to that empirical status. Smith uses plausible but defeasible empirical claims, not metaphysical ones, to underwrite his invisible hand explanations, and his invisible hand itself consists in a set of social rather than metaphysical forces. The beneficent tendencies nudging individual economic decisions in the direction of a society's good arise from general facts about human nature. None of these facts are underwritten by metaphysical guarantees. None of them are even universally true: for which reason the invisible hand works, as Smith says, only "in many cases," not in all.

11.7 Summary

We've seen that Smith's great economic treatise is also a polemical tract against government programs for directing investment towards particular industries or sectors. At the same time, we've seen that the terms he uses to structure his analysis—even "natural price" and "real price," "productive labor," and "the invisible hand"—have a purely descriptive function, rather than a normative one. They serve as imaginative constructs that connect together particular economic observations, so as to produce a scientific system in economics, just as notions like gravity serve, for Smith, to produce systems in physics (see Sections 2.4 and 2.7). And Smith's science of economics is just as naturalistic as Newton's physics. It is free, in particular, of any religious underpinning: the invisible hand that he invokes is a metaphor for wholly explicable social forces, not mysterious divine ones.

Notes

1 John Simmons, *The Lockean Theory of Rights* (Princeton: Princeton University Press, 1992), 9 and footnote 4 on that page. The internal quotation is from Andrei Rapaczynski, *Nature and Politics* (Cornell, 1987), 15.

2 Henry Dundas, a friend and mentor of Smith's, said exactly this when advocating a renewed charter for the East India Company three years after Smith's death. See my *On Adam Smith's Wealth of Nations*, 261–2.

3 It includes a sharp critique of apprenticeship requirements, for instance.

4 See especially Jennifer Pitts, *A Turn to Empire* (Princeton: Princeton University Press, 2005).

5 Note that the "system of natural liberty," here, entails just that governments should not promote any particular industry or economic sector; it has nothing to do with welfare policy.

6 See WN, chapters v and vii.

7 Jack Weinstein, *On Adam Smith* (Belmont: Wadsworth, 2001), 74. Weinstein wants to align Smith strongly with medieval just price theory, saying that Smith does not include profit in natural price and that one is therefore "forced to wonder whether profit is somehow 'unnatural,' and whether or not this is implicitly one of Smith's many criticisms of greed." It is, however, not true that Smith leaves profit out of natural price:

> When the price of any commodity is neither more nor less than what is sufficient to pay the rent of the land, the wages of the labour, *and the profits of the stock* employed in raising, preparing and bringing it to market, … the commodity is then sold for what may be called its natural price.
>
> *(WN 72, my emphasis)*

Moreover, the profits involved in bringing something to market, as the next paragraph makes clear, include the profit "of the person who is to sell [the finished product] again"—the profit of the merchant, who "buys" the good from the workers and sells it "again" in the market—which Smith calls "the proper fund of [the merchant's] subsistence." Smith's point in these paragraphs is indeed precisely the opposite of the one Weinstein attributes to him: he aims to show that "common language" makes a *mistake* when it excludes profit from sales from the proper cost of a commodity. Only commodities that someone is willing to trade regularly will anyone else be willing to produce, so the profit of merchants is essential to the long-term production of commodities, and thus very much part of their natural price. The importance of commerce to production is a central teaching of WN, and one of the ways in which it is most concerned to overcome long-standing popular prejudices.

8 But see Schliesser, *Indispensable Hume*, who argues that the analogy to gravitation would really hold only if market and natural prices gravitated towards *one another*. I think Smith explains himself badly but does want to use an analogy with

gravitation. A better way to put the analogy might be as follows: market prices will gravitate towards one another—buyer's prices and seller's prices will attract one another towards an equilibrium point—and natural price expresses, not the source of gravitation, but the point at which the two types of prices meet.

In his chapter 4, Schliesser provides a brilliant account of how "natural price" provides a theoretically-useful gap between ideal conditions and empirical reality.

9 A small point, here: Some commentators have made heavy weather over Smith's apparent wish to define the labour price of an object both in terms of the labour needed to *make* an object and in terms of the labour that the sale of that object can *command*, pointing out that these need by no means be the same (see for instance Richard Teichgraeber, *'Free Trade' and Moral Philosophy* (Durham: Duke University Press, 1986), 182n12). But Smith was not confused on this issue: he quite clearly meant the latter, not the former. The exchange value of any commodity, he says, its value to a person who means to exchange it rather than use it, is "the quantity of labor which it enables him *to purchase or command*" (WN 47). The first line of the next paragraph may seem in tension with this definition—"[t]he real price of everything … is the toil and trouble of acquiring it"—but in the rest of that paragraph Smith makes clear that he is talking about the "real price" of an object we *wish to acquire*, not of an object we have already acquired. So once again he is defining real price in terms of the labour we can command, by way of the objects we already own, not of the labour needed to make those objects. He does say that the object we offer in exchange for one we want to acquire "is supposed… to contain the value of an equal quantity" of labour, but the accent here is on the word "supposed" and later on in the text Smith will say explicitly that the labour needed to make an object will be in "proportion" to (even here: not *equal* to!) the labour that that object can command only in the earliest state of society, the state that "precedes both the accumulation of stock and the appropriation of land" (WN 65). When societies move beyond this primitive state, rent and profit, which are not reducible to labour (66–7), will make up part of the price of almost everything, so the labour an object can command need not be at all proportional to the labour required to produce it. In both this and the earlier condition, moreover, real value lies in command over labour, not in the labour "contained" in objects:

> The real value of all the different component parts of price … is measured by the quantity of labor which they can, each of them, purchase or command. Labour measures the value not only of that part of price which resolves itself into labour, but of that which resolves itself into rent, and of that which resolves itself into profit.

(67–8)

10 "Or whatever else is the common and favourite vegetable food of the people": WN 95–6, 206, 258–9.

11 There is something a bit circular in this argument. Smith uses a common language definition of "cheap" as "easy to come at" and "dear" as "hard to come at," while acknowledging himself that "easy to come at" is just a synonym for "costs little labor" and "hard to come at" is a synonym for "costs much labour" (50–1). The argument does not primarily depend on this equation, however—the point about the proper order of empirical explanation does most of the work—and I think Smith would say that common language generally reflects the facts about our natural and social worlds, and that the common meaning of words like "cheap" and "dear" reflects our common understanding that when we exchange goods we are simply "coming at" them, indirectly, through our labour, as we might once have "come at" them directly by making them ourselves.

12 On the importance of sectoral analysis to the argument of WN, see Brown, *Adam Smith's Discourse*, 164–82, 196–206.

13 Although he does remark, snidely, that rent comes about because "landlords, like all other men, love to reap where they never sowed" (WN 67).

14 Itself a consequence of the division of labour, according to Smith: WN 19–20.

15 See Chapter 2, above.

16 This is not entirely true: it might add to *your* value, and if you are off to a job interview, that might be of real significance. But Smith is presumably thinking of aristocrats who do not seek or take jobs, and for them the services of their valets probably does lack economic value.

17 But see Bladen, *From Adam Smith*, 65–7, who provides an interesting re-interpretation of the distinction between productive and unproductive labour that sheds light on why menial labour is so prevalent in under-developed economies, and why such labour is both rarer and better recompensed in better developed ones.

18 I discuss this distinction further, and examine its connection to Smith's interest in "independency," in *On Adam Smith's Wealth of Nations*, section 33.

19 In connection with this section, see Emma Rothschild's chapter on the invisible hand in ES (116–56). Not only is Rothschild's own reading of the nature and role of the invisible hand metaphor an extremely intriguing one, but her footnotes contain the most complete survey of literature on this topic I have ever seen. Whether one agrees with her own views or not, there is no better source for materials on this issue.

20 Passages that express the same view, but without the vivid phrase, include WN 374, 524–5, 530, 630.

21 Athol Fitzgibbons maintains that "Smith's invisible hand was the hand of divine Providence" (Fitzgibbons, *Adam Smith's System*, [Oxford: Clarendon Press, 1995], 89; see also 193–4). I disagree strongly. Rothschild shows that this view was held by nineteenth-century *opponents* of Smith (ES 118), and argues that Smith himself opposed the Stoic notion of "providential order" that Fitzgibbons attributes to him (131–6). I would modify this latter point a little. As I argued

in Chapter 8, I think it is clear that Smith did hold out the possibility of a providential order as a reasonable element of a moral faith, but that he never relied on such a possibility in his scientific accounts—in his descriptions of how our sentiments, or society, or markets, work.

22 "Nothing but exemplary morals can give dignity to a man of small fortune," he says (WN 810), so an institution that needs to be served by morally exemplary people will do well to discourage the profit-motive in its employees.

23 See also Nathan Rosenberg, "Some Institutional Aspects of the *Wealth of Nations*," *Journal of Political Economy* 18/6 (1960) and Muller, *Adam Smith in His Time and Ours*, chapters 5 and 9.

24 See note 21 above.

25 Peter Minowitz stresses this point: *Profits, Priests*, chapters 7–9.

26 See Section 10.5, above.

27 Implicitly, this argument depends upon Smith's analysis of sympathy in TMS. We build trust and understanding of other people through sympathy, but sympathy is a highly particularized mechanism, which works most effectively between people who see each other often. As a consequence, people will always tend to trust those they know more than those they don't know—their neighbours more than unfamiliar fellow countrymen and unfamiliar countrymen more than unfamiliar people from foreign countries.

28 See above, Section 7.1.

29 Although they *may* be so rooted: see the discussion of Smith's religious views in Section 8.9, above.

Further reading

Vincent Bladen, *From Adam Smith to Maynard Keynes*, Book I
Samuel Hollander, *The Economics of Adam Smith*
Emma Rothschild, *Economic Sentiments*, chapters 3–5

Twelve
Liberalism

I'd like to close this book by bringing WN together with Smith's moral philosophy. We'll revisit some themes already canvassed in Chapter 10, about Smith's moral purposes in developing a theory of political economy, and expand them in ways that can address the question of the extent to which Smith belongs under the political rubric that today we call "liberalism."

12.1 Speech and freedom

Let's begin by returning to the famous lines in the beginning of WN that have been (mis-)used to represent Smith as advocating that we act only on our self-interest:

> It is not from the benevolence of the butcher, the brewer, or the baker that we expect our dinner, but from their regard to their own interest. We address ourselves, not to their humanity but to their self-love, and never talk to them of our own necessities but of their advantages. Nobody but a beggar chuses to depend chiefly upon the benevolence of his fellow-citizens.
>
> (WN 26–7)

I argued in Chapter 10 that these lines, especially when taken in the context of the paragraph in which they appear, cannot possibly make the case that people are thoroughly self-interested.[1] The passage does not even say that we are self-interested in our interaction with our butcher and baker: just that we address ourselves to *their* self-love.

We may seek bread for a dinner in which we hope to show our love for our family, or nourish homeless people or support an NGO. Nor need the butcher or baker be self-interested, even if that is the aspect of him that we address: he may want the money we pay him to help his family or an incapacitated neighbour or an NGO. It is something about *economic relationships*—about the relationship we stand in to those with whom we exchange products—not about human nature, that leads us to "talk of… their advantages" rather than our own needs: to abstract from their, and our, familial and neighbourly and civic feelings and duties. Nothing here suggests that either party to the exchanges in question *lacks* those familial and neighbourly and civic feelings and duties.

Once we recognize that Smith's point has to do with the structure of economic exchange, rather than the character of the people who engage in such exchange, we can put these famous lines back into their context and understand what the paragraph in which they feature is really about. That paragraph begins by saying that "it belongs not to our present subject" to inquire into whether our propensity to exchange things is simply a basic principle of human nature that cannot be further explained or whether, "as seems more probable," it is a "necessary consequence of the faculties of reason and speech." In the parallel passages in LJ, Smith is not so coy about answering this question. He instead declares that "the principle in the human mind" on which the propensity to exchange is founded "is clearly the naturall inclination every one has to persuade" (LJ 352, 493–4). Offering a shilling, he says there, "is in reality offering an argument to persuade one to do so and so as it is for his interest." And he goes on to note how often we try to persuade others of everything we believe; he claims, indeed, that "every one is practising oratory on others thro the whole of his life." Other animals "have no notion" of how to address themselves to the self-interest of other members of their species—how to persuade them that a particular action could be in the joint interest of several of them. As a result, even when they seem to co-operate in, say, "rob[bing] an orchard," they will "fight (even unto death)" over the spoils. Human beings, by contrast, can bring each other to understand that an action is in their mutual self-interest. We can therefore exchange, hence divide labour, hence increase the goods available to everyone. It is not that we *are* self-interested, but that we can *co-operate even when* we are self-interested, that distinguishes us from other animals and makes possible the vast wealth of goods that only human beings produce.

Despite the fact that Smith downplays the connection of exchange to speech in the butcher-and-baker paragraph in WN, he makes a very similar argument there. The importance of speech runs through the paragraph. "Nobody ever saw one animal by its gestures and natural cries signify to another, this is mine, that yours; I am willing to give this for that," Smith writes. Further down he says that "Give me that which I want, and you shall have this which you want is the meaning of every... offer" to bargain. That is followed by the lines about "address[ing] ourselves" to the self-love of the butcher, brewer, and baker. And these snippets of conversation are held together by the claim that we human beings, unlike other animals, "shew [others] that it is for their advantage to do for [us]" what we want of them. We can speak to one another, hence persuade one another, that an exchange of goods is in our mutual self-interest. That is Smith's point in this famous early paragraph. And his arguments throughout the rest of WN depend similarly on our ability to *address ourselves to* one another's self-interest, not on our *being* self-interested.

There is an additional point about motivation that runs through WN, however, which is also signalled in the paragraph we have been examining. Trying to persuade others to enter a mutually beneficial exchange gets contrasted repeatedly, in that paragraph, with "fawning" on others. "A puppy fawns upon its dam," says Smith, and a man without other means of getting others to do what he wants similarly "endeavours by every servile and fawning attention to obtain their goodwill." The association of "servility" and "fawning" with efforts to win over the goodwill of others suggests that the beggar, further on in the paragraph, who "depend[s] chiefly on the benevolence of his fellow-citizens" must also take on a servile and fawning manner—as indeed beggars often do. Attempting to persuade others that an act you want them to perform is in their own interest as well comes off in this context as the behaviour of a dignified, independent being, while trying to win the benevolence of others goes with indignity and dependency. Once again, Smith is elevating not self-interest per se, but a kind of *relationship* in which neither party needs to depend on the other in order to satisfy her self-interest. Relationships in which both parties can rely on persuasion, rather than fawning, to arrive at a common end are relationships among free and dignified beings.

Smith associates persuasion with freedom elsewhere in WN. When trying to explain why people hold slaves, given that slavery, on his view, is economically inefficient—and obviously so, since slaves lack an incentive to work—Smith says, "The pride of man makes him love to domineer, and nothing mortifies him so much as to be obliged to condescend to persuade his inferiors" (WN 388). If I have to persuade you, I must presuppose that you might not agree with me, and that only your agreement will mark success in my efforts. There is then an implicit equality in a relationship that depends upon persuasion. We hold slaves because we don't like to see others as our equals: our pride is better satisfied by making them do what we want whether they like it or not. But ideally we shouldn't act like this. The impartial spectator, which presumes a basic equality of all people, rejects such behaviour. It calls on us, instead, to stand always ready to persuade. Persuasion contrasts with both fawning and forcing, and is the appropriate vehicle for human beings to use if they are to work together while maintaining their freedom.

Now the form of freedom that most matters to Smith is not the bare possession of political rights, but the socio-economic condition that he calls "independency." In LJ, he says that "Nothing tends so much to corrupt and enervate and debase the mind as dependency, and nothing gives such noble and generous notions of probity as freedom and independency" (LJ 333; see also 486). Having many "retainers and dependents"—many servants—is indeed a source of crime (332–3): when people who have long been servants are turned out of the homes they work for, they have no skills and no sense of how to run their lives—they "are the most helpless set of men imaginable" (333)—and therefore turn to crime to support themselves. Smith doesn't make quite such strong claims in WN, but he does say that servile work renders people "idle, dissolute, and poor" and that, where it is prevalent, it "corrupts... the industry" even of those who would otherwise be hard-working (WN 335–6). He also praises the agricultural life for "the independency which it really affords" and says that a colonist in America will turn from being an artificer to being a planter because "he feels that an artificer is the servant of his customers, from whom he derives his subsistence," while "a planter who cultivates his own land... is... independent of all the world" (WN 379).

These are not stray, offhand comments. Recall that Smith describes commerce and manufactures as having taken people out of "servile dependency upon their superiors" and calls this "by far the most important of all their effects" (WN 412).[2] In LJ, he praises commerce as "one great preventive" of dependency (LJ 333), and says that, by bringing about independency, it is "the best police for preventing crimes" (487). In WN he explains in detail how feudalism bred servility while commerce brings independence. Under feudalism, each person, "being fed entirely by [the] bounty" of a single master, had to obey that master in peace and war. In the commercial world, by contrast, "each tradesman or artificer derives his subsistence from the employment, not of one, but of a hundred or a thousand different customers" and therefore, while being "in some measure obliged to them all, is not absolutely dependent upon any one of them" (WN 413, 420). Increase in independency—we are never *absolutely* independent—is for Smith not just one advantage of commerce but its most important advantage: the main reason for preferring it to other economic systems.

I propose that underlying these claims are two deep themes of Smith's moral theory: that self-command is basic to the development of any other virtue, and that virtues are developed by practice, not just by an orientation of the will. A person who is dependent on others, like a servant or a beggar,[3] does not get much chance to shape his own life. Constantly at the beck and call of his master, he makes few choices even about when and what to eat, and none about what skills to develop. Such a person will have little opportunity to develop self-command. But in that case, he is unlikely to have any other virtues—we need self-command in order to gain control over any of our passions. (For which reason, Smith says, "self-command is not only itself a great virtue, but from it all the other virtues seem to derive their principal lustre" (TMS 241).) A form of political economy that makes room for people to run their own lives is therefore better for the virtue of those people than other forms of political economy. Independence makes possible self-command, and Smith values commerce above all for that independence.

That is not to say, of course, that Smith is uninterested in the material consequences of economic systems. He begins his examination of what he calls "police" in LJ by delineating the aspect of it of interest to jurisprudence as "cheapness or plenty" (LJ 331, 486) and both there and in WN, he is centrally concerned with how goods become maximally "comeattible" (343). It is noteworthy that Smith *defines* wealth or opulence, in a nation, as this availability (cheapness) of goods,[4] not as the possession, by the sovereign or a privileged class, of great treasures. A country counts as wealthy, for him, when the poorest labourer can afford a decent share of food, clothing, and lodging.[5]

Still, Smith's claim that "by far the most important" effect of commerce and manufactures is the way they enabled people to achieve "liberty and security," and free themselves from "servile dependency," suggests strongly that, given two systems that are roughly equal in the degree to which they make basic goods available, Smith prefers the one that most fosters freedom and independence. Such a view also fits well with the contempt Smith shows, in both TMS and WN, for the pursuit of material goods above and beyond food, clothing, and lodging. The rich are fascinated by trivial objects of vanity, he says in TMS (181–5)—"baubles and trinkets"— and in WN he recommends that "carriages of luxury" pay higher road tolls than vehicles carrying freight so that "the indolence and vanity of the rich is made to contribute... to the relief of the poor" (WN 725). This attitude towards material wealth makes it unlikely that Smith had much interest in the goods provided by economic systems beyond those that go towards everyone's basic needs. Once these are satisfied, what is far more important is whether the system enables its participants to work independently: whether it enables them to do without a "master." And Smith thinks that the commercial system (what we today call "capitalism") does that better than any other system.

This might seem surprising. Isn't Smith aware that workers under capitalism have been extremely dependent on their employers—so much so that they could be forced to work for extraordinarily long hours, or locked in their rooms, like the employees of the Triangle Shirtwaist Company in New York in 1911, 145 of whom burned to death in a fire as a result? What "independence" does he think the workers have in the pin factory that he describes at the beginning of WN, and why on earth would he suppose that they were freer in their work choices than a farm hand, in the agricultural age that preceded commerce?

I think the answer to these questions is that Smith did not anticipate the shape that labour in industrial capitalism was going to take. The fact that WN opens by illustrating the division of labour with a pin factory is misleading. The example was a stock one in the literature on the division of labour that preceded Smith,[6] and Smith distances himself from it before and after using it.[7] Indeed, as he explicitly says, it doesn't serve his purposes very well. He wants to show how labour *spontaneously* divides itself, as people realize they can make a living specializing in one craft. That is the point both of the description of the trades going into a woollen coat, at the end of the opening chapter, and of the account of how the division of labour arises in the second chapter (WN 27–8). In a pin factory, however, the division of tasks is not at all spontaneous: a master manufacturer splits up the tasks and assigns them to his workers. Smith says that he uses the pin factory example because it makes the division of labour *perspicuous*: it collects the various tasks going into a pin "into the same workhouse" and places them "at once under the view of the spectator" (14). But he doesn't consider it typical of how labour gets divided.

More generally, Smith is thought not really to have anticipated the Industrial Revolution, which got underway a little after he wrote WN (1780 is generally taken to be its starting point).[8] Few of his examples in the book, after the opening chapter, come from factories, and he usually mentions street-porters and day-labourers, not factory workers, as typical examples of the poor. He is also most concerned about the atrophy of courage and judgment among the poor, in an advanced division of labour (WN 781–8), not about their loss of independence. That again suggests that he is thinking primarily of street-porters, lugging packages all day long, rather than workers in a factory. The street-porter's work is mind-numbingly dull, but he is an "independent contractor," as we would say today: he does not have any single master.

With that in mind, I think it is fair to say that Smith expected commercial society to bring about a world of small independent artificers, shopkeepers, and day-labourers, not large firms controlling the conditions under which practically everybody works. He saw costs to the narrowness of many workers' occupations, but expected there to be a clear gain in independence for most of them. If so, he might well have been disappointed in the actual structure of capitalist societies, especially in the period between the early nineteenth century and the institution of the first governmental worker protections in the early and mid-twentieth century. At any rate, the terms Smith gives us for praising commercial society can readily be used to *criticize* some aspects of it. A capitalist world in which workers are highly dependent on their employers is not what Smith was promoting.

12.2 Affinities between Smith and libertarianism

Bearing these points in mind, let's turn now to Smith's political recommendations in WN. The first point to stress about them is that they do not neatly fit any major political position around today. As Charles Griswold has written, "[It is] impossible to see Smith as either 'conservative' or 'liberal,' 'right' or 'left,' in the contemporary American sense of these terms" (AVE 295n64). This is partly because of changes in political issues since Smith's day. But it is partly because of features intrinsic to Smith's way of writing on politics. Griswold stresses the degree to which Smith's writings are not ideological: "If we expect social philosophy to have a … rigorous structure, then all of [Smith's recommendations] will seem hopelessly unsystematic and ad hoc" (296).

That said, Smith is certainly a liberal in the broad sense of that term—the sense in which it includes anyone, from Milton Friedman to John Rawls, who sees protecting individual liberty as central to the work of government—and he is often identified with a view on that spectrum that has a very rigorous structure: the libertarian view by which governments should interfere with our lives as little as possible, perhaps doing no more than defending our country against outside attackers, and preventing and punishing violence and fraud. Some libertarians grant a limited role for governments in providing infrastructure, or at least acknowledge that Smith, who listed "erecting and maintaining certain publick works and certain publick institutions" as one of the three main tasks of government, would allow for such a role. When they claim Smith for their ideology, what they think he would oppose, and what they invoke him in order to oppose themselves, are government-run welfare programmes. Smith, they say, would agree with them that the private sector can run such programmes better than government agencies and that government programmes to carry out such tasks, whether or not they are effective, constitute an unjustifiable interference with private property rights. To what extent is it true that Smith anticipated this programme of extremely limited government?

Well, there is certainly some truth to it. As we have seen, Smith devotes much of WN to arguing against mercantilist and Physiocratic proposals for governments to promote particular industries, or one sector of the economy over others. He also concludes his polemic against these systems by saying that the best way for a government to promote its nation's economic health is to leave

> Every man, as long as he does not violate the laws of justice, … perfectly free to pursue his own interest his own way, and to bring both his industry and his capital into competition with those of any other man, or order of men.
>
> (WN 687)

So far this is just a recommendation not to micro-manage the economy, however—not to subsidize any industry or sector with "bounties" nor to disincentivize any industry or sector with tariffs. But Smith discourages other kinds of government interference in what individuals do. He criticizes sumptuary laws, as we have seen (Section 10.1). He also opposes laws that restrict the movements of the poor (WN 157), that require workers to go through an apprenticeship before they can set up business on their own (138–9), and that impose caps on how much people can earn (99–100). It is interesting that in all these respects Smith is particularly interested in laws that interfere with the lives of poor people, a point to which we will return. But he does also think that governments should not try to limit assemblies of "masters," even though these conduce to conspiracies against the poor (145).

In addition, Smith does not think that government support for university education is of much use (WN 759–81), and he thinks that ideally governments should not support churches (792–3). This latter point is quite striking. Most people before Smith, including his teacher Hutcheson, thought that governments should support some churches, as part of a larger project of nurturing virtue in the citizenry. Smith rejects the idea that government officials are either well-positioned to teach moral and religious principles or are needed to promote virtue. We acquire virtue, he thinks, primarily by way of our family upbringing, and our sympathetic interactions with our neighbours.[9]

We might add that Smith takes a dim view of the virtue of politicians. His description of the statesman as "that insidious and crafty animal" (WN 468) is perhaps his most famous swipe at politicians, but there are many other passages, in both WN and TMS, where he indicates that political office tends to attract, and produce, vain, arrogant, and otherwise unadmirable people. He tells us that successful warriors, statesmen, legislators, and founders of political parties tend to be filled with "excessive self-estimation and presumption," and that when they are successful, we enter into their self-admiration by sympathy and therefore overlook their imprudence and injustice (TMS 250–2). He grants that successful political leaders are often courageous, but warns that their courage tends to go together with cruelty and violence (TMS 55, 64–5, 152–3). Even where it is not accompanied by violence, moreover, the vanity of politicians is likely to lead them into wasteful projects, spending large amounts of the public's money on their own glorification (WN 342–6), and to arrogant attempts at imposing their will on the populace. Politicians are apt to be "wise in [their] own conceit" and therefore try to impose "systems" that fail to respect the independence of the people they are supposed to serve (TMS 185, 233–4). This arrogance is enough to mark political leaders, on Smith's terms, as less than virtuous; humility is essential to being a truly good person.[10]

Finally, Smith thinks that politicians, even when well-meaning, cannot know enough to carry out large projects of social engineering. He says that

The statesman, who should attempt to direct private people in what manner they ought to employ their capitals, would... assume an authority which could be trusted, not only to no single person, but to no council or senate whatever, and which would nowhere be so dangerous as in the hands of a man who had folly and presumption enough to fancy himself fit to exercise it.

(WN 456)

And he praises the system of natural liberty because under it

The sovereign is completely discharged from a duty, in the attempting to perform which he must always be exposed to innumerable delusions, and for the proper performance of which no human wisdom or knowledge could ever be sufficient: the duty of superintending the industry of private people, and of directing it towards the employments most suitable to the interest of society.

(WN 687)

The point in both cases has to do with micro-managing an economy, but it can in principle be extended to other large-scale political projects. Given the particularistic nature of human decision-making—a point that Smith stresses throughout his writings[11]—it is hubris for politicians to suppose that they can adequately predict the effects of any fine-grained intervention into human lives. In making this cognitive point about political planning, Smith anticipates Ludwig von Mises and Friedrich Hayek, as their contemporary followers like to stress.

12.3 Why Smith is not a libertarian (I)

So there is certainly a case to be made for Smith as a fore-runner of a limited, anti-interventionist approach to government activity. But it is a mistake to over-emphasize this side of him. In the first place, Smith makes a number of explicit recommendations for governments to intervene in economic matters. In the second place, the third task that Smith says that governments should take up allows for the establishment of all sorts of large-scale social and economic institutions. And in the third place, what lies behind Smith's anti-interventionist stance is very different from what lies behind the views of most libertarians.

The first of these points can be illustrated by the fact that Smith unworriedly accepts a role for government in setting standards for various kinds of goods and services. He regards the "publick stamp" that guarantees the quality of money to be essential to the prevention of fraud (WN 40), and endorses, for the same reason, official stamps testifying to the size or quality of linen and woollen cloth (138–9). He suggests, in the interest of restraining speculation, that private banks be prohibited from issuing promissory notes for small sums of money, comparing such a regulation to laws that require the building of walls to stop the spread of a fire (323–4). In the name of combatting religious fanaticism, he proposes that the state require that people study science and philosophy before being licensed to exercise any of the "liberal profession[s]" (law, medicine, academia) or indeed to hold "any honourable office of trust or profit" (796). He also allows for some restrictions on trade in the name of defence (464–5),[12] and even though he regards restrictions on the exportation of grain as generally a bad idea, he concedes that they may be necessary where there is imminent danger of a famine otherwise (539).

There are thus a number of exceptions to Smith's anti-interventionism. Some are justified by the very commitment to liberty that underlies his anti-interventionism. Lack of information reduces our freedom, after all, and deliberate distortion of facts relevant to another's decisions (fraud) is universally seen as an offense against liberty. Other proposals are things that Smith acknowledges to be violations of natural liberty to some extent, but considers necessary for an important social purpose. The fact that Smith makes exceptions of this second type, especially, makes clear that his anti-interventionism is rooted in pragmatic concerns rather than a strict principle. As Griswold says: "A burden-of-proof argument suffuses Smith's writing in political economy; the state may intervene in all sorts of ways, but those who would have it do so are required to show why it should in [each] particular instance" (AVE 295).

Consider now Smith's third task for government. Having said that governments must protect their citizens from external attack (the first task), and must protect each individual in their societies from "the injustice or oppression" of the others (the second task), Smith adds that they have a duty to

> erect [...] and maintain[...] certain publick works and certain publick institutions, which it can never be for the interest of any individual, or small number of individuals, to erect and maintain; because the profit could never repay the expence to any individual or small number of individuals, though it may frequently do much more than repay it to a great society.
>
> (WN 687–8; see also 723)

Smith spends by far the largest chunk of his discussion of what governments should do on this task (91 pages in the Glasgow edition, as compared with 34 pages on the first two tasks combined), and includes within it the making and maintaining of roads, canals, and postal services, support for education, anything the state does to protect or promote particular industries, and anything the state does to support or shape churches. Many of these projects Smith *opposes*—this section of WN includes his extended critique of the East India Company, as well as his proposal that governments refrain from funding churches—and he suggests that some of them can be well carried out on the basis of private funding (maintaining canals, for instance, and educating middle-class and wealthy people). But others he thinks must be run and/or funded by governments, either because they will be carried out in an unsafe way otherwise (WN 726) or because the people they are meant to help will not be able to establish and maintain them on their own. This latter concern underwrites Smith's proposal for a small public school system throughout Britain, something that would have involved a massive expansion of government spending at that time.[13]

Smith's distinction between what governments should and should not fund seems again wholly pragmatic. There is no easily discernible unity either among the kinds of projects he favours—roads, a post office, public schools for the poor—or among the ones that he opposes, except that he thinks the former will not be adequately run by the private sector, while the latter will be. Smith says explicitly that both schools and churches can be "beneficial to the whole society" and that they can therefore be publicly funded "without injustice" (WN 815), but that that expense might "perhaps with equal propriety" be borne by those who benefit from them.[14] His point seems to be that the government may in principle build and fund these or any other institutions that benefit the whole society, but should in practice be wary of doing so if private sources can do so as well or better.

Smith's third task for government therefore leaves, in principle, a hole in his anti-interventionist programme large enough to drive a welfare-state-sized truck through.[15] It's unimaginable that he would have supported public health care in his own day—most doctors were little more than quacks—but had he known of modern medicine, and been convinced that only the state could ensure that the poor have equal access to it, he might well have put universal health care, in some form, under his third task. As for public housing, food support, unemployment insurance: the question to ask in each case is whether these goods can be adequately be supplied to the poor by individuals or whether they will only be supplied, or supplied in an adequate way, with the help of state funding. This is a pragmatic question, not a question of principle, and it may well be answered, in many cases, in favour of the welfare-statist view, not the libertarian view.

Of course, this point cuts in the other direction as well. If the question we need to answer is whether a good like housing or education or health care is most effectively made available to the poor by way of government action or by way of private markets, then it may turn out that the evidence supports the libertarian rather than the welfare-statist position. Some such goods may also be best provided by way of a public-private partnership: by way of incentives to private operators, or regulated markets, or a combination of publicly and privately funded institutions. There is also room to argue over whether a particular welfare programme, or any other government project, actually helps the people it is intended to help. What follows from Smith's pragmatism about these issues is that there is no *a priori* reason either to condemn or to commend government projects. Our answers instead must depend on detailed considerations about how they work, in each social and historical context.

This approach is well-suited to Smith's particularism.[16] His polemical agenda in WN is directed just at the question, raging in his day, over whether governments should use tariffs, bounties, and colonialist adventures to support manufacturing over agriculture, or vice versa. We cannot infer from this what he would have said about a world in which the main politico-economic question has to do with whether governments should institute welfare programmes to help the poor, an idea remote from the practice of virtually every government in his day.[17] Nor can we know what he would have said more generally about commercial economies in a world that has seen all the economic, social, and legal changes that have come about over the past two centuries. If, as Smith seems firmly to believe, our systematic economic and political knowledge is rooted in what we grasp of the economic and social particulars around us, then we cannot expect to make any very useful inferences from the conclusions Smith drew in eighteenth-century Britain to what he might have to say about policies appropriate to our very different context.

12.4 Why Smith is not a libertarian (II)

We come now to the deepest difference between Smith and contemporary libertarians: he does not arrive at his anti-interventionism in anything like the way they do. He does not, for instance, start from a belief that private property rights are sacred. There are just three mentions of "sacred" rights in the whole of WN and two of them argue for a right to labour and exchange freely, rather than for a right to property. In the first, Smith takes for granted that his readers will believe in a right to property on more or less Lockean grounds, and uses that belief to argue for a more basic right to labour: "The property which every man has in his own labour," he says, "as it is the original foundation of all other property, so it is the most sacred and inviolable" (WN 138). The second refers to "sacred rights of private property" in a more standard way (188), but the point is a minor one, tacked on to a generally utilitarian case against governmental obsessions with the mining of precious metals. And the third again describes, as "the most sacred rights of mankind," just the ability of individuals to employ "their stock and industry" in the way they judge to be "most advantageous to themselves," without mentioning property at all (582).[18] Moreover, even when Smith explicitly takes up the right to property in LJ, he defends a basic right in the state of nature just to the property one actually holds in one's hands,[19] treating all property rights beyond that as conventions or creations of the law. Nowhere does Smith give property rights the foundational role that it plays in the libertarian conception of freedom.

It goes without saying that Smith also does not promote the radical individualism of libertarians who take their cue from Ayn Rand. For Smith our very identity, as individuals, comes about only when we see ourselves through the eyes of others,[20] and the main task of our moral lives is to develop our ability to aid, and feel with, our neighbours. "To feel much for others and little for ourselves, to restrain our selfish, and to indulge our benevolent affections," he says, "constitutes the perfection of human nature" (TMS 25). Rand would shudder. Smith is notable for his attempt to bring together individual freedom with a socially structured conception of the self,[21] and if he believes that governments should generally leave us alone economically and religiously and morally, that is because he thinks that everyday surveillance by our neighbours, and the approval or disapproval they administer to us, will suffice to ensure that we develop socially oriented habits and attitudes.

Smith is also uninterested in the accumulation of material goods for their own sake. He is deeply concerned that everyone be adequately supplied with food, clothing, and lodging, and he recognizes that a thriving economy is necessary for that. He also remarks that "noble palaces, magnificent villas, great collections of books, statues, pictures and other curiosities, are frequently both an ornament and an honour... to the whole country to which they belong" (WN 347). In addition, he thinks that the wide availability of "painting, poetry, musick, [and] dancing," and especially of "dramatick representations" that poke fun at fanatical religious figures, can serve as a counterweight to the "temper of mind" that gives rise to "popular superstition and enthusiasm" (796–7). And his personal interest in the arts[22] gives us reason to think he would not be dismissive of the luxury that enables them to flourish. But as against this we need to bear in mind his animadversions against luxury,[23] and the view he held throughout his life, never more so than in the final edition of TMS,[24] that the pursuit of great wealth makes for neither happiness nor virtue. Nor does he ever marvel at the advance of technology, presenting it as a great accomplishment for humankind. So it is highly unlikely that his anti-interventionist view of political economy rested on a desire to see either individuals, or his society as a whole, accumulate as much material wealth as possible.

Finally, Smith, unlike modern libertarians, does not have an unequivocally rosy picture of the private sector. He believes that the market, unrestrained by government, will bring about social goods just "in *many*... cases," not in all (WN 456, my emphasis), and he is fully aware that oppressive restrictions on individuals can come from private agents as well as government officials. Many modern libertarians respond to the problems inherent in government agency by suggesting that social issues be turned over to corporations, churches, and other non-governmental organizations. By leaving such issues up to the private sector, that is, they do not necessarily mean that individuals can solve their problems of poverty or environmental degradation by themselves. Rather, they believe that the interests of large businesses, and the beneficence of churches and other non-governmental organizations, will lead them to help solve these problems, and that these private groups are more likely to act effectively and efficiently than the government. Smith would surely have rejected this view. It is not clear that large organizations like Amazon or the Catholic Church should count as "private" entities at all,[25] and Smith's analysis of what is wrong with politicians in any case applies to the leaders of these entities as well.

Smith makes clear that large churches and corporations are much like government, wielding power that interferes with the way individuals would otherwise act in their local situations, and that where they compete with government for control over the society, it is better to put that control in the hands of government. Government is after all a body entrusted to use power for secular, civic ends, and a body that in most nations is to some degree restrained by the citizenry. Neither churches nor corporations need be restrained in this way, and they are certainly not entrusted by the citizenry with secular, civic purposes. Smith stresses, moreover, that the interest both of churches and of merchants can be, and often is, opposed to the public interest (WN 266–7, 797). When these groups achieve secular power, they tend to use it to promote absurd, factious doctrines, in the church's case, and private, material gain, in the merchants' case. The rule of merchants, Smith says, "is, perhaps, the worst of all governments for any country whatever" (570; see also 637–8, 752), and he describes the medieval Catholic church as "the most formidable combination that ever was formed against the authority and security of civil government" (802). The extreme incompatibility between business habits and concern for the public good is a major point of WN. Smith is very worried about the influence merchants had over political decisions in Britain and intends his separation of economy and state at least as much to protect the state from the corruption of economic interests as to protect the economy from the ineptitude of political forces. He regards the political influence of churches as just as baleful as that of merchants, however, and for similar reasons supports a separation of church and state (792–6). Indeed, he compares churches to corporations: "The clergy of every established church constitute a great incorporation" (797). He then devotes much of his chapter on religious institutions to the politics by which church leaders get selected, and to the ways in which large churches have tried either to subdue the temporal sovereign or to ally themselves with it. He describes churches as rivals to political sovereigns, pointing out that the Catholic Church's medieval role in supporting the poor gave it "the command of a great temporal force" (802). From the point of view of the public good, it was a great victory when governments finally wrested control back from the church: "the liberty, reason, and happiness of mankind ... can flourish only where civil government[, as opposed to the church,] is able to protect them" (802). Smith recommends that governments in future take care not to delegate any part of their power to business and religious interests—that they keep those interests from "the performance of [any] part of the duty of the sovereign" (733).[26]

This is largely because Smith sees church and business leaders as being liable to the same moral problems and cognitive limitations as politicians. He presents church leaders as self-centred, vain, factious, and power-hungry throughout his discussion of the clergy at WN 803–8. He offers moral criticisms of business leaders at WN 267:

they are "an order of men, ... who have generally an interest to deceive and even to oppress the publick, and who accordingly have, upon many occasions, both deceived and oppressed it." Their line of work inclines them to an extremely narrow focus on their own interests, to the exclusion of the interest of the public (144–5, 266–7, 456, 461–2, 734). This narrow, very selfish, uncitizenly attitude—what Smith calls their "mean rapacity, the[ir] monopolizing spirit"—means that merchants are particularly unsuited "to be the rulers of mankind" (493).

In addition, the cognitive problems in judging what will be best for every individual in a great society are just as severe when the people who try to direct those individuals are merchants or church leaders as when they are politicians. Smith draws our attention to parallels between running a large corporation and running a state. A "spirit of faction" can run through the stockholders of a joint stock company, he notes (WN 741), just as it may run through the citizens of a state. The stockholders employ others to direct the day-to-day affairs of the company, moreover, and these directors, "being the managers rather of other people's money than of their own," cannot be expected to "watch over it with the same anxious vigilance" that a person would show if he were taking care of his own interest (WN 741; see also 737, 739–5). Smith believes that self-interest normally motivates attention to detail.[27] Since corporate leaders will often lack the proper motivation for their job, their capacity for attentive judgment will not be properly engaged. "[E]very individual ... can, in his local situation, judge much better than any statesman or lawgiver can do for him" (WN 456), but this crucial premise for the success of the invisible hand holds only where an individual regards a local situation as "his," not where he is carrying out the orders or looking after the interests of someone else. Consequently, "[n]egligence and profusion ... must always prevail, more or less, in the management of the affairs of [a joint stock] company" (WN 741). Smith claims that this is the reason why joint stock companies are anxious to secure a monopoly over the trade in which they engage: they are so poorly run that that is the only way they can succeed (WN 741, 755).[28]

So Smith's opposition to having governments run people's lives does not come from any belief that we would do better to have churches or business enterprises take over that task. On the contrary: Absent any sort of alliance with government, Smith believes, both business and church groups will naturally split themselves up into smaller and smaller entities over time, and he looks forward to this diminution of gluts of economic and religious power. Accordingly, unlike many libertarians who claim his mantle, Smith would never propose a delegation of tasks like welfare or education to for-profit or religious enterprises.

12.5 A liberalism of virtue

If we now put together the various things Smith says about government and about the private sector, we can, I think, attribute the following general view of politics to him:

Both the economic well-being and the moral health of a nation can in general be left up to the spontaneous workings of society. The judgment of ordinary people, as regards their own affairs, is far better than politicians and political theorists generally assume, and far more likely to be sensitive to the details of their local situations than decisions made on their behalf by a legislator or government bureaucrat. The interactions of ordinary people also provide each of them with signals (indirect ones, in the case of prices; direct ones, in the case of moral approval and disapproval) that help guide them towards actions that benefit their society as a whole. And the agendas of "men of system" who want to control how the members of their society act not only overlook those members' freedom—the "principle of motion of its own" that activates "every single piece" of the great chess-board of society (TMS 234)—but tend to be either self-serving or driven by fanatical religious concerns. The cognitive and moral limitations of those who would direct the rest of society rather than letting individuals act on their own therefore give us good reason to favour free markets, avoid moralistic legislation, and withhold public support from churches. As a general matter, we should be suspicious of government intervention into our lives, limiting it mostly to the protection of citizens against military invasion and crime.

But this general presumption against interventionist government can be overridden whenever it is clearly untrue that the unguided interactions of individuals can solve major social problems, and especially when those social problems particularly affect the weak and vulnerable. The presumption can certainly be overridden when disaster looms otherwise: when a market is not providing people with enough food to avoid a famine, say (WN 158, 539). Market interactions also produce outcomes that all their participants want only when those participants know what they are buying or selling; government protections against fraud, or warrants of quality, may be needed to ensure that precondition. And there is no reason to expect participants in the market to benefit from it who are too generally ill-informed, or incapable of judgment, to bargain intelligently, or who are too pressed by dire need, or threats of harassment by their masters, to bargain freely. That is the condition of the poor in many societies—especially, as Smith recognizes, where there is an advanced division of labour, and the work of the poor tends to be mind-numbing. Consequently, providing poor people with the education that enables them to judge competently[29] is part and parcel of a commitment to individual freedom, not a derogation from that commitment. Giving some material support to the poor may also be intrinsic to that commitment (see, again, 725, 842). In any case, there is a clear asymmetry, for Smith, between government intervention on behalf of those who already have wealth and power, and government intervention on behalf of the weak and vulnerable. He notes at one point that when there are conflicts between "masters and their workmen," it is the powerful party to these conflicts— "masters"—who can lean on legislators to get laws passed in their favour. As a result, "when the regulation … is in favour of the workmen, it is always just and equitable; but it is sometimes otherwise when in favour of the masters" (157–8). The same asymmetry, I submit, runs through Smith's view of politics. Intervention on behalf of those who do not have the means or training to pursue their ends in an adequately free way can be justified in the *name* of freedom: on the very grounds, that is, that otherwise underwrite anti-interventionism. Smith's liberalism is one that allows for government intervention whenever it is needed to enable the freedom of the powerless. Exactly when occasions of this sort arise—when a government programme would be "beneficial for the whole society," and especially for the poor, but would not come about by individual efforts alone[30]—is a matter of judgment: debates can legitimately break out over whether any particular proposal meets this criterion. But Smith makes clear that some programmes do meet it.

None of this is to say that Smith would necessarily have defended the modern welfare state, or that his latter-day followers are wrong to invoke him when they complain about welfare programmes administered by large bureaucracies. Smith does prefer government to work through clear, general laws rather than officials making ad hoc decisions; he worries about both the inefficiency and the danger to liberty of anything that involves interference in people's lives on a daily basis.[31] Both the occasions that warrant government intervention, and the means that government intervention should take, thus depend on a commitment to individual freedom, for Smith. But he is far less absolutist about this commitment, far more willing to treat it as a rough and ready guide to practical politics rather than an inviolable principle, than are his libertarian admirers.

Once again, moreover, the point of Smith's commitment to individual freedom is to give us the opportunity to develop virtue—to live out lives of beneficence, justice, courage, and friendship. Only a virtuous life is a good life, for Smith, not only in the sense that only such a life suits one out to help others, but in the sense that only a virtuous life is a truly happy life. "[T]he chief part of human happiness arises from the consciousness of being beloved," says Smith (TMS 41). But only virtuous people are truly beloved. Smithian virtue also rests on self-command. But without self-command, we cannot achieve tranquillity in the face of pain or misfortune, which Smith identifies as crucial to happiness. Virtue, not wealth, is thus the basis of happiness, for Smith—even if we also need some material goods (food, clothing, lodging) to be happy and our lives can be enhanced by a society in which other goods, making possible the arts and sciences, are widely available.

We've seen already that free markets can nurture virtue by increasing independency, which gives us the opportunity and the incentive to take control over our lives: to develop self-command. If we return one last time to the butcher and baker passage, we can delineate this nexus of markets and virtue more precisely. In relation to our butcher and baker, Smith says, we "address ourselves" to their self-love. I pointed out earlier that nothing about this claim presumes that we are self-loving. I would now add a stronger point: that in addressing ourselves to other people's self-love, we turn our attention away, if only for a moment, from our own self-love. Which is to say, there is an echo here, if a muted one, of what Smith says in TMS that we need to do in order to win the sympathy of others: lower the pitch of our own feelings to a level at which a spectator can enter into them. Unlike the puppy that "fawns upon its dam," the butcher's customer can appeal to someone else's needs rather than bleating self-pityingly about her own. Smith's usual way of getting at the self only through the other is thus at work here: it is reasonable to assume both that the butcher and baker are more likely to be open to a true understanding of my concerns if I moderate my self-love ("lower" my passion, "flatten its tone"), and that I can achieve a more appropriate, better balanced sense of my just deserts if I force myself to lessen my demands in the presence of others. So market relationships provide us with regular opportunities for the development of self-command.

There is a lot to be said for this suggestion. Especially in societies that no longer emphasize martial institutions, self-command comes about largely through the workings of the market.[32] In exchanging with our butchers and bakers, and in our relationships with our employers, co-workers, sub-contractors, and the like, we need constantly to perceive and appeal to their interests rather than just talking about our own, and this discipline teaches us a great deal about how to gain command over our passions and interests. Unlike some of his more nostalgic friends, Smith knew that the world of universal participation in the military was by and large over, and looked forward to a world in which war itself would become a less and less important element of statecraft.[33] In such a world, the self-distancing process required to navigate market interactions becomes the usual way by which people learn to control their emotions and desires. This provides a powerful justification for the intrinsic value of market institutions, quite independent of their contribution to the growth and spread of wealth.

We should again remember that the poor in commercial societies may not be able to reap these moral advantages from the markets in which they participate. For that very reason, however, a virtue-based justification for market institutions can be deployed in favour of government intervention in society, in some circumstances. In any case, the difficulties faced by the poor do nothing to derogate from what is striking about the virtue-based justification for markets: that it gives us reason to favour them, not because of the individual preferences they satisfy, but because they enable individuals to acquire character traits that involve *subduing* some of their preferences. Smith is leery of government intervention in society because he thinks that on the whole social forces are better able, on their own, to enable each of us to lead a dignified, admirable, and sociable life—not because he approves of people leading whatever life they feel like leading, or seeking to maximize their pleasurable experiences.

In sum, even if Smith's liberalism resembles libertarianism in some respects, it is aimed at very different ends, and grounded in very different moral views, from those of most libertarians. Libertarians are generally suspicious of the notion that individuals ought to develop virtues: beyond, at least, those virtues that are needed for the functioning of the market and the liberal state themselves. Smith does not share this attitude. He is far from an agnostic about what a good human life looks like, let alone an enthusiast for a conception of the good life that eschews virtue in favour of a pursuit of pleasures. He is not a positivist, sceptical of the significance of moral argument, like Milton Friedman, nor a hedonist, like Bentham and his followers, nor a radical individualist, like the followers of Ayn Rand. Any decent human life, he believes, requires certain virtues, and depends on our respecting and loving the people around us. If he encourages governments, nevertheless, to refrain from promoting virtue, that is because he thinks that social forces can effectively achieve that end without government help. So he may arrive at some conclusions that libertarians will applaud, but not for the reasons they offer.

I thus think we can safely say that Smith is not a libertarian. He certainly fits under the broad rubric of "liberalism," however. Protecting individual liberty is the central function of government for him—protecting us against violence that would interfere with that liberty is the point of both his first and his second task of government—and throughout WN he stresses that governments should let people make their own decisions about where and how to work, whom to employ, and what to consume ("It is the highest impertinence... in kings and ministers, to pretend to watch over the private oeconomy of private people" (WN 346)). He marries this very modern belief, however, to a commitment to the importance of virtue in human life that looks more like ancient Stoicism or Aristotelianism than utilitarianism or Kantianism. This makes for an unusual variant of liberalism. For Smith, the importance of freedom lies primarily in the opportunity it gives us to develop virtues. He favours free market economies because they provide conditions, he thinks, that foster good moral sentiments. And as regards both economic and moral matters, he promotes a largely hands-off approach to government action because he sees liberalism, in this sense, as good for virtue.

12.6 Conclusion and summary

The idea that Smith endorses a liberalism for virtue is the reading of his work that best brings his philosophical and his politico-economic writings into a coherent whole. We saw in the beginning of this book that TMS, LJ and WN were originally part of a single project, examining the social aspects of humanity as a whole, and we have noted repeatedly that Smith moves fluidly between moral and descriptive registers in both TMS and WN. The term "moral philosophy," in eighteenth-century Britain, covered much that today we would call "social science." And Smith, like his friend Hume, was a pre-eminent moral philosopher in this broad sense. Over time, the social-scientific aspects of Hume's work have received less attention than the strictly moral ones, in the sense that we use that latter term today, while over time the moral aspects of Smith's work, in our modern sense, have faded from view in favour of a focus on the social-scientific ones. We do better to keep these things together. The professor of moral philosophy at the University of Glasgow never meant for the normative and the descriptive aspects of his work to be pulled apart. And when we do hold them together, we can better appreciate his central achievement: the combination of a socially-oriented virtue ethic that has deep roots in ancient Greek thought with a thoroughly modern, liberal, individualistic approach to politics. This is a project that challenges widely held assumptions, to this day, about both morality and politics. Whether Smith fully succeeded in it is of course open to debate, but it remains eminently worthy of our attention. Smith invites modern liberals to think through how they themselves propose to reconcile their moral attitudes with what they expect from their economic and political systems. Insofar as we take up this invitation, insofar as we wrestle with Smith, we engage with some of the most important questions—still unresolved—of our modern age.

Notes

1 See Section 10.4.

2 See the discussion of this passage above, in Section 10.3.

3 Or a soldier: another example in WN of a person who is prone to idleness and vice (469–70).

4 "[N]othing else can deserve the name of opulence but this comeattibleness" (LJ 343).

5 "Servants, labourers, and workmen of different kinds make up the far greater part of every great political society. But what improves the circumstances of the greater part can never be regarded as an inconveniency to the whole. No society can surely be flourishing and happy, of which the far greater part of the members are poor and miserable. It is but equity, besides, that they who feed, cloath and lodge the whole body of the people, should have such a share of the produce of their own labour as to be themselves tolerably well fed, cloathed and lodged" (WN 96). See also LJ 377-9 for Smith's emphasis on food, clothing, and lodging.

6 See the citations to the *Encyclopédie* and *Chamber's Cyclopaedia* in the editor's note 3 to p. 15 of WN. Smith also says, immediately before he talks about pin-making, that this is a trade "in which the division of labour has been very often taken notice of" (WN 14).

7 Just before introducing it, he says, "[The division of labor] is commonly supposed to be carried furthest in some very trifling [manufactures]; not perhaps that it really is carried further in them than in others of more importance ..." (WN 14), and he describes the example as "very trifling" again in ¶s 3 and 5.

8 See C.K. Kindleberger, "The Historical Background: Adam Smith and the Industrial Revolution," in T. Wilson and A.S. Skinner (eds.), *The Market and the State* (Oxford: Oxford University Press, 1976).

9 See TMS 145, 222. In WN, Smith makes the striking observation that while the Greeks instituted a formal programme for moral education, and the Romans did not, "the morals of the Romans, ... both in private and publick life, seem

to have been, not only equal, but upon the whole, a good deal superior to those of the Greeks" (WN 774). He goes on to respectfully dismiss the views of Plato, Aristotle, and Montesquieu that favour formal moral education (775–6).

10 In general, Smith says, those in the top echelons in society—whether they get there by birth, by money, or by political power—are prone to being less virtuous than those lower down: Smith argues that people in "the middling and inferior stations of life" are more likely to achieve virtue than their social superiors at TMS 54–6, 63–4, and that poor workers are drawn to particularly strict moral systems at WN 794–6.

11 See above, Sections 2.5 and 3.4.

12 Although the extent to which he allows this exception to his free-trading commitments has been wildly exaggerated, by many. The irony in his famous line that "defence is of more importance than opulence" (WN 465)—given that he applies that line to the Navigation Acts which were supposed, by their advocates, to enhance *both* the defence *and* the opulence of Great Britain—is often missed, as is the fact that he elsewhere subjects these same Navigation Acts to a scathing critique (WN 595–614). One commentator who has recognized this point is Peter McNamara:

> Smith's arguments are a response, rather than a concession, to the mercantilists' twin preoccupations of power and plenty. … It is … significant that he posed the defense-versus-opulence trade-off so sharply. … The mercantilists regarded the two concerns as so interconnected that they were seldom in conflict.
> — McNamara, *Political Economy and Statesmanship: Smith, Hamilton, and the Foundation of the Commercial Republic* (DeKalb: Northern Illinois University Press, 1998), 88–9

13 As Gertrude Himmelfarb notes, indignantly: "Having spent the better part of two volumes arguing against government regulation, [Smith] now advanced a scheme requiring a greater measure of government involvement than anything that had ever existed before"—Himmelfarb, *The Idea of Poverty* (New York: Alfred A. Knopf, 1984), 59.

14 Indeed he says that that expense can "be defrayed *altogether*" (my emphasis) by those who benefit from them. What has happened to his proposal that the state bear some of the costs for the education of the poor? Some contemporary libertarians have leapt on this passage to show that Smith was never serious about having the state fund schools (see for instance David Friedman, "The Weak Case for Public Schooling"). That would leave us with a contradiction between this fleeting reference and the extended argument for the state to fund schools on 781–8, and suggest, implausibly, that Smith's real views come out in the fleeting reference rather than the extended argument. A more plausible reading would note that Smith has argued earlier that it is better for almost all educational institutions—all universities and schools for the children of

middle- and upper-class people—to be privately funded, that teachers even in the state-funded schools he proposes should be paid in part by the parents of the children they teach, and that churches should ideally be funded entirely by private sources. So when he says that the expense of schools and churches can fruitfully "be defrayed altogether" by private sources, that is only slight hyperbole even if he thinks there is a role for governments to play in funding the elementary education of the poor.

15 I have employed Smith to make a case for a robust welfare state in my *Third Concept of Liberty* and the Epilogue to my *On Adam Smith's Wealth of Nations*.

16 Discussed above, in Sections 2.5 and 3.4.

17 See the discussion of European poor laws in my *Short History of Distributive Justice*, chapter 2 and "A Right to Welfare."

18 The phrase "sacred and inviolable" is also used at WN (666), but here it describes just an attitude that kings and churches should take up towards the amount of rent that a landlord needs to cover his expenses, in order to maximize their own gains from tithes and taxes. Rights do not seem to be in question here.

19 See above, Section 9.7.

20 See TMS 110–1, and my discussion of this passage above in Section 4.7, and in *Being Me Being You*, chapter 2.

21 See above, Sections 4.7 and 7.1.

22 See above, Chapter 2.

23 In TMS I.iii.3 and IV.1, especially.

24 See I.iii.3, especially.

25 Jeff Weintraub demonstrates that there are actually several different "public/private" distinctions. On some but not all of these, a business or church would count as "private." See "The Theory and Politics of the Public/Private Distinction," in J. Weintraub and K. Kumar (eds.), *Public and Private in Thought and Practice* (Chicago: University of Chicago Press, 1997).

26 I have used Smith to argue against government alliances with religious groups in "Justice Over Charity: Some Dangers in Faith-Based Poverty Initiatives," in Thomas Maissen and Fania Oz-Salzberger (eds.), *The Liberal-Republican Quandary in Israel, Europe, and the United States* (Academic Press, 2012).

27 See above, Section 2.5.

28 For a trenchant analysis of Smith's views of joint stock companies, and its relevance to critiques of global commerce today, see Muthu, "Adam Smith's Critique of International Trading Companies."

29 Smith's explicit concern when he discusses the education of the poor:

> The torpor of [the] mind [of a poor laborer in a mind-numbing job] renders him … incapable of relishing or bearing a part in any rational conversation, … [and] of forming any just judgment concerning many even of the ordinary duties of private life.
>
> (WN 782)

30 That very condition indicates that Smith is thinking about policies that benefit the poor especially: middle-class and rich people can usually take care of their needs on their own.

31 Smith evinces a strong preference, throughout both LJ and WN, for the rule of law over the rule of persons. Brown says that LJ fits in well with the legal writing of its time, "which accepted the superiority of judicial practice over the work of the legislator" (Brown, *Adam Smith's Discourse*, 120). This captures nicely Smith's belief that fair administration of established law is far more important to freedom and security than new laws aimed directly at freedom and security.

32 Nicholas Phillipson makes much this point in "Adam Smith as Civic Moralist," in Istvan Hont and Michael Ignatieff (eds.), *Wealth and Virtue* (Cambridge: Cambridge University Press, 1983), 191. What I say has an obvious connection with the issues both Phillipson and Pocock ("Cambridge paradigms and Scotch philosophers") discuss in that volume. I am not quite sure what to say, however, about Pocock's placement of Smith in response to, and rejection of, the Harringtonian legacy. Certainly Smith does not place political participation at the centre of his conception of virtue. Nor does he share the agrarian emphasis of the Harringtonians, although he nods in that direction several times. But he by no means gives up on the ideal of virtue as "independence," and he deeply retains the vision of the independent person as "practising an austerely virtuous equality with his no less independent peers" (Pocock, "Cambridge Paradigms," 237). What has changed is that this independent person need no longer be first and foremost a *citizen*—moral rather than political concerns are primary, for Smith—nor requires either battle-hardiness (see next note) or an agricultural setting to develop self-command. It is in the latter point that both Smith's sympathy for and criticism of Harringtonian concerns comes out most sharply. Through the "higgling and bargaining" (WN 49) of commercial exchange, even the common labourer can become "alltogether free and independent" (LJ 333), in Smith's sense. He or she may be paid by a "manufacturer," but Smith sees a free labour market as ensuring that wage labour could transcend the dependency characteristic of master/servant relations. So in the commercial era, classical virtue becomes something everyone can attain. In this way Smith adopts the ideals of the Harringtonians while rejecting their analysis of the material conditions necessary for those ideals—thereby bringing what they had to say into line with his own extraordinary respect and sympathy for the lives of the poor.

33 Donald Winch sorts out Smith's views on (1) modern military effectiveness versus (2) the military virtues extremely well in *Adam Smith's Politics* (Cambridge: Cambridge University Press, 1978), chapter 5. I think he is wrong, however, to portray Smith as "always regard[ing] the art of war as the noblest of arts" (105). The main prooftext he uses for this claim, TMS VI.ii, which was added to the book in 1790, is much more equivocal than Winch claims: the military virtues come off as indeed *aesthetically* admirable, but more often than not used

for vile and horrific ends. When we add to this the many disparaging remarks about soldiers in WN (126, 469–70) and descriptions of war as irrational and destructive to all parties (throughout WN II.iii, III.iv, and IV.i, among other places), it becomes clear that Smith belongs firmly with the most pacifist of eighteenth-century writers, not with those who continued to toy with the idea that war is the most glorious arena of human achievement. The point of TMS VI.ii comes out best in its Chapter 3, I think, where Smith uses the glory traditionally attaching to military accomplishments as a metaphor, whereby we might see our entire lives as a sort of military posting to "the forlorn station of the universe" (236). Courage and self-mastery are indeed great virtues, for Smith, but their greatest achievement comes in a stoic acceptance of our place in the world, not on the literal battlefields where nations destroy themselves to serve the vanity of foolish rulers.

Further reading

Sam Fleischacker, "Adam Smith and the Left"
Sam Fleischacker, On Adam Smith's *Wealth of Nations*, Epilogue
Charles Griswold, *Adam Smith and the Virtues of Enlightenment*, chapter 7
James Otteson, "Adam Smith and the Right"
Emma Rothschild, *Economic Sentiments*, chapter 2
Craig Smith, "Adam Smith: Left or Right?"
Craig Smith, "Adam Smith and the New Right"

aesthetics Derived originally from a Greek word for anything that can be perceived, "aesthetics" was used from the eighteenth century onwards for the philosophy of beauty.

antirealism The denial, as regards any area of discourse or thought, that there is an independent reality corresponding to that discourse or thought. As regards science, antirealists maintain that scientific theories are imaginative formations that satisfy the prejudices of our societies, or help us accomplish various practical tasks, while failing to grasp the world around us. As regards morality, antirealists maintain that values and norms are simply projections of our sentiments or ways of speaking, rather than having an independent reality to which those sentiments and ways of speaking should conform.

approbation Smith's word for "approval." TMS is centrally a theory of moral approbation (which is just one kind of approbation: there can also be aesthetic or prudential approbation, for instance).

a priori A concept is *a priori* if it is not derived from experience; a sentence or claim is *a priori* if its truth or falsehood does not depend on experience. Mathematics and logic are prime examples of arenas in which one can expect to find *a priori* concepts and claims. No experience can show "2+2=4" to be false and no experience can show that "2+2=5" is true; the very concept of number, of addition, and of mathematical equality, are also thought to be *a priori*. Debate has raged for centuries over whether moral, metaphysical, and religious concepts and claims may also be *a priori*.

association of ideas David Hume argued that complex ideas are formed out of relationships of resemblance, contiguity, and cause and effect among our <u>impressions</u> or simpler ideas. These relationships merely "associate" ideas, however, rather than establishing necessary connections among them. This loose associationism is a hallmark of Humean thought.

categorical imperative The principle, enunciated by Kant as the basis of morality, that one should act only on those subjective intentions (maxims) that one can also will as a universal law.

cognitive Of or pertaining to knowledge, or the faculties of mind that make for knowledge.

commutative justice The enforcement of our rights against injury, generally carried out by the state in its judicial and penal system.

contagion In the literature on sympathy and empathy today, "contagion" is used for the theory that feelings pass from one person to another while by-passing our cognitive faculties: without the person who is made unhappy or joyful by another's pain or joy necessarily even being aware of why she is experiencing this feeling.

cultural relativism In moral philosophy, "cultural relativism" is used for claims to the effect that whatever a particular culture considers to be right or good is in fact right or good. Strong versions of these claims are widely considered unintelligible by philosophers, although weaker versions—in which "right" and "good" have some cross-cultural meaning but the particular types of actions that fall under those headings may legitimately vary with cultural context—have defenders.

deontology From the word *deon* in Greek, which means "duty," deontological theories of morality derive what we should do from one or more formal principles about the proper shape of our intentions, rather than by assessing the consequences of our acts. The most famous deontological theory is <u>Kantianism</u>.

distributive justice (1) For Smith, and for Hutcheson before him: the sum total of our moral duties to our family and neighbours; (2) For philosophers from the twentieth century onwards: the duty of the state to re-distribute wealth from rich to poor; also called "social justice" or "economic justice."

empiricism The attempt to trace all our concepts to experience and to evaluate all truth claims by their fit with experience. Usually contrasted with "rationalism," which to a greater or lesser extent sees some concepts as built into the process of reasoning and evaluates some truth claims by *a priori* arguments.

epistemology The branch of philosophy that investigates what and how we can legitimately claim to know things. "Legitimate" is important here: epistemology is generally a normative endeavour, unlike cognitive psychology, which is concerned simply with how we *do* come to know things.

equity A term that generally means fairness or impartiality, and is employed in jurisprudence for a turn to general principles of justice when the literal meaning of a statute seems unfair. Smith's use of the term on WN 96 is interesting in both of these contexts.

essence The features of a thing that make it what it really is, as opposed to its "accidental" features. A group of things can also be defined as the same kind of thing if they share an essence. For Plato, essences exist on their own, as "<u>ideas</u>"; for Aristotle, they are real but always embodied in some particular; for nominalists like William of Ockham (and Hume), they are merely one way of characterizing the <u>general ideas</u> by which our minds collect things into groups.

fallibilism Strictly speaking, fallibilism is the doctrine that no belief or claim is certain: every belief can be wrong. Less strictly, a person can be described as more or less fallibilist, depending on the degree to which she stresses our liability to getting things wrong.

Forms The word most commonly used for the abstract <u>essences</u> or <u>ideas</u> that Plato believed exist on their own, and indeed are more real than particular things.

foundationalism The doctrine that all knowledge must ultimately be grounded on a principle or method of knowing that needs no further justification: that is self-evident or for some other reason exempt from further inquiry. There are both <u>empiricist</u> and rationalist forms of foundationalism.

general ideas (also called "abstract ideas") Ideas that represent a kind of thing rather than specific things. A crucial issue for

Hume and Berkeley is how to account for our possession of such ideas.

hedonic calculus The process of determining how much total pleasure a particular action will cause (subtracting from that total any pains that it causes): this is essential to determining whether that action is good or not, for those utilitarians who identify "happiness" with pleasure.

idea (1) In Plato: see <u>Forms</u>, above. (2) In Hume: The fainter, less vivid contents of our minds, formed in memory and imagination out of the direct experiences that Hume calls "<u>impressions</u>."

ideal observer A figure that Roderick Firth proposed in a famous essay (influenced in part by Smith) as a basis for a system of ethics. The ideal observer, for Firth, is supposed to be omniscient and wholly dispassionate, among other things.

immanent critique Criticism from within a system or method of thought (as opposed to "transcendental" critique, which takes up a stance outside that system or method).

impressions Hume's term for those contents of our minds that arise out of direct sensory experience. The contrast term is "<u>ideas</u>" (in sense 2), which are either memories of past impressions, anticipations of future impressions, or formed by combining other ideas or re-configuring elements of our impressions.

jurisprudence The philosophy of law. Smith uses the phrase "natural jurisprudence" for the search for or study of principles that should run through all legal systems.

Kantianism In moral philosophy, "Kantianism" refers to a theory built around the principle that we should always act from the <u>categorical imperative</u>, rather than assessing actions in accordance with their consequences. Kant maintains that the categorical imperative expresses our <u>practical reason</u>, which in turn expresses our free will. Kantian morality is therefore also supposed to be a morality of freedom: in acting on our practical reason, we show that we can transcend the biological and social forces that shape our desires. In addition, Kantianism is supposed to be a morality of equality. All human beings are equally capable of acting on practical reason, for Kant, even if they are unequal in other ways, and by holding one another up to the standards of practical reason, we can respect one another as equals.

libertarianism A political view according to which governments should do little or nothing beyond protecting our liberty, which is in turn thought to be paradigmatically expressed in our property rights. Libertarians are particularly known for opposing programmes that redistribute wealth from rich to poor, both on economic grounds and as an infringement on property rights.

magnanimity In ordinary English today, this word is simply a synonym for being generous, especially generous in one's forgiveness. That is emphatically not what it means for eighteenth-century writers like Hume and Smith. Instead, they use it in accordance with its ancient Greek meaning of "great-souledness," primarily for people who show remarkable strength in restraining the expression of pain or fear.

mercantilism An approach to economic policy based on the assumption that nations should seek a favourable "balance of trade" and maximize their supply of hard currency. This was thought to entail underwriting exports—in the manufacturing sector, especially—with subsidies ("bounties") and restricting imports with tariffs. The discovery of new gold and silver mines, and the creation of new markets, were also thought to be important, both of which might be achieved by colonial expansion.

meta-ethics A relatively recent term, "meta-ethics" encompasses a wide variety of philosophical investigations into the nature of ethics, or the nature of what we know about or how we speak about ethics: as opposed to what ethics actually requires of us (which gets called, in contradistinction to meta-ethics, "normative ethics").

metaphysics The branch of philosophy that investigates the fundamental nature of reality. The book that came after the *Physics* in Aristotle's collected writings was called the *Metaphysics*, meaning simply "after the *Physics*." Since that book covers questions about the nature of being, substance, and God, however, other explorations of those topics have come to be known as "metaphysics."

moral rationalism Views on which morality is ultimately grounded in one or more principles of reason. Contrast moral sentimentalism.

moral realism The view that moral qualities really exist—perhaps as Platonic Forms, perhaps in God's mind—and that we should aim to discover them in our moral reasoning.

moral sentimentalism Views on which morality is ultimately grounded in our sentiments rather than in a principle of reason. Contrast moral rationalism.

natural justice Smith uses this phrase (TMS 341) for the rules or principles, if any, that should ground all legal systems. Natural jurisprudence, for him, is the search for and study of natural justice.

natural theology A theology based purely on reason and empirical observation, rather than revelation.

non-tuism A term coined by Philip Wicksteed (and picked up, among others, by Lionel Robbins) for actions that are neither strictly egoistic nor strictly altruistic: actions in which what I do is not concerned to further the interests of the person or people with whom I directly interact, without necessarily being aimed at the promotion of my own interests.

normativity Normative claims tell us what should be or what we should do rather than simply what is or what we are doing. They can be contrasted with descriptive claims: they *prescribe* rather than merely describing. Importantly, although morality is a prime arena in which people make normative claims, it is not the only one. If I tell you that you should take the highway rather than local roads, I am most likely issuing a normative prudential claim rather than a moral one, and if I tell you that you should hear the Leonard Bernstein recordings of Haydn masses, I am most likely issuing a normative aesthetic claim rather than a moral one. I can even issue a normative claim in the service of an immoral project, telling you, say, that you should exit the bank via the back entrance rather than the front one, after you rob it.

originall Smith's term for the foundation of some area of justice—what property or punishment "originally" was supposed to accomplish (I preserve the spelling of this word that appears in LJ).

particularism An approach to an area of discourse or thought that gives attention to particular things or situations priority over generalizations. Some people are particularists about history but see general laws as crucial to physics and chemistry. Others are particularists about morality but not about science. Still others— including Smith, according to this book—are particularists across the board.

personal identity The view that each of us exists as a unified and continuous being across time, or the topic under which that view is interrogated.

phenomenology A term used for the examination of forms of our consciousness or practice conducted from within that consciousness itself—of what appears to us (the "phenomena" before us) *as* it appears, rather than in terms of whether it is well grounded or not.

Physiocracy An economic theory developed in eighteenth-century France according to which agriculture is the basic source of all wealth.

positivism A term with a variety of meanings, one of which picks out a particularly strong form of <u>empiricism</u>, insisting that all knowledge depends on observational evidence. A twentieth century version of this view indeed insisted that, aside from logical propositions (which were supposed to be true by definition), only sentences that can be verified by observational evidence so much as have meaning. On this view, moral and religious claims, among other things, are meaningless: are expressions of emotion that lack <u>cognitive</u> content.

practical reason Kant's term for the kind of reason we use in practice—which he thought should be governed by morality— as opposed to <u>speculative reason</u>, which we use to construct theories. Kant argued that practical reason can make basic assumptions (such as the existence of free will) to which speculative reason is not entitled.

prescription (in jurisprudence) A technical legal term for a title to ownership conferred by long, unchallenged use and enjoyment of a thing. If I have used a toaster oven for years, without anyone else claiming it, courts will look askance at a former room-mate's sudden announcement that it is really hers. A home originally occupied by force or fraud may thereby come, centuries later, legitimately to belong to the descendants of that occupier.

private access theories of the mind Theories according to which only I can know my own mind with certainty; no-one except me has direct access to what goes on in it.

qualia The qualities of subjective experience that constitute "what it is like" to go through that experience; the distinctive feel or look, to a particular subject, of a thing or event.

rational egoism The view that every human being either does act or should act solely for her own interests, and does or should use her reason just to pursue that interest effectively. As this definition implies, the view comes in both a descriptive and a normative form.

self-command The trait of character by which I exercise control over my passions, especially strong passions (lusts, fears, forms of anger) that are difficult to control.

simulation theory An approach to human understanding in contemporary psychology and philosophy of mind according to which we figure out what others are feeling, and predict their behaviour, primarily by simulating what it would be like to be in their situation. (Compare theory theory.)

scepticism A position that expresses and sows doubts about a subject that most people treat as well grounded. Sceptics about science suggest that the principles underlying it are unsound. Sceptics about personal identity suggest that we do not exist in a unified and continuous way across time. Sceptics about morality or religion suggest that they cannot be adequately grounded in reason. Hume was a sceptic about most of these things, and some say that the same is true of Smith. This book presents Smith in a less sceptical light than other scholars do.

speculative reason (or "theoretical reason") Kant's term for the kind of reason we use to build theories, whether in mathematics, science, or philosophy.

sympathy The term that Hume and Smith use for our sharing of feelings with others. They understand its workings quite differently, however. For Hume, I sympathize with you when I feel what you feel. For Smith, I sympathize with you when I feel what I imagine I would feel in your situation.

system A term that Smith uses as a synonym for "theory."

temperance Today this word is associated with refraining from drugs and alcohol, but in ancient and early modern theories of virtue, it named the virtue by which we exert control over any of our sensory desires.

theory theory An approach to human understanding in contemporary psychology and philosophy of mind according to which we construct a quasi-scientific theory about how the world works out of what we experience and are taught when we are young. As applied to the understanding of other people, this view holds that we use our basic theory in order to sympathize with others, and predict their behaviour. (Compare simulation theory.)

universals A term often used as a synonym for "essences" or "general ideas."

utilitarianism A moral theory or group of moral theories built around the principle of trying to bring about the greatest happiness for the greatest number of people. Some utilitarians identify happiness with pleasure—these are called hedonic utilitarians. Others identify happiness with the realization of basic human drives, or the satisfaction of everyone's preferences; these are called "ideal" and "preference" utilitarians, respectively. Utilitarians also differ over whether every individual action should be assessed in accordance with whether its consequences maximize happiness or whether we should seek simply to follow rules, or cultivate virtues, that in the long run will maximize happiness. The former are called "direct" utilitarians; the latter are called "indirect" utilitarians. Jeremy Bentham was a direct, hedonic utilitarian; John Stuart Mill was an indirect, ideal utilitarian; most economists today are direct or indirect preference utilitarians. Adam Smith, I argue in this book, fell into none of these categories.

virtue ethics An approach to ethics by which the main thing we need to do is cultivate certain admirable character traits—virtues—rather than find a procedure by which to determine what to do in specific situations. As opposed to Kantianism and utilitarianism, virtue ethics teaches that the virtuous person will generally make wise and appropriate decisions without needing to rely on a moral principle.

Whig One of Britain's two main political parties, from the mid-seventeenth century until the mid-twentieth century (by which time it was called the "Liberal" Party). In the seventeenth and early eighteenth centuries, it referred simply to the supporters of Parliament as opposed to the supporters of the king; the latter were known as "Tories," a designation still used for the Conservative Party. Later, it came to stand for a wide variety of causes that claimed the mantle of liberalism, and was often split within itself among more radical and more moderate groups.

Bibliography

Abramson, Kate. "Sympathy and the Project of Hume's Second Enquiry," *Archiv für die Geschichte der Philosophie*, 83 (2001). Pp. 45–80.

Aquinas, Thomas. *The Political Ideas of St. Thomas Aquinas*, ed. D. Bigongiari (New York: Hafner Press, 1953).

Aristotle. *The Complete Works of Aristotle*, ed. J. Barnes (Princeton: Princeton University Press, 1984).

Bagehot, Walter. *Collected Works*, ed. N. St. John-Stevas (Cambridge: Harvard University Press, 1968).

Baier, Annette. *A Progress of Sentiments* (Cambridge: Harvard University Press, 1991).

Ben Moshe, Nir. "An Adam Smithian Account of Moral Reasons," *European Journal of Philosophy* (2019). Pp. 1073–87.

———. "Making Sense of Smith on Sympathy and Approbation: Other-Oriented Sympathy as a Psychological and Normative Achievement," *British Journal for the History of Philosophy* 28/4 (2020). Pp. 735–55.

Berkeley, George. *Principles of Human Knowledge*, in *The Empiricists* (New York: Anchor Books, 1974).

Berry, Christopher. "Smith and the Virtues of Commerce," in NOMOS XXXIV: *Virtue* (New York: New York University Press, 1992).

Berry, C., M. Paganelli and C. Smith (eds.). *The Oxford Handbook of Adam Smith* (Oxford: Oxford University Press, 2013).

Bladen, Vincent. *From Adam Smith to Maynard Keynes* (Toronto: University of Toronto Press, 1974).

Broadie, A. and C. Smith (eds.). *The Cambridge Companion to the Scottish Enlightenment*, 2nd ed. (Cambridge: Cambridge University Press, 2019).

Broadie, Sarah. "The Problem of Practical Intellect in Aristotle's Ethics," *Proceedings of the Boston Area Colloquium in Classical Philosophy*, 3 (1987). Pp. 229–52.

Brown, Vivienne. *Adam Smith's Discourse* (London: Routledge 1994).

Brown, V. and S. Fleischacker (eds.). *The Philosophy of Adam Smith* (London: Routledge, 2010).

Bueno, O., G. Darby, S. French and D. Rickes (eds.). *Thinking about Science, Reflecting on Art: Bringing Aesthetics and Philosophy of Science Together* (London: Routledge, 2017).

Butler, Joseph. *The Analogy of Religion to the Constitution and Course of Nature; also, Fifteen Sermons*, ed. J. Angus (London: The Religious Tract Society, 1855).

Campbell, T.D. *Adam Smith's Science of Morals* (London: George Allen & Unwin, 1971).

Carlyle, Alexander. *Autobiography of the Rev. Dr. Alexander Carlyle, Minister of Inveresk*, 2nd ed. (Edinburgh: William Blackwood, 1860).

Carrasco, Maria Alejandra. "Adam Smith's Reconstruction of Practical Reason," *Review of Metaphysics*, 58/1 (2004). Pp. 81–116.

Chandler, James. "Adam Smith as Critic," in Berry et al. (eds.), *The Oxford Handbook of Adam Smith*.

Clarke, Samuel. *A Discourse of Natural Religion*, in *British Moralists 1650–1800*, D.D. Raphael, ed. (Indianapolis: Hackett, 1991).

———. *A Demonstration of the Being and Attributes of God*, ed. E. Vailati (Cambridge: Cambridge University Press, 1998).

Coplan, Amy. "Understanding Empathy: Its Features and Effects," in *Emotions: Philosophical and Psychological Perspectives*, A. Coplan and P. Goldie, eds. (Oxford: Oxford University Press, 2011).

Craig, John. "Life of John Millar, Esq," in Millar, *The Origin of the Distinction of Ranks*, ed. A. Garrett (Indianapolis: Liberty Fund, 2006).

Cropsey, Joseph. *Polity and Economy* (South Bend: St Augustine's Press, 2001).

d'Arms, Justin and Daniel Jacobson. "The Moralistic Fallacy: On the 'Appropriateness' of Emotions," *Philosophy and Phenomenological Research* 61/1 (2000). Pp. 65–90.

Darwall, Stephen. *The British Moralists and the Internal 'Ought', 1640–1740* (Cambridge: Cambridge University Press, 1995).

———. "Empathy, Sympathy, Care," *Philosophical Studies* 89 (1998). Pp. 261–82.

———. "Sympathetic Liberalism," *Philosophy & Public Affairs*, 28/2 (1999). Pp. 139–64.

———. *The Second-Person Standpoint* (Cambridge: Harvard University Press, 2006).

Debes, Remy. "Has Anything Changed? Hume's Theory of Association and Sympathy after the *Treatise*," *British Journal for the History of Philosophy*, 15 (2007). Pp. 313–38.

———. "Adam Smith on Dignity and Equality," *British Journal for the History of Philosophy*, 20/1 (2012). Pp. 109–40.

———. "From *Einfühlung* to Empathy," in *Sympathy: A History*, E. Schliesser, ed. (Oxford: Oxford University Press, 2015).

———. "Empathy and Mirror Neurons," in *The Routledge Handbook of Philosophy of Empathy*, H. Maibom, ed. (London: Routledge, 2017).

———. "Hume's Peculiar Sentiment" (unpublished manuscript).

Duncan, Ian. "The Fate of Sympathy: Hume, Smith, Scott, Hogg." Talk delivered at *Re-claiming Adam Smith* (Columbia University, September, 2006).

Ferguson, Adam. *An Essay on the History of Civil Society*, ed. F. Oz-Salzberger (Cambridge: Cambridge University Press, 1995).

Firth, Roderick. "Ethical Absolutism and the Ideal Observer," *Philosophy and Phenomenological Research* 12/3 (1952). Pp. 317–45.

Fitzgibbons, Athol. *Adam Smith's System* (Oxford: Clarendon Press, 1995).

Fleischacker, Samuel. "Philosophy and Moral Practice: Kant and Adam Smith," *Kant-Studien* 82/3 (1991). Pp. 249–69.

———. *The Ethics of Culture* (Ithaca: Cornell University Press, 1994).

———. *Third Concept of Liberty: Judgment and Freedom in Kant and Adam Smith* (Princeton: Princeton University Press, 1999).

———. "Adam Smith's Reception among the American Founders, 1776–1790," *William and Mary Quarterly* 59/4 (2002). Pp. 897–924.

———. *On Adam Smith's Wealth of Nations: A Philosophical Companion* (Princeton: Princeton University Press, 2004).

———. *A Short History of Distributive Justice* (Cambridge: Harvard University Press, 2004).

———. "Adam Smith on Self-Deceit," *Adam Smith Review* 7 (2011).

———. *Divine Teaching and the Way of the World* (Oxford: Oxford University Press, 2011).

———. "Smith und der Kulturelativismus," in *Adam Smith als Moral Philosoph*, and published in English as "Adam Smith and Cultural Relativism" in the online *Erasmus Journal for Philosophy and Economics*, 4/2 (2011).

———. "Justice Over Charity: Some Dangers in Faith-Based Poverty Initiatives," in *The Liberal-Republican Quandary in Israel, Europe, and the United States*, Thomas Maissen and Fania Oz-Salzberger, eds. (Boston: Academic Press, 2012).

———. "A Right to Welfare: Historical and Philosophical Reflections," in *Distributive Justice Debates in Political and Social Thought*, C. Boisen and M. Murray, eds. (London: Routledge, 2016).

———. "Adam Smith and the Left," in *Adam Smith: A Princeton Guide*, Ryan Hanley, ed. (Princeton: Princeton University Press, 2016).

———. *Being Me Being You: Adam Smith and Empathy* (Chicago: University of Chicago Press, 2019).

———. "Charles Mills on Deracializing Liberalism," *Journal of World Philosophies* 5/1 (2020). Pp. 259–65.

Forman-Barzilai, Fonna. *Adam Smith and the Circles of Sympathy* (Cambridge: Cambridge University Press, 2010).

Frankfurt, Harry. "Freedom of the Will and the Concept of a Person," *The Journal of Philosophy* 68/1 (1971). Pp. 5–20.

Fricke, Christel. "Moral Sense Theories and other Sentimentalist Accounts of the Foundations of Morals," in Broadie and Smith (eds.), *Cambridge Companion to the Scottish Enlightenment*.

Friedman, Benjamin. "The Influence of Religious Thinking on the Smithian Revolution," in Oslington (ed.), *Adam Smith as Theologian*.

Friedman, David. "The Weak Case for Public Schooling." http://www.david dfriedman.com/Libertarian/Public%20Schools/Public_Schools1.html

Garrett, Aaron. "Adam Smith über den Zufall als moralische Problem," in *Adam Smith als Moralphilosoph*, C. Fricke and H-P. Schütt, eds. (Berlin: de Gruyter, 2005).

Gill, Michael. *The British Moralists on Human Nature and the Birth of Secular Ethics* (Cambridge: Cambridge University Press, 2006).

Goldie, Peter. *The Emotions: A Philosophical Exploration* (Oxford: Oxford University Press, 2000).

Goldman, Alvin. *Simulating Minds* (Oxford: Oxford University Press, 2006).

———. *Adam Smith and the Character of Virtue* (Cambridge: Cambridge University Press, 2009).

Greiner, Rae. "1909: The Introduction of the Word 'Empathy' into English." *Britain, Representation, and Nineteenth-Century History (BRANCH)*, online-only journal (2012).

Griswold, Charles. "Smith and Rousseau in Dialogue," in *The Philosophy of Adam Smith*, V. Brown and S. Fleischacker, eds. (Abingdon: Routledge, 2010).

———. *Jean-Jacques Rousseau and Adam Smith: A Philosophical Encounter* (London: Routledge, 2018).

Haldane, John. "Adam Smith, Theology, and Natural Law Ethics," in Oslington (ed.), *Adam Smith as Theologian*.

Hankins, Keith. "Adam Smith's Intriguing Solution to the Problem of Moral Luck," *Ethics* 126/3 (2016). Pp. 711–46.

Hanley, Ryan. "Commerce and Corruption: Rousseau's Diagnosis and Adam Smith's Cure," *European Journal of Political Theory* 7/2 (2008). Pp. 137–58.

———. *Adam Smith and the Character of Virtue* (Cambridge: Cambridge University Press, 2009).

———. "Adam Smith on the 'Natural Principles of Religion,'" *The Journal of Scottish Philosophy* 13/1 (2015). Pp. 37–53.

———. "Adam Smith and Virtue," in Berry et al. (eds.), *Oxford Handbook of Adam Smith*.

——— (ed.). *Adam Smith: A Princeton Guide* (Princeton: Princeton University Press, 2016).

Hatfield, Elaine. "Emotional Contagion and Empathy," in *The Social Neuroscience of Empathy*, J. Decety and W. Ickes, eds. (Cambridge: MIT Press, 2009).

Hatfield, Elaine, John Cacioppo and Richard Rapson. *Emotional Contagion* (Cambridge: Cambridge University Press, 1994).

Hayek, Friedrich. *Law, Legislation and Liberty* (London: Routledge, 1998).

Herzog, Lisa. *Inventing the Market: Smith, Hegel, and Political Theory* (Oxford: Oxford University Press, 2013).

Himmelfarb, Gertrude. *The Idea of Poverty* (New York: Alfred A. Knopf, 1984).

———. *The Roads to Modernity* (New York: Vintage Books, 2004).

Hont, Istvan and Michael Ignatieff. "Needs and Justice in the *Wealth of Nations*," in *Wealth and Virtue*, Hont and Ignatieff, eds. (Cambridge: Cambridge University Press, 1983).

Horne, George. "A Letter to Adam Smith LL.D. on the Life, Death and Philosophy of His Friend David Hume Esq., By One of the People Called Christians," in Rasmussen (ed.), *Adam Smith and the Death of David Hume*.

Hume, David. *The Letters of David Hume*, 2 vols, ed. J.Y.T. Greig (Oxford: Oxford University Press, 1932).

———. *Essays: Moral, Political, and Literary*, ed. E. Miller, revised ed. (Indianapolis: Liberty Fund, 1987).

———. *Dialogues Concerning Natural Religion*, ed. R. Popkin, 2nd ed. (Indianapolis: Hackett, 1998).

Hutcheson, Frances. *A System of Moral Philosophy* (London: A. Millar, 1755).

———. *An Essay on the Nature and Conduct of the Passions with Illustrations on the Moral Sense*, ed. A. Garrett (Indianapolis: Liberty Fund, 2003).

———. *An Inquiry into the Original of Our Ideas of Beauty and Virtue*, ed. W. Leidhold, revised ed. (Indianapolis: Liberty Fund, 2008).

Ignatieff, Michael. *The Needs of Strangers* (New York: Viking, 1984).

Irwin, Terence. *Aristotle's First Principles* (Oxford: Clarendon Press, 1988).

Israel, Jonathan. *Radical Enlightenment* (Oxford: Oxford University Press, 2001).

———. *Enlightenment Contested* (Oxford: Oxford University Press, 2006).

———. *A Revolution of the Mind* (Princeton: Princeton University Press, 2010).

———. *Democratic Enlightenment* (Oxford: Oxford University Press, 2011).

Jamison, Leslie. *The Empathy Exams* (Minneapolis: Graywolf Press, 2014).

Jefferson, Thomas. *The Life and Selected Writings of Thomas Jefferson*, eds. A. Koch and W. Peden (New York: Random House, 1993).

Jones, Peter. "The Aesthetics of Adam Smith," in *Adam Smith: International Perspectives*, H. Mizuta and C. Sugiyama, eds. (New York: St. Martin's Press, 1993).

Kames (Henry Home). *Essays on the Principles of Morality and Natural Religion*, ed. M. Moran (Indianapolis: Liberty Fund, 2005).

Kant, Immanuel. *Conflict of the Faculties*, trans. M. Gregor (Lincoln: University of Nebraska Press, 1979).

———. *Religion within the Boundaries of Mere Reason*, trans. A. Wood and G. di Giovanni (Cambridge: Cambridge University Press, 1998).

———. *Critique of the Power of Judgment*, trans. P. Guyer and E. Matthews (Cambridge: Cambridge University Press, 2000).

Kennedy, Gavin. "Adam Smith on Religion," in Berry et al. (eds.), *Oxford Handbook of Adam Smith*.

Kindleberger, CK "The Historical Background: Adam Smith and the Industrial Revolution," in *The Market and the State*, T. Wilson and A.S. Skinner, eds. (Oxford: Oxford University Press, 1976).

Kivy, Peter. 'Science and Aesthetic Appreciation," *Midwest Studies in Philosophy* 16/1 (1991). Pp. 180–95.

Klein, Daniel. "My Understanding of Adam Smith's Impartial Spectator: A Symposium Prologue," *Econ Journal Watch* 13/2 (2016). Online.

Korsgaard, Christine. *Sources of Normativity* (Cambridge: Cambridge University Press, 1996).

Levy, David and Sandra Peart. "Adam Smith and the State: Language and Reform," in Berry et al. (eds.), *The Oxford Handbook of Adam Smith*.

Liu, Glory. *Inventing the Invisible Hand: Adam Smith in American Thought and Politics, 1776–Present* (Princeton: Princeton University Press, forthcoming).

Locke, John. *An Essay Concerning Human Understanding*, ed. A.C. Fraser (New York: Dover, 1959).

———. *Second Treatise of Government*, in *Two Treatises of Government*, P. Laslett, ed. (Cambridge: Cambridge University Press, 1988).

Long, Brendan. "Adam Smith's Theodicy," in Oslington (ed.), *Adam Smith as Theologian*.

MacIntyre, Alasdair. *After Virtue*, 2nd ed. (Notre Dame: University of Notre Dame Press, 1984).

———. *Whose Justice? Which Rationality?* (Notre Dame: University of Notre Dame Press, 1988).

Malcolm, Norman. "Anselm's Ontological Arguments", *Philosophical Review* 69 (1960). Pp. 41–60.

Mandeville, Bernard. "An Essay on Charity, and Charity Schools," in *The Fable of the Bees*, FB Kaye, ed. (Oxford: Clarendon, 1924).

McAllister, James. *Beauty and Revolution in Science* (Ithaca: Cornell University Press, 1999).

McCloskey, Deirdre. *The Bourgeois Virtues* (Chicago: University of Chicago Press, 2006).

McDowell, John. *Mind, Value, and Reality* (Cambridge: Harvard University Press, 1998).

McHugh, John. "Ways of Desiring Mutual Sympathy in Adam Smith's Moral Philosophy," *British Journal for the History of Philosophy* 24/4 (2016). Pp. 614–34.

McNamara, Peter. *Political Economy and Statesmanship: Smith, Hamilton, and the Foundation of the Commercial Republic* (DeKalb: Northern Illinois University Press, 1998).

Meek, Ronald. "New Light on Adam Smith's Glasgow Lectures on Jurisprudence," *History of Political Economy* 8/4 (1976). Pp. 439–77.

Mills, Charles. "Kant's *Untermenschen*," in his *Black Rights/White Wrongs* (New York: Oxford University Press, 2017).

Minowitz, Peter. *Profits, Priests, and Princes* (Stanford: Stanford University Press, 1993).

Montes, Leonidas. *Adam Smith in Context* (London: Palgrave Macmillan, 2004).

Muller, Jerry. *Adam Smith in His Time and Ours* (New York: The Free Press, 1993).

Murdoch, Iris. *The Sovereignty of Good* (London: Routledge, 1971).

Muthu, Sankar. "Adam Smith's Critique of International Trading Companies: Theorizing 'Globalization' in the Age of Enlightenment," *Political Theory* 36/2 (2008). Pp. 185–212.

Nagel, Thomas. *The View from Nowhere* (Oxford: Oxford University Press, 1986).

Nanay, Bence. "Adam Smith's Concept of Sympathy and Its Contemporary Interpretations," in Brown and Fleischacker (eds.), *The Philosophy of Adam Smith*.

Newton, Isaac. *Principia*, trans. A Motte and ed. F. Cajori (Berkeley: University of California Press, 1962).

Nuzzo, Angelica. "The Standpoint of Morality in Adam Smith and Hegel," in Brown and Fleischacker (eds.), *The Philosophy of Adam Smith*.

Oslington, Paul (ed.). *Adam Smith as Theologian* (New York: Routledge, 2011).

Otteson, James. *Adam Smith's Marketplace of Life* (Cambridge: Cambridge University Press, 2002).

———. "Adam Smith and the Right," in Hanley (ed.), *Adam Smith: A Princeton Guide.*

Pears, David. *Hume's System* (Oxford: Oxford University Press, 1990).

Phillipson, Nicholas. "Adam Smith as Civic Moralist," in *Wealth and Virtue*, Istvan Hont and Michael Ignatieff, eds. (Cambridge: Cambridge University Press, 1983).

———. *Adam Smith: An Enlightened Life* (New Haven: Yale University Press, 2010).

Pitts, Jennifer. *A Turn to Empire* (Princeton: Princeton University Press, 2005).

Plantinga, Alvin. *The Nature of Necessity* (Oxford: Oxford University Press, 1974).

———. *Warranted Christian Belief* (New York: Oxford University Press, 2000).

Plimpton, George. *Writers at Work: The Paris Review Interviews*, Fourth Series (New York: Viking, 1976).

Popper, Karl. *The Open Society and Its Enemies* (London: Routledge & Kegan Paul, 1966).

Pownall, Thomas. "A Letter from Governor Pownall to Adam Smith," in CAS.

Rae, John. *Life of Adam Smith*, re-print of 1895 edition (New York: Augustus Kelley, 1965).

Raphael, D.D. *The Impartial Spectator* (Oxford: Clarendon Press, 2007).

Rasmussen, Dennis. *The Problems and Promise of Commercial Society: Adam Smith's Response to Rousseau* (University Park: The Pennsylvania State University Press, 2008).

——— (ed.). *Adam Smith and the Death of David Hume* (Lanham: Lexington Books, 2018).

Raynor, David. "Adam Smith and the Virtues," *Adam Smith Review* 2 (2006).

Robbins, Lionel. *A History of Economic Thought*, eds. SG Medema and Warren Samuels (Princeton: Princeton University Press, 1998).

Robertson, John. *The Case for Enlightenment: Scotland and Naples 1680–1760* (Cambridge: Cambridge University Press, 2005).

Rosenberg, Nathan. "Some Institutional Aspects of the *Wealth of Nations*," *Journal of Political Economy* 18/6 (1960). Pp. 557–70.

Rush, Benjamin. "Defence of the Bible as a School Book," in *Essays, Literary, Moral and Philosophical* (Philadelphia: Thos. and William Bradford, 1806).

———. *Lectures on the Mind* (Philadelphia: American Philosophical Society, 1981).

Sayre-McCord, Geoffrey. "On Why Hume's 'General Point of View' Isn't Ideal–and Shouldn't Be," *Social Philosophy and Policy* 11/1 (1994).

———. "Hume on Practical Morality and Inert Reason," in *Oxford Studies in Meta-Ethics*, R. Shafer-Landau, ed. (Oxford: Oxford University Press, 2008).

———. "Sentiments and Spectators: Adam Smith's Theory of Moral Judgment," in *The Philosophy of Adam Smith*, V. Brown and S. Fleischacker, eds. (London: Routledge, 2010).

———. "Hume and Smith on Sympathy, Approbation, and Moral Judgment," *Social Philosophy and Policy*, 30/1–2 (2014). Pp. 208–36.

———. "On a Theory of a Better Morality" (unpublished).

———. "Rational Agency and the Nature of Normative Concepts" (unpublished).

Schliesser, Eric. *Indispensable Hume*, PhD. Dissertation (University of Chicago, 2002).

————. *Adam Smith: Systematic Philosopher and Public Thinker* (Oxford: Oxford University Press, 2017).

Schumpeter, Joseph. *History of Economic Analysis*, ed. E.B. Schumpeter (New York: Oxford University Press, 1954).

Sen, Amartya. *The Idea of Justice* (Cambridge: Belknap Press, 2009).

Shaftesbury, 3rd Earl of (Anthony Ashley Cooper). *An Inquiry Concerning Virtue or Merit*, in his *Characteristics of Men, Manners, Opinions, Times*, L. Klein, ed. (Cambridge: Cambridge University Press, 1999).

Shklar, Judith. "Liberalism of Fear," in *Political Thought and Political Thinkers*, S. Hoffman, ed. (Chicago: University of Chicago Press, 1998).

Simmons, John. *The Lockean Theory of Rights* (Princeton: Princeton University Press, 1992).

Smith, Craig. "Adam Smith: Left or Right?" *Political Studies* 61/4 (2013).

————. "Adam Smith and the New Right," in Berry et al. (eds.), *The Oxford Handbook of Adam Smith*. Pp. 784–98.

Stewart, Dugald. "Account of the Life and Writings of Adam Smith," in EPS.

Taylor, Jacqueline. "Virtue and the Evaluation of Character," in *The Blackwell Guide to Hume's Treatise*, S. Traiger, ed. (Oxford: Blackwell Publishing, 2006).

Teichgraeber, Richard. *'Free Trade' and Moral Philosophy* (Durham: Duke University Press, 1986).

Thompson, E.P. "The Moral Economy of the English Crowd in the Eighteenth Century," *Past and Present* 50/1 (1971).

Vivenza, Gloria. *Adam Smith and the Classics* (Oxford: Oxford University Press, 2001).

Wattles, Jeffrey. *The Golden Rule* (New York: Oxford University Press, 1996).

Weinstein, Jack. *On Adam Smith* (Belmont: Wadsworth, 2001).

Weintraub, Jeff. "The Theory and Politics of the Public/Private Distinction," in J. Weintraub and K. Kumar (eds.), *Public and Private in Thought and Practice* (Chicago: University of Chicago Press, 1997).

Wilson, T. and A.S. Skinner (eds.). *The Market and the State* (Oxford: Oxford University Press, 1976).

Winch, Donald. *Adam Smith's Politics* (Cambridge: Cambridge University Press, 1978).

————. *Riches and Poverty* (Cambridge: Cambridge University Press, 1996).

Wittgenstein, Ludwig. *Philosophical Investigations*, trans. G. E. M. Anscombe (New York: Macmillan, 1958).

————. *On Certainty*, trans. GEM. Anscombe and D. Paul, eds. GEM Anscombe and GH von Wright (New York: Harper & Row, 1969).

Wollaston, William. *The Religion of Nature Delineated*, in British Moralists, D.D. Raphael, ed., (Indianapolis: Hackett Publishing, 1991) volume I.

Wood, Gordon. *The Radicalism of the American Revolution* (New York: Random House, 1991).

Index

Note: Page numbers followed by "n" denote endnotes.

Printed in the United States
by Baker & Taylor Publisher Services